D0742836

YOUTH IN REVOLUTIONARY RUSSIA

YOUTH
IN
REVOLUTIONARY
RUSSIA

❖

Enthusiasts, Bohemians, Delinquents

ANNE E. GORSUCH

INDIANA UNIVERSITY PRESS

Bloomington & Indianapolis

This book is a publication of

Indiana University Press
601 North Morton Street
Bloomington, IN 47404-3797 USA

http://www.indiana.edu/~iupress

Telephone orders 800-842-6796
Fax orders 812-855-7931
Orders by e-mail iuporder@indiana.edu

© 2000 by Anne E. Gorsuch

Manufactured in the United States of America

Library of Congress Cataloging-in-Publication Data

Gorsuch, Anne E.
Youth in revolutionary Russia : enthusiasts, bohemians, delinquents / Anne E. Gorsuch.
p.   cm. — (Indiana-Michigan series in Russian and East European studies)
Includes bibliographical references and index.
ISBN 0-253-33766-6 (alk. paper)
1. Socialism and youth—Soviet Union. 2. Propaganda, Communist—Soviet Union.
3. Communist education—Soviet Union. 4. Youth—Soviet Union—Attitudes.   I. Title.
II. Series.

HX313.G666 2000
305.235'0947'09041—dc21

00-024181

1 2 3 4 5   05 04 03 02 01 00

For Hal, Hannah, and Ellie

CONTENTS

ACKNOWLEDGMENTS

It is a great pleasure to be able to acknowledge the many people who have contributed to this book. I am particularly grateful to Bill Rosenberg, who was a thoughtful reader through many drafts of both dissertation and book manuscript, managing to find just the right balance between critique and empathetic support. I am deeply thankful, both for his wise academic eye, and for his friendship. Geoff Eley pushed me to look broadly and comparatively at issues of youth culture in other national contexts. He was right, and the book is better for his advice. From my first interest in Soviet youth to recent conference collaborations, Isabel Tirado has always been willing to share ideas and archival experience. Many other friends and colleagues have read parts of this book in various stages and made important contributions: Bob Allen, Caroline Ford, Bill French, Michael Kennedy, Lynn Mally, Christine Ruane, Louis Siegelbaum, Allen Sinel, Kelly Smith, Ronald Suny, Judy Wyman, and Glennys Young. Special thanks to Julia Trubikhina, who now lives in New York but who, together with her family, first helped me feel at home in Moscow when doing early research there.

The International Research and Exchanges Board provided support for the original dissertation research in the former Soviet Union and travel funds for further later research. Both dissertation and postdoctoral funding were provided by a grant from the Joint Committee on the Soviet Union and its Successor States of the Social Science Research Council and the American Council of Learned Societies. The University of Michigan, Hamilton College, and the University of British Columbia also provided funding and support. At UBC, I want especially to thank Judy Levit and Jocelyn Smith for their willing help in the necessary details of preparing a manuscript for publication. In Russia, I am especially grateful to those working at the Komsomol archive who have been continually helpful, beginning with their warm greetings when I was the first foreigner to start working there in 1989 to their continued help in today's more difficult economic conditions.

A special thank you for the friendship of Elena Malysheva in Moscow, who has put me up in her apartment more times than I can now count, helped secure archival access, and consistently reminded me of why Russia current as well as Russia past is such a wonderful place. My mother, Bev Gorsuch, and father, Jack Gorsuch, have supported my efforts with love and confidence. My deepest debt is to my immediate family. My husband, Hal Siden, and my daughters, Ellie and Hannah, have supported me in the many years that it took to write this book by simply, and most importantly, filling my life with joy.

An earlier version of chapter 4 appeared as "NEP be Damned! Young Militants in the 1920s and the Culture of Civil War," in *The Russian Review*, Vol. 56, No. 4 (October 1997). © 1997 by Ohio State University Press. All rights reserved.

An earlier version of chapter 5 appeared as "'A Woman Is Not a Man': The Culture of Gender and Generation in Soviet Russia," in *Slavic Review*, Vol. 55, No. 3 (Fall 1996). It appears here with permission.

An earlier version of chapter 6 was originally published as "Flappers and Foxtrotters: Soviet Youth in the Roaring Twenties," in *The Carl Beck Papers in Russian and East European Studies*, No. 1102.

YOUTH IN REVOLUTIONARY RUSSIA

INTRODUCTION

YOUTH AND CULTURE

Young people living in Soviet Russia in the 1920s were far from universally communist. The writer Il'ia Erenberg described the wide variety of questions he was asked at his lectures in this period: "'Why did the revolution backfire in Germany?'—'What are the fashions today in Paris?' . . . 'Who are worse?: The Social Traitors or the Fascists?' . . . 'Do they accept foreign volunteers in India for the struggle for independence?' . . . 'Will communism discover how to conquer death?' . . . 'In what way is the onestep different from the twostep and which is more popular in Berlin?'"[1] Although the revolution and Civil War had solidified the Bolsheviks' physical control over the country, the most important task still lay ahead—that of transforming pre-revolutionary and "bourgeois" culture and social relations into new socialist forms of behavior and belief. To this end, the dictatorial, class-war policies of War Communism were followed in 1921 by the introduction of the New Economic Policy. NEP was in part a move toward a more moderate and "peaceful" economic policy. It was also a move away from the construction of a socialist state through force toward the creation of a new communist society through cultural enlightenment and purification.

The successful transformation of young people was essential to the Bolshevik project. The younger generation was that part of society which might grow up free from the corruption of pre-revolutionary Russia. Youth were the guarantor of future social and political hegemony, insofar as they were able, or willing, to replicate the ideology and culture of the Bolshevik party. As the "new man" and the "new woman," Soviet youth had to be made communist in every aspect of their daily lives—work, leisure, gender relations, family life. But how to do this? What exactly did it mean to be "made communist"? And what should be done if youth did not respond as desired?

In 1914, a third of the population of late Imperial Russia was under the age of twenty-one. The social and demographic factors contributing to this youthfulness—including a decline in the death rate due to better diets and medical care—improved in the post-revolutionary period.[2] These youth often did not behave or believe as the Bolsheviks wanted them to. There was a deep disjunction between idealized Soviet youth and the persistently non-communist cultures shared by many young people. Some young communists eagerly identified with official discourse. Others were less believing but accommodated themselves to Bolshevik domination. Still others appeared indifferent to the revolutionary project, pursuing popular pleasures like flapper dress or the foxtrot, or retreating to the alternative identities of the street; they were largely uninterested in the political issues preoccupying Soviet authorities. Finally, there were those youth who actively resisted the social identities they were assigned, some manipulating official ideology to support their own causes. *Youth in Revolutionary Russia: Enthusiasts, Bohemians, Delinquents* recovers the great variety of activities and interests among urban youth in early Soviet Russia.

What were the implications of the discrepancies between Bolshevik aspirations for youth and the realities of youth? To the modern observer, it will be clear that not all of those youth who "misbehaved" were counter-revolutionaries. Some of their behaviors were ones that many might now think of as "normal," if sometimes unpleasant, phenomena of adolescence. The Bolsheviks, on the other hand, tended to see almost all non-conformist behavior as delinquent and as a threat to the larger political project of revolutionary transformation. In other words, youth were the very real present, but they were also a discursive lens through which the anxieties of early Soviet Russia were exposed and debated. Political authorities, social scientists, criminologists, and educators deployed various conceptions of youth—both idealizing and condemning—in debates about what the Soviet Union should be. Flappers and foxtrotters had special meaning, for example, in this period of great anxiety about pleasure, about consumption, about sex. Youth who drank, played pranks, or refused to pay club dues had a different meaning in late NEP, when they were labeled "hooligans." By the end of 1926, one-sixth of the males in prison were incarcerated for crimes of hooliganism, and the majority of them were in their teens or early twenties.[3]

Youth in Revolutionary Russia explores the relationships between representation and reality, between official ideology and popular culture, and the meaning of these relationships for the making of a "Soviet" state and society. Ideology, popular culture, and politics were intimately interrelated in post-revolutionary Russia. Youthful impurity and misbehavior (as defined by the Bolsheviks) had great implications for the Bolshevik project, and particularly for the fate of the New Economic Policy. According to the tenets of Marxism-Leninism, the new material conditions of the post-revolutionary period should have produced a new kind of person. So what to do if the new man and the new woman were not produced? What to do if the new generation was not cleansed and purified, but decadent and polluted? The nature of NEP, and indeed its very future, depended on the degree to which culture could be transformed. If youth became communist under NEP, this supported those who wanted to continue NEP's economic and political policies. If they continued to behave in ways that were defined

as non-communist, this suggested to many that NEP, and its material economy, were wrong. The successful transformation of youth in the specific
material conditions of the 1920s was a litmus test for the validity of NEP.

BOLSHEVIK MORALISTS

Youth and youth culture are revealed to us in part through the observations and preoccupations of social scientists. In the 1920s, educators, psychiatrists, and criminologists, together with party and Komsomol (Communist Youth League) authorities, were engaged in a social science of society
[*sotsial'naia nauka*]. In late-nineteenth-century Europe and America, too,
"society" was becoming the focus of scientific and governmental study.
Like the early American sociologists and criminologists of deviancy working in Chicago, Russian social scientists in the 1910s, and especially the
1920s, began to make a "scientific" study of youth, using questionnaires,
interviews, and participant observation.[4] The commitment to science also
reflected the Bolshevik commitment to the empiricism of Marxism. Behavior would be studied in a scientific fashion, and then both individual behavior and society would be rationally engineered and radically transformed.
New centralized institutions and apparatuses were set up to bring the study
of youth under the view of "experts." These institutes were mostly based
in Moscow and Leningrad, and many were under the direction of the Commissariat of Education (Narkompros) or of the Commissariat of Internal
Affairs (NKVD). Social scientists studied family life, schools, street culture, and leisure activities. Time budget studies were especially popular;
statistics allowed the regime to organize and conceptualize individual behavior in its relationship to the larger societal whole.[5]

Many social scientists were officially sponsored by Narkompros or institutions under its direction, but there were others concerned with youth
and youth culture who were not under their control. All of these individuals were broadly part of what I have called Bolshevik "moralists." By the
term "moralists" I want to suggest that this was a group of people preoccupied with questions of appropriate behavior and belief. By "group" I do
not mean, however, that these individuals were an organized cohort, or
that they were simply presenting a party line. Some were the social science
experts described above. Many were members of the party or Komsomol;
others were not. Most were older than the youth cultures they were describing or condemning, but young people themselves also sometimes took
on the role of moralist. They did not always agree with each other, and
were sometimes in conflict with others, as this was a period of relative disagreement and debate (especially in comparison with later periods). Broadly speaking, however, they felt themselves to be interpreting, and in some
important way contributing to, the construction of a Soviet state and society by writing about how youth should be talking and behaving. They
shared the common influence and authority of Bolshevik ideology and of

Lenin. And they were uniformly interested in advancing the legitimacy of the Bolshevik project.

There are several challenges inherent in using these sources. One is that social scientists were not just observing youth. Their observations and reports became the basis of actions taken to improve the lives of youth and to correct and integrate them. Their job was to make sometimes alien youth cultures intelligible, a process of definition and description which necessarily involved interpretation. As they articulated their understanding of the moral, social, and economic causes of delinquency or homelessness, researchers took an active role in constructing the identities of the youth they described. They had their own particular "sociological gaze"—informed in part by pre-revolutionary understandings of the adolescent and in part by Soviet constructions of criminality and reform—that shaped how they understood and then described their subjects.[6] The attempt to define and fix the identity of youth privileged some youth (worker, male) and constricted others (peasant, female).

These moralists, in other words, were providing not analytical descriptions of youth, but prescriptive ones. The many expert articles, works of literature, and theater performances ostensibly devoted to describing youth culture were often didactic. They were part of an effort to define what the Soviet Union should be, and as such had disciplinary implications when young people did not behave as they were supposed to. That this is so is suggested by the amount of work on youth (especially homeless and criminal youth) which took place under the authority of the NKVD. My interest in the disciplinary aspects of new social disciplines relates this work to that of others on the relationship of professional expertise and disciplinary authority to the transformative project of the revolutionary regime.[7]

At the same time, bolstered by additional sources, I am more comfortable than some with talking not only about representation, but about reality. Indeed, my study is premised on exploring the relationship between representations of youth and the realities of youth, and the meaning of this relationship for the Bolshevik project. Young people were not only a subject of power; on the contrary, their actions helped shape the discourses about them, and they actively responded to others' constructions of them. Additionally, young people were themselves involved in the disciplining process. Young believers told others how to behave, and in the process helped define themselves as "Soviet."

It will be clear that the Soviet state described in this book is a state actively, and often uncertainly, in the process of constructing itself. There were conflicts about politics and about culture among members of the communist elite, as well as between subordinate youth and the party. Recent work on the state in other places and contexts has shown that a state should be seen not as a coherent and unambiguously united force, but as a *"claim that in its very name attempts to give unity, coherence, structure, and intentionality to what are in practice frequently disunited, fragmented at-*

tempts at domination."[8] As Derek Sayer explains, "the state is an ideological project (rather than an agency that has such projects)."[9] Examining youth in the revolutionary period allows us to consider this thesis in the Soviet context.

CULTURE AND POPULAR CULTURE

In this book, I refer frequently to the term "culture." This single term represents a variety of different concepts used in sometimes conflicting ways by anthropologists, historians, and literary scholars. Cultural theorist Iurii Lotman offers a helpful, synthetic definition of culture in his introduction to a work on Russian traditions and lifestyles in the Imperial period.[10] First, Lotman argues, culture is a social phenomenon, "something shared by any collective"; it is a *"form of interaction"* and communication. To Lotman's description I would add that there can be multiple cultures within a larger culture, including subcultures or divisions based on class or gender which are somehow at variance with the larger collectivity.[11] Secondly, Lotman argues that a given collective will have its own "language" and system of signs. In other words, culture *"signifies something* and therefore can serve as a means of *conveying meaning."* Culture is symbolic and gives complex meanings to texts, objects, and experiences. This is true of a cultural text, such as a novel or a film, which was designed to signify something. It is also true of popular practices, such as dress, dance, and sexual relations. Thirdly, culture is historical—the "'nongenetic' memory of the collective." It is "a particular quantity of inherited texts, on the one hand, and of inherited symbols, on the other." It is this inherited and pervasive quality that makes culture so difficult to transform. But at the same time, culture is "always flexible and changeable." It is not timeless. "In order to understand the *meaning* of the behavior of living persons . . . of the past, one must know their culture." Fourthly, Lotman argues, culture is everyday life, or what in Russian is called *byt*—"customs, the rituals of everyday behavior, the structure of life that determines the day's schedule . . . the character of work and leisure, forms of rest and play." Finally, culture is a way of enforcing certain forms of behavior. "Norms belong to culture, they are reinforced in forms of everyday behavior, in everything about which we say 'That's how it's done; that is proper.'"

When we add the label "popular" to the concept of culture, something changes. The preface "popular" suggests that popular culture is something that is liked by many people. Or maybe it is culture made by the "people." But there are problems with these definitions. Who are "the people"? And how do we understand the "popularity" of certain commercially produced items, such as movies and music? In fact, popular culture need not be liked only by the "masses," nor produced by them. Cultural historians have explored the fluid boundaries between so-called high culture and popular culture too thoroughly for us to now believe that popular culture means only the culture of the "unenlightened masses."[12] We know that in early-nineteenth-century America, Shakespeare was not reserved for the intellectual elite, but was as popular on makeshift stages in rural areas as he was in urban theaters.[13] Similarly, nineteenth-century Russian worker-authors drew upon the cultural values and cultural productions of other social groups (the intelligentsia, popular belles lettres, the commercial print media) to help formulate their conceptions of the "natural dignity and rights of the workers."[14] Popular culture can lessen the divisions between social groups, but it can also shake them, penetrate them, and transform them. Mark Steinberg argues, for example, that the worker-authors' very appropriation of more-elite culture was an act of "social rebellion" in that it challenged the divide that otherwise set workers apart.[15]

Analyses of popular culture have been especially attuned to questions of power and authority. In other areas of cultural history, too, arenas which were conventionally thought of as "non-political" (home and family, the street, leisure and recreation) are now understood to be deeply political. Everyday life provides opportunities for "everyday forms" of conformity and of resistance.[16] But power and politics are especially important to studies of popular culture. Researchers and theorists, especially those associated with the Birmingham Centre for Contemporary Cultural Studies, have incorporated Antonio Gramsci's concept of hegemony into the discussion of popular culture.[17] As defined by Gramsci, hegemony describes the ways in which the ruling classes secure their control over the subordinate groups in society, not through force or coercion, but through manufacturing consent. There is a continual process of negotiation and contestation between the ruling classes and the subordinate ones.[18] Researchers at the Centre for Contemporary Cultural Studies have argued that popular culture (especially youth culture) is an essential site of exchange, and often conflict, between subordinate and dominant groups in society. As Tony Bennett explains:

> [P]opular culture is definable neither as the culture "of the people," produced by and for themselves, nor as an administered culture produced for them. Rather, it consists of those cultural forms and practices—varying in content from one historical period to another—which constitute the terrain on which dominant, subordinate and oppositional cultural values and ideologies meet and intermingle, in different mixes and permutations, vying with one another in their attempts to secure the spaces within which they can become influential in framing and organizing popular experiences and consciousness.[19]

Importantly, this definition of popular culture emphasizes the interaction between what in our case would be a dominant Bolshevik culture and subordinate youth cultures. It focuses our attention on the ways in which popular culture is about politics, power, and relationship.

There are problems with the emphasis on resistance and struggle, however. In some research on youth cultures, the "dominant" culture appears overly fixed and established in comparison to a more fluid subordinate culture. In Soviet Russia, although the Bolsheviks were politically dominant, they were far from culturally so. Theirs was a hegemony only in the process of being defined and made dominant, and youth cultures helped define what this cultural hegemony would be. Additionally, Bennett's formulation overemphasizes the disruptive and resistant aspects of popular culture. As this book will show, youth cultures can be conformist as well as defiant. Some communist youth supported the Soviet project, even as they resisted the Bolsheviks' paternalist attitude toward youth. Neither Bolshevik culture nor popular culture was singular or unified; instead, both demonstrated internal conflicts and divisions, as well as conflicts between "dominant" and "subordinate."[20]

Under the influence of the "linguistic turn," and with the opportunities presented by newly opened archives, historians of the Soviet Union have begun looking more closely at problems of culture, language, power, and resistance.[21] Eric Naiman's interdisciplinary work on discourses of sex and the body is one fascinating example of how some of these questions might be applied to the period of the New Economic Policy.[22] Much of the recent work on the Soviet period has been on the 1930s, perhaps because the more intimate experiences of Stalinist Russia were for so long closed to researchers. Some of these studies focus on opposition to official languages of the state. In her study of popular opinion in Stalinist Russia, Sarah Davies argues that there was a significant body of "dissonant opinion which distorted, subverted, rejected, or provided an alternative to the official discourse."[23] Sheila Fitzpatrick and Lynne Viola have explored expressions of resistance among the peasantry in the Stalinist period.[24] On the other hand, many monographs on culture in the 1920s might still be categorized as social histories of culture rather than cultural history per se. Historians of early Soviet Russia have turned comparatively recently to questions of popular culture and its relationship to politics, social relations, and material conditions.[25] Little has been done on questions of youth culture. The classic works by American and Soviet historians on the Soviet Union's younger generation describe this generation primarily in institutional terms.[26] While this is important, it is no longer enough. Understanding youth, or indeed all of Soviet Russia in the revolutionary era, requires a much broader view of the complex interactions among social and cultural, as well as political, factors.[27]

NEP

I have chosen to focus on the period of the New Economic Policy (NEP) for two reasons. I began this project because I was interested in the processes of social and cultural transformation implied in the revolutionary endeavor. How did the Bolsheviks go about trying to cultivate a new culture and society, to define and instill a "revolutionary" consciousness and a "communist" morality? What was the daily experience of people in this period of transition? How did their values, rituals, beliefs, and conventions affect the struggle for revolutionary transformation? What was the relationship between culture and social, economic, and political conditions? I felt that these questions were best studied during NEP, as it was a period of concerted cultural effort during which the Bolsheviks were unusually forthcoming about the debates and challenges involved in the attempted transition to a "new life" as well as to a new socioeconomic system. Secondly, because it was a period of relative openness, I had access to a wide range of material written by scholars who in the 1920s still felt able to express disagreements and to publish material on a wide range of youth cultures, including those that they felt reflected badly on the new Soviet state, such as juvenile delinquency.

Introduced at the Tenth Party Congress in March 1921, NEP was intended to provide a period of recovery, a "breathing space," after the traumas of revolution, civil war, and famine which had ravaged the country since 1917. Limitations on private trade were reduced, grain and other foodstuffs were no longer forcefully confiscated from the countryside, and a highly centralized industrial system was replaced by a freer market. The nationalization of industry and urban property that had taken place under the earlier period of War Communism was partly reversed. Some saw these policies as an unwelcome retreat from the more hardheaded and fast-moving policies of War Communism, especially when confronted with the dichotomy of high unemployment rates and prospering private traders (NEPmen). Others supported NEP, either because, like party theoretician Nikolai Bukharin, they believed that the moderate course of NEP was necessary for rebuilding, or because they benefited financially or professionally. During NEP the state bureaucracy expanded greatly.[28] Ambivalence toward NEP was reflected in shifting approaches to private entrepreneurs. They were allowed to flourish between 1921 and 1923, but in late 1923 many NEPmen were arrested and businesses closed as the regime backed away from NEP's most liberal economic provisions. The ideological winds shifted again a year later, and private entrepreneurs were enticed back into business with lower taxes and promises of greater cooperation from state officials. Beginning in 1926, and intensifying in 1928, the regime embarked on a campaign to get rid of private entrepreneurs and, finally, of NEP.[29]

Although NEP may have provided a breathing space of sorts for those interested in private trade, it was not a resting point. The 1920s were a period of anxiety and even crisis, during which the very nature of the Soviet state and the "new" Soviet citizen were under debate. The Bolsheviks turned their attention to making a cultural revolution in social relations, in everyday life (including manners, dress, language, and social hygiene), in leisure and recreational activities, and in gender relations. During NEP the Bolsheviks explicitly tried to transform those habits and traditions they felt would inhibit the creation of a new communist system, most of which they associated with the pre-revolutionary period and the influences of the "bourgeois" West. Hundreds of books, articles, movies, and works of art were dedicated to the attempted transformation of daily life. Some described research while others served as guidebooks or even advertisements of sorts. When, for example, one Bolshevik, Mikhail Ostrovich, who was traveling on a boat to America for the first time, saw a book of matches with the ship's name on it, he whispered to his companion, "What a splendid idea! . . . I shall send some of these home. We should adopt this idea. Only we would not use them to advertise private boat companies. We would write on each match: 'Wash your hands before eating' . . . 'Take a bath every day' . . . Eat slowly' . . . 'Keep your dining rooms neat.'"[30] Part of what made NEP so different from the preceding period of revolution and civil war was that this effort to define and control society functioned primarily not by coercion (though that still existed) but by teaching new ways of being through the disciplining of self and of others.

At the same time that the Bolsheviks were trying to transform daily life, however, the relatively open cultural borders of NEP allowed access to "non-communist" forms of entertainment and expression. Control over state cultural production was lessened, and private forms of cultural entrepreneurship—often influenced or taken directly from Western commercial culture—flourished in this period. These and other aspects of moderate NEP made many committed communists anxious. NEP was supposed to bring prosperity, but the values and behaviors that accompanied this prosperity (dancing, expensive dress, fancy restaurants) were at odds with how Bolshevik moralists imagined communism. How the Bolsheviks coped with "non-communist" cultures and relations would have significant implications for the future course of Soviet politics.

SOURCES

This study draws on a wide range of literatures and disciplines, both in its sources and in its theoretical and methodological framework. The study of popular culture is by nature interdisciplinary, and I have used archives, libraries, newspapers and magazines, fiction and autobiography, Soviet sociological and ethnographic works, travelers' accounts, interviews, and visual sources such as films, posters, and photographs. In other words, my "texts" have been not only written documents but also social practices, such as dance, dress, ritual, and language. The Komsomol archive (TsKhDMO) provided valuable source materials pertaining to club activities and rituals, as well as letters and reports from local activists to the Komsomol Central Committee detailing the nature of their work and its difficulties. The Scientific Archive of the Academy of Pedagogical Sciences (NA RAO) contained documents relating to the street culture of youth as well as material on political education, including copies of school essays on political and social topics. The State Archive of the Russian Federation (GARF) provided source materials on activities organized for youth by trade union clubs and documents from the Commissariat of Education (Narkompros) and its affiliates, of which the material on the homeless *besprizornye* was especially helpful. In general, social scientists were especially alert in this period to questions of everyday life. According to one account of 117 studies of working-class youth in the period from 1917 to 1927, 34 were concerned with problems of everyday life. From 1938 to 1957, in contrast, there was not a single study of everyday life among youth.[31]

My sources have helped shape the geographical focus of this book. The vast majority of Soviet researchers wrote about Moscow and Leningrad and published in these two cities.[32] Although I make an occasional reference to rural youth, the centralization of public discourse in urban areas, as well as the enormous differences between rural and urban youth cultures, led me to focus on urban youth (and their representations) in Moscow and Leningrad.[33] Additionally, I do not try to cover every aspect of youth's complex lives. I do not write extensively about youth in the workplace or at school and university. Some aspects of these cultures have been covered by other scholars.[34] I am convinced nonetheless that my discussion of urban Russian youth provides a rich and complex portrait not only of Russian youth cultures, but of the broader problems of social transformation in the post-revolutionary period.

The book begins with a discussion of the Bolsheviks' discursive imaginings of youth as part of the party's effort to shape social identity and establish hegemony. Chapter 1 describes the party's varied visions of youth and the relationship of these visions to party debates about communist culture, and discusses the many debates about the nature of communist culture and morality. Although this book is principally a work of cultural history, the nature of the urban environment is of fundamental importance to our understanding of the challenges of cultural transformation, and chapter 2 grapples with the social and material realities of this period of transition, as well as the cultural. Efforts to create new mechanisms of socialization through political education, youth clubs, and communal housing were long-term projects which co-existed and often competed with the socializing influences of the family, the community, and the street. Poverty, overcrowding, and high rates of juvenile unemployment also affected attitudes about class, career, gender relations, and leisure.

There were some youth who supported the Bolsheviks' efforts, and it was their beliefs, activities, and organizations, including communist youth clubs, sports groups, and educational circles, which came closest to the Bolsheviks' ideal. Chapter 3 describes these youth and their enthusiasms. It also examines the challenges to Komsomol cultural efforts from the pleasurable entertainment opportunities offered during NEP. Chapter 4 looks at the activities of those youth who were inspired by the ethos of the Civil War to take a more radical approach than their elders to questions of morality and everyday life. They challenged the party not with apathy but with a revolutionary enthusiasm which threatened to move further and faster than the party wanted. Chapter 5 explores questions of gender and generation, especially the stubborn culture of masculinity in the Komsomol and the ways it contributed to young women's exclusion from equal participation in the league. This chapter reveals the difficulties of restructuring gender relations even in the most consciously revolutionary environments.

Non-communist youth posed different kinds of challenges to the party. Chapter 6 explores the symbolic language of dress and dance in a study of Soviet flappers and foxtrotters. NEP allowed an influx of commercial culture both Russian and Western, and many youth flocked to Hollywood movies and Western-style dance halls and ignored more didactic Soviet efforts. Soviet moralists defined these pleasures as dangerous, and by doing so tried to discipline them. The street life of youth was also defined as dangerous. Chapter 7 examines the varied cultures of the urban street, including those of working-class youth, young traders, and the homeless (*besprizornye*). It also examines the meanings given to "the street" by Bolshevik moralists, and the discourses of juvenile delinquency and crime. In chapter 8, I look at rising concern about hooliganism and suicide in late NEP. What was the meaning of hooliganism and depression in the context of late NEP? Why was there such a powerful discourse of propriety, discipline, and contagion in this period? Finally, both chapter 8 and the epilogue explore the idea of Stalinism as a reassertion of parental authority over undisciplined and still untransformed youth.

1

THE POLITICS OF GENERATION

In an article on the sociology of generations, Philip Abrams argues that a society's views of age, and specifically of youth, are an important reflection of that society's perception and definition of self. When looking at the phenomenon of youth protest at various times in the twentieth century, what is most important is not so much the actions of the youth themselves but the reasons why the very idea of youth "acquires great resonance for young and old alike" at particular times.[1] Youth, in other words, is more than a social and biological formation; it is also a cultural construct. In the revolutionary period, and in the decade following, the Bolsheviks gave varied meanings to the term "youth." Images and understandings of youth were sometimes positive—youth as innocent, enthusiastic, communal—and other times negative—youth as corruptible, undisciplined, and "infectious." Much of the discourse reflected great anxiety about social conformity, ideological purity, and contamination from "bourgeois" influences, especially as they were manifested in popular culture. The sources of these images and understandings were multiple, including the perceived needs and concerns of the revolution and New Economic Policy, views of proper working-class behavior inherited from the pre-revolutionary period, and Western theories of youth and adolescence. There was no one way of envisioning youth—which reflects in part the diversity of opinions within the Bolshevik party about what a "Soviet" state and society should be.

The Bolsheviks were unusually preoccupied with the younger generation during the 1920s as compared to later years. From 1918 through 1932, there were at least eighty party resolutions on youth, as compared to only fifteen in the next thirty years.[2] The interest in youth can be understood in part as a common response to a period of attempted revolutionary transformation. Many individuals and groups who have hoped to reshape their society have appealed to the younger generation as an embodiment and advocate of everything new and transformative in their respective movements. In the nineteenth century, the Italian nationalist Mazzini demanded that revolutionary leaders place youth "at the head of the insurgent masses,"[3] while Mao, in a more contemporary example, argued that the youth in the May Fourth Movement "played the role of the vanguard."[4]

Mussolini too appealed to youth as the "man [sic] of the future," "a young man not corrupted by the bourgeois and liberal past."[5] In each case, as in that of the Bolsheviks, the discourse of youth suggested the optimistic transgression of ideological, cultural, and political divisions through the unification of youth (and of those who felt young in spirit) against common enemies: age and convention.

Interest in youth was particularly strong in the inter-war period. In Western Europe, as well as in Russia, the pre-war world was seen as the failed product of an older generation—a generation whose values, as well as corporeal bodies, had died on the battlefields. The catastrophe of World War I led many young people to believe that the older generation had brought the world almost to ruin. The new world could be made only by a new generation. Significantly, both young and old embraced this understanding of the regenerative qualities of "youthfulness." Representations of youth reflected the particular needs of different post-war states as they tried to reassert their legitimacy and vision in an uncertain time. In 1919, England's *Daily Chronicle* imagined a British "revolt of the Young against the Old . . . The victims will be those who have not seen the vision . . . rich men who hold on to broad acres, haughty women who distill exotic perfumes from the sweat and toil of the masses, vulgar profiteers with swollen pockets and swollen bellies."[6] As the *Daily Chronicle* described it, the "social revolution" that youth was launching was "not an affair of classes." Instead it was hoped that youth "would bring about a bloodless revolution which would abolish class inequalities and exploitation without class warfare and without socialism."[7] In the Soviet Union, the younger generation was also seen as a revolutionary vanguard, but in this case one which would bring about just that violent class warfare the British feared. In both cases, questions of youth and of their role in cultural transformation were part of a larger process of state formation and solidification. In both cases (and in other post-war nations too), these attempts to use youth to rebuild the nation stumbled against the younger generation's own powerful understandings of its self and status.

The post-war vision of youth as renewal and regeneration must also be put in the larger context of an early-twentieth-century preoccupation with degeneration and decline. Industrialization, spreading cities and urban slums, and the growing numbers of lower-class immigrants, who were said to "breed" at a higher rate than the native-born, suggested to some elites in Europe and the United States that cultured society was in danger. New kinds of statistical information showed supposed increases in "moral defectiveness," criminality, prostitution, and disease. The social hygiene and eugenics movements—two closely related biologically based movements for social regeneration—aimed at curing these evils. Social hygienists in Europe and the United States tried to eliminate "social plagues" such as alcoholism, venereal disease, and tuberculosis. Eugenicists argued that criminality, feeblemindedness, and social deviance were hereditary.[8] The eugenic focus on fitness, on measuring size, strength, and mental capacity, persisted in the inter-war period. In Soviet Russia too, Soviet geneticists and public health specialists pursued eugenics after 1917 and emphasized the biological determinants of behavior. They were challenged (and eventually defeated) by those who argued that education and environment were more important (and more Marxist) than heredity, but their influence was evident in many Soviet analyses of youth, especially of criminal youth.[9] Books and articles on the recreational or reading interests of non-criminal youth also sometimes included discussions and charts of the height, weight, and body measurements of their subjects.[10] Club activities for delinquent and non-delinquent youth alike were justified in biological terms with a focus on energy, health, and the mechanics of the human body. Sports groups were particularly important in this regard, as they combined an emphasis on the healthy outlet of "energy" with the biocriminologists' preoccupation with man as a machine.[11]

Eugenicists were deeply concerned with the quality of future generations. Society could be repaired through biological intervention in individual reproduction, ensuring that future generations would be a source of renewal rather than of further degradation. Concurrent with this interest was a focus on adolescence as a particular period in the biological life cycle, a period which was thought to exhibit certain key biological, psychological, and sexual characteristics.[12] One of the most influential advocates of adolescence as a particular age category was G. Stanley Hall, an American psychologist and child study enthusiast. Hall argued that the development of the individual recapitulated the development of society in its progression from a condition of primitive wildness to one of civilized maturity. Adolescence was a period of great importance because young people were being torn between these two extremes: "back to the primitive states of stone age baby, and forward towards the rational and enlightened state of 'modern man.'"[13] The supposed transitional status of adolescents was thought to make them especially malleable and educable, but also to make them particularly vulnerable to unhealthy outside influences (however these were defined). For this reason, the upbringing of the adolescent was thought crucial to a society's future.

Though there were challenges to Hall's theories of adolescence, his emphasis on adolescence as a period with special needs and requiring special attention was widely influential. Social theorists in Soviet Russia were similarly preoccupied with the importance of the adolescent life stage. In his book *Adolescent Workers*, V. E. Smirnov argued that the study of adolescence was one of the most important tasks of contemporary "pedology," as it was during adolescence that the "physical and spiritual foundations are laid for an entire lifespan, the person's constitution is formed, his personality and individualism."[14] The new Soviet discipline of pedology studied the developmental stages of human life in what was called a "psychophys-iological synthesis."[15] In Smirnov's book, and in the work of other social scientists, the idea of adolescence was not as specifically defined in terms of age as it is now, however. Social scientists sometimes referred explicitly to those aged from thirteen or fourteen to eighteen or nineteen [*podrostok*], but they were as likely to use the term "youth" [*molodezh'*], which suggested more generally those between childhood and adulthood. Komsomol members were between the ages of fourteen and twenty-three, but the Komsomol was mostly composed of those older than seventeen; in 1922, only about a tenth of the league were between fourteen and sixteen. People in their twenties made up most of the Komsomol leadership. Perhaps this was not only because they were more experienced, but also because they would (in theory) have left behind the particular instabilities and dangers of the adolescent period.[16]

YOUTH AS ENTHUSIASTIC VANGUARD

Ideas about adolescence were made "Soviet" both in terms of how young people were imagined and in the interventions and institutions that were designed to help them. In a powerful congruence of contemporary psycho-logical theory with revolutionary need, early Bolshevik reformers empha-sized the malleability of adolescents in their enthusiastic accounts of the importance of youth. For the early Bolsheviks, youth were a blank slate on which could be written the revolutionary image of the new socialist man or woman. Children are an "extraordinary plastic material," wrote the psy-choneurologist and Bolshevik moralist Aron Zalkind. They yield to educa-tional pressure "much more flexibly than the adult part of the population, [and] in the conditions of our revolutionary-Soviet environment constitute the richest soil for the growth of exactly those principles which are neces-sary to a revolutionary education."[17] The "new man" was championed (and sometimes lampooned) in literature too. In Iurii Olesha's book *Envy*, the modernist hero Andrei Petrovich Babichev describes his young eighteen-year-old protégé Volodia Makarov as "a youth absolutely unlike any oth-er . . . The important thing is that he is the completely new man."[18] Party theoretician Nikolai Bukharin argued similarly that what the party was in the process of creating through youth was "a new type of person . . . with new relations, new habits, new aspirations, a new psychology and a new ideological system."[19]

Many of the most adulatory images of the younger generation come from the period of revolution and civil war, when some of the qualities typically associated with the category of youth by the late nineteenth cen-tury—enthusiasm, energy, optimism, and rebelliousness—were just those qualities thought necessary to the forging of a revolutionary state and soci-ety. In the discourse of this period, as articulated in the press, in political documents and speeches, in literature, and in agitational propaganda, youth were an important metaphor for the desired social transformation, symbolizing the energy and initiative needed to carry out the revolution as well as being that group of new socialist men and women who would actually live to see a new socialist future. The party attempted to create a dominant culture of revolution through appeals to youth and youthfulness, making an explicit connection between the imagery associated with youth and the images and ideals they hoped would be associated with the revolution. In other words, for many Bolsheviks in this period, "youth" meant something far more than a stage in human development. It implied a "youthful" state of mind, a revolutionary way of perceiving the world. While age was associated with the corrupt values of Tsardom and a dying world, an appeal to youth implied a kind of social optimism. The younger generation embodied a world just being born. Lenin described himself and his party as youthful: "Is it not natural that youth should predominate in our party, the revolutionary party? We are the party of the future, and the future belongs to the youth. We are a party of innovators, and it is always the youth that most eagerly follows the innovators. We are a party that is waging a self-sacrificing struggle against the old rottenness, and youth is always the first to undertake a self-sacrificing struggle."[20]

Indeed, in appealing to "youth," the Bolsheviks were in some ways simply affirming themselves. The Bolshevik party was itself a party of youth, particularly in the early years. The median age of those present at the Sixth Party Congress in 1917 was only twenty-nine, and close to 20 percent of those joining the party in Petrograd were under twenty-one.[21] Although the average age of those in the party leadership was thirty-nine in 1917, they had had their formative revolutionary experiences when they too were young, and therefore perhaps thought of most young people as being as innately rebellious as they were.[22] As Lenin explained, "Things are harder for our generation than they were for our fathers. But in one respect we are luckier than our fathers, *we have begun to learn and are rapidly learning to fight* . . . We are fighting better than our fathers did! Our children will fight better than we do, and *they will be victorious.*"[23]

The militaristic language Lenin used here was typical of the early period of Bolshevik agitation and rule. Party documents from the period of War Communism emphasized youth's "battlefield virtues" of "bravery, and self-sacrifice," as well as those of "strength, endurance, toughness, and dexterity."[24] These early official images of youth converged with the Komsomol's view of itself. The party and Komsomol both described youth as warriors and rebels and praised traits of "energy, strength, courage, and determination."[25] In his role as Commissar of War, Trotsky put a particular emphasis on youth as fighters. He described them as fulfilling the heroic goal of destroying the enemies of socialism, be they the Whites (as they were during the Civil War) or the bureaucrats (as they would become in

1923).[26] There were repeated efforts throughout the Civil War to encourage young people, especially Komsomol youth, to join the Red Army. The first all-Russian mobilization of Komsomol members occurred in May 1919, and there were five more before the Third Komsomol Congress in October 1920.

This militaristic discourse was noticeably gendered. Young women in the Komsomol were required to go through military training, though very few, except nurses, were sent to the front.[27] But despite stated ideals of equality, the political and cultural identity constructed for the ideal young communist was overwhelmingly masculine. This emphasis on masculinity had a pre-revolutionary heritage. Memoirs of politically conscious male workers in the pre-revolutionary period describe a fraternity of men who often chose not to marry or have a family.[28] The ideal of "the conscious worker" was an explicitly masculine one not only in its ambivalence (at best) toward women in the workforce, but in its hostility to the arenas of home and family. This is an example of what Judith Butler describes as a "dialectical reversal of power" in which masculine identity is defined against the female "other."[29] Such reversals continued in the post-revolutionary era, when communism was sometimes imagined as a society of men. As the enthusiast and writer Andrei Platonov wrote, "No mother gave birth to us / None of us has held the hand of a sweetheart."[30] There was also an ageist aspect to this discourse. Although many male activists were adults, some sought a kind of prolonged adolescence in which they would strengthen and maintain their commitment to the larger revolutionary brotherhood by staying free from the burdens of family responsibility. Young male communists manipulated this discourse rather explicitly. As we will see in chapter 5, young men defined themselves as revolutionary because they could more easily maintain a heroic adolescent persona, while young women were constructed as less revolutionary because of their familial responsibilities.

It was not only women who were marginalized in the discourse of revolution and war. The Bolshevik appeal to youth favored some young people over others. Working-class youth were the object of greatest affection and adulation, while student youth and children of the intelligentsia were often condemned as counter-revolutionaries.[31] In this respect, Bolshevik attitudes were the reverse of Western European middle-class approaches, which praised the patriotism and good citizenship of the Boy Scout and worried about the dangers of working-class delinquency. The first program of the Communist Youth League described proletarian youth as the "most active and revolutionary part of the working class," moving "in the front ranks of the proletarian revolution."[32] They were portrayed as the vanguard of the vanguard, working in the cities to lead the working class over the barricades to revolution, in the countryside to ensure that peasants supported the efforts of the workers, and in their own families to make sure that their parents followed their revolutionary example. Young workers, Lenin argued in 1920, are a "shock force" on the front lines of revolutionary activity, "helping in every job and displaying initiative and enterprise."[33]

THE NEW YOUTH OF NEP

With the introduction of the New Economic Policy (NEP), the active, iconoclastic qualities of the young (male) revolutionary were no longer valued. The ideal young activist of NEP was no longer the eager and aggressive military hero but the steady, disciplined, and even cautious study-cell organizer. Encouraged now were the more "adult" qualities of self-discipline, moderation, patience, and mastery. Young people now had to go through training in order to take their place in the revolutionary panoply. In 1922, the Komsomol journal *Young Communist* [*Iunyi kommunist*] ran a series of cartoons satirizing the ideal new communist youth of NEP. In the first cartoon the aggressive young Komsomol member from the revolution strides forward with a rifle and handgun. Waving from the end of his rifle is a banner reading, "All power to the Soviets." In the next, the Komsomol youth from 1919 has abandoned the ragged dress of 1917 for a leather jacket, shock boots, and worker's cap, but he too steps forward, pistol in hand. In contrast, the puzzled young communist from 1921 has dropped his gun and is standing in front of a wall of questions reading, "the New Economic Policy?" "Marxist education?" In the final drawing, the Komsomol member from 1922 is shown astride a small wagon being drawn by a turtle. He is no longer actively stepping forward into the future but sits with his head buried in a book. In the background is a large signpost reading, "toward a new kind of work."[34]

As is obvious from these images, the transition from War Communism to the New Economic Policy in early 1921 involved a change not only in politics and economics but also in the identity and iconography of the young communist. At the Third Komsomol Congress, in late 1920, Bukharin argued that while the party still needed "conscious communists who have both a fiery heart and a burning revolutionary passion," it was now especially important to develop young communists "who have calm heads, who know what they want, who can stop when necessary, retreat when necessary, take a step to the side when necessary, move cautiously, weighing and calculating each step."[35] The emphasis on the emotionality of youth quietly receded, to be replaced by a decidedly non-militaristic (and, some young militants would later complain, non-revolutionary) attention to education and learning. A contest held in Saratov for the best Komsomol youth reflected the new demands. The candidate was to be an energetic worker, exhibiting the necessary popularity and authority to be a leader, especially among non-party youth; he or she should exhibit irreproachable conduct, participating in the struggle for exemplary everyday behavior and morality; he or she had to be active in local meetings and educational circles, politically literate, a subscriber to important newspapers and journals, a participant in Komsomol sports organizations, interested and active in Pioneer work, and a good worker at his or her enterprise.[36] When trying to destroy an older order—as had been the case during the revolution and the Civil War—the Bolsheviks encouraged disorder; the stabilizing goals of NEP now demanded discipline. At issue now was containing and controlling the enthusiasms of youth in the aftermath of War Communism and its mobilizations.

These measured goals for youth reflected the particular demands of NEP. The economic disarray stemming from the Civil War, a new hesitancy about the possibility of European revolution following the failure of the German revolution of 1918, and the weariness of a war-worn Russian population imposed a new timetable on the transition to Soviet socialism. It was now obvious to many that there would not be an immediate transition to communism. The gradual building of a socialist society rather than a rapid political and military transformation to a socialist state meant a "radical modification" of the Bolsheviks' "whole outlook on socialism." Whereas before the main emphasis had been placed on the "political struggle, on revolution, on winning political power," now the emphasis was on "peaceful, organizational, 'cultural' work."[37] The "locus classicus" of this position was Lenin's speech to the Third Komsomol Congress in October 1920, in which he argued that while the older generation had destroyed the old order, it was up to the younger communist generation to "build a communist society" on the grounds of the old one.[38] This approach was particularly attractive to those like Anatoly Lunacharsky, Commissar of Education, and Aleksandr Bogdanov, head of the Proletarian Culture Organization (Proletkult), who believed that cultural and educational tasks had to take precedence over economic ones. However, even Trotsky, who otherwise continued to emphasize a "revolutionary heroic" belief in the primacy of economic transformation, concurred with Lenin's new exhortation to youth to focus on learning: "Before all else, comrades, we have to learn, before all else learn. And as the struggle will be long drawn out, up until the victory of the world working class, then we have to learn not in a hasty way but seriously and over a long time."[39] The eventual triumph of a socialist society and economy over a capitalist one was understood to be dependent largely on making the new generation communist.

Although there were varied, and often conflicting, representations of youth during NEP, the dominant view was one of moderation, discipline, and rationality. This was embodied in the new hero of the 1920s—the engineer. "[S]ystematic work must be done to create in this new generation a serious urge to master science and technology," resolved the Twelfth Party Congress in 1923. "The revolutionary energy and enthusiasm of youth must find their broad application in achieving success in the areas of specialized knowledge."[40] While the military enthusiast had been energetic and even emotional, the new engineer was supposed to be as rational in his or her daily life as he or she was at the workplace. "Man will make it his purpose to master his own feelings," wrote Trotsky in *Literature and Revolution*, "to raise his instincts to the heights of consciousness, to make them transparent, to extend the wires of his will into hidden recesses, and thereby to raise himself to a new plane, to create a higher social biological type, or, if you please, a superman."[41] Trotsky's startling images of the new person as engineering a new society and a new self combined rationality and practicality with continued utopianism. The engineering image suited a society that, like youth itself, would be built from the bottom up; the engineer would help construct both society and a new, rational self. The elevation of the engineer also reflected a fascination with technology as that which could bring the new Soviet Union in line with the more industrially advanced West.

The utopianism of Aleksei Gastev, the founder of the Central Labor Institute and an advocate of Soviet Taylorism, similarly portrayed man as a machine who could control his individual impulses in the service of a more rational and scientific organization of society. Gastev appeared to be struggling in particular against adolescent abandon. In a 1923 article in *Young Communist*, he encouraged young communists to develop their machine-like qualities, to learn "to react quickly," "automatically," and yet with self-control: "The development of maximal automatism . . . together with will-power and self-possession, means that one is hardened against any kind of panic, and against epidemics of cowardice which characterize the uncultured man."[42] The pedagogue B. S. Sigal similarly described youth as a "living machine" and as a "steam engine." There was a time, he said, when people looked to understand man through his "spirit," but now they look to his physical and chemical processes. Sigal himself focused on supposed correspondences between the kind of factory work a young person performed and his height, weight, and chest size.[43] All of these factors, not incidentally, contributed to the gendering of communism, as measurements of size and strength favored young men.

Many literary and artistic images of the new man and the new woman emphasized the rational, obedient, and even mechanical qualities of the ideal young communist. Posters and official art from the 1920s show stern young soldiers, attentive students listening to lectures, and crowds of faceless youth marching across Red Square in formation. The building of communism is something to be taken seriously; there are few smiling faces in these portraits.[44] The stern, mechanized image of the ideal Komsomol youth was also evident in didactic works, such as Netaiev's "The Diary of a Girl Propagandist." In it the young teacher Anna, who works at a party school in a Moscow factory, is portrayed as a machine, a very intelligent but completely soulless machine. She is self-sacrificing, working without stop at teaching "class-conscious fighters."[45] In the novels of Evgenii Zamiatin and

Listening. Drawing by E. A. Katsman (1925) in *Dorogi iunosti. Komsomol v iskusstve 1920–1930-kh godov* (Moscow: Sovetskii khudozhnik, 1988).

Iurii Olesha, the new man is an engineer who will build a society and simultaneously shape a new self; he is a rational, orderly being who can even create a new body free from death. In Olesha's sardonic novel *Envy*, one of the major "engineers" of the new society is Andrei Petrovich Babichev, Director of the Food Industry Trust, inventor of a sausage which will sell for only thirty-five kopeks, and builder of "The Quarter," a massive kitchen destined to "put an end to do-it-yourself-cooking." In Zamiatin's novel *We*, the "new man" is a mathematician in charge of building the spaceship *Integral*. Olesha's imaginary society can be described in engineering terms: the building of massive restaurants, the development of new foods, the manufacture of a great revolution. Zamiatin's world is understood mathematically: walking in straight lines, structuring the day in hourly tables, and obliterating all "unreasonable" imagination for the revolutionary world of happy obedience.[46]

Of course, in contrast to Trotsky's sparklingly clear visions, these novels also present the murky underside of the new man, showing him as automated and without feeling, as having lost his individuality in the sea of the masses, and, most cynically, as a simple and horrible recreation not of a new man, but of the worst elements of the old. This ambivalence is a good reminder of the plurality of perspectives that existed during NEP. Though much of the official discourse about the New Economic Policy, and about youth's role, was dominated by a desire for order and rationality, there were those who questioned this approach. Lunacharsky warned that some youth had taken these new ideals too far: "We even hear among our youth voices of those who believe that we don't need passion, pathos, enthusiasm . . . these are harmful voices . . . this is fordism, not Marxism."[47] Young people too sometimes objected. The new emphasis on cultural tasks had the effect of removing youth from more active participation in the political efforts of the party. In the earlier period many young people had achieved a new level of independence and engagement both in the workplace and in the political sphere. In contrast, the policies of NEP effectively depoliticized them, returning them to a state of advanced childhood rather than incipient adulthood. Not all young people willingly agreed to this.

Additionally, NEP itself was not without controversy, and the controversy was reflected in approaches to youth as well as in debates about economics. The militant image of revolutionary youth did not go away, but coexisted uneasily with the image of the measured NEP youth. These two understandings coincided in part with conflicting political positions. Lenin called NEP a "retreat" and argued that it would be followed (at an unspecified time) by "a stubborn move forward."[48] However, there was great debate during NEP about how far this retreat should go, and about when the state should begin again to move in a more "revolutionary" direction. Views of youth often mirrored the broader left/right tensions in the party: Trotsky described the younger generation as the revolutionary savior of an increasingly bureaucratic party, while Stalin perceived militant youth as a possible threat to the stability of the new Soviet system.[49] In fact, young people were remarkably diverse in their social and cultural qualities. As we will see, this multiplicity made it hard for either Trotsky or Stalin to use the younger generation as they desired.

ANXIETY AND THE POLITICS OF POPULAR CULTURE

If, as a period of transition, adolescence was thought to be a time of great possibility, it was also seen as a period of danger. Over the course of the 1920s, Bolshevik moralists became increasingly concerned that as-yet-unformed youth were vulnerable to "infection" from unhealthy threats and influences, especially with the reintroduction of "bourgeois" pleasures under NEP. "These young people are our hope," observed a *Pravda* editorial in 1923; "These young people will be the replacement of our old guard. But at the same time it is just these young people who . . . can much more easily than any other group . . . be subjected to ideological influences alien to Marxism."[50] In contrast to European and American social scientists, who most often attributed problems of juvenile delinquency to psychological problems or to defective family relationships, experts in Soviet Russia most often described delinquency as an imported influence, a form of pollution that infected youth from the outside.

In this context, the emphasis during NEP on the cultural tasks of youth, rather than on their physical prowess or political abilities, has to be understood as deriving not simply from necessity but also from anxiety. In late NEP in particular, youth were as likely to be a symbol of danger as of optimism. In part this may have reflected changing demographics. Over the course of the 1920s a generation gap gradually grew between party "elders" and Komsomol-aged enthusiasts. "Youth" were always those under the age of twenty-three (although the specific people involved changed), while the highest-ranking cadres kept getting older. This gap may have contributed to increased anxiety about youthful misbehavior in the late 1920s. Complaints about youthful decadence in this period suggest that some authorities no longer saw youth as only a slightly younger and less-experienced version of themselves, but instead as an entirely new generation, significantly younger and almost unintelligible to the middle-aged moralists they themselves had become.

More crucially, Bolshevik discourses of adolescence as a dangerous transitional period also reflected larger fears about the instabilities and dangers of NEP as a transitional era. Precisely because it was a period of relative economic and cultural tolerance and diversity, NEP was also a time of great anxiety for the ideologically committed. Even those, like Bukharin, who supported NEP were at times uncomfortable with it, and others, like Trotsky, were openly hostile. The fears of disorder and infection, and of decadence and individualism, so evident in much of the official discourse of this period reflected anxieties not only about the vulnerabilities of youth but about the uncertainties of NEP, the future of the revolutionary process, and the political loyalties of Soviet citizens. Eric Naiman persuasively argues that the Bolshevik discourse of "infection" was symptomatic of anxiety about the "vaccinating" nature of NEP. A limited amount of capitalism was reintroduced into the healthy body of the Soviet state so that "communism could master its tools and use them for anticapitalist aims," but there was always the danger that the state would be overcome by the vaccinating agent and become ill itself.[51]

Throughout the 1920s, expressions of both optimism and anxiety about youth focused particularly on questions of everyday life, or *byt*. Lunacharsky defined *byt* as "that which is left if we remove government and economics." Nikolai Semashko, Soviet Commissar of Health, argued that "by *byt* we usually mean the sum total of traditions, habits, customs, beliefs, and, in part, convictions, which are held by a single individual or by a collective such as classes and social groups."[52] Trotsky published a series of essays devoted to "Problems of Everyday Life" in which he said that while the revolution had once and might again require "readiness to fight fearlessly under the banner of communism," today it demanded "sewing on Soviet buttons."[53] Unlike the period of the Civil War, when good communists were defined by their revolutionary enthusiasm, or the 1930s, when communists were largely defined by their attitude toward work, in the 1920s what was essential was their everyday behavior. Entire areas of youth's everyday lives—manners, language, dress, and sexual relations—were made a part of the public realm and subject to public discourse. As Komsomol moralists V. Dmitriev and B. Galin wrote in their book *On the Path toward New Forms of Everyday Life,* "We no longer consider only the Komsomol member who works and studies well as a good Komsomolets, but also he who is able to live correctly."[54]

In large part, the preoccupation with questions of daily life reflected a deep attention to culture as an integral aspect of the revolutionary process. Young people were the ideal subject for this preoccupation with everyday life, as the daily lives of youth were optimistically understood to be "greatly more mobile than those of the older generation."[55] The effort to define new rules of behavior and communist conduct for youth also reflected anxiety about the dangers of adolescence as well as uncertainty about the social and cultural instabilities of this period of great flux. When communists still lived side-by-side with "bourgeois intellectuals" or "decadent" NEPmen, as they did in the 1920s, then guidelines for behavior, dress, and language were thought necessary to distinguish communist from non-communist. Controlling daily life, making it "communist," may have made anxious communists feel that other aspects of Soviet reality—economic and political—would come under control too.

Although many committed communists agreed that qualities of daily life were important, there was great disagreement about how best to establish the new communist culture, and more fundamentally, about how to define this culture. What was appropriate behavior for the new generation? Who determined what was "communist" and what was not? Could a communist culture emerge from the socioeconomic struggle, or was it necessary to establish prescriptive rules of behavior from above? An underlying anxiety about working-class culture contributed to these difficulties. Some early advocates of the proletarian culture movement (embodied in the Proletkult) had emphasized the creation of a working-class culture truly animated by workers' own interests and priorities. But many Bolsheviks, including some in the Proletkult, believed that the party had to take a more activist role in raising the cultural level of the working class.[56] Existing forms of proletarian culture were often felt to simply perpetuate regressive prerevolutionary patterns, such as drinking, swearing, and smoking. Workers were thought all too vulnerable to "uncivilized" and "undisciplined" behavior, such as the "vulgar" speech criticized by Trotsky in his *Problems of Everyday Life,* or the unhealthy living conditions and dirty working-class clothing condemned by Semashko. Semashko argued, for example, that Russian workers should emulate the "more cultured" workers of Europe who wear one shirt to work and change into a clean one when they get home.[57] Young people were particularly likely to be attacked on these grounds, both because of the associations made between their age and problems of disorder and lack of discipline, and because of their symbolic importance to the revolutionary process.

The new ideal for youth was described as communist, and certainly it reflected the particular concerns of Soviet communists in this period, but it had other roots as well. Some of what the Bolsheviks co-opted was a pre-revolutionary dialogue about improving the working class. "Conscious" workers and union leaders in the late Imperial period were, like the Bolsheviks, disturbed by the "drunkenness, indiscipline, and crude manners" that they felt were "widespread in workers' everyday lives." Among Russian printers, for example, there was "a virtual obsession with sobriety and self-discipline."[58] Russian and Soviet approaches also resembled those of the European socialists, many of whom sought to remake the working class in a certain "civilized" image. In post-war "Red Vienna," the workers were also to be educated into a higher awareness and given the tools and trappings of a more civilized life.[59]

Bolshevik ideals reflected not just those of other socialists, however. The qualities demanded of youth in this period, as well as the anxieties adults had about youth, were also similar in interesting ways to those advocated by the European middle classes. We will see this most clearly in the discussion of flapper dress and dance, when Bolshevik moralists condemned the "frivolous" and "uncivilized" nature of 1920s fashion in much the same terms as European and American observers. One is struck by the similarities too when reading about pre-war British educators' efforts to develop "discipline, obedience, self-control, and self-respect in their youth before admitting them to the public domain."[60] These similarities are not so surprising. Historians of Europe have argued that European socialists resembled the middle classes in their preoccupation with "lifting" the morality and minds of the working class though the improving influences of "rational" recreation.[61] On the other hand, there are obvious important differences between Bolshevik ideals and those of the European middle classes. The focuses on revolutionary transformation, on class conflict, on collectivism rather than individualism, on the subversion of religious authority, on the educational advancement of the proletariat—to name but a few—all marked Soviet goals as different from those of the middle classes.

What some Bolsheviks and the middle and elite classes held most in common was an anxiety about popular culture. The 1920s were a period of intense critique (in Europe and North America) of popular culture as symptomatic of social disorder and decline.[62] Similarly, although there were great debates in Soviet Russia over what exactly was meant by "communist" forms of everyday life, or "communist" morality, it was generally agreed that this did not mean the "unenlightened" and "frivolous" low culture associated with the popular traditions of the masses in the minds of many Bolshevik intellectuals. Although notoriously ambivalent about the role of the intelligentsia in cultural transformation, many Bolshevik leaders, including Lenin, felt most comfortable either with standards of classic Russian culture similar to those embraced by the pre-revolutionary intelligentsia or with a kind of middle-class industrialist culture which emphasized standards such as "cleanliness and punctuality."[63] Although those like Lunacharsky recognized the potential of some popular forms, such as the movies, many Bolsheviks retained the familiar distaste of the elite for the culture of the masses.

The anxieties many Bolsheviks displayed about the effect of popular culture on youth—and of youth on Bolshevik culture—have in other times and places been called "moral panics." Stanley Cohen first introduced the concept of "moral panic" to describe the perceived threat to "societal values" from the culture of young mods and rockers in 1960s Britain. British moralists, including most importantly those writing in the mass media, labeled these youth "juvenile delinquents," creating a national moral panic about youth, and in the process encouraging deviance among youth as they reacted to their labeling.[64] Sociologists interested in questions of youth culture and juvenile delinquency have since described repeated moral panics about youth culture in Europe and North America in the last century. In the nineteenth century, North American educators condemned dime novels; in the 1920s they sounded "the alarm" about the "dire effects on the young" of silent movies; and in the 1950s "comic books, along with Elvis and rock music, became the great threat." Certain assumptions have been shared, among them that children's play should in fact be educational. "In a society [North America] that sees itself as rational, scientific, and ruled by self-control, pop culture is the repository of pleasure, of the forbidden, of gratification and freedom from inhibition," writes one observer of late-twentieth-century youth culture.[65]

Moral panics have often developed in periods of confusion, when, as Jeffrey Weeks has argued, "the boundaries between what are seen as acceptable and unacceptable behavior become blurred, and need redefinition."[66] NEP was definitely a period of boundary blurring and of attempted redefinition, and there are obvious, if perhaps surprising, similarities between the moral panics described here and the Bolsheviks' anxieties about the multiple, and often unacceptable, popular cultures of youth. In the Soviet 1920s the question raised was that of discipline. Who would control the formulation and development of Bolshevik culture? Would it be the party, by directing and dominating youth? Or would it be youth, who were supposed to represent the socialist future, but whose impact on Soviet society and culture might not be what the Bolsheviks wanted, nor be fully susceptible to their control? And if more control was needed, how should it be achieved? What, in other words, were the implications of the multiple and sometimes resistant cultures of youth for Bolshevik policy and for the politics of generation?

These questions should not lead us to conclude that ideals for communist culture were imposed only from above. As Diane Koenker notes in a history of working-class culture during NEP, asking whether working-class culture was "dictated from above" or was "an autonomous reflection of indigenous working-class values" is a "false dichotomy." Many activists (young and old) were ordinary workers, and their cultural goals "frequently coincided with the aspirations of broader worker society."[67] That said, there were differences between "adult" responses to Bolshevik cultural ideals and the responses of youth. On the one hand, some Komsomol youth may have been among the most eager to adopt the sober and disciplined culture of the Bolsheviks as their own. They came of age during NEP and were at least in part the "blank slates" the Bolsheviks so desired. On the other hand, others continued to perceive Bolshevik culture as an agenda and an ideology introduced from above, rather than something to which they had contributed or over which they had control. This was especially so because the didactic aspects of the Bolshevik approach to culture were often exaggerated when they "spoke" to youth as if from parent to child. As we will see in the chapters to follow, the Bolsheviks' antipathy toward existing non-elite youth subcultures had important implications for the Bolsheviks' efforts to successfully transform Soviet youth cultures and, ultimately, Soviet society.

2

THE URBAN ENVIRONMENT

In a speech in 1918 to the First All-Russian Congress of Women, Bolshevik activist Aleksandra Kollontai deplored the condition of working-class youth in the struggling families of pre-revolutionary Russia. Workers' families, she said, were rarely able to fulfill their parental duties. Small wages meant that children did not get fed enough, and long hours prevented parents from raising and educating their children with careful attention. "It was believed," Kollontai said, "that the family raised the children. But was that the case? Proletarian children are raised on the street. Proletarian children already do not know what family life is, as our mothers and fathers knew it."[1] Fortunately, Kollontai argued, the solution was at hand. Communist society would relieve parents' "difficult burden," helping families raise their children by providing nurseries, kindergartens, children's cafeterias, free books, and warm clothing. "Make way," she exclaimed, "for healthy, blossoming children, for a strong, life-loving generation . . . !"[2]

Unfortunately, the reality of the younger generation's urban experience was very different from the hopeful intentions of Soviet planners. The combined traumas of revolution, war, and famine devastated millions of families and overwhelmed the new state's ability to implement the kinds of revolutionary programs Bolshevik visionaries had dreamt of. Of the sixteen million adult males who fought in World War I, at least two million died and one million more were wounded. An additional one million died in the Civil War, and millions more men, women, and children were claimed by raging epidemics of typhus, scarlet fever, and cholera after 1917. The famine of 1921–1922 added to the trauma. Tens of thousands died because of a poor harvest and a failed transportation system. The demographic and social crises were particularly hard on widowed mothers and young children.[3] As Lenin noted at the Tenth Party Congress in early 1921, Russia was like a man beaten "to within an inch of his life."[4]

The new economic and social policies introduced in 1921 were meant to encourage a rapid recovery from the devastation of World War I and the Civil War and ultimately, of course, to improve living and working conditions from what they had been in the pre-revolutionary period. There were some definite improvements, including lower mortality rates and better medical care.[5] In many important ways, however, urban conditions and family life remained much the same as in the pre-revolutionary period, and were sometimes worse. The economy would not be restored to pre-war levels until 1926.

NEP was intended to help Soviet Russia recover from the devastation of war; however, its economic policies—especially the emphasis on productivity—explicitly undermined the social welfare goals and activities of the previous few years. In her work on the New Economic Policy's unhealthy impact on women, Elizabeth Wood argues that the basic principle of the relationship between state and society was "reformulated" under NEP. Social welfare programs for women and children were no longer supported unless they made a clear contribution to economic production.[6] The decline in state revenue (following from the increase in private trade and the attempt to balance state budgets) meant that agitation and education efforts were also sharply cut in the early 1920s. In 1923, there were far fewer libraries and reading rooms than there had been two years earlier. The number of young people who went to school also declined; there were fewer young children in school in 1923 than in 1914.[7]

All of this is important to our understanding of the challenges of cultural transformation. Bolshevik efforts to create new mechanisms of socialization through political education and youth clubs were long-term projects (and not always well-funded ones) that initially influenced only a minority of young people. This meant that the family, the neighborhood, and the street remained vital sources of socialization. We need to ask, therefore, what kinds of attitudes, behaviors, and cultures were cultivated by the social and economic experiences of revolution, war, and NEP. How did crowded living conditions, poor health, and meager resources affect gender and family relations? What effect did high rates of juvenile unemployment have, for example, on attitudes about class and career choices? We know that some young enthusiasts participated eagerly in the revolution and the Civil War, but there were others for whom the fighting meant not so much revolutionary heroism as violence and famine. According to S. A. Zolotarev, who wrote a comparative account of youth before and after the revolution, many young boys and girls emerged from the war not as revolutionaries but as "reactionaries," so scarred by their experiences that all they wanted was to return to the relative calm and comfort of the pre-revolutionary period: "Red flags, songs, crowds, alarms, laments. New searches, arrests, exiles. Scars from these early confused childhood impressions included fearfulness, dislike of crowds, nervousness." "I want everything that existed before the revolution," said one child; "white rolls, and hard shoes." "Tired people physically slide toward conservatism," concluded Zolotarev. "Evolution, progress, and revolution demand activity."[8]

Zolotarev was not alone in his preoccupation with nervous exhaustion. There was a general interest among psychiatrists and other professionals in the 1920s with "illnesses" of apathy and despair. To some degree, this preoccupation with "nervous exhaustion" says more about the moralists than about youth, reflecting Bolshevik anxiety about the questionable potential of youth to advance the revolutionary project.[9] But, of course, some youth must truly have felt upset, confused, and in despair following the trials of revolution and war, and amid the continued uncertainties of NEP. A central argument of this book is that culture had a vital impact on the socioeconomic and political relations of NEP, but clearly behavior and belief were also influenced by the social and material experiences of this difficult period.

FAMILY LIFE, HOUSING, AND HEALTH

To understand youth's experiences in the family, we need to look first at women's lives and gender roles. Under Bolshevik socialism the state was supposed to take over family responsibilities traditionally performed by women. Communal facilities such as dining rooms and day-care centers would make it possible for women to work away from the home on an equal basis with men. Eventually marriage would become unnecessary, and the family itself would "wither away."[10] The right to a quick divorce was a first step toward the establishment of a new kind of family and a new kind of marriage, based on love rather than economic needs and women's subordination. Following the implementation of the 1918 Code on Marriage, the Family, and Guardianship, the divorce rate rose quickly, especially in urban areas like Moscow.[11] However, women's precarious material conditions, especially the high rates of female unemployment, meant that many could "ill afford the personal freedom inherent in Soviet divorce law."[12] Despite the progressive intentions behind the new laws, the principal casualties of divorce were women and their children. High rates of female unemployment during NEP (resulting in part from economic austerity measures that discriminated against less-skilled female workers) made it difficult for a single mother to successfully support a child or children.

Of the single mothers who found work, many had a difficult time finding adequate child care. Many creches and day-care centers had opened during the Civil War, but more than half of them closed in the first few years of NEP because of the new financial exigencies of this period.[13] When creches were available, as in Moscow's Red October candy factory, Komsomol women were among the first to use them, overcoming the concerns that made many mothers hesitate to place their children in state-run child care centers. In some centers, however, conditions were so poor that no one wanted to leave children there. The Dukat factory in Moscow had a creche, for example, but it was "very small and very nasty, and, in addition, was far away from the factory."[14] For these reasons, many children were left with little or no adult supervision for the whole day or for the period after school. Some mothers could afford to pay a neighbor a few kopeks to keep an eye on their children, but in the most desperate cases, the young children of single mothers and impoverished homes joined the ranks of the homeless children or *besprizornye*. "It is not difficult to trace," wrote one well-known juvenile criminologist, "how a child coming from a poverty-stricken proletarian family unable to give him an education and job training, finds himself willy-nilly on the job market and, left to his own devices, becomes a *besprizornik*."[15]

The economics of family life were a challenge even in two-parent homes. Typically both the mother and father worked a full day, because the family could not survive on the father's salary alone.[16] In a small (but suggestive) survey of thirty-six Moscow working-class families, only five had a mother who stayed at home to care for the children. In families with very young children, the mother also sometimes left the children with an elder daughter or relative, or less frequently at a nursery if she could find a place. In fifteen families both parents worked, and in some of these the older children did too. In nine cases the younger children worked as well, and in four they were the only source of income.[17]

Household responsibilities in a period of no refrigeration, little running water, and poor sanitation contributed to the challenges and left even the most devoted mothers little time for careful child care. Collective enterprises such as cafeterias [*stolovye*] were intended to relieve women of the job of food preparation, but cafeterias too suffered with the introduction of NEP. Toward the end of the war, Moscow cafeterias were feeding 93 percent of the population, but when rationing ended in 1921 cafeterias began to close, and many of those that were left had less than optimal conditions.[18] A young female factory worker in Moscow's Dukat factory reported that although one of the two cafeterias available to her had food that was "tastier than that prepared at home," the other was noisy and dark, crowded with six thousand workers from her factory and other cooperatives. At the Trekhgornaia factory, the cafeteria had been reported for its rotten cabbages and bad vegetables as well as its dismal basement conditions.[19]

With few public resources to help her, a factory woman working an eight-hour shift faced another five hours of cooking, cleaning, and washing once she returned home.[20] One survey of women and men who worked an eight-hour day showed that they each spent just twenty-four minutes a day on "child care."[21] The author of a similar survey noted that for families in this situation there was almost no effort to create any kind of special environment for children.[22] Sensitive to the hardships and exhaustion of daily life, some boys and girls even suggested that they might be better off in a children's home. "It is better to live in a children's home," one schoolchild said, "where cooking is done communally, as is the washing of sheets and floors. At home the mother does all of this and gets very tired."[23]

Meager resources and busy parents also meant less-than-ideal conditions for adolescent youth. Economic difficulties allowed most working-class youth only four years of schooling. Many working-class families could not afford the fees required for early education and found it more "profitable" to keep girls at home to help with the housework and child care, while largely letting boys run free. Although proletarian youth were the largest social group in urban primary schools, children of white-collar workers were more numerous after fifth grade.[24] A large number of proletarian youth had finished primary school but had not yet started work or an apprenticeship at a factory school, and were free therefore to enjoy the entertainment and adventures of the street. In 1923, there were one million urban youth between the ages of fourteen and seventeen who were neither at work nor in school.[25] As we shall see in chapters to follow, the large number of unsupervised and unemployed adolescent boys was a cause of great concern to contemporary observers, who worried that they too often turned to petty crime or joined a "delinquent" gang.[26]

Conditions of economic deprivation also reinforced certain traditional gender roles. Young women found their freedoms circumscribed because of their parents' poverty and household needs. Young men were much more likely to avoid the same kind of family responsibilities. Young women living in Moscow commonly did half again as much housework as young men. Although working-class girls were more likely to be literate than their mothers, it was common for them to be taken out of school to work at home when a new baby was born. Young women often served as surrogate mothers to other children in the family, especially when both parents worked. Boys consequently had more free time. In one study, out of every one hundred days, the boys had 230 free hours and the girls just 169.[27] The fifteen-year-old son in one family had time to go to the movies, read books, and participate in a youth club, while the thirteen-year-old daughter carried "on her shoulders all the simpler household tasks: looking after a child, feeding her, washing, sewing, and cooking."[28]

Overcrowded and unhealthy housing conditions were another common element of the experience of urban youth. The small apartments or communal living situations that most working-class youth shared with their parents were often cold, damp, dark, and overcrowded.[29] The situation was even worse for those youth who lived with their families in crowded factory barracks, where they suffered from a complete lack of privacy and unsanitary conditions little different from those of the pre-revolutionary period.[30] Finally, there were hundreds of thousands of young people who had lost their families in the aftermath of revolution, war and famine and who had no permanent place to live. Some of these homeless youth lived in children's homes. Others spent the night in night hostels, which were usually filthy. The majority slept on the street, in doorways, alleys, even tar cauldrons. Most of these youth were part of the roving bands of *besprizornye*; however, occasionally even poor students found it so hard to find a place to live that they too were forced to sleep on the street or in cold and dirty Moscow night hostels, such as the Ermakovka or the Iul'ianovka.[31]

During the Civil War, the shortage of wood had meant that many families were not able to use their large Dutch tiled stoves and resorted instead to building small stoves of brick that they kept fired with whatever wood they could find, including furniture, beams and framework from ruined houses, and even floorboards from their own apartments. Complaints continued after the war. In 1923, more than half of the working-class youth questioned in Leningrad and Moscow said that their living conditions were unsatisfactory. The following year, close to 70 percent of Leningrad youth complained about their housing.[32] Many said that their rooms were too cold and damp. Indeed, few apartments had central heating, and much of the shoddily constructed new housing lacked the double panes of glass necessary to keep the apartments warm. Most basement dwellings in Leningrad had uncomfortably damp walls and were very dark. Almost a quarter of them had no light whatever, and in the others it appeared "not further than the window sills, and, all in all, for a quarter of an hour possibly."[33]

Many Moscow working-class youth also complained that their living quarters were too crowded.[34] Living space had actually increased during the Civil War as working-class families benefited from a massive redistribution of upper-class housing; however, as the urban population increased during the 1920s, housing again became scarce. Families slept in cellars, in lofts, in corridors, and in poorly divided rooms that other families had to cross to reach the communal bathroom or kitchen. The majority of urban adolescent youth shared a crowded room, or at the most two rooms, with their parents, younger brothers and sisters, and perhaps a grandmother or aunt. Although crowded living conditions gradually contributed to smaller working-class families, close to half of all urban adolescent youth lived in a room with four or more people, and almost a quarter shared a room with six or more.[35]

Many apartments had little more than a table, a few stools, a bed, and perhaps an icon hanging in one corner. The shortage of beds was one of the most serious problems. Young people slept on the floor, on a trunk or chest, or on a bench alongside the stove. Those who had a bed often shared it with a parent or sibling, or sometimes with their entire family if they lived in factory barracks.[36] Students living in the hostels or dormitories attached to Institutes of Higher Education, worker schools [rabfaki], or technical schools were no better off. Some students in one Leningrad technical institute had no bed at all, sleeping instead on their coats or blankets in cold corridors. Others of them slept two to a bed.[37] The lack of beds and the attendant problems of hygiene and fear of tuberculosis were so severe that in 1924–1925 the Leningrad Health Department, together with the party and Komsomol, ran a campaign calling for "[a] single bed for every citizen, especially every adolescent."[38]

The chronic shortage of housing meant that many children continued to live with their parents past the age of eighteen. Intimate relations were particularly difficult in such conditions, and scarce housing contributed to a tendency to postpone marriage. In 1925, men were on average twenty-eight when they first married, and women were twenty-four. These ages were two to three years higher than they had been at the turn of the century.[39] Of course, unemployment and difficult economic conditions, as well as the new morality of revolutionary Russia in which marriage was criticized by some as a bourgeois institution, may also have encouraged some young men and women to forgo a permanent commitment.[40]

Housing problems and a poor family life were not the only challenges that urban youth faced. Although the food situation improved during NEP, some working-class youth still struggled to find enough to eat. About one-fifth of the adolescents questioned in one Leningrad survey complained that they did not get enough to eat and had no hot meals.[41] Forty percent said that they were not satisfied with what they ate. Poor working-class families might only have cabbage or meat soup, kasha, and bread for lunch and dinner; however, the problem was particularly acute for youth who did not eat at home, which was about 20 percent of the total adolescent population. Four percent of these youth ate at a boarding artel attached to a factory, 7 percent at a cafeteria, and 10 percent "on their own."[42]

Students at worker schools, technical institutes, and universities had a particularly difficult time. Young people at one Leningrad institute spent half of their monthly stipend on food and still went hungry. Only about half of them ate every day.[43] It was not uncommon for students to go without food altogether at the end of the month, until they received their next stipend. In Moscow worker schools and institutes of higher education the average daily caloric intake was only 800 calories, or 1,000 calories if the student managed to afford breakfast.[44] Not surprisingly, the lack of food made it difficult for even the most dedicated students to participate in political and social activities. The potential power of economic constraints on political participation is suggested in N. Ognev's novel about Russian students, *Diary of a Communist Undergraduate*, in which the young hero Kostya complains to his friend, "Look here, Vanka . . . I realize quite well that I'm not quite up to the scratch [*sic*], that social and political work is going ahead everywhere, and that the whole of life is wonderfully interesting; only, tell me, how can one get into it when one has to worry all day about where one's going to get a meal. They've already started calling me an 'entertaining fellow' because others have to entertain me to dinner."[45]

Bolshevik reformers were concerned about the ways in which the traditional practices and values of the domestic sphere inhibited revolutionary change. Difficult living conditions were to be improved under a socialist economic system, but family life, traditional gender relations, and persistent religious belief also inhibited the transmission of new values to the younger generation. Ivan Bobryshev, the author of a book on "petit-bourgeois" influences on youth, argued that even youth who had grown up under communism were vulnerable to corruption. "The filth from the old world comes to them from their family, from the older generation familiar with capitalist 'charms'."[46] Indeed, there was often a great difference between everything that was considered important at home—"religion, tra-

The Soviet family as it was supposed to be. The original caption reads: "Family of Communards: The mother and father are Leninists, workers in the Number 1 printed cotton factory. The eldest son is a Komsomol member. The daughter is a pioneer. The father is 'initiating' the youngest son into the pioneers by putting on his red bandana." *Chelnok* 8 (May 1925), p. 13.

dition, the patriarchal way of life, respect for private property, and local patriotism"—and what was taught in the new curriculum—"militant atheism, the criticism and condemnation of accepted traditions and outdated family morality, Communist internationalism, and opposition to private ownership."[47] However, while culturally imbedded biases from the past certainly did affect the ways in which the new Soviet order could be imposed, these biases were not those of the family alone. Like the economy and culture, families too were in a state of transition and often embodied a mixture of the old and new. Witness this description of the inside of a working-class apartment: "There were two decorated corners in the room: one belonged to O. [the wife], where she hung icons with traditional cotton curtains and paper flowers. The neighboring corner . . . was put together by her husband. In this corner there was a portrait of Lenin with red trimming, [and] a chess set . . . The entire corner was trimmed with red material."[48] Though stereotypical in its attribution of revolutionary characteristics to the man and religious ones to the woman, this is a likely example of the kinds of contradictory influences that youth were exposed to inside the home as well as outside. The contradiction between these two images, like the contradiction between the promise of a better future and the hard realities of life in the 1920s, is central to what defines NEP as a transitional era.

UNEMPLOYMENT

For many adolescents and young adults, housing and health problems were overshadowed by the high levels of juvenile unemployment during NEP. During the war and revolution, adolescents had little trouble finding work, since much of the adult labor force was sent to the front, first for the Tsarist army and then for the Bolsheviks. In Moscow, a quarter of the working class was under the age of seventeen.[49] Nationally in 1921, 120,000 adolescents worked in industrial enterprises. By 1923, however, there were only 5,000 juvenile workers. One reason for the high rate of juvenile unemployment was the demobilization of the Red Army, which flooded the work force with adult males. Between January 1921 and January 1924, more than three and a half million soldiers, out of approximately four million altogether, were demobilized, many of whom went to urban centers in search of work rather than returning home to their villages.[50] Moreover, NEP was accompanied by new austerity measures that ended the state subsidy of many industries considered less vital for state interests. Labor productivity and profitability were emphasized, resulting in state-sanctioned labor cutbacks, especially of unskilled workers. This practice was particularly harmful to young workers and women. These policies, along with structural problems such as the fuel crisis, famine, the destruction of plant facilities during the war, and migration to urban centers like Moscow, contributed to a general explosion of unemployment after 1921.

Young people made up a substantial portion of the unemployed. Throughout the 1920s, youth under the age of eighteen made up only 5 percent of the work force, but around 15 percent of the total number of unemployed.[51] By 1926, more than two-thirds of the country's adolescent workers were jobless.[52] Older youth also had problems finding employment. In late NEP, close to half of the nation's unemployed were between the ages of eighteen and twenty-four.[53] In mid-NEP, only 20 percent of adult trade union members were without work, as compared to almost half of young trade unionists.[54] "In those years," one historian of youth has explained, "not every young person knew where the Hermitage and Russian Museum were; however, any one of them could explain how to find the Labor Exchange."[55]

Of the unemployed juveniles who registered at the Labor Exchange in Moscow and Leningrad, at least half were children of workers.[56] Those whose fathers had died during the war were sometimes the only source of income for the entire family. Factory committees received desperate petitions from these youth, begging for employment. "I am completely unable to find a means of subsistence," wrote one. "My mother and my young brothers and sisters depend on me. I beg you to give me work of any kind in your factory."[57] Some unemployed adolescents and young adults sat for days on the sidewalks outside the Labor Exchanges, and even slept there, "leaning against the wall."[58]

This high rate of unemployment was particularly difficult for young adults, as it came at a point in their lives at which they were normally expected to get married and begin supporting their own households. Unemployment effectively kept them in a state of permanent adolescence by preventing them from taking on adult responsibilities. It was especially traumatic because many of these young people had already received job training, had been employed for a number of years, and now were suddenly out of work. As one worker recalled in his memoirs of the period, "It was difficult being unemployed when you were twenty-five years old and you had been in the habit of working ever since childhood, having gotten the hang of the machines and long ago having chosen your profession because you loved it. Now you dreamed of only one thing—getting into a factory."[59]

Not surprisingly, unemployment contributed to disillusionment among some youth who felt that the revolutionary promises of 1917 were not being fulfilled. Economic security had been one of the principal promises of the revolution—a promise which must have felt closer to fulfillment during the heady days of revolution and War Communism. "Having finished my ninth year in Soviet schools I have given up all hope of finding work for myself," wrote one young man. "Thirty people from our school have finished the ninth grade this year and not one of them . . . has found work . . . these youth are universally depressed."[60] Desperate appeals to the Komsomol for employment or other kinds of material assistance often remained unanswered. One young woman, who had left home in 1923 in order to join the Komsomol, wrote to its Central Committee about her many unsuccessful attempts to get help from local Komsomol officials in Rostov and her now desperate fear that she would have to turn to either prostitution or suicide. In their response, the Central Committee in Moscow only referred her back again to the local committee.[61] In a form letter of sorts sent back to youth who had requested assistance, the Komsomol regretted that it could give no help, "just as the [Komsomol] Central Committee can give no help to any of the thousands of unemployed youth. The Central Committee has no money for that." It admitted that unemployed Komsomol youth could "often be in as bad a situation as non-party youth."[62]

Both party and Komsomol were acutely aware of the problems of youth unemployment. A lengthy discussion was held at the Eleventh Party Congress.[63] In May 1922, the party passed a law requiring a certain proportion of juvenile workers, ranging from 2 to 13 percent, in different enterprises.[64] Like the 1922 labor code, however, which had tried in a more general way to protect the rights, wages, and health of workers in the face of driving demands for labor productivity, the law protecting young workers was frequently violated. In 1922–1923 alone, the Komsomol Central Committee discussed problems of violation of the law fourteen times.[65] This should not surprise us. Although the party made some efforts to help young people, party policy, as Lenin himself described it, was aimed at raising productivity even if policies threatened egalitarian or social welfare goals.[66] The Komsomol could not compete against factory directors and party authorities determined to implement policies that emphasized profitability and productivity. Industrial enterprises continued to streamline their operations and increase the number of highly qualified older workers at the expense of unskilled and inexperienced young workers.

Komsomol authorities had reason to worry, however, not only about those youth who could not find a job, but about the working conditions of those who did. A survey of over a thousand juvenile factory workers in Leningrad found that 51 percent worked in overly high temperatures and 60 percent worked in dust. More than 80 percent of the young women stood while they worked. Close to a fifth complained of being tired after just two hours, and half said they were tired after four. The author of the survey worried that these young workers already lived and worked like adults, thinking only of wages, "and already oppressed by their monotonous life."[67] Juvenile workers were supposed to work no more than six hours a day, so that they would have time to study. In this respect, conditions did improve as compared to the pre-revolutionary period. In 1923, adolescent youth worked on average just under six hours per day, as compared to 1913, when the vast majority of working youth worked at least eight hours and usually more.[68] Some youth in desperate straits were still forced to work as long as fourteen to fifteen hours daily in bad conditions in small, less-regulated businesses such as bakeries, cafés, and cafeterias.[69] A more serious problem was the pay of these juveniles. They were supposed to be paid for a full day even when they worked just six hours. Often, however, adolescents worked an eight-hour day like adults, but got only part of an adult's pay. In 1925, a young worker made on average only 40 percent of what an adult worker did.[70]

Many working-class youth, especially in the early years of NEP, did not have a choice as to what kind of jobs they took. Unemployment had effects, however, not only on the kind of jobs youth were forced to take, but on the kind of careers they imagined for themselves in the future. On the one hand, Bolshevik ideological, economic, and educational policy emphasized the vital importance of the working class. On the other, children from proletarian families were finding it hard to get jobs. There is some evidence that, despite the emphasis on the importance of the working class, many working-class youth did not want to work in a factory. Of 150 working-class youth studying in a Moscow factory school, only just over half said they wanted to be workers or engineers (45 percent and 13 percent).[71]

More striking is a 1927 survey that asked more than 1,000 students aged nine to seventeen in four Moscow schools what kind of work they wanted. These were not the children of white-collar workers; two-thirds of them were working-class. The largest number of students chose to be workers, but this was only 19 percent of the total. Younger students were most likely to choose this profession. Not one seventeen-year-old wanted to be a worker. The survey's author argued that younger children were most likely to chose the same jobs as their parents or older siblings. It is also possible that they were more optimistic about joining the working class because they had not yet experienced unemployment. Older youth were more familiar with the difficult conditions and low pay of factory work, as well as with unemployment.[72]

What did young people want to be, if not factory workers? Sixteen percent of those surveyed wanted to be white-collar workers (shopkeepers, dressmakers, "employees"). Over two-thirds of the seventeen-year-olds chose this kind of work. It was especially popular among young women, who said they preferred it because it was "clean," not too hard, and well paid. Other popular choices were artistic fields, such as music, ballet, and art. Almost one-fifth of the sixteen-year-olds wanted to work in these fields. In contrast, one of the least popular jobs was that of party or Komsomol functionary. Just 4 percent of all those interviewed wanted to find a job in social-political work, or to be employed as a Komsomol secretary or Pioneer activist. Although these professions were more popular among working-class youth than among the children of white-collar workers, again older youth were much less interested in them. Not one sixteen- or seventeen-year-old wanted such a job.[73]

Youth who were seventeen at the time of this survey had been ten years old in 1917. They had grown up hearing about the value of the working class. That not a single seventeen-year-old wanted to become a factory worker in 1927 suggests that the difficult realities of working-class life and unemployment had made a more profound impression on some of these youth than the agitation and propaganda efforts of the Bolshevik party. The desire to work as an office employee or artist can be understood, however, not just as a desire to escape, but as a dream of self-betterment inspired in part by the new educational and economic policies. Proletarian youth now had the opportunity to go on to secondary school and institutes of higher education. They could dream of becoming office workers or artists, rather than working in a factory as their parents had. That their dreams of self-betterment were the dreams of the middle classes reflects the challenges of trying to create a new culture even among supposedly revolutionary youth.

The discrepancies between the promise of a better future and the hard realities of life in the 1920s made the Bolsheviks' task of educating and inspiring the new generation difficult. Bolshevik moralists and educators were aware of the challenge that unemployment, poor living standards, bad health, and insufficient housing posed to the new government. Lev Sosnovsky, a journalist and prominent social commentator, admitted that it would be hard to create a new socialist culture in such poor conditions: "If you have never been in these [working-class] bedrooms, then you can't imagine how one could raise a pioneer in a room where three families live, each sleeping on one bed—father, mother, and young infant."[74] The irony, of course, was that it was just these kinds of conditions which were previously thought to be necessary to create the Pioneer. Unlike before the revolution, however, when they had seen their task as primarily political, the Bolsheviks were now necessarily more sensitive to the challenges as well as the opportunities posed by the working-class cultures cultivated in such conditions. It was not just that it was difficult for youth to participate in the grander schemes of a new society when so many of them were preoccupied with the day-to-day realities of urban life, although this was certainly true. The day-to-day realities themselves—the tribulations of revolution and war and the environment of deprivation and unemployment—created their own attitudes toward class, toward gender relations, toward family, toward political and economic priorities, which had the potential to resist as well as support Bolshevik efforts at state-directed cultural transformation.

3

MAKING YOUTH COMMUNIST

The importance of youth, along with their supposed malleability and vulnerability, made them particularly important targets for a whole range of Soviet educational, recreational, and correctional activities. Youth clubs and political cells (as well as juvenile courts and labor homes) were meant to address the particular needs of those hovering between childhood and adulthood. In addition to encouragement, these activities were meant to provide the direction and discipline which youth's vulnerability and malleability were thought to require. The Komsomol was the central organization for Soviet youth. It supported those who had already committed to communism, and tried to convert others. The Komsomol used education, agitation, and ritual to explain how new social relations were to be structured and how young communists were expected to behave.

Its work was not easy. Although NEP was intended as a period of cultural transition and transformation, the very character of NEP—its emphasis on stabilization, centralization, and moderation—worked against the kind of rapid and enthusiastic mobilization of youth that had taken place during the revolution and Civil War. While many young people conformed to official definitions of the ideal young communist—speaking and behaving according to the language and rituals of the new state—for some this conformation was not deeply felt, but an example of what Stephen Kotkin has called "speaking Bolshevik."[1] Additionally, the relative economic and social freedoms of NEP made it difficult for the Komsomol to engage youth, because some preferred the "bourgeois" pleasures of the NEP street to the communal discipline expected in the youth league. Finally, certain youth were both particularly encouraged to become active members of the league and particularly likely to do so. Proletarian males were at the top of the ladder of Bolshevik virtue, while peasants, students, and women of all classes were on lesser rungs.

There were additional challenges to Komsomol discipline. Even young people who identified themselves as communist were not always compliant subjects. Young people held a range of opinions about what it meant to be a good communist. There were disagreements and negotiations between party and Komsomol and between Komsomol members. Many Western

accounts of communist youth have focused on the Bolsheviks' manipulation of the Komsomol, describing a coercive relationship between a mon-
olithic party and a weaker youth organization.[2] It is true that the party
intended the Komsomol to be its auxiliary, and the early history of the
subordination of youth and youthful interests to party demands is particularly illustrative of this. This does not accurately represent the whole of
communist youth culture, however. During NEP, at least, Komsomol culture (like Soviet society) blended new ways of life with old ones, and officially approved activities with barely tolerated ones. The Komsomol was
an organization for youth, through which the party tried to remake them
into Bolshevik images of the ideal young communist. It was an organization of youth, in which some young people identified with official communist culture while others defended alternative expressions of what it meant
to be communist. It was a site of agreement, negotiation, and resistance
between and within generations about what a communist should be and
how best to make one.

"WE FELT OUR POWER"

The Komsomol was founded in 1918 with just 2,500 members.[3] Two years
later there were 400,000 members, or about 2 percent of the country's eligible youth between the ages of fourteen and twenty-three. Following the
death of Lenin and the introduction of an ambitious membership levy in
1924, Komsomol membership rose further as young people petitioned the
Komsomol to take them as members to "fulfill the behests of Ilich."[4] By
the mid-1920s, a large majority of Komsomol members had joined after
the period of revolution and war. By the end of the decade the Komsomol
was almost twice the size of the party.[5] There was a high rate of turnover in
the Komsomol membership, though it was less at the highest levels. Some
of this turnover was to be expected as the original members grew older
and younger people joined. Some turnover was related to periods of political conflict. In 1924 and the first half of 1925—when youthful supporters
of Trotsky were purged—the Komsomol lost 150,000 members (some to
purges, some leaving voluntarily). In the same period, 400,000 new members joined. A year later the Komsomol calculated that 70 percent of its
members had entered in 1923 and 1924. As we will see, the turnover of the
Komsomol membership, and the continual and steady increase in the number of new members, posed significant educational and political challenges.[6]

Young people joined the Komsomol for many different reasons. Some
joined because of the drama groups, choral societies, sports groups, movies, and concerts offered by the youth league. Like the early informal youth
groups of the revolutionary period, the Komsomol provided a "community of peers" for urban youth who were developing their own generational subculture.[7] Komsomol cells and clubs were a convivial gathering
point. "Everyone loved to be together," remembered one woman. "I loved

Demonstration on International Youth Day. *70 let VLKSM* (Moscow: Molodaia gvardiia, [c. 1923–28] 1988), pp. 28–29.

the meetings and demonstrations, the music and the dancing."[8] The Komsomol had this function in part because all other youth groups—the Boy Scouts, Menshevik youth groups, and Jewish and Baptist youth organizations—were suppressed.[9] Komsomol clubs and activities provided a place to be and things to do for youth seeking release from cramped and adult-dominated home environments, and from the uncertainties and boredom of juvenile unemployment.

The Komsomol was more than just a gathering point, however. The league's activities and ideology offered a new identity as well as new opportunities. Many youth appeared to have willingly embraced this revolutionary identity that promised them a part in the building of something glorious and hopeful. In her memoirs, the Komsomol activist Vera Ketlinskaia recalled the enthusiasm she had felt for the revolutionary effort: "The Soviet republic . . . everything happened before our eyes, filling our childhood and youth. We felt like victors—begging, hungry, but victorious."[10] "Whatever new dangers threatened us," she said, "[w]e felt our power, the power of our revolutionary country."[11] While many Soviet youth did not embrace communism and its ideals, those who did appear to have experienced the exhilaration of the revolution, and the struggle of civil war, with a sense of great personal involvement. For these eager and ambitious young men and women the utopian ideals and revolutionary norms of the October Revolution were an intimate part of their everyday lives, influencing the kind of lives they imagined for themselves and their attitudes toward politics, leisure, and daily life. "We sincerely believed that we had nothing to lose, apart from the freedom which we had won, and that there was nothing but a fine future ahead of us," an enthusiast remembered. "We were ready to cut the throat of anyone who raised a hand against the Soviet regime."[12] One Nikolai Bocharov recalled how the apparent dedication and comradeship of the Komsomol'tsy inspired him to join: "The enthusiasm of the Komsomol members . . . was infectious. I made new friends: boys and girls who were inspired with feelings of comradeship, who were ready to devote all their efforts to the cause of the Revolution . . . The atmosphere of the Komsomol meeting, where youth held sway and where serious political questions 'on an all-Union scale' were discussed, carried me away. I decided to enter the Komsomol."[13]

For some young people, imagining themselves as communist meant not only that they would operate in a new world, but that they would be entirely different people. "Without the revolution I should never have left my village!" explained one young woman. "I should never have learned even to read or write. I'd have married at 15 like my mother, borne children, cooked and washed and worked in the fields all my life . . . Now I can learn something of what the universe holds."[14] Her new self would be active and able to control her environment; she would be an agent of her own destiny. Though the reality might prove to be otherwise—most young women had a very hard time being accepted as equal and independent—revolutionary ideology shaped notions of personal identity and possibility in transformative ways.

The Komsomol also made some young people feel important and grown-up. One Komsomol member (who in the 1930s broke with the youth league) remembered how excited he felt when as a nine-year-old boy he was given the honor of making a speech at a town meeting devoted to the anniversary of the October Revolution: "I was filled with delight and excitement. Just imagine—I was to stand by the side of the secretary of the city Party committee and the leaders of the city soviet. I was to speak as an equal of the grown-ups! When my turn came, Sokhikyan, the First Secretary of the Party city committee, lifted me up above the rostrum. I remember my first speech to this day . . . What else could I think at that instant except that we were starting out in life as its sovereign masters, and that the future depended upon us alone? I felt in seventh heaven."[15] For its youngest members in particular, adventure and heroism had great appeal. Bocharov (who was only thirteen when he joined the Komsomol) admitted that "it was not only the wish to take an active part in building a new life" that led him to become a member. The fact that some older members were soldiers in a special unit, and carried pistols, played as great a role in his decision. "These pistols, which to our youthful imaginations seemed to be the distinctive insignia of a specially chosen and trusted category of young people, roused burning envy in me and in my classmates . . . In our minds the special purpose men were heroes ready to die in the struggle with the enemies of the workers and peasants."[16]

Of course, autobiographical reminiscences of the 1920s must be read with care. Memoirs can reflect certain conventions, and only some people feel compelled to recall their life in writing. Some of those whose memoirs are cited here use their early experiences as a foil for later disillusionment; their memoirs describe a fall from youthful innocence.[17] And, of course, joining the Komsomol could also have a more practical reward. Like joining the party, becoming a member of the youth league could confer economic and political benefits, and it helped pave the way to eventual party membership (though it did not ensure it). During the revolution and Civil War, youth activists and Komsomol members were awarded important political and agitational positions. The possible advantages of membership may have been especially attractive during NEP because it was a period of such grave economic uncertainty. In this environment, joining the party of the working class may have seemed one way to help find a spot on the factory floor or gain entrance to a training school. We know that Komsomol youth expected help from the youth league by the many petitions for economic and employment assistance received at every level of the Komsomol hierarchy.[18]

Despite a difficult economic situation that prevented many youth from finding a place on the factory floor, Komsomol rhetoric emphasized the active proletarianism of the youth league. In the public presentation of revolutionary credentials common to this period, young people emphasized their working-class backgrounds (or those of their families) if at all possible; this was the best chance for membership in the Komsomol, or entrance to an educational institute. "Please take me as a member of the Komsomol as I am the daughter of a worker and I want to get a political education to keep up with the rest of youth," wrote one such applicant.[19] Young people without a working-class background had a hard time rising above their past. One eighteen-year-old complained in a letter to Trotsky that no matter his revolutionary efforts, the class background of his parents limited his opportunities for advancement. Despite the best efforts of this young man to reject the "unhealthy" influences of his family, revolutionary organizations doubted his capacity to truly start life as a blank slate:

> Comrade Trotsky, this is not a letter; it is a confession. I write you what I have never told anyone . . . the first of January I finish school, the first of January I will be 18. My parents are NEPmen. That says it all . . . there is no worse stigma . . . I want to work, but no one trusts me, no one will take me into any organization . . . I curse the day that I was born, born into a non-working-class family . . . why can't I be a revolutionary having stewed seven years in the revolutionary cauldron? Our house is a nightmare because of my revolutionary beliefs; my parents really stink . . . but what am I going to do. I have already studied and worked in a hospital for two

and a half years, but I don't like the hospital. I'm attracted to a factory or
enterprise, damn it! . . . it is very difficult to be 18.[20]

The proletarian identity of the Komsomol was a particular point of
both emphasis and anxiety following the Civil War, when the working-
class base of the entire revolutionary enterprise was threatened by the number of workers who returned to the countryside for food and employment.
In early NEP, only about 25 percent of Komsomol members were working-
class. Even in urban centers like Petrograd, the percentage of working-class
youth was only just equal to that of white-collar and student members of
the league.[21] Uneasiness about the overrepresentation of white-collar youth
led to efforts to increase the number of worker youth, and in 1924 the Komsomol initiated a campaign to enroll 100 percent of working-class youth.
By July 1926, close to 80 percent of the Leningrad Komsomol were said to
be members of the working class, though some, it must be assumed, by
virtue of family background rather than any significant experience on the
factory floor.[22] Working-class activists tried various means to emphasize
their special claims to revolutionary legitimacy, including clothing. In a
protest against the NEPman style of living, and in emulation of the military traditions of the Civil War, young male communists in early NEP often wore bell-bottomed trousers and a sailor's pea-jacket. Even more popular was the leather coat, which, although it had been worn by pilots and
drivers in the war, became a visual symbol of revolutionary commitment
and proletarian identity. The discursive power of clothing was such that
urban youth from non-working-class backgrounds soon also adopted the
leather coat as a sign of their revolutionary intent.[23] Proletarian identity
may have been especially important to young people in a period when so
few of them could work. Because so few could develop a sense of working-
class identity through real experience in industry, they may have held even
more tightly to the "proletarian" identity granted them by joining the youth
league.

For many urban Komsomol'tsy, proletarianism was central to Komsomol identity. However, according to the party, membership in the youth
league was not supposed to be limited to workers, nor even to communists. Though the party too praised worker youth over non-worker, it argued that the Komsomol was a training ground, and as such had to attract
and admit "the broad masses of still uncommitted worker and peasant
youth" for purposes of making them communist in belief and in behavior.[24] Not surprisingly, there was tension between the party's effort to use
the Komsomol to make all youth communist and many Komsomol activists' own belief that some young people were simply closer to being communist than others. Both the centrality of working-class identity to young
urban communists' senses of self and the dilemmas this centrality caused
are especially evident in discussions about admitting peasant youth to the
Komsomol. From 1923 to 1925, as part of the party's effort to reestablish

A cartoon of the rural Komsomol member. *Iunyi kommunist* 13–14 (August 1922), p. 55.

and improve relations between city and countryside, party authorities repeatedly instructed the Komsomol to integrate the peasantry into the league's public and political life. Half of the peasant population was aged nineteen or younger, and the party needed the Komsomol in order to reach these youth.[25] "The Party is a workers' party, not a workers' and peasants' party," Stalin declared in 1924, "while the Young Communist League is a workers' and peasants' league."[26] The Komsomol leadership was itself split over the policy of rural expansion. Many urban Komsomol'tsy feared that diluting the proletarian core of the youth league threatened its vanguard role, especially as the party itself had a more restrictive admissions policy. Angry activists argued that including more peasants would mean "throwing out" the principle of the dictatorship of the proletariat in favor of the "dictatorship of the peasantry."[27] Despite objections to rural expansion even among some in the Komsomol Central Committee, however, party authority prevailed. The number of peasant members increased until by 1926 peasant youth formed close to 60 percent of the Komsomol.[28] However, although peasant members made up more than half of the Komsomol, still only about

6 percent of Komsomol-aged peasant youth joined the league, as opposed to more than half of working-class youth.[29] To the detriment of relations between working-class and peasant youth, some urban youth persisted in seeing themselves as better than their rural relatives.[30]

Like peasants, students were ideologically and iconographically subordinate in the Komsomol. Although worker and peasant youth were admitted unconditionally, students were accepted only on the recommendation of two members of the party or Komsomol and had to pass through a six-month candidacy period. Suspicion of students stemmed in part from questions of class origin. Many communist students in secondary schools and at institutes of higher education were still from white-collar or professional families. Class was a matter of culture as much as of employment or family history, however. Even proletarian students were suspect, considered more vulnerable to ideological deviation because of their contact with the bourgeois world of the university.[31] In 1923, the student newspaper *Red Student* [*Krasnyi student*] concluded that 15 to 20 percent of the students at Petrograd University were "clearly anti-Soviet," 10 percent were completely apathetic, 60 percent were non-party, and only 10 percent "actively" supported the revolution.[32] In other institutes, particularly those formed after the revolution, the social and political differences were less severe and there were more young communists, but in every case students had to strive harder than their worker comrades to demonstrate their devotion and incorruptibility. Many, again, wore distinctive clothing that marked them as proletarian by conviction if not in reality. They called each other "comrade," while students who did not belong to the Komsomol continued to address each other as "colleague."[33] Komsomol newspapers praised those who, like Comrade "Z," combined scholarship with political agitation. Comrade "Z" joined the Komsomol at eighteen, then traveled from city to city as part of an agitational campaign. In 1919 she went to the front. When she was demobilized in 1921, she entered the literature department at Moscow State University, where she lived in very poor conditions, but worked hard and even studied French on her own at night. She worked as the secretary of the party cell in her Department, agitated among non-party students, fought against illiteracy and against "reactionary professors," and founded a new cell to study "positive ethics." All the while she continued to provide material support for her mother.[34]

CHILDREN WITHOUT FATHERS

Although proletarian youth were considered closer to being communist than peasant and student youth, most Bolshevik authorities assumed that all youth—proletarian, peasant, and student—needed education and guidance from adults to become good communists. There were two obvious sources of authority over youth—parents and the party—and both were problematic for many communist youth. Komsomol'tsy commonly embraced an image of themselves as free from parental influence and control. "Our generation has October as its birthday. It is the first generation in Russian history not to have ancestors. We are children without fathers," explained one such enthusiast.[35] This statement of independence had both symbolic and psychological importance as a declaration of independence from the corruption of pre-revolutionary Russia and as an adolescent assertion of almost-adulthood. The emphasis on independence from parental control also reflected early Soviet discourse, much of which was directed against the family, especially the oppressive proletarian family of the pre-revolutionary period. Communalism will replace the nuclear family, Aleksandra Kollontai explained, creating "a big, universal working family, in which those who work, men and women, will be brothers and comrades above all."[36] Enthusiastic early members of the Moscow Proletkult passed a "Declaration of Children's Rights" which guaranteed that "children could pick their own form of education, their own religion, and could even leave their parents if they chose."[37]

For some would-be Komsomol'tsy, rejection of parental control was also pragmatic. Young people were sometimes forced to leave the parental home when they joined the Komsomol. Rural parents in particular went to great lengths to prevent their children from joining, because they objected to its anti-religious propaganda and other challenges to authority. The mother of eighteen-year-old Feodor Shamalin declared that she would never allow her son to join. She convened all their family and friends in a family "council" to discuss the issue and then forbade him to join, threatening to drag him into the street and tell the entire village if he persisted. When Feodor joined despite these injunctions, she repeatedly stole his membership ticket from him, forcing him to buy new ones. Finally, in desperation she brewed a batch of liquor [*samogon*], got her son drunk, and dragged him in front of the Komsomol secretary so that he would be expelled. Eventually, Feodor left the village altogether, found work in a factory, and rejoined the Komsomol there.[38]

Some young enthusiasts wanted to be free from party authority as well as parental. Those active in the revolutionary period had already experienced considerable independence. This helped fashion a collective self-image often different from that which political authorities desired. Young people, especially young factory workers, had actively participated in the strike movements and protest marches of 1917.[39] They also played an important role in the Red Guards—over 40 percent of Red Guards in Moscow and Leningrad were under the age of twenty-five.[40] Besides joining adults in the larger cause of working-class revolution, young workers had fought to protect their own political and economic interests and had formed separate youth unions, clubs, and organizations. Various groups of factory youth (some Bolshevik, others more broadly socialist) had struggled to develop young workers' class consciousness and had agitated for a minimum wage for youth, voting rights for eighteen-year-olds, and a six-hour day for minors under the age of sixteen. Youth committees, specifically organized to monitor the working conditions of younger workers, mushroomed in many of Petrograd's large factories. In a demonstration of their strength, one hundred thousand young workers marched in their own coalition on May Day 1917.[41]

Although political authorities desired the voluntarism of youth, they were also afraid of it, torn between their need for youthful initiative and their desire to maintain control over the actions of youth and their revolutionary imaginings. Although the party praised youth's spontaneity, it did not allow independently organized youth groups to exist. In 1917, Petrograd youth were forced to dissolve their group "Labor and Light" [*Trud i svet*] in favor of a smaller, Bolshevik-controlled group. Following the revolution other independent youth groups were also gradually suppressed. However, early debates on the nature of the Komsomol suggest that there was not a single blueprint for youth, but an evolving pattern of relations between communist youth and the party. At the first congress of the Komsomol, party authorities still maintained that the youth league was officially independent of the party. In 1919, a joint resolution of the party's Central Committee and the Komsomol stated that the league was to be under the party's control, but that the party was not to interfere in the Komsomol's organization or prevent its "spontaneous" work. This can be seen as an effort to appease those young communists who insisted that the Komsomol should be an elite organization equal to the party. By 1921, party documents increasingly described the younger generation as part of a larger proletarian army that had as its principal task the fulfillment of the party's goals, not the protection of youth's own interests. It was now clear that the party did not intend the youth league to be an advocacy organization agitating for the needs of its youthful constituency, but a means of organizing and educating youth, of making them communist, and of insuring that party leaders and youth held a common perspective. Dual membership was one mechanism of party control. Generally, about 10 percent of Komsomol members were also party members, and in some Komsomol strongholds, such as Leningrad, the proportion was as high as 30 percent.[42]

There are similarities between issues of party control over the Komsomol and party control over the Zhenotdel (women's department): Should women (or youth) be encouraged to "organize for their own sakes" and in their own separate interests, or should women (or youth) be seen as "not having any goals and tasks separate from the goals and tasks of the working class as a whole"?[43] These issues were debated with some intensity during the period of War Communism and the early years of NEP, but the question of the Zhenotdel, like that of the Komsomol, was officially resolved in favor of integration rather than separation. By 1924, according to

Elizabeth Wood, "there was little pretense that work among women was being done primarily for women's sake." The women's sections had become "dutiful daughters" working to bring women into the ranks of the party.[44] In the Komsomol, on the other hand, while the issue of separatism had been settled officially by the beginning of NEP, there was more resistance from Komsomol members to the seeming capitulation of the youth organization to adults in the party. As late as 1927 and 1928, militant Komsomol'tsy continued to complain aggressively that the youth league had abandoned its commitment to advancing the particular needs and causes of youth.

It is not surprising that party authorities wanted to control work among women and youth. Many believed that both women and youth had to be educated into full consciousness, and both received some special dispensation in law and in the workplace to protect their theoretically more fragile physical and moral selves. At the same time, there were important differences between the treatment of women and youth (especially male youth). While young men would eventually rise into adulthood, women were always seen as "just" women, with all of the implicit backwardness this category implied.[45] Perhaps because boys would soon inherit the rights and responsibilities of men, their lifestyle and ethics had particular meaning. To male party authorities, women were fundamentally "other" while male youth were younger versions of "self." While the party was notoriously ambivalent about the need for a separate women's organization, political authorities did not appear to question the necessity and importance of a separate youth organization. At the same time, they were very anxious about youthful deviations from official ideology, as it was young people who were expected to implement the policies of their elders.

QUESTIONS OF EVERYDAY LIFE

With the introduction of NEP and the new focus on education and social transformation, the smallest details of *byt* became as important in defining Komsomol identity as enthusiasm and youthful bravado had been during the Civil War. In striking contrast to the passionate exhortations to revolutionary action found just a few years earlier, in the mid-1920s Komsomol newspapers like *Young Leninist* [*Molodoi Leninets*] debated problems of a much more prosaic kind: How many bottles of beer may a Komsomol member drink? Does a young Komsomolets have to give up his seat to a woman in the tram? Is it wrong to wear makeup or a tie?[46] "Each Komsomol member must now be evaluated not only by how much political grammar he has learned, and by how successfully he participates in socialist production," wrote moralists Dmitriev and Galin, but also "by his ability to construct his own *byt*."[47] Komsomol clubs—with their political cells, drama groups, and agitational efforts—were to be on the front line of the effort to erase all vestiges of a "non-communist" lifestyle and values. Specialized study cells were formed in which young people discussed problems of "hooliganism, drunkenness and flirtation" and dedicated themselves to creating new forms of daily life.[48] The Komsomol even considered establishing a nationwide organization, "The Society to Improve Everyday Life," which would, for example, study the problem of eating in dormitories.[49]

Behavior and belief no longer belonged to the individual, but to the greater Komsomol collective. "The basic characteristics of the new man are collectivism, the steadfast strength to struggle for the general, collective interest, the absence of petit-bourgeois egoism," A. Stratonitskii wrote in his book on questions of everyday life in the Komsomol.[50] Being a young communist, Nadezhda Krupskaia argued in 1922, "means that the communist puts his personal interests aside, subordinates them to the common interest."[51] Although the new guidelines had obvious disciplinary aspects, they were not dictates directed solely at others; enthusiastic young people tried to realize the principles of communalism in their own lives. A former Komsomol member remembered the fervor of these early years, when "not to share an extra smoked fish which had been gotten hold of somewhere or cigarettes taken in exchange for a lighter, not to help a comrade in need, was looked upon as a disgrace, as behavior unworthy of a Komsomol member."[52]

Not everyone was wholly enthusiastic, however, or knew just how to behave. Encouraging new forms of behavior and belief required both education and regulation—the first to teach people what to do and the second to monitor their success or failure. New ways of living and new ways of thinking were meant to become internal to the individual, but until they did, the discipline required to master these new forms of everyday life would have to come from the outside. Komsomol comrade courts and the Komsomol militia were two ways of regulating behavior. During the Civil War, comrade courts had fought against class enemies and counter-revolutionaries. During NEP, courts in Komsomol clubs and youth communes continued to struggle against "enemies of the state" (now usually defined as NEPmen, kulaks, and bureaucrats) but paid increasing attention to problems of daily life within the Komsomol itself, including issues of abortion, religion, and marriage.[53] Judicial decisions often centered on the individual's supposed violation of the larger needs of the collective, and condemned youth were encouraged to admit that they had been wrong to put their own priorities and selfish interests above those of the communist community. "Now I understand that my personal life is not something separate, belonging to me alone," repented one such accused. "Being in the Komsomol means that the whole organization bears the responsibility for each of my actions."[54] The Komsomol community asserted jurisdiction over even the physical body of a Komsomol member. One young married worker who had an abortion was expelled from the Komsomol for two years because "she did not understand that the question of childbirth is not entirely a personal affair, but concerns the entire society." When the young woman argued that having a child would leave her no time for Komsomol work and meetings, the court reminded her that she could put the child in a nursery (a collective institution) and thus not miss a single meeting. "What will happen to our new society," concluded the court, "if every healthy communist and Komsomol member proceeds from the same reasoning as the defendant, and the bourgeoisie, being free, continues to grow?"[55] The right of the collective to control the individual could extend even unto death. Party theoretician Evgenii Preobrazhenskii warned Komsomol'tsy that the league might order them to lay down their dead bodies so that others could advance over them. "If this death is ordered by our party and League, we must accept it in the interest of the common cause."[56]

Besides the courts, two groups—the "militia for the struggle against hooliganism" (ODK) and "friends of the club"—were responsible for enforcing new codes of behavior and for taking action against inappropriate activities. While they had some educational functions, these two groups were largely policing units that kept order in the club, made sure youth sat quietly in club reading rooms, watched over Komsomol behavior in the street, and organized "trials" of hooligans. At meetings or evening events, a few members of the ODK or "friends of the club" might show up to prevent rowdy and drunk members from entering the room or disturbing the group's activities. These squads were largely made up of Komsomol youth, although sometimes adults also participated. In one factory, of fifteen people in the ODK, five were from the factory club, five from the factory itself, and five from the surrounding neighborhood.[57] The militia was not very popular. At a 1926 meeting of Komsomol factory representatives, there were complaints that the militia was not effective at combating hooliganism and drunkenness. Squad members tended to be bullies who were not liked or respected by other youth because they worked with the militia, exploited their situation, and often themselves got into fights with "hooligan" youth.[58] Concerned Komsomol'tsy argued that the squads needed a different, more educational role to offset the anger other youth felt at being bossed about by members of their own generation.

Although policing and punishment were by no means absent in the 1920s, NEP was predicated on a different kind of discipline which demanded a remaking of the self and not just control of the other.[59] Youth communes were a more popular way to encourage young people to live according to the collective interest and to inculcate new forms of daily life. In 1919, the Komsomol press called on youth to organize housing communes among young communists, and then among all youth. This early appeal emphasized the superior role of the commune as compared to the family; youth communes would serve as a "socialist reversal of the style of life of the people." Parents were encouraged to put their own children into communes for which they could then serve as "elder contributors" (although the ambiguous nature of this possible contribution is obvious in the case of the youth commune where the mother of one of the members is praised for her work as a "culinary specialist").[60] Both worker and student youth responded to this call. Communes were popular because they combined a pre-revolutionary heritage of rural communes, artels, and student groups with new revolutionary dreams of a communist individual forged in the communal fire. Communes were also attractive to unemployed and underemployed youth.[61] The students who formed a commune in 1924 at the Leningrad Electrotechnical Institute were committed to "introducing the habit of collectivism in everyday life" but also noted that it was easier to live as a collective when so many students did not have enough money to survive by themselves.[62] Finally, communes offered a way for young people to move away from crowded living situations at home. Generational conflicts over how young adults spent their free time were likely to be exaggerated in such close quarters, and Komsomol groups sometimes urged their members to move into communal apartments, dormitories, or other independent living situations to gain freedom from parental control.

According to the author of an article in *Young Communist* [*Iunyi kommunist*], youth communes were meant to "organize the life of commune members with the principle of building new forms of everyday life."[63] This transformation was supposed to take place both organizationally (with communal cooking arrangements, for example, so that women were freed from meal preparation) and within the individual. Each member was supposed to surrender to the commune in every area of daily life, so that there was not "a single even very small issue" that the commune member could claim was a "private affair."[64] The lack of any individual interest was concretely represented in the lack of any personal space or belongings. Just as there could be no "private affairs," so there would be no privacy. Committed to this end, the young communards associated with the *Freedom* factory shared four common rooms: a large sleeping room where they slept and did physical exercises, a combination dining room/reading room, a kitchen/smoking room, and a cloak room/changing room.[65] Student members of the Leningrad Commune of 133 (a commune with 133 members based in an Electrotechnical Institute dormitory) debated whether a communard could hold anything in private: "Is it allowable to say: my room, my linen, my book, my money?" They worried that separate rooms with doors encouraged too much privacy and declared that anyone could now enter any room without knocking. When this was not enough, they knocked down all the interior walls so that the commune would be as "one family."[66]

All these actions had as their goal the weakening of individual desire and the strengthening of commitment to the community. We can see a relationship between penetrating and rearranging physical space and "rearranging" human consciousness. By regulating physical space, the group insured that there was no "room" for alternate loyalties or languages that might threaten the desired discourses of communality. Regulating space within the commune and within the individual was also more generally related to rearranging the body politic. It was not just the commune that was supposed to be as "one family," but also the larger collective of the new Soviet state.

Relationships were also at issue within the commune. Those most committed to the communal ethic argued that personal relationships had to take second place to the greater needs of the group, and could be permitted only insofar as they did not threaten the larger Komsomol community. Even platonic friendships were suspect for some eager Komsomol'tsy, because they might create a "weakening in the comradely cohesion of the entire collective."[67] Dyadic and family relationships were particularly suspect. If members of the Moscow State University commune noticed that a girl was attracted to a certain boy, "both were attacked, during a heated sitting lasting all night, as subverters of communist ethics on account of this 'offense.'"[68] Some communes forbade marriage and sexual relations and restricted sleeping areas to large single-sex dormitory rooms.[69] In many communes, sexual relations outside marriage also caused problems because of the lack of private space. Three-quarters of the communards in the Leningrad Commune of 133 had had sexual relations before joining the commune, but once they joined some felt forced by circumstances to practice celibacy, while others had quick affairs usually consummated in the dormitory room of a fellow student (but non–commune member). Most saw absolutely no way to resolve the problem within the confines of the commune as it was then established.[70] Some communes did allow marriages (although the young couples often continued to live separately, still sleeping on bunks in single-sex rooms), but forbade children. When they permitted children, they might be regarded as the "commune's children," to be raised communally and brought up at general cost. One commune questioned whether communards leaving the commune had the right to take "their" children with them, or whether they should remain behind as part of the "communal property."[71]

The community also owned most material belongings. In the commune at Moscow State University, overcoats, shoes, sheets, and underclothes were held and washed communally. At the Commune of 133 the commune's "Customs Commission" divided up any incoming package equally. Communards pooled their money—sometimes all of it and sometimes some proportion—and then spent hours debating whether to spend it on new overcoats or on renovations of the commune's facilities. Some young enthusiasts hoped to regulate and mechanize not just money, but time. In both the Commune of 133 and a Mining Academy commune in Moscow, the local Soviet Taylorists established precise timetables for every activity, including getting dressed, brushing one's teeth, and reading the newspaper:

7.30	reveille
7.30–8.45	dress, breakfast, tidy up
8.45–2.00	college
2.00–3.30	dinner and rest
3.30–9.00	college and homework
9.00–9.30	supper
9.30–11.00	rest, reading
11.00–12.00	reading the newspapers[72]

The Taylorists at the Commune of 133 constructed a large board with lists of activities and gave each member a marker with which they could indicate where they were and what they were doing. "I have left the Commune," read one such marker. "I am in room number 10," read another.[73]

Group budgeting of money and time served idealistic goals of equality, but was also meant to change the smaller habits of daily life. Indeed, communes sometimes boasted most of how they changed personal habits of hygiene—that the communards now cleaned their teeth every day, and changed their underclothes and had a bath every week.[74] A major reason the members of the Moscow commune *Red Rubber* shared their money was so that they could learn how to budget their salaries to prevent them from spending it all in the first two weeks and then going hungry. The young men in this commune were also learning to wash their hands before meals, to sleep with an open window, and to put their dishes away after meals.[75] Evident, if unspoken here, is the fact that someone who was already educated must have been teaching those who were not yet as cultured as they should be. There were degrees of revolutionary preparedness, with those in the vanguard rapidly trying to transform themselves before raising up others. Not surprisingly, the differences between the "enlightened" and the yet-to-be-enlightened could cause tensions, sometimes manifested in conflicts between the original members of a commune and those who joined later.

Not everyone could adapt to the rigors of communal existence and the accompanying restrictions on private lives. Communards complained most heartily about the detailed restrictions of the Taylorists, and their efforts did not last long. "I will study where I want and sit where I want," said one such opponent.[76] There were also cases of communards stealing from the communal money pot, refusing to clean or cook, and hoarding their own private supplies of food and money.[77] In such tight quarters disagreements were common. In the Leningrad Commune of 133, some complained that the girls had "too much underwear" and wanted it washed "too often," while others fought about how much money should be spent on baths, or whether school books should be shared among the group.[78] Difficult living conditions intensified these struggles. The commune journal of one group of five young men and five young women suggests the disorder that some young communards lived in:

> October 29th.—Again no breakfast. Also no supper. Nothing has been washed up yet. The larder has not been tidied, nor has the lavatory (indeed the lavatory is hardly ever tidied). There is a thick layer of dust everywhere. The door was left unlocked when we went to bed. The light was left burning in two rooms (a usual occurrence). Our amateur photographer developed his negatives at two o'clock in the morning, contrary to everyone's wishes.

> October 30th.—We have begun to tidy up. Everything is thrown about over the floor, on the windowsills, on the chairs, on and under the beds. In the Club, newspapers, inkpots, letters and penholders are strewn all over the room . . . The kitchen table is packed full to the limits of what it can hold. The outlet-pipe is stopped up with a filthy layer of grease. The larder is an inferno. The communards are apathetic and calm; some are even content. Shall we build a new life like this?[79]

Like many other communes, this one resolved its problems by returning to less-revolutionary methods—it hired a housekeeper to keep the place clean.

Despite these difficulties, however, the communal life was popular among many young communists in the 1920s. Though encouraged by the party and the Komsomol, joining a commune was a voluntary act, and those who joined were in significant ways imposing communal norms on themselves. Some had clearly internalized the authority and ethic of sacrifice required to live in a youth commune; they saw it as a necessary part of the process of self-transformation in a revolutionary era. Communes differed from the other-directed efforts of Komsomol agitation campaigns in that communes were mostly places for revolutionizing the self, rather than the other. By living communally, committed young communists tried to teach themselves what it meant to be Soviet.[80]

THE KOMSOMOL CLUB

"The Komsomol club is the center of educational work in the Komsomol . . . and the spiritual center of all working youth," wrote an optimistic contributor to a book on new ways of life. "It is here in various study circles . . . that new people are educated in new ways."[81] In 1924 there were over five thousand Komsomol clubs in the Soviet Union, under whose auspices were organized literature, drama, and art circles, political study cells, demonstrations, and excursions.[82] Most of these clubs were associated with a factory, but there were also clubs in primary and secondary schools and in institutes of higher education.[83] Besides joining these clubs, which were designed specifically for Komsomol members, youth were among the most active participants in trade union clubs. Of the over seven million factory club members, close to four million were young people.[84]

Like the commune, the Komsomol club established a new space for the making of a new society, although this space was more explicitly a public one. Some of this new space was appropriated from the previous owners of private property: many worker and Komsomol clubs were set up in the homes of the pre-revolutionary elite. Other club activity did not take place in a separate club building; instead the Komsomol established "Red Corners" in existing working-class dormitories, barracks, and communal houses. The appropriation of physical space was the first step toward the ideological "appropriation" of the individual, as the Komsomol moved into, and thus tried to dominate, space and those in that space. Like clubs, these "Red Corners" served as a place for both education and relaxation, with room for political books and belles-lettres, and a table or two with newspapers, magazines, and a chess set.[85]

Komsomol groups also organized cultural events in factories during the lunch break, to encourage more "productive" forms of recreation than the usual "horseplay," rowdy talk, or games of checkers. The Komsomol'tsy in the factory *Stormy Petrel* held lunchtime meetings on problems of everyday life, discussions of poetry and literature, and an occasional sing-along accompanied by an accordion or balalaika. At the *Red Hercules* factory, where close to eight hundred young people worked, a lunchtime meeting was set up especially for young women, at which typically twenty-five to thirty women met to read and discuss literature, mostly belles-lettres.[86] Not all these instructional activities took place indoors. When reading about "the earth and the sun," Komsomol'tsy might go to an observatory, or when studying about "electricity in the service of mankind," they would visit an electric station, a trolley line, or the Dinamo factory. Excursions were also planned to sites of local interest (events from the 1905 revolution, monasteries, and a tour of "bourgeois Moscow") and to factories and enterprises, geological sites, museums, and woods and rivers.[87]

Club education was combined with practical experience and labor. "Only by working side by side with the workers and peasants can one become a real communist," argued Lenin at the Third Komsomol Congress in 1920. "[W]e shall organize detachments of young people who will help to assure public hygiene or distribute food, who will conduct systematic house-to-house inspections, and work in an organized way for the benefit of the whole of society."[88] Komsomol members taught workers and peasants to read, collected money for homeless youth, brought Komsomol theater and chorus to factories, cleaned schools and streets, and went out into the village to try to teach the peasantry new agricultural techniques.[89] Agitational campaigns also moved beyond the boundaries of the local club and encouraged participation by non-Komsomol youth. In 1924–1925 alone, there were two hundred agitational campaigns in Leningrad, in which 260,000 youth participated.[90] Most were linked to current political campaigns. Two popular campaigns in 1921, "Youth Go Study!" and "NEP and Youth," were designed to direct attention to Lenin's speech at the Third

Komsomol Congress, in which he called on young people to focus on learning. Others corresponded with revolutionary holidays and anniversaries. On the first "Holiday of Red Revolutionary Students," which was held on the 104th anniversary of the founding of Petrograd State University, communist students gathered in a crowded hall where they sang the Internationale and loudly saluted the revolution, shouting, "Greetings to the revolutionary students! Greetings to the revolution!"[91]

Many activities supported by the Komsomol were educational. Clubs helped direct political and union campaigns, arranged excursions to sites of professional, industrial, artistic, and historic merit, published weekly and wall newspapers, provided libraries and reading rooms, and arranged exhibits on problems of everyday life, including hygiene, sexual relations, and health. They also ran study groups on sewing and nutrition, organized physical-culture campaigns, helped teach illiterate workers to read, and sometimes taught foreign languages.[92] In much of this they resembled the pre-revolutionary workers' clubs that had also offered lectures, libraries, and evening schools (and in one case something called the "First Society for Sensible Entertainment") to contribute to the intellectual and moral development of workers.[93] Komsomol clubs struggled to make youth politically literate. They held sessions on party history, the role of youth in the revolution, political economy, the Soviet state, and capitalism. By 1925, over sixty thousand young men and women, or 90 percent of Leningrad's Komsomol youth, participated in political study groups of one kind or another.[94] Even the youngest children were encouraged to learn about social and political issues. *Pravda* reported a debate on Soviet marriage law in which the debaters were just nine years old.[95]

Not all of the Komsomol's activities were so intellectually oriented. Communist ritual and "revolutionary countercelebrations" were designed to appeal to both the emotions and the intellect.[96] "Splendour, grandeur, and pomp have an extraordinary effect on the psychology of people, especially on children and the young," the Smolensk Party Committee argued in 1920. "It is not in vain that priests of different religions take care that their ceremonies be surrounded with splendour and pomp . . . One way of influencing the young is to organize magnificent revolutionary holidays."[97] "Splendor and pomp" were thought particularly useful during NEP, when they might compensate for the relative lack of revolutionary excitement. Demonstrations, torchlight processions, mass meetings, banners, and songs could make Komsomol efforts more engaging and effective. Popular hymns from the Civil War, such as "The Young Guard," were meant to reinforce in emotional terms important lessons about communist identity and authority. The lyrics of "The Young Guard" made a familiar comparison, for example, between the darkness of the pre-revolutionary period ("We carried chains around our hearts—The legacy of darkness"), and the enlightenment of the Soviet system ("Comrades in the struggle! Go forward, meet the dawn").[98] As an instrument of what Christel Lane has called "cultural management," new songs and new celebrations were meant to help the Komsomol and the party to consolidate their authority and legitimize the Soviet state.[99]

Theater offered especially effective opportunities for participation in the creation of the new order, as well for communal recitation and ritual. Local drama groups were consistently among the most popular of all organized club activities. In thirty-one out of thirty-three clubs organized by the Moscow metallist union, the drama circle was among the most popular, followed by chorus, orchestra, and physical culture.[100] Drama also accompanied and underscored many other club functions in its role as celebrant, educator, and entertainer. It was powerful and popular because youth were involved in theater not only as spectators but as participants, and not always in an official setting or performance. The language of the youth theaters was usually not that of the public ceremonies of state, but more popular, spontaneous, and sometimes contentious. Adrian Piotrovskii, an active supporter of youth theater, described this theater (perhaps optimistically) as emerging "organically from the rituals and festivals of the lower classes" to challenge traditional theaters, even Soviet ones.[101] Although some plays put on by communist youth were pre-revolutionary classics, many drama circles rejected these plays in favor of new productions about contemporary topics, often written by their members. These plays were also staged in new ways. There were "living newspapers," satirical music hall revues, literary montages in which participants constructed performances from the writings and speeches of others, and agitational courts where the audience and actors together passed judgment on contemporary issues.[102] By writing and producing their own productions, Komsomol enthusiasts affirmed their own role in the creation of a revolutionary culture.

One of the most popular theater groups was the Theater of Working Class Youth (TRAM), founded in the Leningrad House of Communist Education for Youth in 1925. Unlike the well-scripted ceremonies accompanying official events, TRAM performances were non-professional, with actors, authors, and directors drawn from enthusiastic youth who worked in the factory during the day and in the theater at night.

> DEAR KOMSOMOL'TSY!
> Strike up a song
> With every voice!
>   We stand at the bench
>   Each and every morning,
>   But at night our commitment
>   is to TRAM![103]

Insisting that both professional theaters and the plays written for these theaters were too bourgeois, amateur actors and writers instead wrote and performed plays that focused on contemporary issues said to be "taken directly from 'life as it really is'": "What the Komsomol'tsy talk about, the TRAMtsy bring to the stage." "Morning in the papers, evening in satirical songs."[104] TRAM instructed young people about their new identities, but it tried to include them in the process of revolutionary transformation by tying these new identities to the stuff of daily life. There were plays on work in the factory, gender relations, family life, problems of hooliganism, and "historical" topics such as the fight of the red partisans in the Civil War. TRAM productions also showed their viewers a new kind of hero, the young worker. Typical in this vein was a 1923 play about the murder of a young Komsomol woman who blew the whistle on an embezzler in a factory administration. TRAM's approach was clearly well liked. From its origin in Leningrad TRAM soon spread to other regions, and by 1929 there were close to sixty TRAM groups throughout the country (including in Voronesh, Baku, Irkutsk, and Rostov, among other cities), with three in Moscow alone. One Moscow troop had two hundred applications for just forty positions.[105] TRAM performances were also well attended, attracting both well-dressed youth and unkempt street youth, and succeeding, if only for an evening, in bringing together a diverse audience under a single roof.[106] Good theater combined entertainment with education, satisfying a desire for relaxation and pleasure in an officially sanctioned fashion. Close to two million people came to the eight thousand shows, concerts, and "evenings" performed throughout the Soviet Union in March 1923. Less than half that many attended the seven thousand lectures and discussions held in the same period.[107]

THE KOMSOMOL IS BORING

Demonstrations, theater, parades, reading groups, and political education courses were part of a hegemonic project that sought to teach youth a common language of communism. For some participants and some observers, these efforts were very effective. A former young communist remembered how a simple Pioneer song turned him into a believer: "It is hard to describe the effect that this new song had on us. The words, the exalted mood, seemed to fill our hearts with enthusiasm. We forgot about the narrow limits of the schoolyard. We felt that the horizon had opened, and that we were marching above the city . . . We sang the song five times, and even then we felt like going on and singing it."[108]

For others, however, the results were more disappointing.[109] The existence of a hegemonic project does not mean that hegemony was (or could be) achieved. In a survey in the mid-1920s of over three hundred young people living in the Vyborg region of Leningrad, A. G. Kagan found that favorite leisure activities included the movies, nighttime strolls with groups of friends or persons of the opposite sex, kissing, beer bars, and fighting (for boys). "My rambles [*progulki*] usually end either with success with a girl or a fight," explained one young man. This was not a group of disaffected youth—close to 90 percent of those interviewed in this survey belonged to the Komsomol, and the Komsomol clubs were also a destination point. Close to a third of the boys said they ended in the club at night, though only 11 percent of the girls did.[110] For the most part, however, the favorite leisure activities of these adolescents and young adults were beyond the borders (both literally and figuratively) of the Komsomol. Dissatisfied Komsomol'tsy were unlikely to be enthusiastic participants in the youth league. Indeed, the Komsomol generally acknowledged, if deplored, the fact that a small number of activists did the majority of work in the youth league.[111] As Derek Sayer reminds us, the state may talk and talk, but we cannot be sure that the intended audience is listening. Instead, "they may be snatching their 'half-hour of pleasure' in whatever form."[112]

The problems with Komsomol clubs appear to have intensified in the mid-1920s. This may have reflected in part the large number of new members. Between July 1924 and December 1925, Komsomol enrollment increased by close to a million.[113] Some of these youth were of a different cohort than those who had participated in the revolution and Civil War, and their expectations, interests, and perhaps abilities may have been different. But the problems were broader than this, and it appears that it was long-term members who were especially disappointed. In newspaper articles and in letters to Komsomol authorities, young communists complained that they felt the youth league to be increasingly irrelevant because it did not address their interests, both personal and political. Some complained about the lack of revolutionary inspiration and purpose, and others about a lack of interesting leisure activities.

For some Komsomol members, the once inspiring and perhaps spontaneous verbal and visual evocations of revolutionary enthusiasm had become stiff, didactic, and uninteresting. Komsomol meetings now seemed like dreary lessons rather than the rousing call to arms they had been. "But look how Komsomol'tsy speak . . . it is an unbroken riddle that is impossible to make out! Or, in the best case, it is dry officialese that makes the entire group yawn and fall into a dead sleep," one worried observer explained.[114] Despite efforts to imbue clubs and study circles with revolutionary enthusiasm, many clubs had retreated into a stupefying routine of endless lectures and meetings. A single performance of the *Internationale* at the beginning of a meeting could be moving, but repeated recitations following every lecture were boring. Much of the new ritual and celebration was highly orchestrated. Komsomol initiations, graduations, and revolutionary celebrations were often scripted educational events. One guidebook to revolutionary events described step by step how clubs should celebrate anniversaries and births. The outline for a sample "celebratory meeting" for graduates of a literacy course ran to three pages of small type,

"At the party everything was stern and serious; at 9 o'clock everyone fled in different directions." *Iunyi proletarii* 3 (February 1928), p. 12.

with especially detailed instructions on the material to include in the lecture.[115] The Komsomol, as one Petr Volkov complained, was "boring."[116]

Not everyone was willing to practice the kind of single-minded self-denial demanded of them in the youth league. "I want very much to be a Komsomolets. I am interested in the Komsomol's work," explained one young man. "But I want to live. And do you really live? At the Komsomol it is just lecture after lecture."[117] In Kagan's survey of over three hundred Leningrad youth, close to three-quarters said that their Komsomol collective did "nothing" to organize their leisure time. Only 4 percent said that their clubs made a good effort in this regard. When Kagan made the rounds of Komsomol clubs one night to see what they offered, he was distressed by how limited their programs were. In the *Karl Marx* club he found a handful of young people listening to a lecture on the health of women and infants. Another club had an evening of questions and answers on "new" apartment buildings built a half-year before, while *Red Beacon* had an evening program devoted to Chekhov that was "boring" and required tickets. Only a club holding a dance was full of young people. "Of course," Kagan concludes, "not finding anything of interest in the clubs, youth head off to various other places," including, most often, the beer bar or a party at home.[118] Nikolai Bocharov, who had been an enthusiastic early member of the Komsomol, asked repeatedly in 1925 to be relieved of his many Komsomol responsibilities so that he could "enjoy life." "I, who had started on my work with great enthusiasm and pride in my appointment, very soon lost interest in it . . . I longed to have a drink with my friends, to sing, to dance, and to court a girl."[119]

ASCETICISM AND DISCIPLINE

As Kagan's comments suggest, many in the Komsomol recognized the problems it faced. The Komsomol Central Committee admitted in 1925 that clubs were "the weakest urban location for workers' education."[120] However, there was great disagreement within the Komsomol over how best to address these complaints. Kagan himself favored providing more recreation for youth, but many Komsomol leaders and activists still insisted that club activities should contribute to the improvement of society rather than to the simple entertainment of the individual. Komsomol'tsy disagreed over whether the Komsomol should require complete abstinence from the "unhealthy" pleasures of NEP, or allow some forms of popular entertainment in the hopes that this would draw youth into the clubs and make them available for more educational efforts later.[121] Advocates for these positions could be found among both the leadership and the rank and file. This was not simply a matter of the leadership imposing its ideas about communism on a recalcitrant membership, but a struggle at all levels over the purpose, methods, and identity of the Komsomol.

In place of the kinds of "dangerous," "frivolous," or "popular" activities that many in the party and Komsomol associated with the "uncultured" elements of proletariat and peasantry, educational advocates argued that clubs should offer "healthy" diversions from the common vices of hooliganism and drunkenness. This approach had its roots in the revolutionary period, especially in the utopian enthusiasm of the early Proletkult movement, which emphasized the role of clubs as intensive study centers.[122] Komsomol'tsy were expected to teach communist values of selfless devotion and self-denial to others—to "direct the petit-bourgeois element with benefit to the party, but not be penetrated by this element."[123] Komsomol and workers' clubs would make this easier by teaching young people what should make them happy and relieving them from any false understandings or attractions to non-communist pleasures. Educational advocates in the Moscow Komsomol hoped, for example, that healthy evening entertainments would strengthen communist influence over the nighttime leisure activities of youth and distract them "from beer, from purposeless roaming of the streets, and from hooliganism."[124] "Workers come to a club to expand their knowledge," explained Semashko, "to better understand their needs, to understand how best to struggle and work for a better future. Relaxation for male and female workers is now connected with real enlightenment and genuine pleasure."[125] "Genuine pleasure" was not the private and decadent pleasure of the NEP bourgeois, but the communal pleasure of education and communist advancement.

The best way for young communists to advance the Bolsheviks' cleansing and purifying project (and also to avoid becoming polluted themselves) was to avoid purposeless entertainment. Educational advocates criticized cultural activities that did not satisfy didactic goals. Western films were thought particularly dangerous for a vulnerable younger generation. Before the revolution, the most popular films had been romances and "salon dramas."[126] To the dismay of many educational advocates, even after 1917 adventure movies, detective stories, dramas, and comedies continued to be more popular among youth than Soviet agitprop or avant-garde films. Movies were the most popular form of entertainment among urban youth both male and female. In Moscow, over 80 percent of the younger generation went to the movies regularly, and by late NEP, it was estimated that every day more than twenty thousand young people went to the movies.[127] To many moralists, however, Hollywood films and those Soviet films which sought to imitate their popular features—violence, adventure, sex—not only failed to teach young people about socialist values, but actively encouraged young people to imitate the inappropriate and even hooliganish behavior of their favorite film stars. Educators worried that action and adventure films overstimulated youth, encouraged them to behave aggressively, and made it difficult for them to work calmly and productively at school.

Theater was also thought to be vulnerable to "bourgeois" influences. One irate observer complained that too many Komsomol plays were works by "lascivious directors" or the "monastery of the blessed Magdalene"— plays which were dangerous for youth, as they led to pessimism and mysticism.[128] The Briansk factory club was condemned by an enthusiast who wrote secretly to denounce it for performing the plays "Princess Turandot" and "Blue Bird," the latter said to combine "two elements characteristic of the decadent intelligentsia—a completely petit-bourgeois [*mesh-chanskoi*] 'practicability' and a dyed-in-the-wool idealism."[129] These activities were especially worrisome because they were happening within the walls of the Komsomol club, a space that should have been used to inoculate youth against deviance, not contribute to their infection. With concerns like this in mind, the Cultural Department of the Trade Union instructed drama groups to make their own work more explicitly didactic. They were to work with the political study cells to present plays on "internal and external political developments," with the professional circles to perform plays on the history and growth of the Trade Union, and with the natural science cells to dramatize scientific discoveries.[130]

The directives from the Trade Union are just one example of the ways in which young people were instructed how to perform and how to play.

"Comradely get-together."
Iunyi proletarii 3 (February 1928), p. 11.

The scripted educational efforts of some Komsomol educators suggest that while they were hopeful about the capacity of young people to become communists, they were anxious about what would happen if young people were not directed carefully. Even communist youth would return to the more anarchistic aspects of non-official youth culture if not given precise instructions on how to organize themselves. There were complaints in this vein about the "undisciplined" atmosphere in Komsomol club rooms in which the revolutionary elements common to every club—the red carpet, communist banners, and portraits of revolutionary leaders—were overwhelmed by the smoke and noise of energetic teenagers. The student newspaper *Red Students* [*Krasnoe studenchestvo*] described such a club in disparaging terms:

> Smoke is the main adornment and decoration in the "club," that is if you don't count the cobwebs, the filthy puttee stuck on the stove, and the spittoon whose main task is to spread infection. As usual the club is full. Through the smoke you can just make out the figures of students. One, without a shirt, is bitterly making some argument about physical culture, while others, lying on the floor, on bunks and on the table, occasionally exchange a few remarks either for or against.[131]

Of particular concern was the dirt—as in the "infectious" spittoon and the smoke. The dirt itself may have been disturbing, or talking about "dirt" may have been a powerful way to express disdain for and disgust with the "unclean" (and thus unhealthy) recreations of club youth. The lack of useful activity was also distressing. In the club at Ivanovo-Voznesensk there was said to be "a group of kids telling each other jokes, 'salty' ones of course," while in a nearby room, "a Komsomolets banged away endlessly on the keys of a piano." "All of this, together with card playing, is called a 'pleasant' and 'wholesome' use of time," complained the authors of a book on old and new forms of daily life.[132]

In part these complaints suggest discomfort with the coarseness of everyday life and with relaxational activities that appear to be pleasurable rather than purposeful. They also resemble the anguished voices of adults everywhere when confronted with the disorderly living habits of their children. Indeed, much of what was inadequate about this emphasis on purpose over mere pleasure was its very adultness, which could not compensate for the comradeship and culture of adolescent youth. Again, this is not to say that advocates of this approach were all adults. Some Komsomol'tsy themselves took a serious approach to questions of leisure. Their rigorous efforts to define what kind of entertainment was appropriate for the up-and-coming communist, and to inculcate others with this belief, were part of an effort to advance and defend their own (new) revolutionary selves. They saw in this seriousness a sign of their commitment to their own vanguard role and a sign of their almost-adulthood.

THE CAMPAIGN AGAINST ALCOHOL

The Komsomol's anti-alcohol campaign is a good example of the effort to instill "ideologically correct" forms of everyday life in an instructional fashion, and of the challenges this kind of effort faced.[133] The ideal qualities of the non-drinker were qualities particularly valued during NEP—restraint, rationality, and self-control. In contrast, drunkenness was said to induce a lack of control leading to "hooliganism" and "other unpardonable activities," especially sex.[134] Vodka took one "out of the world of reality into a world of illusion."[135] The Komsomol fought against drinking in agitational campaigns which reminded young communists that the "Komsomol is the enemy of drunkenness. Komsomol'tsy must not drink!"[136] Factory clubs sponsored lectures and meetings about the dangers of alcohol and local "sanitary commissions" put up posters showing the effects of alcohol on the human body. Newspaper articles on alcohol described the undisciplined qualities of those who drank too much. "A group of drunks showed up at an evening get-together at MGU's [Moscow State University] club number two," began one such article. "One of them . . . became rowdy, started swearing, and tore up the furniture."[137] This article made a common association between the destruction of the individual body brought on by alcohol and the destruction of the Komsomol. Those who drank were not just hurting themselves but hurting the larger collective as well. "Each one of our com-

Student participants in a demonstration against drunkenness, Moscow, November 7, 1928. *1917–1932. Agitatsionno-massovoe iskusstvo. Oformlenie prazdnestv* (Moscow: "Iskusstvo," 1984).

rades who is drunk," wrote A. Stratonitskii, "is an evil agitator against our very core, against our affairs."[138]

Much effort focused on turning the energy and impetus for drink toward other, less-harmful pursuits. The crude insensitivities of the drunk were contrasted with the disciplined efforts and energy of the abstainer in one Komsomol poem:

> With sorrow,
>   or with happiness,
>   we drank vodka,
> With swearing,
>   and obscenities,
>   we tossed back the drinks,
> Drunk or sober,
>   who gave a damn.
> To hell with,
>   the tavern,
>   and the beer bar.
> To be picked up,
>   off the stove.

> To knowledge.
> To work.
> To the right path,
> We move toward a new kind of daily life.[139]

Student newspapers encouraged young people to donate the money they normally spent on alcohol and cigarettes to help fund political and social campaigns. In public confessions of remorse and redemption these regenerates then put notices in the newspaper: "I have stopped smoking [or drinking] as of November 25 and will now donate the two rubles 50 kopecks that I have saved for the airplane 'M[oscow] Univ[ersity]' and call on the 3rd year students to follow my example."[140] Komsomol groups organized non-drinking circles that encouraged entertainments not revolving around drink. Some clubs forbade certain kinds of music associated with drinking, and substituted new communist songs and dances written for the accordion.[141] Other Komsomol groups concentrated on eliminating factors that were thought to encourage drinking. A group of Leningrad Komsomol'tsy tried to decrease the number of bars near large factories.

Komsomol anti-alcohol campaigns were meant to counteract the archaic influences of family, community, and street that Komsomol and party authorities believed encouraged drink and prevented revolutionary transformation. This was clearly an enormous task, and not surprisingly, the campaigns were largely unsuccessful. For one thing, the anti-alcohol effort was puritanical. It told youth what to forgo but too often offered little of equal recreational and social value to take its place. For another, because drinking was an important aspect not only of youth culture but of the adult working-class experience, drinking (or not drinking) had ramifications for acceptance into the adult world. Even the most dedicated young communist felt pressure to drink with others on the factory floor if he wanted to be accepted and not derided as an "intellectual" or a "baba" [backward woman].[142] The Komsomol recognized the power of the adult example, and also campaigned to stop adults from drinking (including holding mass anti-drinking demonstrations just outside the factory walls). These campaigns were no more successful than those among youth in an environment where alcohol had long played such a fundamental cultural and social role.[143] Consequently, there was little real support for the anti-alcohol policy among Komsomol youth, and anti-alcohol activities were only episodic.[144] Surveys of Komsomol youth show that a significant percentage continued to drink despite the campaigns and despite threats of expulsion.[145] They still organized drinking parties in their homes, in the woods, or on river banks during the summer.[146] Activists did appear to recognize that they should not use alcohol; they tried to hide their drinking so that non-party youth and Komsomol leaders would not find out. But even those who took Komsomol pledges not to drink did not always stick to their commitment.[147] They had learned to "speak Bolshevik," but not yet to act it on it, let alone believe it.

ANTI-RELIGIOUS CAMPAIGNS

The Komsomol's anti-religious campaign was at first a more popular and less didactic effort, but it too was taken over by advocates of rationality and discipline and became in turn less popular. The first Komsomol Christmases were carnival-like productions. On Orthodox Christmas in January 1923, Komsomol'tsy, students, and other sympathizers staged alternative celebrations in more than four hundred towns throughout Soviet Russia, and there were close to two hundred special carnival processions and parades in city squares.[148] Komsomol'tsy in Tiflis sponsored a "grandiose" torchlight demonstration by close to three thousand young people, some of them mockingly dressed as priests, who carried banners through the city. A crowd of twenty thousand working-class youth, party members, students, and Komsomol members gathered to meet the parade in the city's central square, where there were speeches and songs, culminating in a rousing rendition of the Internationale. Similar events were held in rural areas, such as the small town of Alekpole where local Komsomol'tsy demonstrated outside the church and again paraded about costumed as priests and princes. In the local club there were meetings and lectures, and a special "court" in which religious representatives, "scientific" experts, workers, and peasants gathered to pass judgment on religion.[149] Like alcohol, religion was said to provide an unscientific and fuzzy-headed view of reality, drugging the mind much as alcohol drugged the body.[150]

Much of this early anti-religious behavior is reminiscent of the Bakhtinian carnival, with its critique of the official through parody and the inversion of traditional hierarchies. Komsomol'tsy degraded sacred text and persons by explicitly associating them with the profane. At an anti-religious carnival in Moscow there were floats with false rabbis and others with mock priests singing parodies of church liturgy with obscene lyrics. There was a truck with a figure of God embracing a naked woman.[151] The challenge was not just that of science to the sacred, but of youth to adulthood. Adolescents—who were without much power in other situations—reversed the rules and asserted their newfound ideological superiority over their elders. In this way, too, these celebrations differed from the anti-alcohol efforts that had been primarily directed by youth toward other youth.

Rather than encouraging anti-religious attitudes, however, the antagonistic nature of the Komsomol campaign provoked hostility from many believing adult members of the local (usually rural) population, who sometimes then retaliated. Such was the case, for example, when a group of communist youth tried to perform a special "blasphemous" revolutionary pageant on horseback. The horses they used were from the local fire brigade. When the pageant started across the stage, someone purposefully sounded a fire alarm to disrupt the pageant, at which point the trained fire horses ran into the auditorium, killing over forty men, women, and children and wounding many more.[152] The anti-religious reputation of the Komsomol was a principal reason rural parents would not allow their children to join the league. One such father was very angry when his son returned home at three in the morning from a Komsomol Christmas party held in the village reading room. "And just what do you think you're doing, playing and coming home at three o'clock on such a holiday," he complained. "That's why there isn't any bread. God has seen everything."[153]

What made youth's religious "carnival" not truly Bakhtinian, of course, was that it depended on the sanction of the newly privileged Bolsheviks, who became increasingly unappreciative of popular carnivalesque impulses. In contrast, Bakhtin reminds us, true carnival laughter builds "its own state versus the official state."[154] Given the hostile response of parents to the anti-Christmas efforts of their children, political authorities declared that Komsomol youth had been overly enthusiastic. Afraid of the disruptive effects of these youthful expressions of anti-religious belief, the Bolsheviks tried to tame them. Behavior that had been condoned was now criticized as "unorganized," "destructive," and "hooliganish."[155] Komsomol and party leaders now called instead for "revolutionary counter-celebrations" which were to put aside all mockery and use proper entertainment, and perhaps voluntary labor as well, to encourage anti-religious belief.[156] The party restrained the power of subordinate youth to disrupt the routines and rituals of dominant adults by reminding young people of their "responsibilities." More sedate suggestions were offered for Easter 1923 than for Christmas. Activists were urged to focus on evening club meetings with scientific and historical discussions of religion, and to stage free plays and performances to draw youth away from traditional holiday celebrations.[157] These kinds of more moderate activities would be common throughout the 1920s as school and factory youth clubs sponsored anti-religious study groups, various lecture series on "religion and science," and evening programs with sports events and anti-religious poetry readings.[158] Though perhaps more "appropriate," these activities were also less interesting, and they contributed to an eventual drop in the number of functioning "atheist circles" among Komsomol'tsy in the 1920s.[159]

RECREATION

Both the anti-religious and anti-alcohol campaigns suggest the challenges the Komsomol faced when they tried to instruct youth in a new revolutionary consciousness. Campaigns foundered in the face of tradition; it was hard to change old and established patterns of daily life. The nature of the campaigns was also important. Aggressive and anti-authoritarian efforts were more popular than restrained and structured ones. Although the effort to transform behavior was utopian and revolutionary in its desire for fundamental transformation, its methods were too often instrumental and non-emotional.

Recognizing that many young people were uninterested in the serious educational activities of the clubs, some Komsomol and party authorities insisted that the youth league needed to provide more in the way of popular leisure activities. As early as 1922, M. Neznamov argued in the pages of *Young Communist* that if clubs did not have entertainment (even "the simplest, such as chess, checkers, dominoes"), then they would "lose any stimulating motive for working youth to come to the club. A club must satisfy *all* needs of working youth."[160] Concerns increased in mid-NEP. In 1925 the General Secretary of the Komsomol, Nikolai Chaplin, condemned what he labeled "absurd communist asceticism," blaming it on an enthusiasm left over from the late Civil War. Now we know better, he said, than to try to make "ascetics out of stylish youth."[161] There have been times, he said, "when a guy buys an accordion, plays it and is expelled from the Komsomol, or when a girl who dances is also expelled. This goes too far, comrades. We have to understand that the economic situation of youth is improving, that young people don't want to just sit in meetings and listen to dry lectures about every kind of international and national issue, but want to enjoy themselves, to have fun."[162] The problem for the Komsomol leadership in the non-revolutionary atmosphere of the 1920s was how to keep youth away from the twin shoals of NEP: militant asceticism, on the one hand, and petit-bourgeois hedonism, on the other. Chaplin's approach was a utilitarian one which reflected the moderate practicality of NEP and was designed to steer a course down the center. "Why can't a Komsomolets play the accordion?" he asked. "If we forbid it then he will turn to hooliganism or drink."[163]

The pragmatism of the "utilitarians" allowed for a broader range of human interests and emotions. Whereas advocates of education imagined idealized Komsomol youth who were uninterested in ordinary pleasures, utilitarians argued that they needed to approach youth as living people. For utilitarians, understanding youth in their entirety meant satisfying their desires and being patient with their imperfections. One L. Stal'skii complained, for example, that the Komsomol was so concerned with perfection that instead of helping troubled Komsomol'tsy with support and assistance, the Komsomol too often just "removed them from the League."[164] "Which is better," wrote Komsomol activist Mil'chakov, "to contemplate a semi-deserted club" or to bring youth into the club by giving them the same "civil rights" to gay and cheerful activities in the club as they have outside? "There is only one answer," said Mil'chakov; "it is better to let youth have fun in the club under our direction and with our help."[165]

The pragmatic approach of the utilitarians is an example of the ways in which popular desires could influence official culture. The younger generation's persistent interest in their own forms of recreation and entertainment encouraged some Bolshevik and Komsomol officials to repackage history and politics in more dynamic ways. Movies are again a good example. Bolshevik cultural workers tried to create revolutionary films that would take advantage of youth's enthusiasm for the movies and help "enlarge [youth's] cultural and political understanding."[166] Indeed, the Bolsheviks' awareness of movies as a medium for conveying a socialist message set them apart from West European socialists, who generally condemned film as "the newest and most threatening form of cheap entertainment."[167] It is true that many Soviet movies remained serious and educational; films on the Pioneer and Komsomol organizations, homeless youth, and the Civil War were thought to be especially suitable for youth. Schools and clubs also showed films on problems of everyday life (*Abortion*) and scientific topics (*Electrification, The Port of Murmansk, Ford and Fordism*).[168] But there were again some in the party and in the Komsomol who recognized that in order for Soviet films to compete with Western ones, they too would have to be entertaining. Commissar of Education Lunacharsky wrote the script for the popular melodramatic movie *The Bear's Wedding*. Soviet commercial studios catered to the demand for popular entertainment by producing Soviet films like the comedy/spy series *Miss Mend* (with complicated plots, murders, and chases set in exotic foreign settings) and crime stories like *The Case of the Three Million* (about sex, bankers, and thieves).[169] Certain "revolutionary" films were also popular among youth, if they were full of adventure and not overly pedantic. After all, the same qualities of heroism and daring that young people attributed to Fairbanks could also be ascribed to the idealized Civil War activist. They flocked to the film *Little Red Imps*, which was a revolutionary adventure set during the Civil War with adolescent heroes.[170]

The problem of pleasure was not easily resolved, however. An article in a 1928 issue of *Young Proletarian* complained that clubs still chased young people away with their dreary gatherings.[171] Frequent changes in policy led to confusion in local clubs about the proper approach to entertainment. "A heated discussion has come up among the Komsomol members in our cell concerning the participation of Komsomol members in dances," wrote one confused Komsomol member from the Donbass. "One side says that there is nothing wrong with dancing and that young working people come here from work to find some kind of entertainment . . . The other side argues that dancing is a bourgeois prejudice and that we have already broken from that bourgeois legacy."[172] Another group of puzzled Komsomol'tsy wrote Bukharin asking why they had been told to speak out against dancing in 1921, but now in 1926 the Komsomol was itself sponsoring dances.[173]

Komsomol members were themselves confused, torn at times between belief in a stringent revolutionary asceticism and a longing for pleasure, between the new forms of everyday life that they learned in school and in the Komsomol clubs and the sometimes disturbingly attractive forms of daily life that they experienced in the streets and at home. The tension between official prescriptions and the temptations of youth was captured in a popular novel, *Diary of a Communist Schoolboy*. In the novel, the young hero Kostya asks his friend Sylvia whether she can dance. She says she knows how but claims she does not like to, and yet "her eyes all sparkled, and her face was flushed and her bow hopped up and down to the music." Sylvia then asks to leave, commenting on her way out, "There are all kinds of things one would like to do; but if one did them, where would our ideology come in?"[174] Vera Ketlinskaia's autobiographical novella about communist youth in the 1920s is similarly replete with the challenge of remaining faithful to Komsomol values in this period. During the Civil War, everything was clear; "I knew that there were two classes—the bourgeoisie and the proletariat." But with NEP, "everything became complicated. Confused." This was especially true for poor, and often hungry, young students.[175] "Not far from us," she writes, "sprang up NEPman restaurants, where elegant people went. From the door smells of cooked meat, onions, or fish wafted into the street. Lela and I related to these smells stoically: it was all for NEPmen, so to the devil with them. We didn't want to be with NEPmen . . . But what a bakery in that window. "[176] Difficult economic conditions could force even the most revolutionary of youth to compromise. Komsomol youth worked for NEPmen as salesgirls in fur shops, or were paid to keep older bourgeois women company by reading to them or accompanying them to cafés at night. As Ketlinskaia says: "Work for a NEPman? There was something in that which harmed one's self-esteem, but when there were so many unemployed around, there was no other choice."[177] In this context we might consider whether the extreme asceticism of some communist youth was not in part an effort to make a virtue out of necessity. Having no money to buy fine things or entertain themselves, they made themselves feel better by insisting that it was wrong to have any such things or to enjoy them.

At the same time, for many communist youth the powerful appeal of leisure activities such as dance often outweighed puritanical efforts to discourage them. When allowed, dancing remained one of the most popular activities in factory and Komsomol clubs. Over two-thirds of those in Kagan's survey said they liked dancing and danced whenever possible, and 11 percent admitted they had taken dance classes.[178] Indeed, dancing was so popular that some Komsomol clubs incorporated it into their regular programs. "Small towns are in the grip of this music," complained one small-town reporter. "In every worker's club there is a brass and string orchestra . . . When you pass by a club, you can hear the orchestra playing a foxtrot . . . In another club, that of the metal workers, you can hear the same foxtrot, but under a different name: 'fox-genre.' Next you hear the song 'Little-bells' and after that, again a foxtrot."[179] Even in early NEP, there were reports of Komsomol groups dedicated entirely to teaching popular dances like the waltz. In Odessa, a group of Komsomol youth threatened to leave the organization altogether when the local Komsomol committee tried to close down a dance class.[180] Some factory clubs even sponsored evening balls for young people, and posters and placards advertising these dances were plastered on the walls of trade union and factory clubs:

DIAMOND EVENING BALL
Extraordinary concert
Foxtrot 'til morning . . .
Amazing program with wine, and
Dancing between the tables
Serpentine.[181]

SPEAKING (AND BELIEVING?) LIKE A YOUNG COMMUNIST

An early survey of youth's political views suggests the enormous challenges facing the Komsomol. In 1920, Soviet sociologists questioned 1,127 youth living in Tambov to gauge their attitudes toward the revolution and their degree of political literacy. When asked whom they most wanted to be like, only 5 percent of these primary school students chose revolutionary figures, with Karl Marx the most popular and Lenin second. The author of the study suggested that even this modest number of "revolutionary" responses probably reflected the number of streets, monuments, and meeting halls recently dedicated to Marx rather than any real understanding of who he was. When asked what they wanted to be when they grew up, 8 percent of the students wanted to be communists or commissars. Less than half of them chose these professions for political or moral reasons, saying, for example, "the communist defends freedom" or "they are honest." The majority wanted to be communists or commissars because they could carry a revolver, get a good pair of boots, afford white bread, or just plain "live well."[182] For these students a commissar was essentially a new kind of post-revolutionary nobleman, with privileges stemming from his powerful position rather than his dedication to revolutionary ideals.

A survey seven years later of over three thousand youth aged eight to eighteen suggested some changes. According to the author of this study, N. Rybnikov, all of the school youth surveyed thought Soviet power was better than any other power. Proletarian youth appreciated the working-class basis of the new state, while white-collar youth referred to the "democratic" principles on which the government was founded. Young people were most impressed by the economic achievements of the revolution, specifically the eight-hour day, although they also mentioned political changes including "freedom," "equality," "the right to vote."[183] When asked if they thought anything should be changed about the existing Soviet system, about a third of those surveyed said that nothing needed to be changed: "Tsarist power was bad, Soviet power is better." Young children were most likely to say that everything was fine. Adolescent youth were more likely to mention necessary political and economic changes, although most of them were of a revolutionary nature. Complaints were about activities and people who might jeopardize the complete and rapid transformation to socialism, including capitalists, kulaks, private traders, and priests. Working-class youth, especially young women, were also likely to suggest changes in social relations and everyday life. The most common complaint in 1927—one that clearly reflected the official anxieties of that year—was about hooliganism.[184]

The results of this survey suggest that the Bolsheviks had succeeded in creating a common language among some youth—a common discourse, if you like. We cannot know, however, if these youth believed what they said. Some Bolshevik moralists worried about this; they wondered if young people truly understood and believed what they were saying. For researcher Iu. I. Kazhdanskaia, speaking like a Bolshevik was not enough. Communism was meant to be an integral part of individual identity, not something simply acquiesced to. Kazhdanskaia set out explicitly to uncover those youth who did not understand as completely as they should and who were not, therefore, fully conscious. In September 1924, and again in February 1927, she questioned a group of Odessa schoolchildren about revolutionary history and politics. Kazhdanskaia interviewed the same group both times to see if their awareness and comprehension increased as they grew older and their schooling increased. In 1927, she paid special attention to those responses that she considered "formulaic." These were responses that on first glance seemed satisfactory, but when probed with a follow-up question revealed that the child did not understand what he or she was saying.[185]

Kazhdanskaia asked the schoolchildren questions such as: Who is Lenin? What is communism? Who leads the government now? Who led it before? What is the name of the country in which you now live? According to Kazhdanskaia, in 1924 fewer than 10 percent of the answers were correct. A quarter were what she called "vague," a quarter were "absurd," and almost half of the time the students simply did not know the answer. Fewer than 10 percent of the students clearly knew who Lenin was, and only 2 percent could explain the basics of communism to Kazhdanskaia's satisfaction. In 1927, 12 percent of the answers were correct. This time the students did not know the answer only 16 percent of the time. However, almost 20 percent of the students still did not know who Lenin was or could not say anything significant about him. Most importantly, according to Kazhdanskaia, a third of all responses were "formulaic," suggesting to her that while these youth had memorized certain kinds of information, their understanding was far from complete. For some youth who grew up after the revolution, facts about the revolution and Civil War were already considered history, something to be memorized, rather than a vital part of living memory. Many insisted, for example, that the February revolution occurred after the October revolution, because they learned about the October events in the first trimester of school, but the February revolution in the second.[186]

Kazhdanskaia was not the only one worried about young people's lack of historical and political knowledge. Komsomol leaders were also concerned about the lack of political literacy, even among their most active members. At a Komsomol meeting in 1929, one delegate complained that "a very significant part of the league consists of people who from a political point of view are still only just starting their political lives, who are completely unpolished." He argued that their level of political knowledge was so low that it was "indistinguishable from the level of non-party youth."[187] A 1924–1925 study of 106 Komsomol political cells totaling almost three thousand members showed that most of the groups were not very active, and 40 percent of the members participating had "less than average" levels of political knowledge. The report blamed these problems on low levels of literacy, a lack of materials, and weak cell leaders who were themselves often poorly educated.[188] Some young people were also simply uninterested in politics. While some young men and women did things which would teach them about political events—frequented a Komsomol club or political circle, read newspapers, or participated in student meetings—others could not have cared less. "Politics don't interest me," said one at the beginning of the decade, and another, "I don't understand and I don't believe."[189]

In many ways it should not surprise us that young men and women had a difficult time articulating the political lessons of 1917. Because many working-class youth attended only a few years of primary school, the descriptions they received of socialism, new class relations, and appropriate forms of everyday behavior were necessarily watered-down, popularized versions of complex party policies. The non-traditional educational methods popular in Soviet schools in the early to mid-1920s also contributed to political illiteracy. In these early years, educators focused on experiential learning and on creating new forms of social behavior. It was only in 1927, when consistently poor results on university entrance exams alerted teachers that boys and girls entering secondary school and institutes of higher education were not prepared well enough, that the emphasis shifted back to more traditional methods and disciplines, including history, economics, and political theory.[190] The economic crisis during NEP, which resulted in financial cutbacks in education programs, also made it more difficult to forge ahead with visionary plans to ensure that every member of the new generation was politically literate. Financial cutbacks and distribution problems meant that schools often did not have enough books and supplies, or that the available ones were politically suspect. Even Komsomol cells, which played an important educational role, complained about a lack of good political literature. In a survey of 106 working-class political cells, over 80 percent of them had libraries but only 30 percent had enough books to allow them to circulate.[191]

For believers like Kazhdanskaia, however, the lack of political literacy signified not only that political education had failed but that young people were not fully communist. Understanding, belief, and the thoughtful articulation of both mattered to Kazhdanskaia. This is consistent with the particular revolutionary agenda of the early Soviet period and the emphasis in this period on penetrating and transforming individual identity from the inside out. The Bolsheviks of the 1920s were trying to create a revolution "inside people's minds," a cultural revolution of consciousness which they believed was not just an important aspect of the creation of a communist state and society, but a necessary prerequisite.[192]

Kazhdanskaia would have disagreed with many of those writing today about state authority. Belief, Derek Sayer writes, is "neither here nor there." "Rule is not centrally about either inculcating beliefs or securing consent." What is demanded are performances. "Believers or not, participants are by their very actions affirming the power of what is sanctified." The state, Sayer argues, depends on "people living what they much of the time know to be a lie."[193] James Scott too has famously argued that rule does not depend on ideological consent or consensus, but on power. Acquiescence does not mean allegiance. The people who are dominated "know they are dominated, they know by whom and how; far from consenting to that domination, they initiate all sorts of subtle ways of living with, talking about, resisting, undermining, and confronting the unequal and power-laden worlds in which they live."[194] In other words, a common language reflects the power of the state to shape discourses, but that language tells us little about the individual's personal allegiance to the official.

This may be true. In this chapter I too have explored the ways in which Soviet power was talked about, resisted, and sometimes undermined, and yet the state continued. Young people had questions, suggestions, and preferences; some Komsomol activities were clearly more popular than others. There were young people who remained simply uninterested in the educational efforts of the youth league. Even believers could publicly complain about the Komsomol in the 1920s. Some argued not only about how the Komsomol went about its business, but about what that business should be. Even the supposedly most loyal of communist youth sought out and expressed rival discourses. They also used official discourses, such as those of the anti-religious campaigns, to further their own desires and goals. Communist youth are a surprisingly good example of the range of contradictory opinions an individual (or a group of individuals) can hold, including support for some aspects of Bolshevik policy and criticism for others. Even revolutionary beliefs can vary, be partial, or be at odds.

But Kazhdanskaia was on to something too. The fact that belief is partial does not mean that it does not exist, or that it is not important. While it is difficult to determine belief, belief does matter, just as resistance does. Intent, personal choice, and individual action on behalf of the Bolshevik ideal clearly contributed to the revolution of 1917. So too in the decade following. Although Bolshevik language was only unwillingly accepted by some, for others it was integral to their own sense of self. Without belief, the impetus to transform others would have been far weaker and less vital, a pale version of the intense drive to revolutionize culture and consciousness we see in the 1920s. Indeed, as we will see in the next chapter, it was the very depth of this belief that led some young militants to challenge party practice as they pushed the party to fulfill their youthful understandings of the revolutionary promises of 1917.

4

EXCESSES OF ENTHUSIASM

Young communists did not always have the same understanding as older ones of what it meant to be a good communist. The German visitor Klaus Mehnert recalled how the Komsomol youth he knew referred to NEP as "damned NEP" and "devilish NEP," disappointed by what they saw as a retreat from the goals of Civil War socialism.[1] While some young people proudly repeated the language and lessons they had absorbed about their role and that of the youth organization, young militants resisted what they saw as the Thermidor of the Russian revolution. For these young enthusiasts, the Civil War and the New Economic Policy represented two very different kinds of communism—the first promising cultural confrontation, utopian experimentation, and youth-generated forms of cultural expression, and the second, discipline, cultural pluralism, and moderation. The persistence of militant understandings of communism and communist culture raises new questions about the multiple meanings of communism, about the relationship between personal identity and official ideology, and about notions of popular versus party authority. What did it mean to be a young communist? How should young communist behavior be defined? Who would control these definitions? Could the party permit the young militants their popular expressions of revolutionary meaning? Or did revolutionary meaning need to be defined (and the militant enthusiasts disciplined) by a party better able to judge what was necessary and appropriate?[2] For Bolshevik moralists, discipline of the body was as important as discipline of the mind: this chapter explores both intergenerational political struggles and debates about dress and hygiene.

THE POLITICAL CHALLENGE
OF MILITANT YOUTH

Eight years after the end of the Civil War, Bolshevik Vladimir Slepkov described a persistent subculture of dogmatic young communists whom he called the *bratushki* ["little brothers"]. Slepkov defended the moderation of NEP against the aggressive, and to his eyes self-indulgent, excesses of these young people. The *bratushki* still wanted to do battle, he wrote, and were protesting against "peaceful conditions and narrow-minded pragmatism."

Accustomed to the free and unorganized life they had known during the Civil War, they could not tolerate even "elementary laws" and restrictions, but insisted on acting as their own bosses. The war invalids among them would not even put up with hospital routine, because every "regimen" seemed despotic to them, and they saw "counter-revolutionaries in every corner." One young metalworker whom Slepkov described showed an "inexplicable" hostility to his foreman, constantly ignoring his orders, verbally abusing him and calling him names. When called in front of a Komsomol court, the *bratushka* called his boss a "bloodsucking exploiter." In contrast, when the foreman took the stand, he was (according to Slepkov) "quiet, modest and exceptionally gentle."[3]

Some young people had felt themselves adrift after the end of the Civil War. At the Fifth Komsomol Congress in 1922, both party and Komsomol leaders openly acknowledged the growth of apathy and disillusionment in the post-war period. Activists from Smolensk complained that it was difficult to organize even the smallest events, because of youth's lack of interest in tasks and topics which they now found largely unrelated to their own interests and needs. Others described exhausted youth who preferred to play checkers rather than go to lectures on new NEP topics such as "the need to reduce the currency supply."[4] Young members of the Red Army had particular problems adjusting to the peacetime environment.[5] Russian and Western observers both described a significant increase in the number of Komsomol youth whose disillusionment and depression led them to suicide. In her book *My Lives in Russia*, Markoosha Fisher described "a wave of suicides which [swept] the ranks of youth," while according to Victor Serge many young men who were "expelled from the party for having opposed the 'new line'" got "hold of revolvers—to turn against themselves" while young women used veronal.[6] Some Komsomol youth were said to be sympathetic to the despair which led to suicide, and there were those who defended suicide as understandable in conditions of such revolutionary despair.[7]

Many young people responded to the changing circumstances not by withdrawing, however, but by articulating a politics and a culture which actively aimed at resurrecting the heroism and militancy they associated with the Civil War. A crucial aspect of this civil-war culture was the continued attachment, even in late NEP, to the idea of an "other." Officially, identity constructed through opposition was less tenable than it had been in 1918. During NEP, the enemy was no longer the clearly defined "other" of the White Army officer, but the far more amorphous "enemies" of illiteracy, religion, and disease. Peasants and workers were to reestablish a link [*smychka*] based on market relations, and even bourgeois NEPmen were officially tolerated. In the new environment, the Bolsheviks addressed themselves to converting, rather than to banishing, the "other." The diminished sense of difference between "us" and "them," between communist and non-communist, made identity less certain than it had been, and led to both disillusionment and anger among some young people. "In the period of the Civil War there stood before youth a colossal task of unprecedented beauty," explained Bukharin sympathetically. "It captivated them; their relations to it were unusually clear and obvious: they had to kill the common enemy—world capitalism." In contrast, "the switch over to the rails of the New Economic Policy immediately tore out this pivot," because it did "not set before youth any vigorous, colorful, sharply defined, militant, heroic task."[8]

NEP became the new "enemy." The resurgence of "bourgeois" capitalists, of restaurants, and of casinos with their "money-bags stuffed with notes" and "ladies with bracelets and rings" outraged and puzzled young radicals.[9] "The most basic and painful question [I have] is about NEP," wrote one Komsomol member to Trotsky. "When you walk along the street and see the satisfied well-fed faces and patent-leather shoes alongside some adolescent worker, 90% of whom have tuberculosis, then straight away you . . . become ashamed. Was it really necessary to have the October revolution, during which so many young people were killed, only to return to the past?"[10] How are we to understand, asked another, why "[s]ome scrimpy registrar" gets "40–50 rubles for writing numbers on paper" while an unskilled worker with children receives only 30 even though he works "twice as hard"?[11] Some wondered, too, about party elites who were paid more than others and worried about the effect this embourgeoisement would have on the "masses," who would see these people "working not for the good of the masses, but for the good of themselves."[12]

NEP was not the only enemy. For young enthusiasts one of the most telling, and disturbing, aspects of Slepkov's description of bratushki would have been his assumption that adult-like behavior was more appropriate than the enthusiasms of youth. The inherent conservatism of this message was underscored by the fact that the foreman was vindicated at the expense of the worker. Some young people disagreed, and began to transfer categories of class from enemies of the people to the party itself. Young militants blamed the older generation of Bolsheviks for the failures implied by the introduction of NEP. For them it was not that the revolution had failed to occur as promised, but rather that adults had failed to follow through, retreating from revolutionary action to the bourgeois and bureaucratic world of the NEPman and the apparatchik. NEP symbolized the older generation's lack of courage and conviction, and proved, to some at least, that the "old ones" were "psychologically unfit" to direct a revolutionary government. "One cannot make too much of a fetish of the 'old ones," communist students wrote to Pravda in 1924; "too many are already invalids."[13] In the Red Army, too, there was a generational split between an older cohort of senior political staff (often married and of non-worker origin) who overwhelmingly favored NEP, and a younger group who condemned their elders as part of a new NEP "bourgeoisie."[14] The juxtaposition of vital youth with an impotent older generation echoed the language of revolution and war, when the bright new days of a communist future were often compared in poetry and song with the "old, powerless, and putrid" Tsarist order.[15]

Finally, enthusiasts condemned not only NEP and the older generation, but the Komsomol as well, in its new post-war incarnation as a bureaucratic organization dedicated to fulfilling plans rather than helping youth. It is certainly true that the Komsomol had become more bureaucratic. The rise of the party apparatus and the growth of the party's Central Committee during NEP have been well documented, and much the same was true in the youth league; the process of stabilization under NEP encouraged bureaucratic tendencies in both party and Komsomol.[16] Of twenty-six activists working in one Komsomol cell, for example, all went to at least ten meetings a month, and one went to fifty. Provincial activists spent an average of three hours a day in meetings.[17] "In our organization," wrote one Leningrad activist, "there are commissions, meetings, conferences, plenums, circulars, resolutions, protocols, subscriptions, relations, committee work, membership cards, questionnaires, the coordination of questions and problems, and so on and so on. For this reason, activists first of all, never study, secondly, never spend time with working youth, and thirdly, create conventionalism and red-tape."[18] If the activist was a member of the party, the Komsomol, and the Trade Union, he or she was expected to go to the meetings of each. As another activist complained, "At one and the same time I was nominated to the party meeting (for my report), the meeting of the Trade Union (for my financial report), and the bureau of the *Volraikoma* KSM (for my report). I decided to go to the Komsomol meeting but I sent my certificate materials to the rest. On my certificate they replied: 1) you are a party member, so do not forget party discipline, 2) you are a member of the trade union, and you must not forget trade union discipline. How does one find a way around this?"[19] It was not uncommon for a Komsomol activist to work eight hours a day, go to night school from six to eleven four times a week, and attend meetings on top of this.[20]

Most troubling to young militants was that many of these meetings seemed to have no value. While the meetings passed "tens and hundreds of every kind of resolution" and people spent many hours and made "many good resolutions," some Komsomol'tsy protested that there was "absolutely no control over the fulfillment of these plans," meaning that there was "work without any result."[21] The author of an article in *Young Communist* [*Iunyi kommunist*] complained that Komsomol lectures and club activities did "not provide youth with knowledge, but with formulas, slogans, schemas, and empty phrases, from which has already fled any real essence, and all genuine thought."[22] Political education courses, too, seemed to many to have retreated from agendas informed by the practical realities and emotional immediacy of the revolutionary period into theoretical formulas. This was particularly frustrating when Komsomol'tsy faced so many concrete problems, such as high rates of juvenile unemployment.

Some militants who protested that the youth league was not doing enough to defend the economic and political needs of working youth suggested that the Komsomol could be revitalized. "Youth must be called to battle" with new slogans designed for NEP, argued one such enthusiast. The usual slogans, such as "The communist education of youth is the main task of the League," were too "conventional." Instead he proposed "Fight against the NEPman" as a slogan that would portray the Komsomol as still a revolutionary organization. "The Komsomol is not a school. Its most important tradition is struggle. To retreat from this tradition . . . is to put an end to the League."[23] Young militants like this one used earlier official representations of communist youth as a foil for newer definitions of youth which they disliked.

Other young people were so frustrated that they suggested that the Komsomol should be done away with altogether. They created new groups which were intended to better address the interests of the younger generation. Some of these new, unofficial, groups had political agendas. An "anarchist-communist" group in Voronezh condemned the "current leadership of the party over the Komsomol," while members of a syndicalist youth movement argued that, because the communist party defended only the interests of adult workers, it was necessary to create "professional youth unions" and even non-party "youth collectives" to protect the special interests of youth.[24] Other groups responded to the Bolsheviks' sober seriousness with an apolitical fatalism and with laughter. One such group declared its allegiance to the positivist teachings of Immanuel Kant and called itself the "All-World Association of Foolish Ones [*Erundistov*]." These disillusioned youth dedicated themselves to the belief that "everything in life is rubbish [*erunda*]." Apparently quite successful, they spread to other locations, where they adopted such nonsensical names as "Hooligan gravy." Laughter in the face of official seriousness has a long history, and can, as Bakhtin reminds us, have subversive significance.[25]

Although there were complaints throughout NEP, peak periods of opposition were related to the larger political environment and specifically to conflicts within the party leadership. Trotsky became very attractive to certain communist youth when in 1923, in *The New Course,* he assigned the younger generation a special role in the regeneration of Bolshevism, which he said had fallen into uninspired bureaucratism. He argued that the younger generation was the "barometer" of the party, registering through its discontent the problems of a party which had increasingly prohibited youth from participating in positions of leadership. The tendency of the apparatchiki to "turn up their noses at youth" was a great mistake, Trotsky insisted, as "youth are our means of checking up on ourselves, our substitutes."[26] It was a mistake, however, not only because youth were a barometer indicating what was wrong with the party, but because the initiative and idealism of youth were important means of pushing the party in the right direction. If the revolution was to be a continual process, and not simply a single act, Trotsky argued, then it was necessary to involve the younger generation fully and to encourage their participation and capacity for critical thought.[27] Trotsky's description of youth's role coincided with the young militants' understandings of self—they were supposed to be the young saviors of an anti-bureaucratic and energetic Russian revolutionary movement, not steady builders of bourgeois NEP. By late 1923 approximately 40 percent of Moscow Komsomol members were said to support Trotsky.[28] Support for Trotsky and for the leftist opposition was especially strong in Moscow, Leningrad, and the Urals, and in the institutes of higher education. The period 1923–1924 was, as one student commented, "a golden time for the Trotskyite opposition."[29]

For those in the party who, like Stalin, were committed to moderation and stabilization, and who were opposed to Trotsky's vision of revolutionary renewal, young enthusiasts posed a significant problem by virtue of both their youthfulness and their militancy. As general secretary of the party Secretariat, Stalin derived much of his power from his development and manipulation of the bureaucracy. In addition, Stalin and Bukharin both advocated moderation in the party's agricultural and industrial policies.[30] However, the often energetic and sometimes oppositionist qualities of young people (and not just young militants) meant that many were ill suited to the bureaucratic demands of a period of stabilization. As many young people themselves recognized, NEP signified the explicit rejection of the more spontaneous and destructive environment of the revolution and Civil War for a more orderly, controlled, and "improving" moral culture. In this environment, behavior which could not be fully controlled, excesses of enthusiasm, and spontaneous rather than conscious militancy were condemned by political authorities interested in stabilization. There may have been something about being a young person, on the other hand, that made it hard for many youth to appreciate the process of deliberate stabilization and solidification.

Militant youth, and their alliance with the more radical elements in the party, were an explicit challenge to those who supported the more moderate course of NEP. Although Stalin had described youth as the vanguard of the party in 1901, he now repudiated this idea. Youth were neither the barometer of the party nor the element that would save it. Instead, "the barometer must be sought . . . in the ranks of the proletariat." According to Stalin, "only those who want to drive a wedge between the cadres and the younger party element" would insist that the question of generation was so crucial.[31] Bukharin (himself a member of a group of young oppositionists in 1917) likewise condemned Trotsky's approval of youth's taking it "upon themselves to conduct the old" as a "demagogical viewpoint sufficiently remote from Leninism."[32] The militants' "disorderly" behavior was disturbing because it appeared to elevate youth's own interests at the expense of the stabilizers' political goals. By doing so, youth challenged the party's role as the principal creator (and enforcer) of revolutionary meaning.

Political authorities took direct action against student supporters of Trotsky by purging a quarter of all communists in schools of higher education in 1923–1924.[33] Encouraged by the party leadership, the central Komsomol leadership also initiated action against oppositionists in its ranks. There were some expulsions and, more generally, numerous "educational" efforts, including lectures in Komsomol clubs and articles in the Komsomol press. Not all in the Komsomol leadership were opposed to Trotsky; the powerful Leningrad Komsomol organization harbored many supporters of the leftist opposition and tried to call a country-wide conference to discuss their ideas. But the highest leadership of the Komsomol generally supported Stalin's position, and indeed remained in power partially because they did so.[34] Following these efforts, explicit support for Trotsky appeared to taper off for a few years, but the purge did not create a wholly enthusiastic student body. Instead it contributed to disaffection and hostility among student youth, leading to a round of depression and suicides in late 1924.[35]

The sense of alienation created by NEP and youthful enthusiasm for Trotsky's policies did not end in the mid-1920s. The Komsomol archive contains letters from young people resigning from the league in late NEP who complain that the Komsomol is "ill" and that the country is "further from socialism than it was before."[36] In 1926–1927 rebellion surged again, rejuvenated by the new alliance of prominent party leaders Zinoviev and Kamenev with Trotsky. *Red Students* [*Krasnoe studenchestvo*] noted that student agitators "ran through every district, stirring discussion and winning supporters."[37] This time the movement was centered in the Leningrad Komsomol collectives, but it was also strong in the Urals ("Regional Committee of Young Trotskyists"), Armenia ("Trotskyist Union of Youth"), Azerbaidzhan ("Trotsky Union of Defenders of League Democracy"), Georgia, and Belorussia. Five hundred and seventy oppositional speeches, appearances, and performances were recorded throughout the country in the first two weeks of October 1926 alone. In speeches and platform proposals in 1926 and 1927, youth protested the lack of "democracy" under Stalin. "We know that this declaration will bring persecution and victimization," concluded two members of a Leningrad Provincial Committee in an oppositionist resolution. "But this won't stop us . . . If intra-party arguments are decided with the help of the GPU . . . then we young revolutionaries announce that we are not afraid."[38] Even when traveling to prison in the back of a Black Maria, some sang anti-Stalin songs—defiant and unrestrained songs that one suspects only the young would sing:

> Greetings to you, Uncle Stalin,
> Ay, aya, ay,
> You're disloyal, full of malice,

> Ay, aya, ay
> Lenin's testament, you stuck it,
> Ay, aya, ay,
> Deep inside your big side pocket,
> Ay, aya, ay.[39]

Reading this song, we would do well to remember what Lev Kopelev recalls in his memoirs, namely that oppositionists were not always attracted only by "theoretical considerations" and "faith in the program of the Opposition." Also important, he notes, was "the enticement of the *underground*, the revolutionary conspiracy: in essence, the same passion with which a short while ago we had invented Pioneer war games, played 'Cossacks and brigands.'"[40]

Students continued to be a principal source of support for the opposition. "Towards the end of 1927," one Komsomol activist remembered, "the situation in the YCL [Young Communist League] organization of Moscow University reached [a] white-hot pitch. Komsomol meetings and sessions of the University and Faculty YCL bureaus would drag on for several days."[41] The militants' efforts to involve working-class youth enjoyed success as well. In Leningrad connections were made with Komsomol groups in the factories *Red Triangle* and *Fast Runner*. The Kharkov factory *Red October* had close to four hundred Komsomol members who supported the opposition.[42] As before, most activists objected that the party was doing little to alleviate the difficult economic and material position of working youth and complained about the level of bureaucratization in the Komsomol and the party.[43] The journal of the Leningrad Komsomol organization published an article in 1927 called "Where is the Komsomol going?" in which the author argued that the Komsomol was losing its edge; that it was no longer the kind of revolutionary organization it had been, but was mired in bureaucratic lethargy and too narrowly focused on unproductive kinds of cultural work. The Komsomol needed to attend to the needs of youth and could best do so by becoming once again a sharp-edged force for political change.[44] This author, and others like him, used the left opposition, in other words, to forward their own agenda of revitalizing the Komsomol and advancing the interests of working-class youth.

THE CULTURAL CHALLENGE
OF MILITANT YOUTH

The young militants' evocation of the civil-war ethos was as evident in the area of culture and everyday life as in that of politics. They put forward their own definitions of appropriate forms of everyday behavior based on the legacy of the Civil War, using the languages of dress, speech, and style to define themselves and the nature of their beliefs in a period of great transition. For all communist youth during NEP, debates about wearing lipstick or a tie or drinking beer had great significance, because personal habits helped distinguish communists from non-communists. The enthusiasts' behavior differed not only from that of NEPmen and NEPwomen, however. They also challenged "official" conceptions of communist youth culture based on cleanliness, politeness, and discipline. Instead, not unlike the nihilists of the 1860s, these youth revered coarse manners and clothing, afraid that fine clothes and good manners made them unrevolutionary.

Clothing and behavior have more than just symbolic meaning in a revolutionary period. As Lynn Hunt explains in her history of politics and culture in revolutionary France, clothing, colors, and other outward symbols "did not simply express political positions." Rather they were "the means and ends of power itself," because to have power "meant to have some kind of control, however brief, over the articulation and deployment of outward manifestations of the new nation."[45] Like the French revolutionaries, the Bolsheviks themselves contributed to the power of the everyday with their constant efforts to create revolutionary signs and symbols for the new Soviet state. But while this preoccupation offered new possibilities, it also offered unexpected challenges. The politicization of daily life meant that through their behavior and dress, enthusiasts offered alternative articulations not only of the everyday, but of the nature of the new state. The conflict between different definitions of communist culture reflects questions crucial to the early Soviet endeavor. How was Soviet society to understand the legacy of the Civil War? What was the best way to advance the revolutionary cause now that the revolutionaries were in power? What was communist culture and what did it mean to be "cultured?"

For the young enthusiast, the most powerful tool for self-definition and identification of the other was the concept of *meshchanstvo*. A pre-revolutionary term connoting petit-bourgeois vulgarity, it was used in the 1920s to label all kinds of "non-communist" behavior, dress, language and manners.[46] Exactly how to determine what was non-communist and what was not remained a matter of great debate, however. Young enthusiasts used the terms *meshchanstvo* and *meshchanin* ["philistine"] to describe anything that reeked to them of the old order and of pre-revolutionary bourgeois traditions. Bolshevik moralists and Komsomol moderates proposed a more limited and, one might even argue, conservative definition of appropriate behavior. The confusion was evident in Komsomol newspapers, which published conflicting information on all aspects of everyday life. A club newspaper might condone dancing, while an evening speaker at the same club criticized it as bourgeois. "Gather around you ten young men and women in any VUZ [Institute of Higher Education] and you will hear how often and in how many forms and different hues they use the word 'meshchanstvo.'"[47]

Komsomol militants insisted that they could best demonstrate their devotion to the higher causes of communism through a complete disdain for nice clothing, good manners, and even clean living areas. Theirs was a kind of radical iconoclasm, which refused to accede to any "idols of the establishment," including not only pre-revolutionary privileges but the post-revolutionary, semi-bourgeois culture of NEP as well.[48] For these youth, dress was one of the most obvious ways to represent one's own revolutionary intent and to determine the political character of others. In order to be a good communist one had to practice the most severe kind of cultural asceticism. Enthusiasts accused working-class leaders who wore ties of "careerism" and argued that girls who had long hair were "undemocratic."[49] In their minds even the most minimal adherence to traditional standards of dress symbolized a retreat from the more radical efforts of the revolution and Civil War.

> Even now a necktie, brooches and bow are regarded as signs of petty-bourgeois individualism. An orderly, hygienic way of life means banishment from the Komsomol. An undisciplined, slovenly appearance, boisterous manners, a "lad in worker's blouse" is considered essential for the "solid" Komsomol member. All this echoes from the old, bygone days of war communism.[50]

Young women as well as young men saw attention to clean and fashionable dress as unrevolutionary, and Komsomol girls, like Komsomol boys, wore "leather jackets, crumpled skirts, and patched shoes."[51] One young female factory worker criticized the well-paid women in her factory who liked to dress well, arguing that "[t]heir style of dress outside of the factory [was] completely unproletarian."[52] In early NEP "there was a passion for dressing like a slob so that you could show everyone that you were a *'komsomol'ka.'*" A purposeful lack of attention to appearance was a marker, positive for the enthusiast and negative for others. Workers "give a hard look at Komsomol girls," argued one female activist. "As soon as they see dirt they still burst out, 'there goes a Komsomol girl.'"[53]

With their leather jackets, worker's caps, and lack of grooming, young people were distinguishing themselves from NEPmen and -women with their fancy furs and flapper dress. This was again a generational critique in that they were criticizing older Bolsheviks who had "inherited," along with their new bureaucratic posts, the neckties of the pre-revolutionary elite and had "begun to look cleaner than the bourgeoisie."[54] The enthusiasts also rejected the revolutionary "costumes" designed by experimental artists such as Liubov' Popova. Perhaps they recognized not only the impracticality of such outfits (few were actually produced), but also the implicit elitism of the constructivist costumes, which, although meant to be revolutionary, had more in common with European flapper fashion than with working-class dress.[55]

Any behavior which smacked of refined living was also severely criticized. Komsomol members in Kiev almost rioted when they found that a new club had hooks for coats and a hall porter to take their galoshes and heavy winter clothing.[56] Others deliberately cultivated a "coarse and debauched way of talking," using rough expressions and street slang.[57] Despite the Komsomol's admonitions not to smoke, some continued to do so. At the Fifth Komsomol Congress, when Bukharin suggested that Komsomol youth should give up smoking and drinking as an example to non-communist youth, some delegates refused, expressing fear "that Komsomolites would become sissies." "They protested that smoking was not really such a terrible sin; and they argued that rough worker youth would not take to such petty 'rules of conduct.'"[58] In *Diary of a Communist Schoolboy*, a young schoolboy scorns the school wall-newspaper, called the *Red Scholar*, in favor of an alternative paper, *Ex*, produced by the students. About the *Red Scholar*, the schoolboy says: "At first everyone was interested, but it all turned out to be bunk. The articles are stupid—all about studying and good behavior." *Ex* is far preferable, he declares, because "in this *Ex* everybody gets it in the neck—the skworkers [school workers], Dalton, the girls who dance on the quiet, and above all, the *Red Scholar*." He likes a supplement to the *Ex* even better as it "is full of dirt and it's funny like the dickens."[59]

The association made here between disorder and the revolutionary enthusiasm of youth had a pre-revolutionary heritage. The nihilist students of the 1860s and 1870s were similarly committed to breaking "all ties with the social order and with all educated society, with all manners, accepted customs and morality of this society."[60] In the pre-revolutionary period, when the typical upper-class clothing was a tie and starched collar or a lacy dress with hoop skirts, young nihilist women "made a sensation" by going in public with "short hair, blue tinted glasses, sloppy dress, uncombed and unwashed" while the young men wore "working-class clothes —red shirt or greasy coveralls—together with long hair and the usual dark glasses."[61] Both the nihilists and the young militants of the 1920s recognized the power disorder had to disturb the assumptions of civility and culture held by the well-established. Their lack of attention to the personal may have also signified to them a deeper commitment to the political.

It is not surprising that the nihilists were successful in angering "respectable" Russia with their provocative dress and behavior. In Russia, as in Western Europe and North America, the late nineteenth century was a period of particular anxiety about attacks on "civilization" and morality by the lower classes or by any who threatened the fragile security of the civilized elite.[62] Suggestively, after 1917, and especially after 1921, the Bolsheviks responded in much the same way to perceived threats of "disorder" as had the pre-revolutionary intellectual elite. Older party members themselves disagreed about definitions of communism and appropriate communist behavior, but many were united in their opposition to the young militants' idealization of the unclean and the disorderly. They were wary of the younger generation's enthusiastic condemnation of every young man wearing a tie as a philistine and every well-dressed young woman as a petit bourgeois. "You hear youth, especially Komsomol'tsy, call people philistines when they keep themselves clean and have a nice haircut. This, of course, is not *meshchanstvo*."[63] The anxiety was not just about youth in the Komsomol. Political workers in the Red Army worried similarly about young recruits who were overly aggressive in their campaigns against "petit-bourgeois lifestyles" among senior officials.[64]

Bolshevik moralists (and many in the Komsomol leadership) opposed the young militants' approach to communist behavior on two accounts. The first was its emphasis on the external. For example, the editor of *Komsomol Truth* [*Komsomol'skaia pravda*] argued that what was crucial was not external characteristics, but the young communist's "relation to his comrades . . . to social work . . . to women . . . to his relatives . . . to society . . . "[65] The most threatening characteristic of the "philistine" was not that he wore a tie or that she wore makeup, but the danger that this kind of cultural individualism posed to the communist collective. Using makeup or wearing gold jewelry was wrong because it insensitively emphasized the implicit inequalities between those who could wear gold bracelets and others who had little to wear at all. It gave an external expression to the wearer's separation from the working-class masses. Secondly, and more fundamentally, Bolshevik moralists objected to the basic principle behind sloppy dress and poor hygiene. Rather than seeing them as revolutionary, they argued that the militants' slovenliness inhibited the development of a more advanced and cultured working class. Instead of criticizing cleanliness and good hygiene as bourgeois characteristics, prominent authors on problems of everyday life described them as two of the most fundamental characteristics of a good communist and a crucial step in the creation of revolutionary forms of everyday life. Scores of books published for wayward Komsomol'tsy reminded them that nothing was wrong with neat clothes or a clean apartment and insisted that the first step toward a new life was the "struggle for cleanliness in Komsomol dormitories."[66] The newspaper *Blue Blouse* [*Siniaia bluza*] instructed youth that "keeping your body clean and brushing your teeth is a revolutionary act."[67] As A. Stratonitskii explained, it was not that Bolsheviks were against "refinement and beauty," but that one simply must not overvalue it. "You must dress cleanly and well . . . Suits should be clean and up-to-date . . . attractive, but not so luxurious that you stand out from the larger working masses."[68]

The Bolsheviks' focus on cleanliness and good hygiene reflected their understanding of the central tasks of cultural construction. As Richard Stites explains, Bolshevik moralists criticized "the inner *kul'tura* of the intelligentsia," with its "self-doubt, soulful introspection, and universal humanitarianism," but respected and desired *kul'turnost'*, which included "the external values of cleanliness and punctuality."[69] In this environment, the appropriate and distinctly moderate tasks of the young communist were, according to one Bolshevik, to "see women as friends and comrades . . . spend money on books instead of beer, and not 'show off' but dress cleanly, handsomely and well."[70] This reflected, in part, the very different agenda of a regime that now had to govern a state and a society, as opposed to a party that sought to destroy them. There may have been something inherently conservative about the new tasks faced by the Soviet government, tasks which could be made easier by sobriety and self-discipline. Thus Bukharin would argue that while rebellious behavior might have been understandable and even appropriate under the old system, now that the revolution had occurred it was inappropriate for communist youth to continue with these undisciplined and negative acts. In 1922 he spoke out against the continual use of tobacco and alcohol by Komsomol youth, insisting that whereas before the revolution it had been "fun to walk right by the superintendent with a cigarette in one's mouth," now this had to be ended, as tobacco and alcohol were "of direct harm" to the body and implicitly, therefore, to the revolution.[71]

At the same time, though, as I have suggested above, these attitudes were not new. The rather conventional, almost middle-class attitude of socialist revolutionaries reflected the larger European socialist tradition, which had long emphasized the values of cleanliness and sobriety over the disorderly realities of much of working-class life.[72] Although the Bolsheviks rejected the kul'tura of the intelligentsia, their enthusiasm for kul'turnost' suggested that they, like the European socialists, still longed to "lift" the working classes into the ranks of the clean and "cultured." By insisting that the militants' behavior was inappropriate, the Bolsheviks again helped identify Soviet culture-in-the-making as "civilized."

The struggle here between disorder and cleanliness suggests something more than just Bolshevik appropriation of bourgeois proprieties, however. Peter Stallybrass and Allon White describe the late-nineteenth-century preoccupation with cleanliness as a new place onto which Victorian moralists could focus their concern with control. E. Chadwick, who was the "leading exponent" of the "sanitary ideal" in nineteenth-century Britain, wondered "how much of rebellion, of moral depravity and of crime has its roots in physical disorder and depravity." He suggested that "new forms of propriety must penetrate and subjugate the recalcitrant body," retraining "bodily irritability and thence uncontrollable mental irritability."[73] The Bolsheviks made similar connections between "disorders" of the body and disorders of the mind by associating dirt and physical disorder with a lack of enlightenment. This association had implications for Bolshevik control over the revolutionary agenda as well as larger implications for the place of the popular in revolutionary Russia. By connecting communism with cleanliness, Bolshevik moralists could reassert their control over the revolutionary definitions of young militants. This was particularly important because enthusiasts were not just repudiating conventional forms of behavior by identifying dirt and disorder as positive, but doing so in the name of communism. "Cleanliness" and ideological purity would become even more important to the party during the 1930s, when it increasingly relied on "public rituals of cleaning" to purge itself of the impure.[74]

Sociologists distinguish between behavior appropriate to the age of an individual, such as the particular developmental stages of adolescence which every individual goes through, and that which reflects "the distinctive collective experiences" of a particular group or generation.[75] Youth's experiences in the Civil War were representative of both kinds of behavior, linking "personal time" and the everyday experiences of the life cycle to "social time" and historical experience. Although not all young people who went through the revolution and Civil War had the same experience, those described here might be included together as part of a generation, molded by a common central experience which shaped their socio-cultural perspectives.[76] This generational effect was not limited to those who had been directly involved in the war. Through discussion in the Komsomol club and in the newspaper, and through the "languages" of dress and behavior, young people who joined the youth league in the 1920s were also exposed to the heroic vision of communism. They reenacted a narrative about Civil War asceticism and heroism even though they had not experienced it themselves. For participants, as well as those who wished they had participated, the dichotomy between the various definitions of communism was one not just of economics and politics, but of self-definition as well: what did it mean to be a communist in 1919 versus 1925? In this way, feelings about the relative virtues and failings of the Civil War reflected images and understandings of self. They also reflected understandings of others, as enthusiasts saw the shift to NEP as a failure on the part of a "weak-willed" older generation.

To some degree it may have been the very nature of adolescence which encouraged young people's idealization of certain Civil War attributes. The characteristics they attributed to the revolution and Civil War—exuberance, destruction, explosion, and disrespect—were similar to those of adolescence. NEP, on the other hand, represented responsibility, sober maturity, and patience—characteristics usually associated with adulthood. Some Bolsheviks themselves described the transition in just this way. Bukharin, for example, made a comparison between the "infantile psychology" of War Communism and the sobriety of NEP when "the illusions of the childhood period are consumed and disappear without a trace."[77] As adolescents, these young enthusiasts were not interested in moderate, "grown-up" activities, but in the rough-and-tumble of the revolution. The heroic aspects of the revolutionary process were appealing to youth who were themselves often energetic and spontaneous. They are "young and noisy," wrote journalist Walter Duranty about one group of communist youth, "evidently enjoying themselves immensely. You can hardly tell the boys from the girls—the popular outfit for both sexes is a high, buttoned-up, black leather tunic and a mop of unruly yellow hair. They shout across to each other or break out in dissonant choruses. They cheer like college boys when the flag of the Red fleet is entrusted to their keeping."[78] Duranty commented on the striking contrast between the young Komsomol'tsy in the theater "huddled in groups of five on three seats or in clusters of twenty in boxes meant for eight" and the political leaders on stage who, he said, might have been members of a chamber of commerce. He implied what militant Komsomol'tsy repeated as well: that it was youth who were acting like the true revolutionaries.

Yet for many of these young people their admiration for the Civil War was not simply a reflection of their age and immaturity, but had political significance as a symbol of their revolutionary intent. The mentality and goals of the Civil War shaped their perceptions of self and other, and their zealous approach to questions of politics and everyday life can be seen as an attempt to maintain and even advance their view of communism and communist man in the face of a changing social order. By identifying with the Civil War, however, the enthusiasts placed themselves outside the mainstream of official policy in the 1920s. This was most obvious in the case of student supporters of Trotsky, who were often treated as "alien," but it was also true for those working-class war veterans who idealized the Civil War, and who should otherwise be "considered a base of social support for the Bolshevik Party." As Sheila Fitzpatrick has noted, the introduction of NEP created outsiders out of those previously very much on the inside.[79] The sense of betrayal implicit in this transformation must have contributed to the degree of disappointment we saw evidenced above. It also fueled the self-righteousness of young people eager to identify and correct the "mistakes" of their elders.

The militancy of some Soviet youth and the responses it engendered in the party expand our understanding of the complexities of Soviet society "in the making" in the 1920s. The Bolsheviks experienced serious challenges to their domination not just from the many non-communist elements remaining in Soviet society but also from dismayed and disappointed youthful supporters of radical Bolshevism. Young militants served as keepers of the Civil War legacy—as persistent reminders of alternative definitions of communism and communist man, some aspects of which were re-evoked and celebrated during the period of the First Five-Year Plan. The generational struggle over cultural definitions was also a crucial part of a larger political debate about NEP. Anxious about youth's own "non-communist" forms of dress, language, and behavior, the Bolsheviks encouraged them to dress neatly and talk politely. Young militants resisted this attempted domination. In the contested environment of the 1920s, the symbolic languages of behavior, of dress, and of the body had political meaning and

provided an important forum from which youth could challenge the Bolsheviks' right to define the revolutionary agenda. In the next chapter we
will see how another symbolic language, that of gender, was also a point of
contestation in the 1920s, though this time among members of the Komsomol rather than between youth and adults.

5

GENDER AND GENERATION

Many young women joined the Komsomol in the 1920s hoping that in the young communist organization they might find the equality and opportunity for women that the revolution had promised. In a 1928 survey of a thousand school youth, the authors noted that young women were even more eager than young men to join the league. "They sought authentic equality, and a society that refrained from the scornful relationships and hooliganish escapades [typical] of the male part of the school."[1] As representatives of the younger generation and as members of a revolutionary organization, Komsomol women should have had unprecedented opportunities for political and social participation, and young men and women might have been expected to be on the forefront of the effort to forge new standards of gender equality. In the same year as this optimistic survey, however, the journal *Kommunistka* [*The Communist Woman*] reported that despite a history of Komsomol resolutions aimed at increasing the number of women in the youth league and bettering their condition, in fact "the status of work among women has not only not improved but in the majority of cases has become worse."[2]

That this was the case will not be a surprise to historians of women in revolutionary Russia. Very good works on women in early Soviet Russia have explained the many material reasons why overburdened and economically vulnerable women did not participate wholeheartedly in the political life of revolutionary Russia.[3] In this chapter, I also briefly discuss the ways in which parental opposition and young women's household responsibilities contributed to positioning them on the periphery of the Komsomol. My principal focus is on a different aspect of this marginalization, however: the relationship between the culture of the Komsomol and young women's participation in the political life of their generation. What happened when young women did try to take part in politics, to join the Komsomol, to participate in the creation of a new state and society? How did the masculinized culture of the Komsomol marginalize and exclude them?

First, it must be acknowledged that there were many changes in relations between young men and young women following the Russian revolution. Some resulted from legislative actions such as the 1918 Bolshevik Code on Marriage, the Family, and Guardianship, which together with other early legislation mandated equal economic, marital, and civil rights. Young men and women also had opportunities to mix in different ways in communist clubs and communal houses, and could meet in popular dance halls and movie theaters, which flourished after 1917. These opportunities may have been greater for young people than for mature adults. Many of the new entertainments and educational opportunities were dominated by youth. In 1926, young women made up close to 20 percent of the Komsomol.[4] The league thus compared favorably with the party, where by 1927 women made up only about 12 percent of the total membership.[5] In these and other ways, gender differences between young men and women were being leveled, as women were now considered in theory to be the same as men, and young women and men worked and played together in new ways and new places.

This supposed sexual equality was limited, however, and reactions were mixed. As we will see, much of the language and practice of the Komsomol emphasized instead the differences between men and women. The culture of gender difference, with its assumptions about men and women (and about the nature of the Komsomol), was one of the most significant factors inhibiting young women's active participation in the youth league. Much of this differentiation was based on fundamental associations: women with the private sphere of home and family, and men with the public sphere of politics. The gendering of private and public was not particular to this period, nor of course was it confined to Russia, but the meaning of this construction needs to be explained in a revolutionary environment otherwise committed to sexual equality. My material suggests the difficulties of restructuring gender relations even in the most conscious of revolutionary situations. When considered together with recent work describing similar kinds of gendered hostilities among adult workers, we gain a new appreciation for the power of entrenched cultural forms to resist transformation in multiple areas of urban life and work after the revolution.[6]

Of course, discriminatory conceptions of what it meant to be a woman were not particular to youth. In many ways young people reproduced the gender representations and discriminatory behavior of adults. However, youthful conceptions of gender (and gender relations among youth) were not always the same as those among adults. In Soviet Russia, as in many cultures, adolescence and early adulthood were crucial periods of "settling" issues of sexual identity and of deciding just what it meant to be a "man" or a "woman." In the uncertain and unstable environment of NEP, when there were important generational factors at play as well as gendered ones, this task was particularly complex. As we will see, young men defined themselves as revolutionary in part because they could more easily maintain a heroic adolescent persona, while young women were seen as less revolutionary because their familial responsibilities (and the nurturing nature required for them) were thought to make them more "adult." Gender and generation were intimately interrelated in the construction of sexual identity among Soviet youth.

Sources on gender relations in the youth league include Komsomol Central Committee reports on the status of women and articles in Komsomol and student newspapers on relations between young men and women. Soviet sociologists wrote about the daily life of youth on the basis of questionnaires, interviews, and participant observation, and educators prepared instruction books and pamphlets for young people on questions of sexuality. Valuable as it is, most of this material captures young women as they were represented "on the page." It is more difficult to find them as they appeared "on the streets" and in the clubs, and my discussion of what Komsomol women did, and how they saw their lives and opportunities, is therefore more limited than I would have liked.[7] That said, there are some good sources on the culture of young women, including interviews and observations; the best information was gathered by older Komsomol and party women about their younger colleagues. Unfortunately, the Soviet sociologists and ethnographers whose research is such a good source for other areas of daily life among young people were interested primarily in young men, who they felt were principally responsible for the most serious problems of adolescence, including hooliganism and juvenile delinquency. Compounding the problem is the fact that girls' culture was more likely to center on the less visible arenas of home and family, whereas boys were more likely to be visible on the streets and in youth clubs. We have to be especially sensitive, therefore, to the marginalization of young women implicit in the sources and to the gendered qualities of the discourse on young people in the effort to recover young women's own voices.[8]

We also have to be aware that there were sometimes larger, if unspoken, meanings to some of these materials, especially those that detailed transgressions against women. Public campaigns against the mistreatment of women increased in 1927 and 1928, probably reflecting a related campaign against hooliganism, larger concerns about corruption, and failed efforts to transform daily life. Conceptions of gender were clearly a part of this campaign. This is not to say, however, that the troubling descriptions of young women's lives that pour forth in this period are only constructs. In her work on women and the family, Elizabeth Waters argues that an increasing preoccupation with daily life in the mid- to late 1920s had a freeing effect on the women's press as "inner tensions [in the proletarian family] were admitted, their causes and effects explored." "More critical about the failures of government policy" and more willing to identify men as "the agents of oppression," the women's press now "highlighted cases of wife-battering, rape, sexual harassment—topics they had almost completely ignored in the first half of the decade."[9]

ECONOMIC DEPRIVATION
AND PARENTAL OPPOSITION

Despite changes in law and rhetoric after the revolution, conditions of economic deprivation reinforced traditional gender roles. As described in chapter 2, young women's responsibilities at home made it more difficult for them to join political and cultural organizations such as the Komsomol. Young factory women complained that while boys were allowed to do as they pleased, girls were only reluctantly permitted to attend club meetings: "Boys enter the Komsomol much more freely. Their families do not force them to work. They couldn't care less whether they go out biking or to a meeting. Therefore all [the parents'] anger falls exclusively on the girl."[10] According to one female activist, in order to get along with her family and still go to Komsomol meetings, a girl had to show her family that she was not going to "sabotage" family life. This meant going to bureau meetings and club gatherings just three days a week, while the most dedicated activists went daily.[11] Another activist said that she and her mother got along well because, although she had work to do in the Komsomol, when she was free she could do all that was necessary at home: "On Sunday I am free and can always do the wash." Parents were not always pacified by these efforts to find a compromise, however.[12] For this reason, one young woman suggested that young women who were truly committed to the Komsomol might be better off leaving home to join a commune or to live in a dormitory.[13]

Economics was not the only factor keeping young women away from the Komsomol. Some parents forbade their daughters to join the Komsomol not only because of their household responsibilities but also because they did not see any reason why a girl should learn politics or participate in social work when her principal task was to learn how to care for the household and raise children. Some young women would attend Komsomol meetings, but would not join the Komsomol for fear of their parents' reaction: "I have attended Komsomol meetings for four years, but I'm not a member. My parents won't allow it. I just barely mentioned my decision to enroll in the drama club, and they looked at me as a hopeless good-for-nothing. And the Komsomol—I'm afraid to even discuss it. When I cry or curse, the old folks threaten to throw me out of the house. But where would I go? That's why I haven't joined the Komsomol."[14]

To many parents, particularly peasants, the Komsomol seemed like an immoral organization, because it removed young girls from adult control and then required them to attend meetings that were often held at night. To many rural parents, the Komsomol was associated with corruption and hooliganism because of its urban heritage (and its supposed connections, therefore, with sexual depravity and big-city decadence) and because of its strong anti-religious tenets. Urban and rural parents alike worried that young women who joined the Komsomol were "looser" than their non-communist counterparts. Mothers dropped in on Komsomol meetings to make sure that their daughters were really in attendance and not out at a party. In one case, a young woman's factory organization had to go visit the girl's mother at home to convince her that her daughter was not out wandering the streets, but working in the factory club. Dislike of the Komsomol was so great that some mothers who heard that their daughters had joined the Komsomol disowned them.[15]

Finally, boys had wider opportunities than girls: "Boys are experienced: they enter the army, do seasonal work, meet intelligent people, attend lectures . . . They have the knowledge that they gained in school . . . Girls have none of this," explained one observer of youth.[16] For these reasons, not only were boys more likely to be allowed to join the Komsomol, but they were more likely to want to. With fewer opportunities, young peasant women were more likely to maintain contact with village traditions and young urban women were more likely to stay within the circumscribed world of family.[17] Young women both urban and rural were also more likely to see themselves as intellectually or politically unprepared to join the youth league: "Why would they take me? I don't know anything." "I don't understand anything in the newspapers; the Komsomol wouldn't let me join."[18] Or they might insist that it was men's work anyway: "Oh, that's for the boys; it's not any of our business."[19] As one group of peasant girls explained, "We don't refuse work, we always help by cleaning the floors and sewing decorations and cleaning the club so that generally we do everything that is within our ability."[20] Even in some largely female factories there was a "tradition" which said that for "public, responsible work you need boys."[21] Unfortunately, participating in the Komsomol would do little to alter these young women's opinion of themselves as unprepared and unable; indeed, in many cases, it only reinforced it.

THE FRATERNITY OF MEN AND
THE SUBJECTION OF WOMEN

As Carol Pateman has argued in another context, "To explore the subjection of women is also to explore the fraternity of men."[22] Through language and behavior, male Komsomol'tsy created a masculine identity that was separate from the female sphere; indeed, this separation was central to their own definition of self. In the pre-revolutionary work-floor environment, "locker room" talk had united workers "as men as well as workers." "Workers' common sexual identity—at least its presumption—was one of the bonds that united them," and female relatives "were often spurned" because they "represented competing identities" of "family and kin."[23] Language and joking were used to much the same purpose in the post-revolutionary Komsomol. Women were commonly called "baba" ["backward

The masculine culture of civil war. *70 let VLKSM* (Moscow: Molodaia gvardiia, 1988), p. 15.

woman"] rather than "comrade," even when they had been in the Komsomol for a long time—a term that excluded and devalued them. Teasing and practical jokes made young women feel uncomfortable, particularly when they were so outnumbered—a typical cell might have thirty to forty young men and only six young women. One young woman who came to join the Komsomol was welcomed by the club secretary, who offered her a seat but then pulled the chair out from under her. The group laughed at her embarrassment, and she ran out of the room.[24] Jokes like these expressed the group's perception of young women as interlopers. They also reinforced the young women's own anxiety about joining a group that was so overwhelmingly male in culture and in composition.

To some extent, young men were replicating traditional pre-revolutionary patterns. But they did so in some new ways, and with new "revolutionary" justifications. For some young men in early NEP the "fraternity" of men (and exclusion of women) stemmed from their experiences in the revolution and Civil War. Some young women did enter into new and more public roles during the war, but most Bolshevik women found that "a gender-based division of labor and power" still restricted the kind of jobs available to them.[25] Although a few women participated in military training programs, and fewer in military actions, the vast majority were directed to work in traditionally female support positions, managing home, kitchen (even if now a public cafeteria), and family.[26] In ideology, too, it was primarily young men who were shown as active, engaged, and important. The revolutionary image of "youth as a warrior and a rebel" was a male model; there were almost no female images of the revolutionary militant in the early period.[27] During NEP, defiantly maintaining the maleness of the Civil War model and disdaining the private world of home and family may have been a way to preserve the fighting spirit of the youth league, even among those young men who had not been active participants in revolutionary events. It helped some young men maintain their own identity in a period of great political and personal transition. This militancy differentiated male Komsomol'tsy from adult Bolsheviks, for despite the party's ambivalence about the place of women, the aggressive and oppositional aspects of this Komsomol culture were opposed by the Bolsheviks, who were trying to create a new kind of "cultured" communist who was disciplined, obedient, and "sensitive to the needs of others."[28]

In contrast to young men, young women were thought to embody the dangers of a reactionary past by virtue of their association with the private spheres of home and family. So fundamental was the public-male versus private-female construct that even when young women were involved in activities outside the home these activities were somehow suspect, tainted as they were by women's association with the private. In the women's bureau of the party, the Zhenotdel, activists described uninvolved women as "backward," but in the youth league, even female activists were described as such. Thus male delegates to one Komsomol meeting complained that young women rarely participated in political meetings or joined club circles that required some technical skill, gravitating instead to sewing circles and drama and chorus groups that were less important and in which "nothing serious occurred." There was little recognition that sewing clubs, with their exclusively female constituency, must have offered a rare forum for like-minded women to meet and share their problems. Even "women's work"— among Pioneer youth or in health campaigns—was seen as a sign of women's backwardness, linked as it was with family and private issues of home and health. Similarly, work organized specifically for women was derided as "baba work," devalued in comparison with men's efforts to organize the factory floor or increase production.[29]

Young women's fundamental "otherness" made them less than the equals of men: less-fortunate individuals who had to be educated into political awareness and given something "practical" to do. Direction from above, from male Komsomol'tsy, was all that prevented young women from backsliding into unawareness, and sometimes even that was not enough. "The girls are all interested in housework, sewing something or patching it; that's what they ask for," noted a delegate in a 1926 meeting. "We didn't give them that and they left the club, fell into the surrounding environment and as a result did nothing."[30] "The political and cultural backwardness" of young women "as compared to young men" is the "principal cause of the slow development of girls' activism," concluded a Komsomol Central Committee report. It is the "past historical development" of women that inhibits them.[31]

The cultural and social construction of "female preoccupations" as backward meant that there was little space in either language or experience for young women who carried the new triple burden of family, work, and Komsomol. Little was done in the Komsomol to address the realities of a young woman's private life, with her responsibility to contribute to her parents' household or to care for her own young children. At Komsomol conferences, which were the most common form of work among young women, presenters typically discussed International Women's Day and the status of women workers, but said nothing about the problems young women faced in their everyday lives. "There was only one conference for girls," complained one young woman, "which gave us nothing." It was all about politics.[32] Women argued that local Komsomol collectives also failed to pay adequate attention to family issues and were often unsympathetic to the particular demands of children and a household. "If you go to the Komsomol and complain that things are difficult for you," Comrade K. noted, "they'll only laugh." A young married Moscow worker, Nadia Borisova, explained: "I want to work and be a productive Komsomol member; I don't want to be left behind in the Komsomol's work . . . but escaping from the oppression of the kitchen is beyond my strength. My husband works during the day and in the evening he goes to classes or participates either in some kind of social work or party work. Alone I have to deal with the everyday cleaning, prepare dinner, run to the cooperatives, clean the swaddling clothes, feed the baby . . . " Borisova blamed the Komsomol most of all for her difficulties: "What does the Komsomol do? Absolutely nothing. We married Komsomol women with children are without hope, in the dark; I am thinking of the future when the baby will grow a bit older so that I can work again. But the Komsomol sleeps, leaving its members behind; if a girl gets married there is no place for her in the Komsomol."[33]

Most young women did not go so far as to suggest that the solution to these problems lay in getting their husbands, brothers, or fathers to help around the house, although some of those with helpful husbands did take pride in that fact. On the other hand, young women asserted that the solution did not lie in simply instituting sewing circles and home economics classes, as some male commentators had suggested.[34] One sympathetic female author noted in late NEP that what young women wanted and needed was for the Komsomol to "discuss not only theoretical questions about the place of the family in socialist construction, but the personal, concrete problems of the home life of youth."[35] The Komsomol had to stop imagining its constituency in statistical terms and start relating to them as "living" people. If they did so, this activist argued, then young women would "understand that the Komsomol will pay attention to and take account of their needs and family affairs" and "they will quickly enter the Komsomol."[36]

The Komsomol did not take this approach, however. The strong asso-

ciation between women and the private sphere of home and family contributed to its masculinization. Many in the Komsomol did not appear eager to help women manage the "private" aspect of their lives. Indeed, statements by male Komsomol members at committee meetings and in reports
suggest that some believed young women were the perpetrators of inequality rather than its victims. In late NEP there are increasing numbers of references in meeting minutes and in Komsomol documents to problems between young men and women, but many of the men in these documents
argue that women are to blame for these problems. Although some delegates to a 1926 meeting concerned with "advancing women to more active work" admitted that the Komsomol was "guilty" of not successfully
interesting young women in its work, others argued that the central problem was not the Komsomol but the young women's own low "cultural
level," which made them interested in less-practical and less-important
kinds of work. They suggested that young women only had themselves to
blame for their lack of genuine participation in the Komsomol because they
were not interested enough in political tasks, and because "in ninety-nine
out of a hundred cases, the girls 'elected' to these organs don't manage to
do any practical work, really only visiting the meetings." The delegates
argued that the "promotion of girls to the leadership organs" would be
"warranted only when they learn to work."[37] This is in striking contrast to
the perspective of female advocates who argued that the problem did not
lie with the young women and their supposed backwardness, but with the
Komsomol organization's failure to address women's specific concerns.

YOUNG WOMEN AS ADULT VERSUS
YOUNG MEN AS ADOLESCENT

The hostility of some Komsomol members to "women's issues" suggests
something particular about their attitude not only toward women and the
"private" sphere of home, but toward the entire range of adult issues associated with women by virtue of their ability to have children and their
household responsibilities. In contrast to the responsible, sober, and sometimes petit-bourgeois family life associated with young women, the ideal
young communist lived in a state of permanent adolescence that celebrated
the exuberant, unencumbered, and communal life of the teenage male. The
adolescent ideal again stemmed in part from the revolutionary period, when
youthful qualities of energy and initiative had been needed and glorified,
and young people had served as full-fledged participants in the forging of
a new society as they stepped into adult roles in factories and fought in the
Red Army. For young men, maintaining a rebellious adolescent persona
despite the transition to more moderate NEP was one way to sidestep the
party's increasingly paternalistic attitude toward young people. Some
young men turned a necessity into a virtue by transforming their marginalization as minors into a glorification of adolescent qualities.

Complications of marriage and children forced young men to confront adult issues and the concrete problems of real life when they often preferred the single-minded, independent, and aggressive identity of the Komsomol adolescent. Male Komsomol'tsy often resisted making changes (either personal or social) that would have facilitated sharing family responsibilities or encouraged young women's full participation in the youth league. Most egregious were the young men who abandoned their wives or lovers when they got pregnant, sometimes skipping from one relationship to the next. In a survey of five hundred young women, 27 percent said that their spouses left them "as soon as they found out they were pregnant."[38] Among those who abandoned their families were not just activists, but members of the Komsomol leadership. One leader was said to have berated others for drinking and sexual misconduct while he got one woman pregnant and went out with two others. Sometimes young men did not just abandon their pregnant partners, but also tried to force them to leave the Komsomol, perhaps because it was then easier for them to avoid their responsibilities. Pregnant girls were accused of having sexually trapped their former partners. A district secretary accused his pregnant former girlfriend of being a prostitute, despite the fact that she had been an active member of the youth league since 1920.[39]

Some of this "adolescent" behavior, especially multiple affairs, was justified as part of the "new communist morality," which at its most extreme refused to admit that love existed and saw sex as "physiology."[40] When confronted with the problem of who was going to raise the children of these unions, some young men answered, "We are communists, and in a communist society there are no families."[41] Sexual freedom and family policy were contentious issues, however, in both the Komsomol and the party. Communist theater groups like the Blue Blouses agitated against "scoundrels" and "riff-raff" who seduced young women and then abandoned them once pregnant. In one such play, the fallen Komsomol member Semyon explains his "tactics" to the virtuous Komsomol member Peter:

Semyon: . . . Let's have a little chat.

Peter: I have no time, I'm off to a meeting, we've got an extraordinary session on today on the question of Komsomol morality. Come along . . .

Semyon: I can't. I'm waiting for someone here. You just use your tongue, whereas I'm practicing morality.

Peter: How do you do that?

Semyon: Oh, I take Katya or Natalia, I suggest a rendezvous on the boulevard. I take her by the waist straight away, and squeeze her petit-bourgeois self-consciousness.

Peter: But what if her waist gets fatter after that?

Semyon: Well, she'll have to cope with that as well as she can. She

"You should be ashamed! You come home from the 'House of Culture' and start looking for a fight! — And so! The 'House of Culture' is one thing, but the culture of home another." *Bich* 7 (February 1928), p. 7.

can give birth or abort, "liquidate," my only job is to agitate. I have a really original system. (*He sings*)

> I must show young ladies,
> That in the USSR—love is free,
> She only needs to give birth twice a year,
> And as soon as the baby appears in the world,
> I shall certainly disappear . . . [42]

Those young men who did not leave their wives or lovers often replicated patriarchal family relations. Aleksandra Kollontai had predicted the death of the patriarchal family with the introduction of communism, and Leon Trotsky, too, imagined a shift "from the old family to the new" after 1917.[43] Instead, when young men did get married it was common for even the most active and educated of them to insist that their politically active wives leave the Komsomol to take care of the house and the children. Despite official rhetoric welcoming women's full participation in the creation of a new state and society, young Russian women were still generally assigned supportive rather than leading roles. Young male Komsomol'tsy believed that by disencumbering themselves of family responsibilities they could devote themselves wholeheartedly to the Komsomol collective. As several young workers responded to a questionnaire on married life: "It's good that my wife prepares everything. She isn't a Komsomol member; she takes care of all the household work. I am the social activist."[44]

Once a young woman entered the "private" world of marriage and family, she was often no longer considered capable of being revolutionary. The case of one Lena Kuippe was typical. Lena joined her local factory Komsomol in 1925, and "in production, in social work, at meetings, in political studies—in everything, Lena was top rank." She then met and married a young man named Slesarev. Her husband did not like it when she read newspapers and told her not to waste her time on them. She agreed. Then he told her to leave the Komsomol, which she also agreed to do. "One often sees cases," concluded a Komsomol report, "of girls who were energetic, active, spirited, before their marriages, [but who] afterward become inert, passive and by stages withdraw from societal life."[45] Male Komsomol'tsy justified their actions by insisting that married women or those with children were less interested in political work and less able to do it well even when they did participate. "Ah, she got married, that means strike her from the list of activists,"[46] said one. "In my eyes my wife has died politically," explained another.[47]

While women were considered too adult in some ways, they never fully came of age in others. For male Komsomol'tsy, the adultness (and backwardness) of women was principally associated with women's reproductive and household roles. However, although more "adult" in their private lives, in other arenas young women were seen as less adult than young men. In the factory, for example, young and mature women alike had long been treated by mature male workers as minors. It was easier for young men to graduate to the world of the adult worker by acquiring skills; women were more often forced to remain unskilled and thus less than "adult." Young women could never fully escape the limits assigned to their gender; they were either too young or too old, and never truly revolutionary.

"CRITICIZED FROM ALL SIDES"

The Komsomol leadership acknowledged that "an uncomradely environment" contributed to young women's low levels of participation and leadership. In late NEP, Komsomol authorities talked about the ill effects of "uncomradely relations" based on sexual desire. Sexual harassment, and more specifically sexual dissoluteness, were discussed as one of a series of increasing problems in the youth league, along with hooliganism and drunkenness, all of which were said to "repel girls" from the Komsomol.[48] However, if young women appeared as victims in some Komsomol reports, in others they were again blamed for the sexual "hooliganism" that occurred in Komsomol clubs. As one delegate in a 1926 meeting complained, "All the girls want to turn some guy's head and rope him in. Then the guys lose their heads and nothing serious can be done with them."[49] Here men are the victims, trapped by the conniving female into relationships over which they apparently have little control. "Roped" into the feminine sphere of individual relationships, these men become no better than women, since "nothing serious can be done with them." In a popular novel of the period, *Dog Lane*, a young women named Vera, who sleeps with four men a week, is described as a spider whose eyes spread "like a web" over the "feelings, thoughts and desires" of young men. A communist medical student, Horohorin, becomes frightened of her for himself and for all men "who were caught in the web of the huge, white smug spider called sex, which was sucking not the blood, but . . . the very best in man—his brain."[50] Other novels instructed young readers about the dangers of women (and the dangers to women) who replicated the sexual adventures of men. In *The First Girl in the Komsomol*, a heroine of the revolution named Sania "loses her sense of proportion" after the war ends and "surrenders" to "unrestrained sexuality" with "one, then two, then half the Komsomol." "When a few youth, who through her have become diseased, are going to thrash her and dishonour her in public, she is shot dead by her best friend, who loved her most and possessed her least of all. Only thus could he save her and the Komsomol too from disgrace."[51]

Though these accounts describe women as the perpetrators, young women themselves complained that they were the ones who were pursued and regularly treated as sexual objects rather than as individuals with intellectual abilities and aspirations. Enthusiastic young women like Liza Kozhevnik, who from the "first moment of full self-consciousness as the daughter of a worker" hoped to "build a bright future" by joining the Komsomol, were too often forced to decide that they had "made a mistake": "Faced with girls, especially Komsomol girls, our Komsomol'tsy don't see comrades, but see only girls who can satisfy their desires."[52] The factory worker Petrova similarly complained that even when a young man behaved appropriately at a Komsomol meeting or in the office, "outside the Komsomol he becomes a completely different person."[53] Sexual jokes were common. "When I was pregnant," Comrade K. complained, "and went to a meeting, all the boys played tricks on me. Of course after that I didn't attend any more meetings."[54] Pregnancy is, of course, the most female of events and as such could be seen as a threat to the masculine culture of the Komsomol. It also signaled that a woman had been sexually active, which may have made her a more likely target for sexual comments, jokes, and unpleasant remarks.

In meetings and in classes, young women's contributions were frequently criticized or dismissed as stupid, and they were often given busy-work to do while their more constructive efforts were rejected. In university classes, young women who tried to speak were sometimes greeted with the response "A lot you know! Stupid! Shut up!"[55] On the factory floor, women experienced hostility from older male workers and from younger Komsomol'tsy who argued, "You can't make a skilled workman out of a baba." When Comrade Dunaevskaia was assigned as an apprentice to workers in the *Red Dawn* factory, all the male workers at first "flatly refused" to take her and then finally "cast lots." At the *Proletarian Work* factory, a young man entering his apprenticeship was treated "just as he should be," while a young woman starting at the same time was "criticized from all sides." Again, local Komsomol cells rarely addressed these problems, as Comrade Bychkoza explained: "One needs comradely assistance, moral support, but these do not exist. It is hard to work with the older workers. Almost every girl who is assigned requests support from Komsomol members, but she frequently doesn't get any."[56] These dynamics are similar to those Diane Koenker has described in her work on men and women on the post-revolutionary shop floor, where men still "retained the power of control" and "women were represented as partial workers, incomplete" and "transient."[57]

Because they were seen not as comrades but as fundamentally less-capable beings or as targets of sexual desire, young women were often not even considered for some kinds of work—sports director, secretary of a Komsomol collective, president of a meeting—but were relegated to more marginal, and more traditionally female, roles, such as working with children in the Pioneer organization or setting up for a club meeting and cleaning up afterward. When they were admitted to leadership positions, it was often only to fill quotas handed down by the higher Komsomol authorities. The existence of quotas suggests that Komsomol authorities recognized the need to bring more women into the organization, and that they had to legislate this desired increase in order to make it happen. A factory worker, Comrade Petrova, recounted a time when she recommended a woman for one position and was told, "Moll, we already have three girls and three guys in the office, and if we choose one more girl, then we won't be 'maintaining the right percent.' Therefore we need a guy."[58] Some women were not willing to be accepted on the basis of a quota. One Dunia, who "was furious because the boys wanted to elect her so as to have a girl on the committee," argued that if she was not "good enough as a human being" she would not "go on the Committee at all."[59] For these reasons, young women greatly admired other women who were in positions of power within the youth league: "In one of our shop sections there was a guy who was a member of the party and a secretary of the section cell but the cell had completely disintegrated; there was hooliganism and so on. Then we moved a girl up to the position of secretary. She has now gathered the activists around herself, raised their qualifications, put work on a really good footing."[60] Komsomol men often objected to being "headed by a baba," however, and even in the case of the successful female cell secretary described above, activists outside her cell rejected her and "tried to show that she couldn't be in charge of work like a guy could."[61]

Gender inequalities in leadership positions were spread throughout the youth league. At the fourth all-union congress of the Komsomol in 1921, only 25 of 614 delegates were women. In the mid-1920s, out of more than three thousand representatives of national republics and other political units (*guberniia, krai,* and *oblast'*) at a Komsomol plenum, only 10 percent (308) were young women. Of these, only thirteen were on ruling committees, and twelve of these thirteen worked with Pioneer organizations. Although the problem was acknowledged, the situation was no better at the highest levels. Of eighteen people on the Komsomol Central Committee in the late 1920s, only one was a woman.[62] The situation could be worse at a local level. According to a 1924 history of the Orsha Komsomol organization, a woman had served as chairman of a meeting or Komsomol gathering only once. Of the 273 women members of the local Orsha organization, only three were activists in the members' bureau. The report noted: "In our district not a single woman has attended one conference. And there have been ten congresses." The author of this report argues that even in the Pioneers, the one area where women were traditionally active, local women from Orsha were "afraid" to participate.[63] The problems remained at the end of the decade. The Komsomol Central Committee itself admitted in 1928, "Despite the fact that much has been said and decided" about the need to have more women in leadership positions, the situation "is still very poor."[64]

One solution sometimes suggested to the "strong inadequacies" in league work was to "organize separate [club] circles for girls as a means of improving [their] psychological and cultural level," and to use International Women's Day as a way to pull in non-party women.[65] There were, however, relatively few successful efforts to provide special activities for young women. "The 8th of March [International Women's Day] is a good thing," observed Comrade Gol'dina, "but it's a shame that it happens only once a year; if it took place five times a year that would be better."[66] Indeed, there was great ambivalence in the Komsomol, as in the party and the Zhenotdel, about developing separate organizations for women. Some thought there should be no special or separate efforts, since they would "put boys and girls in an unequal position."[67] According to one report from late NEP (just a few years before the Zhenotdel itself was liquidated), girls' bureaus [*dev'orgi*] in the Komsomol allowed young women to become accustomed to meetings and helped them maintain ties with the Zhenotdel, but had an unhealthy tendency to separate women's work from men's. The authors argued that the existence of girls' bureaus meant that the Komsomol cells stopped their general work among women, and the women in turn "did not help and did not contribute to the daily work" of the cells.[68] Young women were often discouraged from organizing among other women.

When one young woman who energetically tried to set up a commune for female workers went to the Komsomol for assistance, they would not help her and actively discouraged her from further participation, not just in women's work but in the youth league altogether. In a letter to a Komsomol newspaper she wrote, "I was ashamed and hurt . . . I want to work; I love the organization, but they pushed me aside."[69]

THE CULTURE OF YOUNG WOMEN

The masculine culture of the Komsomol asserted the preeminence and prerogatives of public life over private. This ideal was obviously easier for young men to achieve than for young women. The youth league was generally unable to allow young women to create an identity for themselves that could accommodate both the Komsomol and their familial responsibilities. How did young women respond to this challenge? Many were forced back to the more conventional spheres of female activity. As we have seen, some were urged to leave the Komsomol by their husbands so that the husbands could remain free to pursue their own political work. Other young women left the league of their own accord. One Comrade Revina had been an active worker who had chided other Komsomol women when they left the league after getting married. But when she herself got married, she too left. When questioned, she answered, "What do I need the Komsomol for; my husband works and makes 150 rubles. I work and get 70 rubles and I'm going to live quietly without the Komsomol."[70] The "conservatism" of those who left the Komsomol often reflected economic anxiety. As Wendy Goldman and Barbara Clements have explained, many women who were economically vulnerable, who were unskilled or struggling to survive as single mothers, often supported the preservation of the family (even the patriarchal family) as a lesser evil than abandonment and poverty.[71] The traditional safeguards were all the more important because the Komsomol did so little to address the economic and material needs of women. Many left the league because of inadequate child care facilities and overwhelming household responsibilities. Women will want to remain in the Komsomol, one female activist concluded, "only when we have adequate cafeterias and creches."[72]

Some women did not leave the Komsomol, accommodating themselves instead to the male adolescent ideal. This often meant relinquishing their familial responsibilities. Some of the most committed young women left their children with their parents or in a nursery so that they could continue to be active in the Komsomol. Comrade S. from the *October* factory noted that because she was so busy she saw her sons only three weeks out of the year. One lived in the Caucasus, and the other with her mother. When she asked the Komsomol secretary for a vacation in order to see them, he told her it was "impossible," as it meant "a break" from her work in the youth league.[73] Other young women emulated the "military virtues" of the Civil War and resented "allegations of femininity." The "defeminizing element" of these revolutionary women was displayed in their masculine military clothing—leather jackets, boots, and pants. Thus one young woman combatant, dressed in a leather coat, and carrying a Browning, asserted that she was "not a little girl now," but a "soldier of the Revolution."[74] Finally, some women's sections in some factories replicated men's attitude toward "female questions." In one Moscow factory the women workers met only when they needed to elect someone to the Soviet. They never met to discuss questions of daily life or talked about them in any way.[75]

Active young women could be as disdainful as their male colleagues of women who were involved only in "female" activities, such as drama and sewing groups, or who expressed "female" sensibilities. Women look only at books that have love in them, complained one young female activist.[76] There were two kinds of female factory workers, explained Comrade Petrova. The majority were unskilled workers who were still dependent on their families, since they did not make much money. Eager to get married to escape their parents, they were more susceptible to what Petrova (and communist enthusiasts like her) considered hooliganism, which meant wearing lipstick and powder. The dedicated Komsomol'ka was not supposed to be interested in dressing well; she was supposed to be a lover of books, not of fashion, and the books she read concerned technical topics rather than love affairs. Indeed the Komsomol'ka of early NEP developed a reputation for "dressing like a slob" in order to "show everyone" that she was a communist and not a young woman who adopted the latest flapper fashions. Petrova notes that by the late 1920s, most communist women had left the most extreme manifestations of this behavior behind, although they still rejected makeup and fancy clothes. Petrova makes interesting connections between gender, skill, salary, and political awareness. In her portrayal, the ideal female worker was like her male colleague—skilled, wealthier than other women, and less associated than they with the private sphere of family responsibilities. She says, for example, that because the salaries of skilled communist women were higher, and because they could therefore contribute more money to their families, they were allowed greater independence.[77] Young female enthusiasts like Petrova defined themselves in opposition to "backward," unskilled women in much the same way as young men did.

Not all of what Petrova admired came from a male model. Activist women, too, had images of self that had originated in the Civil War. As Barbara Clements explains in her study of Zhenotdel utopianism, activist women in this early period imagined a "bold, impetuous, practical, prudently intelligent" new woman who was a "strong, free citizen, not inferior to man in anything."[78] This image of the "new woman" was "communicated to a younger generation of communist women" in the early 1920s, especially to "teenagers from the working class and the lower echelons of

A cartoon of the female activist. *Iunyi kommunist* 13–14 (August 1922), p. 60.

the urban middle class."[79] Literature was a powerful transmitter of the ideal of the "emancipated" woman who declared herself in print to be not just the equal of men, but their "superior": "We shall be engineers, soldiers, inventors, artists—we shall beat you at your own game!"[80] The "new women" of Soviet Russia did not want to spend their lives cleaning and cooking. "Is this life?" asked one. "No, life should be built on creative possibilities and not on the ancient structure of family happiness."[81] Like the male adolescent ideal, this alternative ideal of female emancipation had an effect on visions of the ideal marital relationship. Irina Pavlovna, who was twenty years old when the war began, was married (though the marriage was not registered) but said she wanted to "keep her independence," earn her own living, and keep her own room. "The two of us together in one small room would have been unbearable." Her husband wanted them to live together and have children, and asked her to give up her work. "He was a member of the Party, and I wasn't, yet he was so much more conservative than I," said Irina. Finally she left him so as to keep working and to maintain her independence.[82] "I won't have Jura live with me in my room," explained another young woman. "I've only one room, and I don't want to wash and cook and darn for him. Of course, I don't mind if he comes in the evening and washes up his plate and cup, but I don't want him to be there always. I want it to be a fresh conquest every time."[83] One female factory worker described in admiring tones a marriage in which both the husband and wife were so busy with their respective work (she in the Komsomol and he studying) that "they had little time to see each other, and all went well."[84]

These female visions of self suggest a blurring of sexual differences. Despite a rhetoric of equality, however, many male Komsomol'tsy were uncomfortable with this leveling of gender differences. Women should be equal (perhaps), but not the same as men. One Komsomol cell refused to accept one woman's membership application because she swore in an "unbecoming" fashion, and another's because she "went out with boys too much."[85] Both behaviors suggested that these women were becoming too much like men, either in their language or in their sexual behavior. This view echoed that of Nikolai Semashko, who bemoaned the "masculinization" of some Komsomol women in an article published in the Komsomol journal *Young Guard* [*Molodaia gvardiia*]. We too often see young women with "disheveled, often dirty hair; a cigarette hanging from the mouth (like a man); a deliberately gruff manner (like a man); deliberately rude speech (like a man)," he complained. This "vulgar 'equality of the sexes'" was not right, he wrote, because women are naturally different from men and have "their own social functions and their own particular characteristics."[86] Semashko might have agreed with the character Besais in the play *Our Youth*, who explained, "For my part [my ideal woman] may be enlightened about everything; but I should be offended if, while I was stammering out my love she were to clean her teeth with a match-stick and swing her legs—'Good, Besais my darling, I love you too.' In a word the girls may be modern if you like, but they may not lose their capacity for blushing."[87] According to Semashko, it was not only undesirable but impossible to have women act like men, since the characteristics of masculinity and femininity were determined by the functioning of the male and female endocrine glands. The fact that the inherent otherness of women was seen as not just cultural but biological "naturalized" the differences Semashko assigned to the sexual and social behavior of men and women.[88]

Although the fact that they were "different" did not necessarily mean women were unequal to men, in practice that was how young women were imagined and treated. The special characteristics Semashko attributed to women—"kindness, consideration, heartfelt attitude, gentle manner"—

were not qualities highly valued by revolutionary youth. Indeed, what adult Bolsheviks like Semashko valued in women was precisely what young men disliked. The very qualities Semashko desired reminded young male readers of women's "essential" ties to the less important private sphere. "Girls' minds were not made for politics" was a common argument in the youth league.[89] Even when young women were involved in political work, their reasons were thought to be more emotional and less rational than those of men. "This type of Komsomol girl will do everything that is asked of her, but not from a sense of discipline, but simply because she wants to," concluded one observer.[90] In addition, many of the characteristics thought by some to be "natural" to women were not the "positive" attributes described by Semashko. In Komsomol Central Committee documents young women were variously described as lazy, weak, timid, and lacking both stamina and concentration. "In the summer there was absolutely no work [in the club] and absolutely no leadership of the youth section. Of course it is hard to say who was guilty, but the most at fault were the girls themselves who were not very active in this work."[91] "Some of the girls are active, but we don't give them the opportunity to especially develop it," admitted one Komsomolets. On the other hand, he says, "girls are naturally more timid, and afraid to come forward, while guys are different—bolder."[92]

The proposed solution to backwardness was to raise young women's political and cultural level, but there was some ambivalence about this. Could it be done? Should it be done? That the differences between men and women were understood to be partly biological must have contributed to the feeling that it was harder (if not impossible) to persuade women to relinquish the dangerous habits of the past for the revolutionary future. It is true that some of what differentiated young women from young men was biological—they were associated with the non-revolutionary sphere of the private and of the adult partially because of their ability to have children, for example. But this essentialism, and all the differences attributed to men and women, served a larger purpose as young men used these supposed differences to bolster their own shaky senses of self. "A wife should be less developed than her husband," wrote one young man; "then everything will be fine."[93] This sense of self may have been more precarious during the uncertain period of NEP, when definitions of both revolution and gender roles were undergoing transformation. In this environment, all that it took to marginalize young women was their sex, which was constructed by male Komsomol'tsy to mean everything other than what they wanted to be.

6

FLAPPERS AND FOXTROTTERS

A cartoon in the early Soviet satirical magazine *Rowdy* [*Bich*] showed a young couple dressed in flapper fashions dancing the Charleston. One asked the other, "So, Vasia, what class do you consider yourself coming from?" Vasia responded, "Frankly speaking—the *dance-class*!"[1]

With the introduction of the New Economic Policy, cities such as Moscow and Leningrad appeared to change very quickly. Expensive food and clothing stores, flashy nightclubs, gambling casinos, and other manifestations of the changing economic climate resurfaced for the first time since the ending of the Civil War. William Reswick, a Russian who had emigrated to the United States before the revolution and returned as a journalist during the war, wrote that as he made the rounds of Moscow he was astonished "by the great change that the NEP, a comparatively free economy, had wrought in a matter of nine months or so. It was a change from a state verging on coma to a life of cheer and rapidly growing vigor."[2] The *New York Times* Moscow correspondent, Walter Duranty, also marveled at the changes. During War Communism, Moscow

> was a doleful city . . . ill-dressed inhabitants drifted aimlessly through the streets. Almost all the stores were shut, with boarded-up or broken windows. Here and there a listless crowd waited at the door of some state or co-operative supply depot. The buildings lacked paint and plaster and the only means of transport for the public were decrepit hacks or filthy street cars.

By 1923, according to Duranty, old residents agreed that Moscow was "not much different from pre-war days."[3] The stores were well stocked with expensive fruits from the Crimea and wines from Georgia, both far beyond the price range of most residents but satisfying the urges of the new entrepreneur. Restaurants and gambling establishments had reopened for

"So, Vasia, what class do you consider yourself coming from?"—"Frankly speaking—the *dance-class!*" *Bich* 5 (1927), p. 7.

wealthy patrons in evening suits. NEPmen with money to spare threw extravagant dinner parties with tables "laden with platters of caviar, wild game, suckling pigs, and many bottles of vodka and Caucasian wine."[4]

The changing atmosphere was due in part to the legalization of private trade that accompanied the introduction of NEP. With it came a resurgence of entrepreneurs. Some peddled goods on the street, while others opened clothing and food stores, cafés, and restaurants. Private traders lined the streets, selling everything from furs and velvet dresses to Singer sewing machines and Kodak cameras. *Izvestiia* ran advertisements for corsets, fashion magazines, and pianos next to notices about the latest books on problems of everyday life and contests for the best enterprise. By 1926 there were more than a hundred thousand NEPmen in Moscow, many engaged in artisanal or handicraft activities such as baking and dressmaking, and others working as shopkeepers, wholesalers, and small traders.[5]

Although the Bolsheviks legalized private business to rescue a floundering Soviet economy, there were many communists who barely tolerated NEP and NEPmen as a necessary, but temporary, evil. Private trade in food and clothing revived a population on the brink of death, but some wondered if the price was too high. "We wanted to remain a party of poor people," wrote Soviet sympathizer Victor Serge,

> but money very gradually became most important. Money rots every-thing—and yet it also makes life spring forth everywhere. In less than five years, freedom of trade had accomplished miracles. There is no more star-vation; an extraordinary zest for life rises up, carrying us along, but the worst of it is we feel we are rapidly being swept downhill. Our country is a great convalescent body, but on this body whose flesh is our flesh we see the blotches spreading.[6]

Party leaders and Komsomol activists were concerned not just about the economic contradictions of NEP, but about the implications of contin-ued exposure to what they considered bourgeois attractions. The "blotches" Serge saw threatening the body of Soviet communism were spread by con-sumption of Western cultural products. While we do not need to accept the Bolsheviks' definition and denigration of Western commercial culture as "bourgeois," it is true that the relatively relaxed cultural borders of NEP permitted an influx of mass media images from the West that showed young people in the Soviet Union what their European counterparts were danc-ing, watching, and wearing.[7] The most visible, and to the Bolsheviks most problematic, manifestations of this Western culture were the Soviet "bo-hemians," who adopted the flapper fashions of Paris and New York and danced to the seductive rhythms of American jazz. Their bodies—the West-ern clothes they wore and the exotic movements they made—were visible reminders of threats to a healthy communist body politic. Their playful forms of personal expression and entertainment appeared to challenge the serious and more puritanical aspects of Bolshevik culture. Committed to the penetration and transformation of intimate areas of everyday life, Bol-shevik moralists saw the pleasures of dress and dance as evidence of devi-ance and opposition.[8]

The fact that many Bolsheviks thought young flappers and foxtrotters were disaffected does not necessarily mean that they were (though some may have been). But for communists anxious about NEP, bohemian youth were more than just a cultural challenge. The problem with bohemianism was not only pleasure, but the particular meaning pleasure, abandon, and well-being had in the unsettled and contentious environment of the 1920s. Bohemians were especially anxiety-provoking because they exemplified aspects of NEP (prosperity, material pleasures, even luxury) that made many committed communists uncomfortable. Talking about bohemians was a way to represent anxieties about NEP; representations of flapper and foxtrotter youth became another part of the struggle to define what com-munists ought to be like.

SOVIET BOHEMIANS

The term *bohemia* [*bogema*] was first associated with the late-night lifestyle of young people who frequented the busy literary cafés on Moscow's Tverskaia Street during the closing years of the Civil War and the early years of NEP. These early bohemians were identified not so much by their adoption of Western culture as by their appropriation of the more outrageous aspects of the pre-revolutionary salon traditions. "You know, of course," wrote Vladimir Slepkov, "of these elegant and pensive young people, who can dance the foxtrot so well, who with inimitable grace kiss the hand of a lady and drink champagne in cut-glass goblets with toasts to all that is 'elevated and beautiful.'"[9] Poets and painters, writers and artists met and discussed their works in the many small, "ephemeral" cafés that passed in and out of existence in those early years: "Poet's Café," "Music Box," "The Tenth Muse," "Three-Leaved Clover," "Café Bom."[10] At one of the most famous, "Pegasus's Stall," poets began reciting at 11:30 in the evening, while a "motley crowd, poets and their girl friends" ate, drank, listened to poetry, and danced the occasional foxtrot until two or three. Just outside, prostitutes from the Tverskaia bargained with reluctant clients and drunks argued noisily with hack drivers.[11]

The post-revolutionary "prince of Bohemia" was the poet Sergei Esenin, who took a special pride in acting the part of the "tender hooligan." With his friends from the scandal-ridden group of poets known as the Imagists, he hung around noisy cafés such as "Pegasus's Stall," drinking, brawling, and insulting the very audience who had come to hear him recite his already famous poetry. Refusing to adapt to the revolutionary iconography of the working-class costume, he wore a top hat, gloves, and patent-leather shoes.[12] In a 1924 volume of poems entitled *Moscow the Tavern City* (*Moskva Kabatskaia*), Esenin described the underside of Moscow life during NEP:

> And when the moon comes out at night,
> Shining like—God knows how!—
> Hanging my head I set my sights
> Through backstreets to a favorite bar
>
> The filthy den is full of noise.
> But through the night until dawn I shout
> My poems to the whores
> And knock back vodka with the pimps and touts.[13]

Members of Moscow's bohemia were also attracted to the more "comfortable" quarters of the Artist's Club, where they met to "curse or bless the times, predict the future, discuss themselves and each other, organize into groups and movements, and act not altogether unlike the inhabitants of Montparnasse."[14] Moscow's bohemia looked "rather more 'bourjui' than the rest of Europe," one Western observer noted, and indeed the Artist's Club was decorated in mahogany and bronze and had a billiards room, fine food, and a dance floor where artists and ballerinas danced the foxtrot.[15] Less-wealthy poets and their admirers also gathered to read their works in private apartments. In Moscow, young people gathered at Kara-Murza's to hear the poets Lipskerov and Vera Inber. The writer Vladimir Lidin was also there, and later he described such a gathering in his novel *The Price of Life*:

> The room was full of people. Poetesses, with beads on flat chests, shingled, or with bobbed hair brushed in a crescent over their cheeks; girls . . . in vivid jumpers, green or scarlet, and with bright-coloured socks worn over their stockings, wandered to and fro, their painted lips droning verses. There were young things, pupils from the poetry studios, who listened dreamily to the droning voices, their eyes staring as if drugged. There were thin, dignified young men in horn-rimmed spectacles, who were most of them leaders and masters, moving among the crowd of disciples with the stately slowness of the consecrated.[16]

DEBATES ABOUT DANCING THE FOXTROT

Esenin's "young aristocrats" represented the most extreme and self-conscious examples of bohemian subculture. Their innovations and attitudes implied a deliberate rupture with Bolshevik norms, and only a small number of urban youth were fully committed to this kind of subcultural expression and style. However, elements of the bohemian visual and behavioral vocabulary trickled down through other layers of society and were adopted in less-radical forms by working-class, student, and even communist youth. "Different youths bring different degrees of commitment to a subculture," Dick Hebdige notes in his work on British youth cultures. There are the "originals," for whom the subcultural activity is a "major dimension," and the "hangers on," for whom "it can be a slight distraction, a bit of light relief from the monotonous but none the less paramount realities of school, home, and work."[17] For the youthful "hangers on" in the 1920s, one of the most popular elements of "bohemian" culture was dance. A visitor to Moscow in this period noted the raging popularity of the foxtrot:

> From ballet dancers to former princesses, former manufacturers' daughters to former janitors' daughters, every girl in Moscow has one great social ambition—to learn the foxtrot. From former grand dukes' sons to shopworkers, every sprightly young man in Moscow wants to learn to foxtrot—as the sure way to the heart of his galoubushka [darling].[18]

To the dismay of Bolshevik moralists, dancing seemed to take place everywhere: in restaurants and clubs, in schools, on the street, and in reformatories. "So far the only place where they don't dance the foxtrot," wrote one worried observer, "is on streetcars and in cemeteries."[19] The foxtrot was not the only popular dance. Young women students practiced the tango with their girlfriends in dormitory kitchens as they sang the latest Argentinean dance tunes.[20] By the mid-1920s, the latest dances had even spread to the countryside: "If five years ago not many rural youth were able to dance the cracovienne and the polka . . . in 1924 they are already dancing the tango, the pas de quatre . . . and so on."[21]

Some of these dances, including the tango and the foxtrot, had been popular before the revolution. They were introduced to the upper classes by foreign visitors and by Russians traveling to the West, and then filtered down to the larger public.[22] According to journalist Edwin Hullinger, the foxtrot was introduced with new vigor to Moscow and Leningrad after the war by "fifty fox-trotting college boys" working for the American Relief Administration:

> Along with the grain for the starving and food packages, the young American Relief workers brought the fox-trot to Russia. They found an entire city waiting to receive it. And during their spare hours these young philanthropists could easily have kept themselves busy (and many did) introducing ballet dancers or princesses, as the case may be, to the mystic steps and rhythm of Broadway.[23]

In *Red and Hot: The Fate of Jazz in the Soviet Union,* S. Frederick Starr describes how the Charleston came to Moscow in 1926, only months after it was introduced in Paris, via a variety revue act called *The Chocolate Kiddies:* "It began with the latest dances executed by high stepping babes dressed in above-the-knee flapper skirts and their Harlem swells decked out in tuxedos."[24] The decadent appeal of these Western acts was satirized in a cartoon in the magazine *Rowdy [Bich]* in which two men were shown avidly watching three girls in scanty outfits perform the can-can. The caption reads, "Brother, I come here not without purpose. I want to see Europe *in all her unattractive nakedness.*"[25] While concerned Bolsheviks denounced the decadent influences of Western bourgeois culture, eager members of the younger generation flocked to dance the foxtrot and the black bottom to the tunes of traveling American jazz bands. Capitalizing on this appeal, Soviet dance troupes and jazz bands soon advertised their acts as "American."[26]

Before the explosion of "bourgeois" behavior and culture in 1921, there had been few places for young people to meet and dance. Emma Goldman described the shocked expression of one Bolshevik official during the Civil War when she asked him "if the young people could not occasionally meet for a dance free from Communist supervision." "Dance halls are gathering places for counter-revolutionists," he responded. "We closed them."[27] After 1921, dance halls, cabarets, and even private dance studios reopened. Young people from the former upper classes danced at the newly opened foreign missions in Moscow. In the winter of 1922, the British mission held regular dances on Sunday afternoons and occasional Saturday evenings. The Polish delegation held "elaborate balls," at which, according to one observer, "in her pre-war dress, many a young woman who would have been making her debut at the Court save for the accident of the Revolution, looked as charming and pretty as if just home from college."[28] The cafés and cabarets of NEP tried to recreate a pre-revolutionary atmosphere on the dance floor. One café near Petrovka Street in Moscow served fine wines and was elegantly decorated with lush green palms. Patrons wore evening suits, and "obsequious waiters [said] 'please, sir' as in the days of the Empire."[29] At the famous "Eldorado" in Leningrad, Russians listened to "the wild caress of a jazz band," and when they finally stumbled from the restaurant at two in the morning, they could hail a cab with a fancy horse-drawn carriage to take them home. According to one worried Bolshevik, some areas of Leningrad were so full of fancy cabarets and cafés that they were starting to resemble New York's Seventh Avenue.[30]

Many exclusive dance clubs met in private apartments. They were secret hideaways, operating away from the watchful eye of Bolshevik inspectors and open only to those who knew the right password. As with jazz music or the sultry rhythms of the tango, the illicitness of these underground gatherings may have given them a special kind of appeal. Edwin Hullinger described a private cabaret located in the back of an old frame house that during the day served as a doctor's office:

> We tugged at the bell cord beside the padded door, and waited, it seemed, for ages. Inside we heard faint strains of music, so faint as to be scarcely audible, sounds just trembling on the threshold of consciousness. Finally a cracked voice came through the keyhole. "*Kto tam?*" ("Who is there?") "Friends," my guide answered, and went on to give the password, "*Morozova*," the name of the young woman proprietor. The door opened, and we pushed through thick portieres into a hallway . . . At the top we pushed through another pair of thick curtains and found ourselves in a cloak room. As the attendant removed our wraps, we looked over our shoulders at one of the most picturesque scenes I saw in Russia . . . the exact duplicate of one of the "Chauve-Souris" famous gypsy cabaret tableaux . . . In one corner a small gypsy quartette was singing and strumming their guitars. Guests—Bohemians, former bourgeois or Tchekaists weary of duty, were seated at small tables around the walls. Most of them too were singing.[31]

Those who could not afford to go to private dance clubs, restaurants, or cabarets went to dance halls. A dance hall near Red Square was named after a famous pre-revolutionary club for the Moscow elite—the "Yacht Club"—although most of the members were tradespeople and many wore "communist pins in their buttonholes." Instead of caviar and champagne, the club served sandwiches and ice cream in the intermissions.[32] Many young people also danced at small parties held in their apartments or the apartments of friends. They gathered in tiny rooms, pushing the furniture to one side or simply dancing around the tables and chairs while the latest

tangos from Paris played on the gramophone, or, if there was a piano, someone pounded out the foxtrot. Popular novels of the 1920s described the
lively atmosphere of these parties, where young men and women drank
vodka and ate whatever poor appetizers of cabbage salad or cold fish their
host could provide. In a small space cleared in the middle of the room, they
danced the foxtrot or struggled with the Charleston.[33]

Many of the new dances popular among young people were conspicu-
ously sensual. This was particularly true of the tango, which emerged from
the bawdyhouses of Buenos Aires to take Europe, America, and Soviet
Russia by storm. The tango and other popular dances rejected the distant
and formalized steps of figure dances such as the mazurka in favor of ex-
pressive movements and closer contact between men and women. In the
tango, for example, "the male [kavaler] bent his partner in two, untwisted
her like a top . . . and threw her toward the floor."[34] The openly sexual and
slightly "sinful" elements of these dances were also reflected in their tunes'
lyrics. One of the most popular tangos among Moscow students, "Under
the Sultry Skies of Argentina," evoked the "hothouse" atmosphere of Latin
America in which a young man and woman fell in love and danced in a
bar to the "wild and raging" tune of the "teasing tango."[35] Even the titles of
some popular tangos suggested something dark and vaguely illicit: "Tango of Death," "Opium Tango," "Hashish Tango," "Tango of Love," "Exotic
Tango," "Tango of Ecstasy," "Tango of Oblivion," and "Melancholy Tango."[36] The tango was not the only sexually suggestive dance, of course. In
1820, the waltz had been banned from the French court because of similar
associations with "sexual transgression" and eroticism.[37] The tango was
new and more explicit, however, and together with the foxtrot was more
likely to be danced by a wider range of people in places less easily monitored by an older generation.

What role did "bourgeois" dance play in communist Russia? Attraction
to the tango and the foxtrot reflected in part a European-wide rejection of
the sober and self-controlled respectability that had been so common in
the Victorian era. The new dances also gave a playful, public expression to
popular concepts among Soviet youth of "sexual liberation," "free love,"
and the demise of "bourgeois" marriage. These exotic dances embodied
changing sexual mores in which some young men and women felt freer to
explore and express their sexual natures outside the marriage bond. For
many, the vibrant new dances and the lighthearted quality of the new "bourgeois" amusements were also antidotes to the traumas of war and revolution and the post-revolutionary problems of poor housing, hunger, and
juvenile unemployment. The political and economic retreat signaled by
the introduction of NEP was accompanied by an emotional retreat from
the difficulties and challenges of revolutionary upheaval. As one young
woman told Hullinger, "I am trying to live on the surface of life . . . I have
been in the depths for five years. Now I am going to be superficial. It hurts
less."[38]

Many of those who danced may have been indifferent to communism, and others, as we know, were believers who also wanted to dance. For some young people, however, dancing the foxtrot and the tango may have had a more obvious political intent. The symbolic importance of participating in something so clearly antithetic to what the Bolsheviks imagined youth culture to be should not be underestimated. Some young people insisted on modeling their lives as closely as possible on what they imagined the pre-revolutionary or Western bourgeois experience to be. In *The Diary of a Communist Undergraduate,* a young flapper who is challenged by the communist student Kostya defends her interest in dancing in just these terms: "'So you believe in Communism?' said the Zizi girl. 'It's a silly question,' said [Kostya], getting up. 'I'm a student and a young communist.' 'Very well! But remember that I believe in God and the foxtrot!' she cried. 'And no one—do you hear?—no one can stop me. Do you hear, Young Communist?'"[39]

Of course, the foxtrot had meaning not only for those dancing it, but also for those who watched it being danced. In his book on questions of daily life in the Komsomol, A. Stratonitskii condemned dancing as "an abnormal, unnecessary and even harmful kind of entertainment."[40] The provocative pleasures of these "decadent" dances appeared to violate basic norms of respectable behavior, and were seen by some committed communists as the first step on a slippery slope leading to complete immorality. "What kind of youth is especially attracted to 'gypsy' romances?" asked one author of a work on "NEPman music."

> Philistines . . . These are dandies . . . with bows, with fashionable boots, wearing the latest outfits over dirty underwear . . . dancing "American" dances and having only one wish—to find "a good fiancé." These youth stay away from social work, from the active work of the Komsomol, and from the interests of socialist construction.[41]

The "dirty underwear" said to lie under fashionable clothes is important, symbolizing the real corruption many Bolsheviks felt lay under the false glitter of NEP pleasures.

Of particular concern were the immoral influence of dance and its contribution to the "sexual excesses" of the younger generation. Soviet youth were said to be surrounded by sex, including "the foxtrot with its strongly emphasized sexual features, erotic literature, operettas overloaded with sexual images, [and] erotic films."[42] Anxiety about eroticism, and about overly sexualized youth, was a common trope during NEP, when, as Eric Naiman has argued, sexual consumption served as a metaphor for social corruption. Sexual activity suggested that the individual was out of control (just as NEP threatened to get out of control) and was operating from personal desire rather than collective interest.[43] The very nature of the foxtrot and tango, the close physical contact and strange, jerky movements they called for, embodied just this loss of control and "the abandonment of civilized restraint."[44] Thus the Soviet author Vladimir Lidin described the Charleston as a kind of uncontrollable seizure: "The two girls, linked together, began to twitch their legs as though palsied, and to stamp convulsively in one spot, their knees knocking, and their calves slanting outwards."[45] Instead of dancing, the Komsomol was supposed to encourage healthy diversions such as going to the theater and to museums and inspecting factories, all of which would presumably protect youth's physical and ideological "cleanliness." If, despite everything, young people insisted on dancing, then the Komsomol should come up with "dances for the masses" as a healthy form of relaxation that developed physical ability and encouraged a sense of the collective.[46]

Many anxieties about dance were specific to NEP and to the ideological and cultural challenges of this transitional era. But Bolshevik moralists also had much in common with their European and American "bourgeois" counterparts, who also worried about the "decadent" behavior of their youth and described their uncivilized behavior and dress in terms that were strikingly similar. European moralists worried, for example, that "jazz, savage, primitive, rotted moral fiber, spread a whorehouse culture, polluted children, caused illegitimacy and all manner of unspeakable crimes,"[47] while Frankfurt Social Democrats complained about big-city dance halls where the "misled section of the proletarian youth dance[d] its way into depravity."[48] To adults in both East and West, jazz and the flapper dress that accompanied it appeared uncivilized, challenging standards of mature, self-controlled, and sober behavior. European and American moralists also condemned jazz as a product of the "primitive" culture of Black America. "Jazz originally was the accompaniment of the voodoo dancer, stimulating the half-crazed barbarian to the vilest deeds," wrote the *Ladies' Home Journal* in 1921.[49] Similarly, Stratonitskii argued that wearing an "excessive" amount of jewelry was wrong not only because it reflected bourgeois traditions inappropriate for a working-class society, but also because it was "barbarian," common to the Blacks and Aborigines of Africa and Australia. It is "a vestige from primitive, barbarian times," he insisted, "and as advanced and cultured people we komsomol'tsy do not need it."[50] Instead Stratonitskii urged moderation and modesty. That many Bolsheviks held standards for public behavior similar to those held by Western capitalists suggests that some of their fears were not specific to socialism, but reflected a general anxiety (a moral panic) about the meaning of youthful behaviors, styles, and attitudes in the uncertain postwar period.

SOVIET FLAPPERS

In this period of transition and great cultural confusion, appearance was a quick indicator of character and political affiliation. According to the So-

viet Commissar of Health, Nikolai Semashko, the dress of the revolutionary should be simple, functional (allowing for the proper regulation of body
temperature), neat, and hygienic. Semashko condemned any interest in
"bourgeois" fashion, which he saw as too extravagant, elegant, and Western.[51] As we have seen, Komsomol enthusiasts took a different approach,
advocating a severe cultural asceticism that criticized as unrevolutionary
even the most minimal adherence to traditional standards of cleanliness
and neatness, such as a necktie or clean blouse. In both cases, the symbolic
language of attire and appearance helped define who was a communist
and who was not.

With the introduction of NEP, however, there was an explosion of interest in flapper fashions in the latest Western styles.[52] Some of this interest
echoed the pre-revolutionary period, when France and London had been
considered the major centers of fashion and style. From the early nineteenth century on, Russian upper classes had emulated French and English dress, and by mid-century journals such as *Fashion: Journal for Fashionable People [Moda: Zhurnal dlia svetskikh liudei]* had contributed to the
beginnings of a Russian consumer culture with their images of the latest
fashions from Paris. Turn-of-the-century magazines such as *Women's World
[Zhenskoe delo]* combined articles on the "woman's question" with illustrations of European fashions and articles on fine-art exhibitions.[53]

The most important influence on fashion-conscious young women and
men after 1917 was the sophisticated dress of the American movie star. The
favorite movies of this period were foreign films with the great early silent
film stars: Harry Piel, Douglas Fairbanks, Harold Lloyd, Charlie Chaplin,
Buster Keaton, and Mary Pickford.[54] "American films dominate, inundate,
glut, overwhelm the Russian motion picture houses today," wrote a troubled
(American) observer. "Clara Kimball Young has a theater devoted solely to
her in Moscow. In the Arbat, center of the workers' quarters of the Russian
capital, a new building celebrates the glory of Douglas Fairbanks in electric letters three feet high."[55] Leningrad's Nevskii Prospect was lined with
commercial movie theaters with alluring European names. In building
number 48 there was the theater "Soleil," in number 55, "Nirvana," in number 60, "Picadilli," and in number 80, "Parisian."[56] In early 1928 a major
Moscow theater on the Arbat showed twenty-two foreign films and only
seven Soviet films.[57] Movie posters advertising the latest foreign film could
be found all over the streets and public squares, drowning out the political
posters. The ads for commercial theaters were often blatantly erotic and
violent. A poster for the film *Life for a Life* portrayed a woman with tousled
hair dressed in just her bathrobe, while an advertisement for a detective
film depicted several menacing men with revolvers and a third man wearing a black mask.[58] To attract patrons, some commercial theaters resorted
to "bourgeois" attractions such as expensive and well-stocked buffets, free
coat rooms, and even orchestras that serenaded moviegoers with the latest
European dance music.[59]

An advertisement for a
NEP movie theater.
Sovetskii ekran 15 (April
1926), back cover.

Famous costume designers like Adrian of Hollywood created the screen
images of innumerable Hollywood stars, who then served as role models
for young viewers in East and West. Young women "cut back on everything else, so that they can 'look like their screen heroes'," complained Bolshevik moralist Ivan Bobryshev.[60] One young man who had been told he
looked like the actor Gary Pil took to calling himself after the actor, and
grew side whiskers to look a part of the *beau monde.*[61] Young women were
said to admire Mary Pickford, because she made even rags look like a princess's dress: "She was enchanting . . . although she wasn't especially pretty,
she made us believe that she was very beautiful."[62] In contrast to the rough-
and-ready young working-class revolutionary who wore a leather jacket,
shock boots, and a worker's cap, fashionable young women wore bright
red lipstick and narrow-toed high-heel shoes, bobbed their hair, and short-
ened their skirts. Young men wore tight double-breasted jackets, trousers
in the "Oxford" style, and boots called "Jims" [*"sapogi Dzhim"*].[63]

Some of the urban population's information on the latest styles did not
come directly from Western Europe but from Russian fashion magazines,
which provided European images for the Russian reader and were sold in

Moscow stores such as "Fashion World."[64] Two popular examples were *Fashions* [*Mody*] and *Fashions of the Season* [*Mody sezona*], both of which were published monthly in Moscow. *Fashions*, which appeared between 1924 and 1929, had a circulation of close to fourteen thousand. *Fashions of the Season* was even more popular; its circulation reached twenty-five thousand in 1928. Other than the quality of paper and printing, there was little to differentiate these magazines from equivalent fashion magazines in the West such as *Fémina* or *Vogue*. Some images were the same as those in the Parisian émigré journal *Illustrated Russia* [*Illiustrirovannaia Rossiia*]. That the Bolsheviks criticized much of Western fashion but permitted Russian fashion magazines to be published is a vivid example of the kinds of cultural conflicts that flourished during NEP.

The images of the fashionable young woman and man found in *Fashions* and *Fashions of the Season* were at odds with the modest, working-class lifestyle advocated by many Bolsheviks. A 1924 issue of *Fashions* showed models in soft, full dresses that were very feminine—a far cry from the functional clothing advocated by Semashko. The young women wore large, wide-brimmed hats, often with feathers or flowers, and leaned languorously against elegant balconies or strolled in the park holding fancy parasols. There were models in fancy beaded party gowns that were clearly meant for elegant evening parties, not for the neighborhood Komsomol club. In one picture, immaculately groomed children played in a ballroom overlooking a large garden, evoking the leisurely, pastoral lifestyle of Russia's own former nobility. In another, models wore elegant dressing gowns made of the latest Chinese fabrics, suitable only for the wealthy aristocratic woman with plenty of leisure time on her hands.[65] By 1928, *Fashions of the Season* showed the type of clothing more typically associated with our images of the young flapper. The lean, boyish figures wore short dresses that fell to just below the knees and their bobbed hair was covered by close-fitting cloches set with ribbon or rhinestones. In the winter issues they were shown in sleek, fur-trimmed coats, and in the summertime in simple dresses with abstract patterns influenced by the artistic avant-garde. As pictured in these pages, the adventurous and independent young woman of the postwar years had a busy social life, and needed the right kind of clothing for every occasion. In summer 1928, *Fashions of the Season* described "the kind of dresses that Parisian women take with them when they go to their summer houses" and the proper outfits for a game of tennis or a drive in the car. The daring young flapper of the modern era might even take an airplane flight, for which she needed a leather aviator's cap and glasses like the ones shown in the spring issue of *Fashions of the Season*.[66] Men and boys were not immune from efforts to dress Russians in the latest European fashions. The boys, who in these drawings looked like proper British boarding-school pupils, wore shorts, knee socks, and sailor hats. The men were dressed in dapper bowlers and boaters, and double-breasted plaid

531. Костюм из светлой шерстяной или бумажной материи. Отделка светлой материей и вышивкой.
532. Пальто из шерстяной материи, кроится прямое, отделано сутажем.
533. Пальто из светлого сукна. Отделано клетчатым материалом.

Russian flappers. *Mody sezona* 3–4 (March–April 1928), p. 5.

suits. They carried gloves and walking sticks, or posed with a cigarette in hand.

Although the images found in Russian and European fashion magazines showed a lifestyle few if any Russians could achieve, they encouraged young consumers to buy certain kinds of clothing by making an association between clothing and lifestyle, subtly suggesting to the reader that wearing the right kind of clothing could lead to a more desirable way of life. "Lifestyle advertising" of this type evoked dreams of carefree adventure far removed from the daily burdens of revolutionary Russia. The magazines, and the consumer products described in them, appealed to the fantasies of the new Soviet consumer. As Rosalind Williams argues about Western Europe, magazines, movies, and department stores made a link between "imaginative desires and material ones," between "dreams and commerce."[67] The question, of course, is how to understand and interpret the persistence of such desires in a post-revolutionary environment.

Some youth drawn to imitate these "decadent" Western fashions were the wealthy children of private entrepreneurs who feverishly shopped and

Young flapper. E. M.
Newman, *Seeing Russia*
(New York: Funk and
Wagnalls, 1928), p. 32.

traded, knowing that the right to do so was temporary and subject to increasing restrictions. However, the interest in flapper fashions was not limited to the children of NEPmen and their poorer cousins, the Soviet shop
girl and office boy. Many of the young people who were attracted to the
Western fashions pictured in magazines and in Hollywood films were
working-class youth. Factory girls became "avid followers of fashion and

primpers," wearing "stylish checked caps, and coquettish yellow shoes, and beige stockings." Even those who did not make much money wore "nice dresses specially made for them, and always carefully ironed."[68] When they could not afford to buy the new luxuries, they did their best to imitate them. Young women used Russian fashion magazines to reproduce the styles of New York and Paris at home with whatever hard-won materials they could find in public markets or Soviet stores. Journals like *Home Dressmaker* printed clothing patterns "necessary for every family and every woman."[69] Unable to afford expensive imported items, young women bought "imitation silk stockings, lip stick and Soviet substitutes for Coty products—made by the Chinese."[70]

By the late 1920s, girls could buy Russian lipstick, still considered a "bourgeois vice" but so popular that it was now produced by a government monopoly.[71] Hungry for the fancy goods denied them, young women envied the clothing of Western visitors. As one visitor noted: "Some have developed an almost pathological desire for the good-quality clothes they have so long been deprived of. I have had them feel feverishly my foreign clothes, hat, frock, sample the material, stroke the silk, almost pull my underwear from under my blouse in their frenzied hunger."[72] While young people in Paris or London could shop in the latest *grand magasin* or department store, Soviet youth who could afford to buy clothes were limited to small, privately run shops like the popular Moscow stores "Paris Fashions" and "Viennese Chic."[73] In contrast to the noise and flamboyance of European department stores, many of the choicest shops in post-revolutionary Russia were to be found in out-of-the-way private apartments. As one observer described:

> To reach the millinery shop we left our sleigh one evening in the courtyard of an immense white house which was once the residence of a nobleman. We skirted the corner of the house and at the rear turned into a tiny door. My guide led me up the two dark flights of stairs, and pushed a door. We literally fell into a lighted corridor, and picked our way down between a few broken chairs, an old mattress, a bicycle, and a pile of old hats. The milliner herself answered our knock on one of the doors at the end of the passageway.[74]

Some Komsomol girls kept the "leather jackets, crumpled skirts, and patched shoes"[75] of the Civil War period, thinking this demonstrated their revolutionary devotion, but other communist youth succumbed to the lure of fashion, and suffered to do so. One young Komsomol woman who made sixty-five rubles a month working in a factory was said to spend two-thirds of it on "manicures, cosmetics, silk stockings, and dance parties."[76] Komsomol activists in the *Red Triangle* factory reported that there were many cases of female workers who "literally starved because they spent all of their wages on silk stockings, makeup, and manicures," while a Komsomol

newspaper described young women working in another factory who wore "fashionable" low-cut dresses and "scanty shoes that pinched their toes."[77]

It seems likely that by imitating the clothing and manners of wealthy West Europeans even as they toiled away in the heat and dust of the factory floor, young men and women hoped to appropriate some of the modern independence and sophistication associated with flapper fashions. Much like dancing, silk stockings and red lipstick can be understood as a manifestation of some young people's desire for easy and enjoyable forms of everyday life and must have served as a release from the dreary realities of a working-class existence. On a deeper level, however, imitation of upper-class clothing can be seen not only as a search for chicness and sophistica-

МАГАЗИН ИЗЯЩНОЙ
ОБУВИ
ПО ЗАГРАНИЧНЫМ
МОДЕЛЯМ

С.Ф.Котиков

БОЛЬШОЙ ВЫБОР ВЕСЕННЕЙ ОБУВИ
МОСКВА,
Кузнецкий пер., д. № 3
(быв. Кузнецкий п. дом „СОКОЛ")
ГАРАНТИЯ ЗА ПРОЧНОСТЬ

Advertisements for fancy hats, coats "in the Parisian style," and shoes in the "latest foreign models." *Novyi zritel'* 16 (April 1927), p. 29; *Novyi zritel'* 51 (December 1926), p. 17; and *Novyi zritel'* 51 (December 1926), p. 24.

tion, but also as a devaluation of certain traditional forms of working-class culture. Some fashion-conscious factory youth had internalized the message, implicit in some commercial culture, that their own forms of dress, behavior, and language were not as good as those of the middle and upper classes. To this end up-and-coming young Komsomol'tsy used "bourgeois" clothing to segregate themselves from the "masses." Some communist uni-

versity students wore the same peaked cap as the pre-revolutionary intelligentsia, for example, to distinguish themselves from the mass of "uncultured" and uneducated youth.[78] Contemporary observers noted that many
young people did not just try to dress in the latest styles, but made "an
obvious effort to reproduce 'aristocratic manners' in everything they did."[79]
One young Komsomol member named Boris Kliuev tried to escape the
world of workers by leading a double life—honest Komsomol member by
day, young bourgeois dandy by night.

> In the evening after work this Komsomolets can no longer be considered
> your colleague. You can't call him Boris, but imitating a nasal French ac-
> cent you must call him "Bob." If you meet him somewhere in the park
> "with a well-known lady" . . . and start to talk to him about something
> related to the factory, he will cautiously glance back at the "madam" and
> without fail change the conversation.

According to the author of this article, Kliuev did not want to call himself
a worker, but imagined a more "picturesque" appellation: *elektrotekhnik*, or
elektrik.[80] Similarly, there were working-class girls who refused to go out
with factory boys, looking "condescendingly at their comrades at work."
Instead "they moved about in 'high society,' with the children of specialists, . . . NEPmen, and so on."[81] Some still dreamed of marrying young
naval officers. This "vice" was not limited to young women; Komsomol
newspapers also complained about Komsomol men who preferred to go
out with "the made-up daughters of NEPmen" rather than the supposedly
less attractive, but more communist, Komsomol women. One frustrated
Komsomol woman from Kiev complained about the impossible luxury and
sophistication that these young men were attracted to, and described a
"typical" scene in which the daughter of a NEPman "with delicate hands"
played "some romantic piece" on the piano while the young worker sat in
a "deep, soft sofa."[82]

Flapper fashion was a marker of urbanity and as such became a part of
the whole ritual of gender relations and efforts for upward mobility in the
countryside as well as in the city. Before the revolution, the peasant girl
hoping to attract attention sewed herself a fashionable skirt in the latest
style "all covered with flowers."[83] After the revolution, she wore gloves
and carried a parasol, and instead of traditional peasant bast shoes and
work boots, she wore leather boots. Such aspirations to city sophistication
were reflected in some traditional four-line *chastushki* [topical songs in
rhyme]:

> Don't refuse me money, Papa
> Twenty-five rubles,
> To buy a parasol and leather boots,
> Just like cultured people have.[84]

Makeup was also very important, and observers noted that in some peasant trunks one could find "a whole battery of boxes with various greasy materials: powder, rouges, pomades, cream and other cosmetics." For peasant youth and urban youth, nice clothes and an attractive appearance were likely associated with an easy life. The occasional piece of finery or tube of bright lipstick transported these young women from their difficult lives into an imagined world of sophistication. It was not only dresses and dances that did this. Peasant girls in the 1920s enriched their vocabulary with a whole range of "fashionable" expressions borrowed from the formerly French-speaking upper classes, like "merci," "pardon," and *"simpatichnyi."*[85]

We should not overemphasize the purposefulness of this emulation of the upper classes. As Kathy Peiss notes in her history of working-class leisure in turn-of-the-century New York, dress was a "potent" way to "play" with the "culture of the elite."[86] The notion of play is essential here because it reminds us of the pleasure some youth received from dressing up, a pleasure that may have had little explicit political signification. Young people did not always see clothing in the same way as their elders, either. As Diane Koenker writes, "Some women defined their class culture differently from party norms: why should not the fox-trot and cosmetics—living freely and looking good—mean 'modern,' not bourgeois?"[87] "Modern" clothing may have been a way to look up-to-date, but it did not necessarily mean nonrevolutionary.

At the same time, post-1917 Soviet Russia was clearly a very different place than either prewar Russia or New York, and official discourse encouraged the "respectability" of Semashko's neat and functional clothing, not the costumes of the elite or the far-out fashion of the flapper. In this environment flapper fashion did have political significance, no matter what the intent of the wearer, and some youth were conscious of the politics of dress. Non-communist university students in the traditional institutes of higher education, such as Moscow State University, "paraded about" in jackets with white silk linings. Before the revolution, students who wore these coats were called *belopodkladochniki* ["those who wear white silk linings"]. After 1917, this term described students who were considered "political aliens."[88] That some students continued to wear these jackets suggests that they deliberately used the language of clothing to express their resistance to communist norms and to define themselves as anti-Bolshevik. Like militant Komsomol youth who carefully cultivated a dirty and bedraggled appearance to appear more revolutionary, these young students used clothing as a means of self-identification—in this case to remind people that they were against the revolution.

Many Bolsheviks saw the Soviet flappers' open identification with "bourgeois" culture as a threat to the successful socialization of youth. In contrast to the socially aware young communist who was supposed to sublimate his or her own desires for pleasure to the wider concerns of society, fashion-conscious youth seemed to emphasize their rejection of the social-ist agenda through their choice of clothing. The focus on fashion signaled a rampant individualism of personal and cultural expression that threat-ened the collectivist mentality many party and Komsomol leaders felt was necessary to build a new society. They worried that for some youth the "culture of clothing" had become "more important than any other ques-tion."[89] Bolsheviks condemned the sacrifice, both literal and figurative, of Soviet youth to the altar of fashion, and they warned youth to protect them-selves against its dangers. Indeed, some stories about youth and fashion might best be understood as "cautionary moral tales."[90] In one such story, the protagonist, a young Komsomol worker named Olga P., is said to be "consumed" with clothing. As Ivan Bobryshev describes it, "Class, revo-lution, construction—these ideas didn't exist; there was a different 'sun'— a skirt . . . " When Olga discovered one day that her favorite velvet skirt was missing, she cried to a friend: "I have no life . . . they stole my skirt . . . In my velvet skirt I looked like the daughter of a nobleman."[91] She then committed suicide by drinking a bottle of vinegar essence. This story bears a notable similarity to pre-revolutionary "moral tales" told to and about young peasants who were also condemned for "striving to be like the petty bourgeois." In one story from 1910, a young woman goes without food to save money to buy a dress in the shop window. Like Olga, she too dies because of her "unhealthy strivings."[92]

In the "moral tale" about Olga P. two sources of youth's "decadent" behavior are apparent. The first is the dangerously polluted "alien" cul-ture of the bourgeoisie. By labeling flapper fashions bourgeois, party and Komsomol leaders helped create the image of a decadent "other" against which the communist "self" could be developed and defended. In their view, "real" communist youth were not excessively interested in clothing or cosmetics. If they were, it was assumed they had been diverted from their "normal" path and influenced by the bourgeoisie. To claim otherwise would have suggested that communist youth were themselves interested in fashion and external appearance, and in this way not so different from the very youth and youth culture that they were expected to oppose.

Femininity was the second source of "decadence." The overly fash-ion-conscious "bourgeois" youth were frequently, though not exclusively, female. An article titled "The Girl in the White Scarf" described the ap-pearance and shallow life of the "typical" daughter of a private entrepre-neur, who "loved her body" and "valued her physique."[93] Superficial and self-absorbed, she and young women like her were "dangerous" because of their ability to distract men from the more serious tasks of communist construction. To some, flappers recalled the dependent, unliberal, and un-equal female of the pre-revolutionary period. The unliberated NEPwomen described in the fiction of Aleksandra Kollontai were, for example, very like the "frivolous" young flappers described here.[94]

On the other hand, for Bolsheviks worried about immorality, the linking of women and fashion may have suggested, not dependence and inequality, but a shocking independence and proclivity toward excessive eroticism. Cosmetics, which were still associated with a kind of "moral ambiguity," and the new shorter dresses and bobbed hair suggested degrees of sexual liberation (by which I mean both the liberation of women and the liberation of sexuality) which may have made some Bolshevik moralists uncomfortable.[95] In her discussion of the meaning of the new style in inter-war France, Mary Louise Roberts argues that the short hair of the "femme moderne" was interpreted by many French critics as "evidence of a refusal among women to pursue traditional gender roles."[96] In revolutionary Russia, such a "blurring of sexual difference" might have been thought to be a good thing, given the ostensible focus on gender equality. And yet, as I have argued, many Bolsheviks, Komsomol'tsy, and non-communists alike were still uncomfortable with women's equal participation in the cultural sphere or elsewhere. For these individuals, the provocative post-war fashion of the flapper may have had much the same meaning it did in France, where it was seen as a threat to "traditional notions of female identity."[97]

Western films, fashion magazines, and traveling artists and performers helped structure a consumer mentality similar to that of Western Europe and the United States. Although this alternative youth culture was in conflict with many Bolshevik and Komsomol ideals for youth, it is not surprising that so many young people enjoyed the lively, imaginative, and exotic aspects of the new culture industry. The beauty, fun, and adventure of dancing the foxtrot or slipping on a pair of silk stockings apparently answered a need that was not fulfilled by the disciplined, and sometimes puritanical, leisure activities prescribed by Bolshevik and Komsomol moralists. A minority of young people purposefully used the language and gestures of bohemian culture to disrupt the fragile boundaries of Bolshevik hegemony, but many seemed simply to enjoy the fantasies of dress and dance available to them in this transitional era.

Young people did not need to be consciously resistant to have a political effect, however. Dance and dress had particular political meaning in the unsettled and contentious environment of NEP. The policies of NEP were supposed to provide an increase in material well-being; NEP was meant to bring recovery, even prosperity, to Soviet citizens. In 1925, Bukharin encouraged the peasants to "enrich" themselves.[98] Even more to the point, factories in Soviet Russia made lipstick, and Russian magazines printed patterns for the young flapper. But the objectives of NEP, and the relative economic freedoms NEP permitted, were clearly problematic in that they allowed (even encouraged) behaviors and beliefs that ran counter to more serious, sober, and collectivist ideals for youth. Flapper fashion and dance represented the individual consumption of material pleasures rather than collective consumption and accumulation.

The apolitical excesses of bohemian youth may have been particularly problematic for Bolsheviks who imagined youth as a source of revolutionary renewal. While militant youth threatened the gradualist aims of those who supported NEP, flapper youth must have disappointed those, like Trotsky, who appealed to youth to renew the revolutionary flames of what they saw as a lethargic and overly bureaucratic party. For many committed communists, flapper dance and dress violated multiple cultural and political ideals—they were "frivolous," interfering with the development of rational and disciplined forms of recreation; they were "uncivilized," threatening Bolshevik conceptions of proper public behavior; and they were "immoral," sparking fears of uncontrollability. Soviet discourses of dance and dress defined these pleasures of the body as dangerous, and by doing so, tried to discipline them. In this period of great anxiety about social transformation and social control, the popular (particularly when tied to material pleasure and prosperity) could be threatening.

7

LIFE AND LEISURE ON THE STREET

When I was just a small lad
Bell-bottomed jeans I wore,
Straw hat set high upon my head,
And a Finnish knife I bore.

I carved my mother up but good,
And sent my dad to hell,
My sister from the ladies' school
I shoved right down the well.[1]

Streets have long appeared dangerous to moralists of many persuasions because they are so difficult to monitor. Russian criminologists in the late Imperial period described the street as a dangerous "world beyond the purview of respectable society," a world that "lured children and then contaminated them with the immoral and illegal behavior on open display."[2] European socialist parties and middle-class reformers similarly condemned the street, with its unrestrained and aimless freedoms that left a "large number of boys and girls" without "sufficient guidance or care" during "the most critical period in their lives."[3] Social sites next to the street, such as the beer hall and the cabaret, were seen by European authorities and by the church as "places of subversion."[4]

James Scott has argued that subordinate groups use alternative spaces like the street to create a "social existence outside the immediate control of the dominant."[5] Social spaces which are beyond the effective surveillance of authorities become privileged sites for what Scott calls a "hidden transcript." In Europe, the working classes met at the tavern, the cabaret, and the public inn: "Here subordinate classes met offstage and off-duty in an atmosphere of freedom encouraged by alcohol. Here also was a privileged site for the transmission of popular culture—embodied in games, songs, gambling, blasphemy, and disorder—that was usually at odds with official culture."[6] In Moscow and Leningrad, the Bolsheviks too found it hard to monitor the social spaces of the street, such as sidewalks, markets, streetcars, train stations, and movie theaters. Though not all of the young people who gathered in such spaces were as explicitly resistant to dominant culture as Scott describes, the street did provide opportunities for the formation of alternative identities.

In a book published in 1925 on the everyday life of Soviet youth, S. Shkotov proudly noted the difference between pre-revolutionary youth culture and post-revolutionary attitudes and behavior. In the dangerous and depraved urban environment of pre-revolutionary Russia, youth grew up very fast, telling dirty jokes, gathering in gangs, and carrying knives. After the revolution, Shkotov asserted, working-class youth had a very different attitude toward work and leisure: "Among youth the old forms of entertainment have gone out of fashion . . . instead of the former gatherings now most youth spend their time in people's houses . . . parties are now always organized by the Komsomol . . . Instead of the vulgar anecdotes of before, young men sing revolutionary songs."[7] Shkotov optimistically assumed that the post-revolutionary urban environment, as embodied in the new relations of production and in working-class clubs, had only a positive effect on the new generation of proletarian youth.

Many contemporary observers disagreed, however. They insisted that the city still corrupted youth. The "power" of the street leads to a "new type of person," argued educator and researcher A. K. Pokrovskaia—not the new man the Bolsheviks desired, but a criminal.[8] "The conditions in which children grow up in the big city harshly affect their health, morality, and social habits," concluded criminologist P. I. Liublinskii. "Isolation from their parents, who are the majority of the time busy with factory or other work, early acquaintance with the depraved and criminal street, the presence of many temptations . . . these are the characteristics of the life of youth in the big city."[9] As Liublinskii's litany suggests, the supposed dangers of the street were manifold. The failure of working-class parents to monitor their children meant that young people were dangerously unsupervised. Children's "early acquaintance" with the street contaminated them when they were too young to resist its temptations. Seduced by the unhealthy and unproductive entertainments of the street, they became idle, undisciplined, and even "criminal." Evident here again is Bolshevik anxiety about infection by the unhealthy influences [vliianie] of the surrounding environment.

It is interesting that in a period of admiration for the modernizing processes of industrialization, there was also such anxiety about the urban environment. Liublinskii made an explicit comparison, for example, between the crime-ridden environment of the city and the relatively crime-free atmosphere of the countryside, attributing problems in the urban environment to relative differences in "mutual social control[s]," and to the presence "of nervous-stimulating influences."[10] With its "restaurants and cafés, cabarets and gambling clubs, luxurious store windows and smart automobiles,"[11] the NEP street was a concrete reminder of the possibilities of corruption and lack of discipline the Bolsheviks' effort still faced, even from within their own country. L. M. Vasil'evskii compared the revolutionary discipline of streets in the early years of Bolshevik rule—when "the characteristics of the big city street were strictness and work"—to streets during NEP, which had "become thoroughly dirty."[12] For Vasil'evskii, who wrote frequently on problems of sexual deviation as well as juvenile criminality, "dirty" meant something more than just physical filth, pointing again to the rhetoric of pollution. Delegates at the Eleventh Party Congress described the NEP street as a seductress who would tempt youth away from their responsibilities: "This youth is scattered, comes under the influence of dime novels, comes under the influence of the new nep street, and thus, the future cadre of our army, the army of the working class and of communism, is snatched away into strange hands."[13] The existence of "strange hands," even in the middle of a supposedly Soviet city, suggested the need for special vigilance to protect the younger generation and the Soviet state.

Of particular concern to Bolshevik moralists were the *besprizornye*—the millions of homeless youth who lived, ate, slept, and died on the streets of Moscow, Leningrad, and other cities in the Soviet Union. The word *besprizornye*—usually translated as "homeless"—can also be translated as "unattended," which is appropriate for a group that created anxiety about social control. Although there had been *besprizornye* before 1917, their numbers exploded in the early 1920s, following years of war, civil war, epidemic, and famine. Although the famine of 1921–1922 was the single biggest cause of homelessness, certain conditions during NEP—including high unemployment rates and broken families resulting from the new ease of divorce—continued to add to the ranks of the *besprizornye*. In the early 1920s, there were as many as seven million *besprizornye* as compared to a quarter of a million members of the Komsomol.[14]

The *besprizornye* were not the only young people using the street, however. They shared it with other youth who saw the street as a place to play, drink, fight, and work. As we have seen in chapter 6, young people who benefited from the prosperity of NEP traveled in and out of nightclubs. Komsomol and party members who were opposed to the bourgeois prosperity of the flappers also used the streets as they went to school, clubs, and meetings. Working-class youth were the most likely of all urban youth, excepting the *besprizornye*, to spend time on the streets.[15] Children of the intelligentsia often stayed close to home, playing indoors or in the courtyard beside the family apartment. Some of these varied groups (the Komsomol'tsy and the *besprizornye*, for instance) may have made each other uncomfortable. What many of these young people had in common was the anxiety their too often ungovernable behavior created among the adults who watched them.

Much of the information on the everyday life of youth on the street comes from the work of Soviet criminologists, social workers, and educators. They interviewed *besprizornye* in a variety of children's institutions, including children's homes, working colonies, and labor homes. Educational institutes and organizations for the protection of youth also studied

the *besprizornye*. The Office for the Study of Children's Homelessness collected materials written by homeless youth, including diaries, journals, and
poems in which the *besprizornye* wrote about life on the street, their connections with the adult criminal world, their dreams and desires.[16] Material on daily life and statistical data were collected by criminologists, such
as Boris Utevskii, who worked at the State Institute for the Study of Crime
and the Criminal Personality; Mikhail Gernet, who was head of the Department of Moral Statistics; and Vasilii Kufaev, an associate of Gernet's, who
worked in the Department for the Social and Legal Protection of Minors.[17]

Curious about the impact of the urban street on non-criminal youth,
social scientists and moral statisticians also observed and recorded the lei-
sure-time activities of "ordinary" youth in the urban environment. Though
we do not know for certain the intellectual influences that led them to this
project, it is possible they were influenced by the ethnographic work done
at the University of Chicago by the early American sociologists of deviancy. Many Russian experts had been active in sociological and crimino-
logical research before the revolution and had been in frequent contact with
European and American social scientists. Mikhail Gernet was already an
eminent sociologist in the pre-revolutionary period, and had published
numerous books on juvenile criminality before 1917.[18] He participated in a
German seminar on criminology in 1899, where he was influenced by the
work of Franz von Liszt on the relationship between the delinquent's individual qualities and the surrounding economic and social factors. P. I. Liublinskii, who was a specialist in juvenile law and one of the main forces
behind Soviet legal reforms, had traveled to the United States before the
revolution and already in 1912 championed the idea of special courts for
juveniles, aimed at reeducation rather than punishment. Although after
1917 these same social scientists were eager to differentiate their work from
that done in the pre-revolutionary period, many still defended the importance of scientific connections with Western researchers.[19] In a seminal article called "The City," the American Robert Park described a program for
exploring "the customs, beliefs, social practices and general conceptions
of life and manners" of individuals and communities in the urban environment.[20] Very much in this vein, A. Pokrovskaia, together with other educators from the Scientific-Pedagogical Institute of Aesthetic Education,
founded the "Commission for Research on the Street and Its Influence on
Children." They used observation and interviews to study the "typical"
elements of the street in a large city, including posters, architecture, store
windows, teahouses, movie theaters, and the daily activities of youth in
this environment.[21]

Soviet researchers gathered detailed information about every aspect
of the daily lives of their subjects. This material is invaluable for the historian, but it has its limitations. Social scientists admitted that it was difficult to get the *besprizornye* to respond to their questions and hard to know
whether to trust their responses. Utevskii noted that one had to use the

questionnaire data very carefully, because the *besprizornye* sometimes did not remember correctly, lied, or changed the facts every time they were asked a question. They invented new family names to avoid stiffer court sentences for a second or third arrest, and they changed their ages from fourteen to thirteen to avoid the labor homes (for which the minimum age was fourteen). There is also comparatively little information on homeless girls as opposed to boys. In part this was because there were more boys than girls on the street. Girls may have been easier to institutionalize and "reeducate." They were less likely to run away once they were put in a children's home, and may therefore have been of less interest to social workers concerned with removing the *besprizornye* from the streets.[22] However, concepts of gender also played a role here. For social scientists, the problems of sexual delinquency and prostitution associated with girls seemed to pose a different kind of threat than the culture of violence attributed to boys, and appeared therefore to be less worthy of study.

The focus on statistical and empirical information also reflected the particular tasks of the expert in the new socialist state. Rational and trustworthy information was thought vital to the thorough organization and transformation of the individual. If understanding was organized, people could be more easily managed and the Soviet state better planned and developed. As Kenneth M. Pinnow explains in his history of suicide and the politics of social science, "social 'experts' looked upon the social order as something that could be manipulated and guided towards a certain desired configuration, provided that they were given the necessary authority and tools to do so."[23] The Soviet expert did not see himself as a bureaucrat (as in the Imperial period), but as a social worker, who was meant to "apply his scientific knowledge to the benefit of society."[24]

PLAYING, DRINKING, FIGHTING

Much of the language used to describe the dangers of the street turned the behavior of urban youth into something unhealthy. It was seen as "dirty," "vulgar," and "debauched."[25] The research of A. K. Pokrovskaia was an exception. Although she worried about the dangers of the street, Pokrovskaia's descriptions of urban youth also revealed a world of small pleasures. Her first project was a study, conducted from April to June of 1922, of Moscow's busy Arbat Street and its neighboring squares and marketplaces. Twelve observers were divided into teams of two or three to observe youth on the street from early morning to midnight. They began their analysis with a description of the street, which was suffocatingly hot in the summer, dusty, and very noisy: "You can feel the tempo and movement of the Arbat . . . clattering, draft-horses, even the rumble of a few cars. Adults pass by, rushing and hurrying."[26] Human voices were hard to hear over the sound of honking trolleys, noisy wooden carts and wagons, rattling carriages, and, on holidays, ceaselessly ringing church bells. The crowded

Moscow loafers. E. M.
Newman, *Seeing Russia*
(New York: Funk and
Wagnalls, 1928), p. 249.

side streets and courtyards where children often played were quieter and
cooler than the main thoroughfare, although just as dirty and dusty. Only
the small houses furthest from the main street had an occasional patch of
green grass or a tree in front. The Arbat itself swelled with all kinds of different people: children rushing to school, young traders with shoulder bags
scurrying off to Smolensk Market, children going for a walk with their
nannies, boys hawking cigarettes and girls selling breads and sweets. The
street was a study in contrasts. Poorer members of the working-class, traders, and beggars rubbed shoulders with richly dressed men and women
profiting from the legalization of private trade. Wealthy men and women
(or those who hoped to imitate them) wore suits and dresses in the latest
European styles. Young working-class "toughs" strode the streets in wide
trousers and striped sailors' vests, with "brass knuckles" hanging from
their pockets. Working-class schoolchildren often wore clothes reminiscent
of the Civil War, including ankle-high boots with leg-wrappings, and
pointed Red Army helmets.[27]

For young people with little money the street was one of the few places
to play and to gather in groups. Younger children congregated on Arbat

Square and in Smolensk Market, and in nearby alleys and courtyards in the afternoon and early evening. They drew on the sidewalks with chalk and put pieces of wire under trolley tracks to flatten them into different shapes. Groups of boys hung off the sideboards of crowded trolley cars. Boys also gathered on the street to play cards. Both boys and girls loved to window-shop, vicariously enjoying the unaffordable luxuries of NEP. Boys were said to be especially drawn to the expensive sweetshops and the mechanical delights displayed in watch and optical shop windows. Girls stood outside dress and shoe store windows for hours, "admiring the shoes and blouses [and] looking at the little watches."[28] On the Arbat and other major thoroughfares, like Leningrad's Nevskii Prospect, the lights of casinos and well-known late-night restaurants also attracted young people who could not afford to enter but stood outside watching the well-dressed patrons come and go.[29] Although they did not have enough money to go to fancy commercial theaters, many children did go to small inexpensive theaters like the "Iar" in Leningrad, which made its audience wait on the street for the next showing. Movie theaters such as this were among the few sources of commercial entertainment available to even the poorest youth, including the *besprizornye*, who were frequent patrons of the cinema.[30]

At night the younger children went indoors, and the older adolescents and young adults came out to stroll the streets with their friends. Whereas during the day the population of busy city streets was primarily middle-aged, young people dominated in the early evening and night.[31] Much of their time was spent walking around with no particular goal in mind other than to relax and to flirt with the small groups of boys or girls they might meet on the way. Most chose to walk in areas with plenty of people, noise, and activity, such as Nevskii Prospect in Leningrad. While a few discussed life in the factory or the latest theater production, others preferred the perennial adolescent topics—parties, boys, girls, work, and sex. These walks often ended at the movie theaters, less often at a factory or Komsomol club.[32]

In the pre-revolutionary period the public space of the street had included the beer bar and tavern, as well as the crowds and noise that spilled out onto the street from these popular places. Drinking remained an important part of urban youth culture after 1917. Children were exposed to alcohol at an early age. Of 280 primary school youth surveyed by the Institute of Social Hygiene, close to 10 percent said that they drank beer, wine, or vodka every day (boys were twice as likely to drink regularly as girls). Of those who could remember when they had their first drink, half had been seven years of age or younger.[33] The impetus to drink only increased as young people grew older. Because drink had special significance as a symbol of adulthood and of status as a (male) worker, young people (especially young men) often drank in emulation of the adult culture they were striving to join. One survey of young Leningrad factory workers showed that by the time they reached adolescence more than 30 percent drank regularly.[34] Alcohol consumption increased as wages rose, suggesting that even more youth would have drunk if they could have afforded it. In another survey, over 80 percent of those earning more than 90 rubles a month drank regularly, as compared to just about 30 percent of those making 30 to 60 rubles a month.[35] Historians of Europe and the United States have noted a similar trend among the working class in the nineteenth century. Michael Marrus has explained this convincingly in terms of pleasure, arguing that those who drank the most were not the most unhappy, but those with enough money to spend. As working conditions improved and wages went up, "workers naturally turned to drink . . . because they were still adjusting to a more affluent state of affairs. What was new to them was the prospect of having any pleasure at all which was not furtively snatched from the grip of necessity."[36]

Before the revolution, much drinking had taken place in single-sex spaces where young men and old gathered apart from women to reaffirm their comradeship and male identity.[37] The number of taverns decreased dramatically after 1917,[38] and among youth the favorite place for drinking became a party either at one's own home or at a friend's. Some drinking now took place in mixed-gender situations, where alcohol often helped make young women and men less inhibited and more comfortable with each other. Saturday night was the typical time for parties, and alcohol was so crucial to the mood of these gatherings that it was a rare party that did not have bottles of beer, wine, or vodka lined up on the table. "Parties are boring without drinking," complained one twenty-one-year old factory worker. "Without drinks, it's not a party," said another. "I went to a party at someone's place," reported a Komsomol girl; "All us kids gathered and drank until the wee hours of the morning."[39] Drinking made these youth feel different. Young men reported feeling "reserved," "boring," and "quiet" before drinking, while afterward they felt "free and easy," "unbridled," and "very bold." Young women described a similar transformation from "modest" and "mincing" to "laughing and singing."[40] Among the reported results of these transformations were frequent and early sexual relations. In Kagan's interviews of women who had had premarital sex, 60 percent said they had been drinking.[41]

The alcoholic abandon of young people at these parties was the opposite of the supposedly temperate and chaste young communist. The Komsomol press frequently made a connection between the evils of drinking, sex, and the street:

> If you take a stroll on a Saturday evening along the muddy Kolpina street, you will run into groups of overdressed "dandies" . . . among whom you will recognize young men and women workers from the Izhorskii factory, including shock workers and Komsomol members . . . They are going to the usual party. In one of the small houses located on the outskirts, flooded with electric lights, you hear an accordion player or local "jazz" band bashing out music. In the stuffy heat, pairs of foxtrotters knock each other over.

In the next room you are struck by the incalculable number of bottles spread out on the table. Everyone at the party drinks. The girls drink a lot. After about two hours when the majority of the bottles are empty, they open a door to a small dark room to which couples go by turns to "unburden" themselves. Around eight or nine the next morning, the young people get dressed to go home.[42]

The author of this piece appears to deplore the vulgarity of the party-goers as much as their repudiation of communist values: the "overdressed 'dandies'" pick their way through the mud, the small houses are on the outskirts, and the dancers are so inept that they knock each other over.

Drinking was not the only aspect of lower-class behavior that youth retained after 1917. Fistfights also remained popular. Some brawling took place at parties where drunk youth pitched into each other: "Pet'ka, are you my friend or not my friend, friend or not? If you are my friend, hit me, I ask you, hit me!"[43] Fighting also took place between working class youth groups from different regions of the city. Though information is scarce about these fights, they were likely a continuation of the pre-revolutionary recreational brawls common among workers.[44] After the revolution, inter-regional fights were still so common in Leningrad that the local party committee passed a special resolution against fistfights and hooliganism.[45] Sometimes fights were not limited to fists but escalated to Finnish knives, a weapon traditionally favored by the homeless *besprizornye* but now said to be adopted by some working-class youth as well.[46] There were post-revolutionary gangs, too. Some were composed of groups of young traders who worked the streets selling newspapers and cigarettes. They gathered in groups, christening themselves with names like "Cunning Band" and maintaining a wary distance from other groups of youth. Sometimes a whole group of young boys from one apartment building worked together, heading off to sell newspapers together and hanging around the streets in the evening. Group members picked up papers for each other from the dispatchers in the morning, lent each other money, and went to the movies together. They solidified their group identity by calling each other by nicknames, sometimes shortening or making a pun on a family name and other times taking names from the movies, such as Gary Pil or "Red devil." They knew all the "regulars"—other traders, restaurant workers, and the *besprizornye*, many of whom spoke to each other in the same street slang.[47] Other gangs were drawn from the ranks of unemployed youth. In Leningrad the most famous gangs, "Koltovskikh" and "Gavanskikh," were composed almost entirely of youth fired from local factories.[48] Although there is little evidence to explain the attraction of these regional gangs, the extensive literature on young gangs elsewhere suggests that the informal solidarity of these groups may have given youth a way to address feelings of failure and insignificance. The gangs also provided a sense of community for youth who were otherwise adrift from the main body of the working population

and who were denied an opportunity to participate in the culture of production.[49]

Unemployed gang youth did not identify with communist youth, although many Komsomol youth were also often unemployed. Street youth
complained that Komsomol members insulted them and would not allow
them into their clubs. The Komsomol insisted that delinquent youth were
not admitted because they were often drunk. Communist newspapers reported incidents in which parties were broken up and club workers as-
saulted by young "hooligans."[50] Like the pre-revolutionary battles between
worker youth from different parts of the city, these struggles might be seen
as territorial. The street toughs resorted to older forms of domination—
drink and physical strength—in a bid to reclaim positions of informal power that had previously been theirs. The Komsomol'tsy asserted instead a
new kind of moral territoriality over the club (and over the youth inside)
which was the opposite of that of the street youth in its rejection of drink
and fighting. In Komsomol reports these fights took on mythical stature as
examples of the struggle between the "civilized" culture of the club and
the "uncivilized" and unofficial culture of the street. For the hostile non-
communist youth, too, these conflicts were serious, suggesting their dis-
possession from the process of revolutionary state building.

For party and Komsomol authorities, the aimless and sometimes violent activities of youth on the street were a problem. In Leningrad, the Komsomol set up six houses specifically for unemployed adolescents that were
intended to "keep a definite part of unemployed youth away from the de-
moralizing influences of the street."[51] The Moscow Komsomol used evening
entertainments, such as theater, to strengthen their influence over the unhealthy nighttime leisure activities of youth: "Instead of a bottle of beer—
a ticket to the theater."[52] The unstructured time of these unemployed youth
appeared a direct threat to the project of cultural transformation. It removed
young people from the acculturating and disciplining force of the work
place or factory school and exposed them instead to the harmful and less
easily monitored influences of the urban environment. In a survey of 250
newspaper boys, 60 percent said that when they grew older they wanted
to go into trade or handicraft work; only 12 percent said they wanted to
work in a factory. When asked whether they wanted to enter the Pioneers
or the Komsomol, most simply laughed.[53] This was a new generation of
youth who were molded not by images of revolution, but by the harsher
realities of life after revolution and war. They were street-smart survivors,
not members of a new vanguard, and it should not surprise us that they
remained uninterested in the cultural projects of Soviet socialism.

THE *BESPRIZORNYE*

"My father died . . . [and] after a year my mother died, leaving us five
children without bread," explained one young boy in a story typical of the

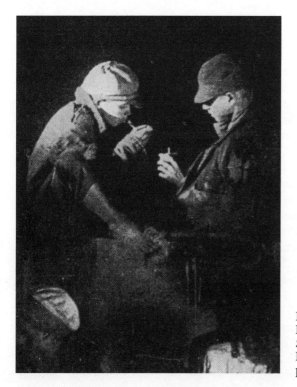

Homeless youth in
Moscow. E. M. Newman,
Seeing Russia (New York:
Funk and Wagnalls, 1928),
p. 129.

besprizornye. "It was bad, so I broke with everything. I went to the train
station and met up with some kids who went by the names of Sen'ka one-
eye and Paska-of-the-missing-left-leg, and I began to run around with them
. . . stealing. I stole for a month, then I left . . . I arrived in Moscow and again
I began to steal . . . "[54] Moscow was a magnet for many homeless youth,
with its opportunities for shelter and thieving.[55] Many escaped from the
South, which had been especially hard hit by the famine, and where they
had often been abandoned by their helpless parents, left on staircases and
in cellars, on the street and in the doorways of makeshift orphanages. Their
ranks were continually replenished by new victims of economic disloca-
tion, unemployment, divorce, and single motherhood. Over two-thirds of
the *besprizornye* were fully orphaned. The majority were between the ages
of twelve and fifteen, although there were older youth, preschoolers, and
toddlers among them. Just over half were the children of peasants and a
quarter were from working-class families.[56] "I saw them in Leningrad and
in Moscow, living in sewers, in billboard kiosks, in the vaults of cemeteries
where they were the undisturbed masters," wrote Victor Serge.[57] At night
they slept piled together in large round tar cauldrons that faintly retained
the heat of the day's work, or in train stations, abandoned railroad cars,
public toilets, or garbage dumps.

Of all the youth cultures discussed thus far, the *besprizornye* provide perhaps the best example of the archetypical subculture—a subordinate group, often of youth, who, through language, behavior, and values, try to find a "'solution' to the problems posed for them by their material and social class position and experience."[58] Subcultures are in part the products of another's gaze: members of a subculture are often positioned as "other," as "deviant or debased," in contrast to the "normal, average, and dominant" ideals of the larger community.[59] Subcultures also participate in their own construction. Dick Hebdige argues that belonging to a subculture is "a declaration of independence, of Otherness, of alien intent, a refusal of anonymity, or subordinate status. It is an *in*subordination."[60] So too with the *besprizornye*, who were not just positioned as different by others but also constructed their own "consciousness of 'otherness' or difference."[61] Powerless, homeless, and often mistreated, the *besprizornye* lived on the margins of "respectable" Soviet society, and coped with their position in part by creating a distinctive subculture. Within this alternative social system, they were the insiders and respectable adults the outsiders, or dangerous other. Homeless youth solidified their own identity through autonomous forms of social organization, language, and ritual. Of course, Komsomol'tsy too used language and ritual to help define themselves, but Komsomol youth clearly had a different relationship to the "parent culture" (meaning that of both adults and Bolsheviks) than did the *besprizornye*. Sworn at, spat on, and condemned as nothing but thieves and bandits, homeless youth often felt themselves apart from the rest of society. In the words of an investigator in Saratov: "People fear the *besprizornyi*, shun him, sometimes avoid him. And he, this juvenile delinquent, learns early to pay back this cold society in the same coin . . . crime in his eyes amounts to a violation of the laws only of these well fed, clothed, and complacent people—not something to trouble his conscience. Anything may be done when it comes to these alien, hostile people."[62]

The *besprizornye* used language to mark their community. Their street slang [*blatnaia muzyka*] was largely the same throughout the Soviet Union, facilitating the frequent migrations of homeless youth and rendering even the most common words, such as ruble, train, and girl, incomprehensible to non-*besprizornye*. A ten-ruble bill was called a *vosh'*, or a "louse"; "fifty lice" meant fifty ten-ruble bills. A train was commonly called a *maidan* (from the word for gambling den), and a thief who worked the trains was called a *maidanshek*. Much of the jargon referred to criminal acts. The word for thief was *khulik*, which stemmed from the word "hooligan." Some slang ridiculed traditional Russian culture. A pack of cards, for instance, was called a *sviattsy*, which in non-colloquial Russian means a church calendar. The distinctness of this vocabulary gave the *besprizornye* a mechanism for expressing, more or less privately, feelings of anger, of otherness, and of subcultural community, which could not otherwise be safely expressed. The slang was opaque enough that police officers needed a dictionary to penetrate this "hidden transcript." To help police officers understand and apprehend the *besprizornye,* the NKVD assembled a two-hundred-page dictionary of criminal slang that was published in a pocket-sized format so that officers could carry it with them on the street.[63]

Names were another way of linguistically constructing community. Communist youth commonly changed their given names to more revolutionary ones, such as Freedom, Victory, and Revolution, as a way of signaling their enthusiastic intent. These new names then helped distinguish communist insiders from non-communist outsiders. Among homeless youth, names also helped establish community boundaries. *Besprizornye* nicknames were often based on physical characteristics, relating an individual's face or body type to an animal or bird, or describing a physical deformity. A young waif without arms might be called a *ruchkin* (from *ruka,* arm) and one without legs a *kul'shkan* (from *kul'tia,* stump). Common animal names included "mouse," "crocodile," and "bulldog."[64] The physicality of these names, as opposed to the ideologically inspired names of the Komsomol'tsy, suggests the different realities (and, perhaps, aspirations) of these two groups.

Ritual behavior also helped seal the bonds among members of the *besprizornye* subculture. A youth who had lost or stolen the belongings of another, such as a pack of cards or a book of matches, might be abused and forced to serve the owner until he had repaid the loss. If, however, at the moment he was confronted the wrongdoer repeated the ritual phrase "Precisely I, when I want, how I want, where I want, what I want," then he was still required to make the loss good, but could do so in whatever way he wished.[65] Such reliance on the magical power of words was vital in a community that had so few formal mechanisms beyond violence to settle disputes or regulate relationships. Mutual guarantees or oaths, such as "May I be a stool pigeon if . . . " and "May I never enjoy freedom if . . . ," were also very important. Although the *besprizornye* often lied to children's-home workers or other adults, they had oaths and other ritual interchanges by which they guaranteed to each other that they were to be trusted.[66]

To work freely and sleep safely, the *besprizornye* needed to mark the boundaries of their space and decide who had access to it. They were possessive of the places where they slept and the markets and streets in which they worked as traders, bazaar thieves, and prostitutes. Territoriality functioned as a form of ownership over streets and spaces for youth who otherwise owned very little. It was also a way of reinforcing community. Often a certain space was not held by an individual, but defended by a small group of fellow homeless. Such groups would collectively protect their sleeping areas, leaving one member behind during the day to defend their rights to a railroad car, a certain corner of the train station, or a particular tar pit. Violation of these territorial boundaries could result in violent skirmishes. One sixteen-year-old boy explained that he and his friends had not gone to the station, "as there was a group of hostile guys there. And if one of us

Homeless youth sleeping on the streets of Moscow. E. M. Newman, *Seeing Russia* (New York: Funk and Wagnalls, 1928), p. 20.

showed up at the station, they would force him out of there pretty quick either by kicks, or by tossing him on his side, or on his ears."[67]

In an inversion of the qualities of honesty, temperance, and cleanliness expected of Komsomol youth, the ideal young *besprizornik* "had to possess all the signs of a real thief—the fellow would have several warrants and convictions, boldly employ thieves' jargon and artistically command swear words . . . and dream of that time when he will achieve his ideal and become an 'elusive bandit.'"[68] There were regular tests of courage involving outlandish dares in which one youth would accuse another of being weak and dare him to do something. If the dared one did as requested, then he earned the right to demand a payment or dare of some kind from the first.[69] Drugs were another kind of boost to courage. It was not uncommon for a group of *besprizornye* to use cocaine before a "job." As one ten-year-old boy told a worker in a *detdom* [children's home]: "You need two grains; once you sniff it, boldness overcomes you and you're afraid of nothing." "Yeah, I like it; you sniff it and then you go crazy," said another.[70] In a survey of 150 youth at one labor home, 70 percent of them used cocaine.[71] Cocaine was popular because it was so easy to get, but homeless youth also used hashish, morphine, heroin, and opium. Young cocaine users met outdoors or in broken-down buildings; they bought cocaine at the infamous Khitrov market, which maintained its pre-revolutionary reputation as an unsavory area.[72]

Homeless youth were sometimes violent with those they robbed for money or goods, but violence was also directed at the weaker or newer members of a group of *besprizornye*. When a group admitted someone new into their ranks, they often submitted him to physical trials before he was accepted. These trials served as a kind of hazing, ritualistically preparing the untested youth for admission into the larger group of the already initiated. Some of this ritualistic violence was similar to the abusive aspects of working-class culture. Apprentices in the pre-revolutionary printing industry were routinely slapped and beaten by older workers in a "rite of passage" in which "enduring beating and humiliation were requirements for acceptance."[73] Among the *besprizornye*, challenges ranged from beatings and insults from the older and more powerful youth, to ritual forms of testing such as covering a new recruit with a pile of branches on top of which was built a fire. James Scott argues that subordinate groups often resort to some kind of regulatory conflict to reinforce group solidarity against authority.[74] It is also possible that the *besprizornye* adopted and then exaggerated certain aspects of rough working-class culture that were condemned as uncivilized by the Bolsheviks, but that were still necessary in the world of the street in which they had to survive.

Once a youth had become a "member" of the *besprizornye*, the injunction against informing was very strong, and the rare informer was dealt with harshly. He or she might be beaten, or forced outside the group and no longer protected from outside violence or arrest.[75] Homeless youth had few positive expectations of respectable society. It was their own who could disappoint them. It was also their own against whom they might have any chance of acting. In a song about an informer, the *besprizornye* sang about the violent retribution they would exact, not against the police, but against the one who had turned them in:

> Middle of the nighttime—
> The wind it was a howling—
> At the hideout was a meeting of the gang.
> These were desperadoes,
> Hooligans and convicts—
> There to find out who it was that sang.
>
> Hello, oh my Murka!
> Hello, oh my darling!
> Hello, oh my Murka, and goodbye!
> You squealed, you turned a stooly!
> You sang on us so cruelly!
> So take your bullet now, for you must die!
>
> Was it all that awful—
> Here with us together?
> Were all the rags we gave you still too few?
> So what was it that made you
> Take to that police dog—
> And go and turn us into the Cheka [secret police]? . . .

Hello, oh my Murka!
Hello, oh my darling . . . [76]

Pre-revolutionary hooligans had been aggressive, but they had directed most of their hostility outward, shouting obscenities, throwing rocks, knocking passers-by to the ground. Despite their alienation from respectable society, however, pre-revolutionary hooligans had comparatively greater power and status than the *besprizornye*, if only because most were attached to the world of work. Some were hooligans only on the weekends, and even those without regular employment usually identified themselves as workers.[77] The *besprizornye*, in contrast, were young, unemployed, and abandoned. They responded to the enormous challenges they faced by turning inward, creating their own community and culture through language, ritual, and violence. So vulnerable to the actions of others, the *besprizornye* might in this way—perhaps only in this way—address feelings of hunger and insignificance, and feel in some small way in charge of their own existence.

PUBLIC SPACE

One of the most threatening aspects of the *besprizornye*, to political authorities and "respectable" observers, was their appropriation of public space. In many areas of Moscow and Leningrad—such as Nevskii Prospect in Leningrad and the train stations in both cities—the *besprizornye* shared the street with other groups and classes. Some spaces were dominated by the *besprizornye*—especially the least favorable parts of Moscow, including the cellars of Prochnyi Lane, a famous "haunt of thieves, petty speculators, [and] market-stall holders,"[78] and the "Catacombs," an enormous acre-wide system of cellars in an unfinished pre-war building in the center of Moscow.[79] Komsomol youth, and other youth from universities and trade unions, penetrated these areas (and the cellars, taverns, and flophouses in them) only when they were sent in to conduct a census of homeless youth, or to round them up and take them to children's homes. But the *besprizornye* proved that these areas did not belong to the uninitiated by the ease with which they avoided these forays into their territory. Homeless youth lived, worked, and played in the public spaces of the new Soviet state, but remained disturbingly independent of authority. With its educational campaigns and scientific studies, the party was trying to penetrate the internal territory of individual behavior. In the case of the *besprizornye*, the party was unable to penetrate and transform even the public territory of the city street. [80]

In 1923, between 40 and 50 percent of homeless children in Moscow and Leningrad practiced begging.[81] They frequented public spaces, such as train stations and market squares, and sometimes invaded more private ones, such as restaurants. Newcomers might stand or sit quietly on the cold pavement, while those who had been at it for longer sang, staged performances, feigned illness, or hobbled after a likely mark.[82] Young thieves disrupted market and street spaces in more dramatic ways. Bazaar crooks swiped goods:

> They were the terror of the keepers of small booths where apples and chestnuts, meat-filled *pirozhkis*, and cheap clothing were sold. Upon such tiny, open-faced shops, and upon the street-vendors, with their baskets set upon the pavement, they would descend in droves; with lightning-like organization one would attack the vendor, one spill over the wares, a third collect the booty, and all would disappear before the astonished shop-keeper or street-vendor had time to collect his wits and call the police.[83]

Others worked the railways, stealing goods from train cars or lifting suit-cases from unsuspecting passengers. Pickpockets worked both the crowded markets and the train stations and designed elaborate "performances" to distract their victims.

Although the criminal acts of the *besprizornye* were deeply disturbing to their victims, the *besprizornye* had few compunctions about theft, ex-plaining that they were forced to steal in order to eat.[84] Three-quarters of the crimes for which children were arrested were property violations, in-cluding theft of food from market stalls and pickpocketing.[85] Crimes against a person were less common, and rarely involved serious assaults.[86] For some *besprizornye* who had been on the street for a time, stealing had a better, more "manly" reputation than begging.[87] For many, too, the criminal world was one they had long been familiar with. "I started studying the thieves' lives from an early age," admitted one boy. "[S]o don't judge me, because I grew up in a home where only thieves lived."[88] Long-term beggars were more likely to be from the countryside. These were children who, because they were less familiar with urban culture and traditions, were more likely to stick with begging as their principal source of income.[89] Some homeless youth began their criminal careers working for adult criminals who used them as messengers, as scouts, as nimble housebreakers, and as drug deal-ers and sellers of homemade alcohol [*samogon*]. Some dreamed of moving up to a "higher level" of criminality. This included those who broke into apartments and stores, who could make between two and ten rubles a day slipping through small windows. Girls sometimes participated in such schemes, working under the guise of laundresses or cleaning women, while boys pretended to be stove-setters. It was only the few most experienced and professional thieves who participated in acts such as armed robbery that provided them with enough money for fancy clothes and a lifestyle that put them far above that of the typical street urchin.[90]

Homeless youth also worked the streets as traders. By one estimate, close to half of the street traders on the Arbat were children and adoles-cents, although not all were without parents or a home. Young boys stood on busy street corners hawking cigarettes, water, fruit, or flowers, some of which they had purchased to resell and some of which they had stolen.

Others shouted out the latest news on trolleys and street corners to sell newspapers. Young women were more likely to sell breads and sweets, a trade traditionally dominated by females. Older adolescents might work these jobs, but could also be seen selling goods off the back of small carts, or running small shoe-shining operations.[91] Especially in the early 1920s, when private stores had yet to reopen in any significant numbers, peddling provided the urban population with many of their most basic necessities.[92] To one Western observer, the major streets of Moscow seemed like a "continuous market-place":

> The sidewalks were lined with vendors of every conceivable kind of merchandise. They stood in close formation, elbow to elbow, holding out their wares . . . The most unlikely things were sold: rouge to barefoot girls, glass beads to women in cotton slips, underwear, chairs, salted cucumbers and slices of watermelon . . . The entire population seems engaged in this kind of private business. They sell everything there is to sell and they sell at all hours: at two o'clock in the morning it is easy to satisfy a whim for a string of imitation pearls, a cucumber, a cigarette, or a briefcase. The strongest competitor of a shop-keeping government is not even required to keep union hours.[93]

Some young traders were sent out to work by their parents, but others were homeless and relied on their income for their own survival. Making money from trading goods or selling newspapers was unreliable, and failure could propel a young person from poverty at home into the ranks of the *besprizornye*. As thirteen-year-old Zhenia explained:

> My father died . . . I have a mother, a sister who is fifteen and a little brother. When my father was alive I studied, but when he died, mama sent me out to trade. I traded but couldn't make enough profit. One day I was unsuccessful with my trading and there was no money. I didn't go home. I lived in the Ermakovka [a night hostel] . . . then I came here [another night hostel]. I see my sister almost every day at the Kursk train station. She and my little brother come. My mother came, but when she saw me she ran away. I am afraid.[94]

Though traders might have been seen by many citizens as a unpleasant necessity, homeless girls made the streets of Moscow and Leningrad feel dangerous to respectable citizens in a different way. They appeared to carry and transmit vice by selling their bodies on the public space of the street corner.[95] As the authors of a 1929 book described their presence, "On a holiday, or especially on a payday, all the neighboring crossroads are teeming with prostitutes . . . They all gather at the bars, at the 'family baths,' at the restaurants like 'Little Star,' and don't let the workers escape, especially the young ones . . . On these days, prostitutes and their 'friends' terrorize the entire region. This disgusting, cynical scene is performed in front of everyone's eyes, right there on the street."[96] Before 1917, prostitutes had often worked indoors, in brothels. After the revolution, such places were officially outlawed and young prostitutes took their trade to the streets and gardens, boulevards and forests of the city, sometimes taking a client inside to a squalid apartment and other times simply completing the transaction on a park bench.[97] In Leningrad, patrons sought prostitutes on Ligovka, in the infamous Chubarov Lane, on Nevskii Prospect, or at the Leningrad port. The most popular sites in Moscow were Tverskoi Square, Strastnyi Boulevard, and Trubnaia Square. Some houses for prostitutes did reopen illegally after 1917, but homeless girls were unlikely to live and work in such places. Instead, as Walter Duranty described, they tried to survive in even less appealing living situations: "In the Trubny district there were a dozen big tenement houses, regular rabbit warrens with deep communicating cellars, which for some reason became the haunt of an alien population—Chinese, Gypsies . . . and a host of so-called students of both sexes. There were corridors in these buildings where the rank, sweet smell of opium smoke hung one might say unnoticed, day and night, and where beside the name and number of the small cell-like rooms was tacked a photograph of its fair occupant in the scantiest of costume."[98] As in the prerevolutionary period, some Leningrad prostitutes (although usually older and better-off ones) again worked at cafés, bars, hotels, and fancy restaurants, like the night restaurant "Universal," the Hotel Evropeiskaia, and the casino at 47 Fontanka.[99]

Young prostitutes engaged in "criminal" acts on the streets to survive. More than half of the young girls selling their bodies in Leningrad were homeless.[100] Eighty-five percent of prostitutes in this city did not know a trade and almost 40 percent were illiterate. In 1923, there were twenty-five thousand unemployed young women between the ages of fourteen and twenty-four registered at the Petrograd Labor Bureau, and many more who were not registered.[101] Many young women who resorted to prostitution remembered the first moment when they realized that they had nowhere to live and nothing to eat. They had often turned to the streets after their parents died. "You don't know what else to do," one explained.[102] Fifteen-year-old Daria was not atypical. Daria's father died early in her childhood and her mother remarried. When one day Daria lost some money on her way to buy goods and was afraid to return home, she decided to run away instead. She went to the train station, where she fell in with some street youth, and then moved in with two prostitutes who were ill with syphilis. She learned the language of the streets and stole to get shoes and clothes. "At first I wasn't used to it," she said. "But then I thought: Go ahead— whatever God gives you. I lived like everyone."[103] The seventeen-year-old "C." similarly began her sexual life at age fourteen and became a prostitute soon after, often servicing five to six men a night.[104] Many young women also had a boyfriend or lover of their own age who lived off their small earnings of one to five rubles a night. Many were abused by the criminal gangs they associated with, by the NEPmen, who exploited them, and by the police, who often swore at them and beat them.[105]

DANGEROUS OR IN DANGER?

The persistent independence of homeless youth had important implications for the urban environment; in the 1920s, Moscow and Leningrad remained motley cities with some spaces transformed by communism and other spaces as yet unchanged. This was intolerable to many Bolshevik observers. Authorities tried to remove homeless youth from the street. Sometimes this meant putting them in "closed" institutions that kept them off the street by keeping them behind locked doors. More often it meant sending them away from the city; many children's homes [detdoma] were established in rural areas. Removing them from the public sphere had multiple purposes. The street was said to contaminate homeless youth, so taking them from this environment was part of the process of reeducating them. If they stayed on the street, the besprizornye also threatened to spread their contamination through the ranks of other children. Schoolchildren, for example, were said to pick up the street slang of the besprizornye by hanging around the marketplace and the movie theater.[106] In other words, healthy youth had to be protected from the already ill. As Aron Zalkind explained, "The struggle against besprizornost' [homelessness] staves off the contamination of healthy youth, youth from normal schools, normal children's institutions, by those harmful influences which seep out toward them from the streets—from the homeless, besprizornye child thieves."[107]

In Zalkind's description, the homeless child is like a germ which travels from the source of disease (the street) to infect new hosts (healthy youth). But Zalkind did not believe that the homeless child was inherently diseased. He emphasized instead the environmental and social factors leading to delinquency. There were others writing on youth and delinquency, however, who sought the causes of criminal behavior in biologically conditioned individual disorders.[108] Biological explanations for delinquency often described criminal adolescents as "sick" or "mentally retarded." In an article on the causes of child criminality, T. Simpson described three types of criminal youth. The first were the "spiritually ill," who lacked a "healthy" spirit and clear consciousness. "Mentally retarded" youth were those whose brains were not "sufficiently developed," making them incapable of distinguishing good from evil. The third group of delinquent youth were the "psychopathic personalities." These were described as "degenerates" whose intellectual development was normal, but who were too stimulated and excited, often having "ill" inclinations of a sexual nature. All of these youth, according to Simpson, needed to be institutionalized in special medical units, children's homes, or homes for "psychopathic personalities," where they would learn "correct moral understanding." The delinquent was seen as a special kind of personality, one inherently different from "normal" individuals.[109] In his book on "criminal types," S. V. Poznyshev similarly distinguished among different types of criminal youth, including the pickpocket, the bandit, and the "impulsive" criminal. He included photographs to reveal how these characteristics were evident in the distinctive features of the delinquents.[110]

Some argued that age was an important factor contributing to delinquency. This was a difference from the pre-revolutionary period, when there had been no discussion of hooliganism as a function of youthfulness.[111] In 1924, in contrast, V. E. Smirnov argued that it was especially important to monitor youth from age fourteen to seventeen, as this was the period in which they were most likely to participate in criminal acts. Adolescence was characterized by a "flood of power." This power was necessary to the development of the individual but made the adolescent vulnerable to instability and internal disruption. "New impulses and desires come up against the now already developed motor apparatus, and there is nothing more distinctive than this combination of awkwardness and dexterity, lack of awareness and intellectual power."[112] The conflict between physical ability and mental development could lead to the "most serious results," including crimes against property and against persons. That girls were less likely than boys to participate in criminal activities was also explained biologically. At this age, Smirnov argued, girls' hearts were "less developed" and their bodies "slower" and "heavier," making them more "passive" and less prone to criminality.[113]

In contrast to these views were those of writers such as Aron Zalkind, who rejected the idea of children's "defectiveness" and emphasized instead the non-biological factors contributing to delinquency and criminality. This approach was more consistent with the optimistic Marxism of the 1920s, which emphasized the fundamental "plasticity" of the "human organism," and by the mid-1920s advocates of this non-biological approach dominated the fields of pedology and juvenile criminology.[114] Even before 1917, there had been some movement away from the biological explanation to the social. In a 1912 book on delinquent youth, Mikhail Gernet focused on the social and legal factors contributing to delinquency. After 1917, experts eager to display their Soviet credentials now especially emphasized social factors.[115] In an article on *besprizornost'* for the *Bol'shaia Sovetskaia Entsiklopediia*, Zalkind and Epshtein agreed that economic conditions created homelessness and criminality, although they mentioned only externally caused problems such as World War I, military blockades during the Civil War, and the pre-revolutionary capitalist heritage.[116] M. I. Levitina, who wrote an important study of the daily life of homeless youth, argued similarly that juvenile crime resulted from the disastrous economic conditions arising from "the squalls of war and revolution" which "broke up families and destroyed the economic base." It was only after this that "before us appeared robbers and bandits and murderers."[117] The Soviet view of youth was reflected in a new legal vocabulary: instead of terms such as "juvenile delinquent" [*maloletnie prestupniki*] and "child delinquent" [*deti prestupniki*], the post-revolutionary expression was "young offender" [*nesovershennoletnie pravonarushiteli*].[118]

In the view of some experts, not only were the *besprizornye* not ill, they were fundamentally good. "The majority [of *besprizornye*] crave a healthy adaptation to life, strive for work, for social independence," Zalkind and Epshtein argued. All they needed were conditions that provided them with the "full possibility of free working and social independence, without violence, without contemptuous, slighted children."[119] Levitina and Zalkind emphasized aspects of the culture of the *besprizornye* that they said prepared homeless youth to become good communists. Their lack of family ties, dislike of religion, love of freedom (which would make them work to be self-supporting), realism, flexibility, "biological hardening," and courage all suggested not only that they could be rehabilitated, but that they might even have a head start on other youth. The *besprizornye* were even said to have the right approach to questions of class: they identified with the working class and scorned NEPmen.[120]

The social scientists' idealization of homeless youth was particularly obvious in descriptions of *besprizornye* "communes."[121] Some described the *besprizornye* as banding together in communal organizations that varied in size from five or ten individuals to groups as large as six hundred. While it is likely that many *besprizornye* lived and worked together in groups, *besprizornye* "communes" as described by Soviet ethnographers became primitive forms of socialist organization. In a novel by Shishkov (based on his research on the street), the homeless heroes relinquish whatever small bits of private property they have, such as shoes or a shirt, to the communal "checkroom." "Smokes," "chow," and booze are also held in common.[122] "The communal bands of the *besprizornye* are *closer* to the collective comradely ethic than is the 'normal' morality of self-love of children from a bourgeois environment," Zalkind claimed. Levitina argued similarly that "[s]uch behavior and such relations to one's comrade are an *indication of a social union*, although of course only to the members of that collective. Our educational task is to deepen this feeling and to push it to the limit."[123]

MAKING COMMUNISTS AND MAKING RESISTANCE

The optimistic appraisal of some Soviet pedologists led them to hope that better conditions, preferably in a healthy, non-urban environment, could help the *besprizornye*. Homeless children were to be removed from the streets, funneled through "receivers" which would provide immediate temporary shelter and medical assistance, and then sent to a *detdom* [children's home]. Both the receivers and the *detdoma* were supposed to be "open" and non-disciplinary, and the latter were supposed to have schools, labor training, clubs, reading rooms, games, and even "days of rest."[124] "What should a children's home be like?" asked Nadezhda Krupskaia. "It should be an institution that provides children with the opportunity for full physical development, with serious stores of knowledge, with skills to adjust to life, giving them work habits, the ability to live and work collectively, an understanding of life and the skills to take their places as useful members of society."[125] Descriptions of the ideal *detdom* sounded very much like a Komsomol club. Teachers at children's homes were encouraged to put on plays, establish wall newspapers, and celebrate "red holidays" by taking the *besprizornye* on excursions to Red Square or to factories.[126] Indeed, model *detdom* wall-newspapers resembled Komsomol club papers, with materials on religion and on holiday preparations. Supplementary articles on life on the streets ("How I ended up in Moscow," "How I traveled on the tram," and "How I ended up in a night hostel") sounded sometimes like exercises in communist self-criticism.[127]

Most homeless youth did not have the kind of *detdom* experience Krupskaia described, however, and of those that did, few appear to have become Komsomol members. There are many reasons for this. Some young people were simply thought by authorities to be unsuited for the open atmosphere of the *detdoma*. The Commissariat of Education (Narkompros) established children's colonies and institutes for "difficult" or "morally defective" children.[128] Like the *detdoma*, these institutions were supposed to provide school and club activities, but discipline was more strict and children in these institutions could not come and go as they wished. Children who were not just "difficult" but had committed crimes were directed to the Juvenile Affairs Commissions, which were meant to replace courts for those under seventeen. Offenders were then often sentenced to labor homes. These were closed reformatories which still emphasized education rather than simple incarceration, but which were run by the NKVD rather than Narkompros and put a greater emphasis on discipline and occasional punishment. The most serious offenders who came before the Juvenile Affairs Commission were still referred to the courts and from there were sent to prison, often because there were not enough places for them elsewhere.[129]

However, even those children who did go to *detdoma* (who were the majority) did not often get the benefit of the kind of program Krupskaia optimistically described. Alan Ball and Wendy Goldman have described the many social and economic problems facing efforts to rehabilitate homeless youth in the 1920s. Despite sometimes heroic efforts, most *detdoma* found it difficult to satisfy basic requirements for food and shelter, let alone communist education. Many institutions could not provide enough to eat, nor enough clothes to wear, nor enough places to sleep. In the mid-1920s, children's camp director Anton Makarenko complained that his charges were so hungry that they resorted to fishing or stealing food from the market when they went to town. Even Makarenko, who was known for his disciplined approach to delinquency, did not punish them for this: "The famished grubby lads, wildly searching for food, did not seem to me suitable material for the propagation of morals of any sort, on such trifling provocation as the snatching of a *bublik* [roll]."[130] *Besprizornye* were often unable to go to school or to the baths, and sometimes had to "sit not leaving their rooms" because they did not have shoes to wear.[131] It was not uncommon for children to sleep two, three, or even six to a bed, and clean sheets were almost unheard of.[132] Finding experienced or even willing teachers in these conditions was difficult. Many reports complained about haphazard teaching methods and materials and, more troublingly, about teachers and administrators who stole from the children to improve their own situation, or got drunk and beat their charges.[133]

The lack of money, materials, and good teachers made it difficult for children's institutions to make homeless youth into the good Soviet citizens educators hoped for, but there were other reasons for their inability to rehabilitate the *besprizornye*. Some educators may have optimistically seen them as future Komsomol'tsy, but few *besprizornye* saw themselves this way. Not unlike the Komsomol clubs, children's homes failed in part because of a discrepancy between the kinds of activities and opportunities they offered and the interests and desires of their clientele. To children so accustomed to the freedoms and pleasures of the street, and so hostile to and suspicious of outsiders, the *detdoma* were to be avoided at all costs. "It is bad there, they don't give you any freedom, they don't let you go anywhere," explained some homeless youth in a night hostel.[134] The *besprizornye* would typically scatter all over the streets and into side alleys to avoid "capture" by the groups of Komsomol youth who would periodically try to round them up and put them into orphanages. Many were put in a children's home only to escape to the streets again. Such was the case with "K.," a war orphan who went before the Juvenile Affairs Commission and district military officer and was sent to a children's institution [*kollektor*]. He soon ended up back on the streets, however, and then again back before a Commission, from which he was sent again to an institution. As Levitina explained, "He wanted to start a new life. However, a series of humiliations and insults in the *kollektor,* boredom and an empty life did their job on him. He ran and . . . started to go downhill."[135]

For some children, poor food and a few clothes from the *detdom* were not enough. "I ran away from the children's home," one boy explained. "They were strict there, didn't let you go anywhere . . . there was nothing good there. They didn't even give you clothes. If they'd let you go wherever you wanted, then maybe [I'd consider it]."[136] Some unhappy youth who were cold and hungry on the street welcomed the opportunity to find shelter in a children's home, but others appear to have enjoyed their independence, or at least to have grown so accustomed to it that they could not imagine living any other way. Soviet experts frequently described the appeal of independence to orphan youth already on the street and even to youth from what observers described as "good" working-class families, who would sometimes leave their homes and jobs to join the street children in search of adventure and excitement. The tendency of the *besprizornye* to move from place to place, traveling on trains from one end of the country to the other, was sometimes a reflection of this wanderlust. Of 480 homeless youth arrested in a Transcaucasian town, only a quarter accepted the offer of a job in government or a factory. The rest preferred to stay on the street.[137] As one fourteen-year-old explained to an inquisitive *detdom* worker:

—And now you don't miss your mother?
—No, I don't miss her; I'm used to it.
—Will you go see her again?
—I don't know, no. I'm used to it this way.[138]

Detdom activities could be boring in comparison with the immediate excitements of the street, as is evident in this conversation between Makarenko and a seventeen-year-old boy named Mitiagan:

I shan't be long in the colony . . .
Why not?
Why should I? I shall always be a thief.
You can get out of the habit.
I know, but I don't consider it worthwhile.
You're just putting on airs, Mityagan!
No, I'm not! Stealing is fun! You only have to know how . . . [139]

Even when they participated in institutional activities, the *besprizornye* rejected the optimistic and heroic language of the Komsomol club in favor of a language and experience closer to their own. When a volunteer in a youth night hostel sat down to tell a group of homeless girls a story, they cried, "[T]ell us a story about robbers, about stealing. We don't need stories about love. A witch story is better, with ogres. Something scary . . . About sorcery. About detectives. About devils."[140] Like the Komsomol clubs, some *detdoma* had to use movies to keep the homeless children from running away. It was not food or clothes, safe shelter or beds that kept them off the street, "but the chance to see, free, Doug Fairbanks and Harold Lloyd."[141]

Contributing to the problem was the *detdoma*'s struggle to provide the *besprizornye* with vocational training to enable them to leave the street. A lack of resources made it hard to provide much in the way of successful training or workshop experience. *Besprizornye* complaints sometimes echoed those of the Komsomol'tsy. "There is nothing to do, it is boring there." "I don't like the life and situation [in the *detdom*] because there are no results."[142] In contrast to the *detdoma*, where children receive "irrelevant" training in rhythmic dance, explained P. Shimbirev in an article on delinquents, outside "they feel like full citizens."[143] As Amelka, the gang leader in the novel *Children of the Street*, explains: "A chap wants to learn a trade and they push a tank with frogs and goldfish in front of him . . . And they tell him to make toys out of clay . . . And then there are rules too . . . We are used to smoking tobacco and eating tasty things. But there it is all different, it's all boring government issue stuff: clubs, pictures, dances. That's nonsense."[144]

The *besprizornye* often looked down on those who were too "good" or too involved in *detdom* activities. Young people who lived willingly in the *detdoma* were considered "pretty boys" and "goody-goodies" by those still on the loose. Young people at the Moscow labor home [*Mostrudom*] looked suspiciously at any one of their members who agreed, for example, to take on the role of group leader [*starosta*], as he was said to have gone over to the side of the administration. Others who might have liked to participate in plays or other club activities often did not because it embarrassed them in front of their friends. "I would like to stay in the children's home but I would be ashamed and could never do it. I am a long-time thief and if my comrades found out that I live 'cleanly,' they would stop respecting me."[145] Many *besprizornye* simply replicated their street habits and traditions in the institutions. Fights were frequent and the *besprizornye* still gambled, now for tasks, chores, and sugar as well as for money. In homes where there were children of both sexes, boys and girls would slip out the windows at night to meet each other.[146] Often the institution did not transform its charges; rather, the *besprizornye* turned the children's home into a version of the street. "The colony was becoming more and more like a den of thieves and cutthroats," Makarenko observed. "The attitude of the boys to their teachers was rapidly crystallizing into habitual insolence and frank hooliganism. By now they were bandying dirty stories in front of the women teachers, rudely demanding their dinner, throwing plates about the dining room, making open play with their Finnish knives, and inquiring facetiously into the extent of everybody's possessions."[147]

Of course, there were some *besprizornye* who adapted to life in children's institutions. The easiest to work with were said to be those who had only recently left home or been abandoned, while the most difficult were those with connections to the criminal underworld.[148] For some tired and frightened youth, the *detdoma* seemed like a wonderful respite from life on the street. "I want to be in a *detdom*," wrote one twelve-year-old boy. "There you live and work well. In the *detdom* children can take walks in the grass, browse like little cows. Comrades ask you not to play tricks; whoever plays tricks won't go to the *detdom*, and it is very nice there. They give you candy there."[149]

Despite all efforts, then, the problem of homeless youth was not solved in the 1920s. In part this was a reflection of economic constraints that made it all but impossible for Soviet reformers to implement the kinds of programs they desired; by the late 1920s continuing problems of *besprizornost'*, and the apparent failure of the *detdoma*, pushed the state to look increasingly to the family as a solution to homelessness and criminality.[150] The problem was not only material, however. Educators and criminologists had also failed to fully understand the culture of the *besprizornye* and how it was necessitated by their living conditions. Although political and moral authorities often complained that it was the *besprizornye* who made the urban environment unsafe, to the *besprizornye* it was not their activities that made the streets so dangerous. From their perspective it was already dangerous, threatening, and violent.[151] The qualities of "hardness," criminality, and vulgarity so criticized by educators and criminologists might be seen instead as the result of homeless youth's adopting and adapting the characteristics they thought necessary for survival on the street. In this environment it is not surprising that the attempted "Komsomolization" of the *besprizornye* would prove unrealistic and ultimately unsuccessful.

This chapter has described youth on the street as if they belonged to many different groups—working class, street trader, homeless. Sometimes, however, these groups overlapped; many were marginalized from Soviet society by their isolation from both the culture of the factory floor and from the "respectable" aspirations of communist authorities. This was not true of all of them. Communist youth also walked the street in groups and went to the movies. But for both communist and non-communist youth, the largely unmonitorable spaces of the street contributed to the formation of alternate identities and values. Some young people developed identities based entirely on the culture of the street. Others used the street as a temporary respite from the more serious disciplinary efforts of the Komsomol club or even the factory floor. In the eyes of the educator and communist moralist, all these youth were at risk because they were not under the civilizing eye of the school, youth club, or workplace. Their use of the street also put the city itself at risk by making portions of the urban environment feel unsafe and, as yet, uncommunist.

However, even if the street was dangerous (or had a dangerous influence), most Soviet social theorists in the 1920s still believed that the youth themselves were worth saving. However unsuccessful Bolshevik educators and criminologists may have been, they had a striking and apparently genuine optimism about youth and their capacity for fundamental change. This was very different from the attitude that followed. Responding to another wave of *besprizornost'* following the collectivization campaigns and famine of 1932 and 1933, the Stalinist justice system replaced the special children's commissions with regular courts, lowered the age of legal responsibility from sixteen to twelve, and set up a system of work camps and labor homes for youth under the direction of the secret police. The fear of unsupervised youth was so great in the mid-1930s that even children who had homes, whose parents were alive, who had committed no crime, were sometimes detained and arrested. The head of the security apparatus, Iagoda, suggested that children caught skating on winter streets should be sent to labor camps.[152] The Commission for Improving Children's Welfare ordered the seizure of all children under the age of sixteen who were on the streets on the night of November 3, 1934, in order to evaluate them and decide if they should be sent home or detained.[153] However, although it did not reach these Stalinist extremes until later, this anxiety was already present in the 1920s. Adolescents were put in special juvenile facilities during NEP not only because the Bolsheviks had hopes for their redemption, but also because they were thought immature, irresponsible, and in need of extra supervision. The next chapter discusses the Bolsheviks' anxiety about these and other non-productive and "non-communist" values, and their efforts to reestablish communist control over wayward youth.

8

DISCOURSES OF DELINQUENCY

In 1926 and 1927, a rash of articles and books appeared in the Soviet Union describing disturbing increases in "hooliganism" and suicide among youth.[1] According to A. A. Gertsenzon, who was the author of a work on the causes and growth of hooliganism, crimes of hooliganism in Moscow Province more than quadrupled from 1925 to 1926.[2] There are many reports from local Komsomol organizations in the same period documenting and deploring rising rates of drunkenness, sexual depravity, suicide, and political withdrawal. These reports—so similar in format and detail—appear to have been filed in response to a request from the Komsomol Central Committee for information about "problems of drunkenness and hooliganism."[3] In 1926 and 1927, institutes including the Moscow Bureau for the Study of the Criminal Personality and Crime and the State Institute for Research on Crime and Criminals also began studying hooliganism. They published statistics, case studies, and surveys focusing on the sociological, psychological, and physiological characteristics of supposed hooligans.[4] Hooliganism was an object of popular as well as official preoccupation and imagination in late NEP. It was reported that there was "not a single workers' collective, a single organ of the worker-peasant press that [did] not discuss the problem of hooliganism and measures to fight against it."[5] Authorities in Soviet Russia did not just talk about the increasing problem of delinquency; in late 1926, one-sixth of the male prison population was incarcerated for supposed crimes of hooliganism.[6]

These reported increases in delinquent behavior came at a time of increasingly bitter debate about the future of the New Economic Policy. NEP as a period of reconstruction was ending as economic indicators finally returned to their prewar levels in many key areas. To ensure continued economic growth, some party officials urged rapid industrialization, including a renewed campaign against the private sector and against the peasantry. Others, most notably Bukharin, still supported moderation and restraint. The political struggles that lay behind the economic debates were intensifying and becoming more rancorous. The United Opposition (including Trotsky, Zinoviev, and Kamenev) demanded a renewed offensive against NEP's "bourgeois" characteristics and condemned the party leadership for weakening the Soviet Union. Struggles between the party leadership and the opposition dominated the discussions at the Fourteenth Party Congress in December 1925 and continued through 1926. In July 1927, with the support of the majority of the Central Committee, Stalin asserted his authority and condemned the United Opposition for encouraging factionalism; in the fall of 1927, many of its leaders were arrested, and Trotsky was expelled from the Central Committee. In early 1928, having taken care of his major rivals, Stalin himself switched to a more militant position and initiated aggressive policies of rapid industrialization and forced collectivization.

For some in the party and the Komsomol, the struggle against hooliganism was intimately linked to the struggle against "Trotskyite influence" among youth. The desire for greater control over the personal lives of youth reflected growing concerns about the lack of discipline in the political lives of youth. Indeed, youthful support for Trotsky and the Opposition did revive in 1926 and 1927. In speeches and platform proposals Komsomol youth openly criticized Stalin for his "anti-Leninist policies within the party." They demanded a return to the "old Leninist accomplishments of the Komsomol," its "military traditions and international proletarian principles." Seventeen Moscow Komsomol members wrote a letter breaking with Stalin's policies. "In our opinion," they concluded, "Stalin is not a Leninist." In 1927, on the tenth anniversary of the October revolution, oppositionists in Leningrad and Moscow organized noisy protest demonstrations.[7] Much, though not all, of this activity originated from the Leningrad Komsomol, which angrily attacked the Moscow Komsomol and the party for their support of the wealthy peasants at the expense of the working class and proclaimed themselves the defenders of true Leninist principles.[8]

It is difficult to know for certain how many young people really felt themselves to be part of an opposition, and were not merely characterized as such by the regime. Various elements within the Komsomol were used by both party and opposition in their struggle against each other. Although the information on youthful support for Trotsky comes from new archival material which documents in convincing detail a wide range of nonconformist behavior, this data might still reflect the preoccupations of those collecting evidence, rather than the interests of youth themselves. Individuals and groups could be easily tarred by accusations of support for Trotsky, and such accusations sometimes reflected other, more fundamental concerns about discipline and disorder. In a 1927 survey of close to three hundred and fifty thousand Komsomol activists, fewer than two thousand were willing to openly admit that they supported the opposition. It is hard to know for sure what "reality" this represents, however, as those who supported Trotsky faced at the very least official disapproval, and more likely expulsion. Another 2,418 (0.7 percent) did not vote either for or against the opposition.[9]

That said, evidence of discontent is widespread, and not limited to support for Trotsky. There were letters written to the Komsomol Central

Committee; there were strikes and demonstrations. We know, for example, that there were more strikes in 1926 and 1927 than in any year since 1921, and Komsomol and party activists sometimes directed the protests.[10] Militant youth increasingly complained, both in letters and openly at Komsomol meetings, about the bureaucratization and creeping irrelevance of the youth league. Young people wrote to the Komsomol Central Committee in 1926 and 1927 complaining in bitter terms about severe economic hardships. Young people also formed associations, some with explicitly anti-Soviet names: "Down with the Bolsheviks!" "Down with the Komsomol," and "Society for non-party youth," and others with more lighthearted (though, to the Bolsheviks, just as disturbing) ones: "Society for those who love to drink and eat," "Central committee of hooligans," and "Circle of gamblers," whose motto was "Your money will be our money" [*Den'gi vashi—budut nashi*].[11]

Anxieties about so-called "hooliganism" went beyond even these complaints, however, and most importantly, beyond the specific case of youthful support for Trotsky. Individual cases of "hooliganism" were often generalized and used to point out larger failings in the Komsomol and in the younger generation as a whole. There was a sensationalist aspect to much of the reporting that emphasized the anti-Soviet aspects of behavior which may in fact have been little more than irreverent or simply disinterested.[12] Indeed, what was called "hooliganism" did not always have any obvious connection to the kinds of political opposition described above, although the use of the label was deeply connected to anxieties about discipline, corruption, and control. A typical report on hooliganism from the late 1920s described rowdy behavior on the street and in the youth club, including drinking, swearing, fighting between Komsomol and non-Komsomol youth, assaults on club officials, and the general disruption of club and school activities. There were complaints about harassment of women and girls by hooligans who hid on the side of the road or in the bushes, waiting to scare them as they went to and from work.[13] There were also multiple reports of sexual assault.[14] Schools and universities were said to be particularly vulnerable to hooliganism. Aron Zalkind described "growing problems" of fights between students, rudeness toward teachers, and "sexual unruliness."[15] An official at Moscow State University complained about students "smashing chairs at the local club, scribbling graffiti on walls, terrorizing their neighbors in the dormitories by forcing them to engage in drinking games, and intimidating provincial girls."[16] In late NEP this kind of behavior was increasingly criminalized, as is evident from the active involvement of institutes for the study of the criminal personality in research on hooliganism and from the rising numbers of those sentenced to prison.

Hooliganism had not always been defined this way. During the period of War Communism, hooliganism was described primarily as a political threat. The first post-revolutionary legal reference to "hooliganism," in May 1919, was a directive from the revolutionary tribunals referring to "the struggle against pogroms, bribes, forgery, the improper use of Soviet documents, *hooliganism* and espionage."[17] A circular a month later from the Court of Appeals division of the All-Russian Central Executive Committee (VTsIK) underscored the threat hooliganism was thought to pose to successful state formation. It promised to punish as "hooligans" all who "offended the moral feeling or political beliefs of those around them with the explicit goal of contributing to the disorganization of Soviet power." "Provocateurs," former secret police, and other members of the old regime could also be tried as "hooligans" in the new Soviet courts.[18] Over the course of the 1920s, hooliganism was increasingly associated with offenses against public morality. Statute number 176, introduced in 1922, defined hooliganism as "mischief, linked with explicit disrespect toward the functioning of society."[19] Editorial changes in 1924 drew attention to the "aimlessness" of this "excessive and unruly behavior."[20] By late NEP, hooliganism was described as a "pedagogical problem, a cultural problem, a problem of daily life."[21]

This chapter is concerned with the relationship between culture and politics in late NEP—between particular definitions of hooliganism and concerns about the failings and future of the Soviet endeavor. Historians of other times and places have shown that fears of hooliganism often coincide with rising anxieties about state stability and cultural hegemony. Stephen Humphries argues that the key factor in the "law-and-order" campaigns to control working-class youth in pre–World War I Britain "was not so much a rapid increase in delinquency *per se* as the increased public sensitivity to law-breaking that followed from internal and external threats to the power and stability of the state."[22] Joan Neuberger has argued similarly that hooliganism was an obsession in late Imperial Russia because it symbolized "the erosion of the unity, authority, tradition, and optimism that had characterized the last decade and a half of the imperial era."[23] In the case of the Bolsheviks, "hooliganism" was a convenient target for a state increasingly worried about cultural hegemony and about controlling undisciplined youth. A decade after the revolution most young people were not yet "communist." Rather than decreasing, the non-official interests and non-controllable pleasures of youth appeared to be increasing. This chapter explores how discourses of hooliganism were used to talk about and respond to the particular anxieties of late NEP: anxieties about the victory of "primitiveness" over "civilization," anxieties about corruption by an alien, bourgeois West, and anxieties about the "unhealthy" withdrawal of youth from active participation in Soviet political life.

HOOLIGANISM

Although they were revolutionaries, the Bolsheviks clearly hoped to be among the civilized peoples of the world. Hooliganism, on the other hand, was understood to represent the victory of the "primitive" over the "civilized." Criminologists described hooligans as a "primitive part of youth culture." Particularly primitive were so-called "malicious" hooligans. These irredeemable young "psychopaths" were said to hate the city "of which they themselves [were] an ugly product" and to feel "hatred and contempt toward culture, toward society."[24] Lunacharsky argued that hooligans turned the city street into an urban jungle: "[I]n big urban centers like Nizhnii-Novgorod, it is dangerous to walk in the gutters at night. You can find yourself an adventure on the streets the likes of which you could never find in the actual jungles of Brazil."[25] The undisciplined life of the young delinquent was again connected to the unhealthy influences of the urban street. At the same time, the primitive was not only an urban phenomenon—the idea of the primitive may have been especially meaningful, and especially frightening, to urban Bolsheviks confronted with a vast, as-yet-untransformed, "primitive" peasantry. Officially NEP was more tolerant of the "primitive" and the "backward" than the revolution and Civil War had been. As Yuri Slezkine explains, "NEP constituted a temporary but deliberate reconciliation with 'backwardness'—backwardness represented by peasants, traders, women, all non-Russian peoples in general and various 'primitive' tribes in particular."[26] Living among "backwardness" had the effect of making some communists more anxious to assert their civilization, however. Additionally, some worried not only that backwardness was being transformed too slowly, but that it was increasing under the inattentive eye of NEP.

The idea of the "primitive" was not only a Russian one, of course, but a powerful part of European and American discourse in the 1920s. Critical early works in anthropology were published in the late 1920s, including Margaret Mead's *Coming of Age in Samoa* (1928). Freud too was fascinated by the primitive and published *Totem and Taboo* (1913) and *Civilization and Its Discontents* (1930). Malevich, Stravinsky, and other Russian artists in the modernist movements experimented with "primitive" motifs in art and music. In film, Sergei Eisenstein's work revealed a fascination with ethnographic materials at the same time as an apprehension about them. In popular culture, too, the primitive was ascendant in E. R. Burroughs's Tarzan novels. These were extremely popular in the Soviet Union, to the dismay of Soviet educators.[27] No single meaning was attributed to the "primitive" in all these works. For artists the primitive was often positive, but for many others it was associated with the "simple," the violent, the developing.[28]

In the Soviet context, as in the European, the discourse of primitiveness served many purposes. The idea of "bestiality" served to dramatize the hooligans and to emphasize their supposed difference from "civilized" society. P. I. Liublinskii complained about the "hottentot" mentality of the hooligans, their "zulu customs" and "arabic tricks"; these linguistic devices emphasized the alienness of the young delinquent. To some degree these terms may have been adopted from the racist language of Western delinquency theorists; the term "arabic tricks" is presumably related to the phrase "street arabs" commonly used to describe juvenile delinquents in England before the introduction of the word "hooligan."[29] But in Soviet Russia too there were biological aspects to the discourse of hooliganism. Liublinskii was co-editor of a Russian journal of eugenics, as well as the author of articles on hooliganism. A biological association was also made between hooliganism and age. Young people were thought to be particularly vulnerable to the temptations of primitive hooliganism because of certain inherent qualities associated with their youthfulness. Although the precise figures differed, most experts agreed that the majority of hooligans were younger than twenty-five.[30] Many were adolescents, whose particular biological and psychological instabilities were said to make them more likely to be "in conflict with the social structure." Those aged twenty to twenty-five were said to suffer from the contrast between the revolutionary enthusiasms of their adolescent years and the moderation of NEP.[31] Liublinskii argued that the hooligan was one in whom the natural and age-appropriate inclination toward protest had been deformed and exaggerated. Both the "primitive" and youthfulness were sometimes seen as transitional states: Freud described the primitive as "a necessary stage of development through which every race has passed." In a famous early text on adolescence (of which Soviet delinquency theorists were well aware), Stanley Hall argued that "the transition from childhood to maturity corresponded to the leap from barbarism to civilization."[32]

The "primitive" hooligan was sometimes "bestial." In his book *Hooliganism as a social-pathological phenomenon*, I. A. Bulaiskii complained about the animalistic behavior of Komsomol hooligans, who sometimes took off their pants and pranced around naked. He described them urinating in halls, in auditoriums, and in foyers because they "could not bother going to the work of walking to the bathroom."[33] Nikolai Semashko compared those who wore flapper fashions to animals: "To become more like a lady or gentleman, people turn into monkeys, buying all kinds of stupid things."[34] Soviet observers wrote with concern and wonder about Edgar Rice Burroughs's primitive "monkey": "The ape—the Tarzan ape—has risen to its full height and has overwhelmed us. The ape has caressed the Russian reader. The reader is captive in the ape's paws."[35] Here again the ape is the "primitive," but is also the West that threatens to overrun Soviet Russia with its decadent, erotic, and disturbingly appealing popular novels. The "primitiveness" Soviet experts described was not only that of the African native, but could also be that of the bourgeois NEPman. Sometimes these two images were combined. Certain aspects of Western bourgeois culture were said, for example, to be originally the products of "primitive" cultures. In a condemnation of excessively fine dress among some young Russians, Stratonitskii argued that wearing jewelry was wrong both because it was bourgeois and because it was "a vestige from primitive, barbarian times," common to the Blacks and Aborigines of Africa and Australia.[36]

Comrade Semashko: "Citizen hooligans! Don't kill. This is not hygienic!" *Buzoter*
21 (November 1926), cover page.

The supposed primitiveness of the delinquent mind and body served
to point out through contrast the culture and "civilization" of the Soviet
elite. In this respect, there are important similarities between the anxieties
of late NEP and the obsessions with crime and "public rowdiness" of the
late Imperial period. Joan Neuberger argues persuasively that pre-revolutionary hooliganism illuminated a cultural conflict between the upper and
lower classes, the object of which was to "determine whose cultural norms
would dominate on the streets."[37] Hooliganism was a challenge to cultural
authority, a challenge that was particularly painful because it came at a
time when the Russian middle classes were striving expressly to "'raise
the cultural level' of Russian society."[38] In this context, explains Neuberger,
hooliganism "symbolized the failure of the whole culturalist enterprise to
raise the moral and intellectual level of the people, to assimilate them into

society.[39] Although the Bolsheviks were trying to establish a new kind of culture rather than to shore up an old one, we have seen that they also had an acculturating agenda. This is not to say that their values were the same as those of the pre-revolutionary elite (although there were similarities), but in both cases the educated classes persisted in seeing the other classes as people to be made more cultured. This was evident in Bolshevik approaches to the working class, which Bolshevik elites worried had not become fully communist in dress, language, or belief. So too in their views of the peasantry. The young rural hooligan was said to be even less civilized than his working-class cousins. Criminologist E. K. Krasnushkin described the typical rural hooligan as a "strong, energetic" young peasant boy who got involved in hooliganism because he was "uncivilized" and did not know any better.[40] From this perspective, primitiveness, like peasanthood, was a kind of early, uneducated state that required acculturation into proper behavior and understanding.

In these discourses, peasant, "primitive," and hooligan were all portrayed as "other." The image of the hooligan as an alien or "outsider" was represented metaphorically in the typical journalistic account of the hooligan as someone who stood *outside* the door of the Komsomol club and threatened those who wanted to go inside. The depiction of the hooligan as an outsider was related to the Civil War image of the hooligan as provocateur or spy; both images depicted the hooligan as an obvious opponent of Bolshevik domination. The hooligan as alien also embodied a more general concern about dangerous and barbarian "external" influences on the vulnerable Soviet state, especially those of the bourgeois West. The hooligan himself was thought to have been corrupted by these unhealthy influences, including most especially those bourgeois influences that had taken root under NEP.[41]

The creation of the alien "other" facilitated Bolshevik control of "hooligan" youth. This is not unexpected. Foucault has described how nineteenth-century European regulatory agencies used discourse to monitor and control undesirables, and later scholars have explored the disciplining of youth, of homosexuals, and of women in both the nineteenth and twentieth centuries.[42] Between 1925 and 1926, the number of youth expelled from the Komsomol for drunkenness, hooliganism, and other "illnesses" rose by 10 percent.[43] As Table 1 shows, the proportion of prison sentences handed down for hooliganism relative to other punishments sharply increased in the second half of 1926. This followed the introduction of a new statute in June 1926 that punished hooliganism more severely. In comparison, before 1926 concern about hooliganism had seemed to decline. Just two years earlier, the legally mandated punishment had decreased from one year of compulsory labor or a one-year jail sentence to one month of labor or a fine of fifty rubles. But in June 1926, although some still argued that education and cultural work were the best ways of fighting hooliganism, this trend was reversed, and the number of prisoners serving time for hooliganism

TABLE 1. Sentences Imposed for Hooliganism (per 100 convictions)

	Jan.–June 1926	July–December 1926
Suspended sentence	3.7	8.7
Fixed prison sentence	29.1	81.5
Hard labor	1.9	3.9
Other (fines, reprimand)	65.3	5.9

Source: V. Iakubson, "Khuliganstvo i sudebnaia repressiia protiv nego," in *Khuliganstvo i khuligany. Sbornik,* ed. V. N. Tolmacheva (Moscow: Izd. Narodnogo Komissariata Vnutrennikh Del RSFSR, 1929), p. 88. See also Peter H. Solomon, "Criminalization and Decriminalization in Soviet Criminal Policy, 1917–1941," *Law and Society Review* 16 (1981–1982), pp. 16–17.

TABLE 2. Number of People Held in RSFSR Prisons for Hooliganism

	1/1/1926	7/1/1926	1/1/1927
Absolute numbers	1,406	4,381	12,851
Percentage	100	312	914

Source: Iakubson, "Khuliganstvo," p. 86.

rose dramatically (Table 2). [44] These figures are especially striking when compared to the period of War Communism. In a 1918–1922 study of 23,200 men in prison, only 79 were there for hooliganism, or 0.3 percent of the total. In December 1926, in contrast, one-sixth of the male prison population were imprisoned for hooliganism.[45] That the change happened in 1926 is no accident; there was rising concern in 1926 about the threat youth posed to the Soviet project, and an effort was made to use both law and discourse to reassert the power of the state. It was in the summer of 1926 that Trotsky and Zinoviev officially allied to form the United Opposition. Sergei Esenin committed suicide in December 1925, and while in the first half of 1926 comparatively little was said in the press about his death (and about the wave of copycat suicides said to be following it), by mid-1926 great concern was being expressed in both the Komsomol and the party press. Similarly, in September 1926 the great public agony began over the gang rape of a young woman by Komsomol youth in Chubarov Alley.[46]

If left alone, hooligans threatened to spread their disease among other youth. "Club work is dying down permanently," complained the author of a 1926 article in *Pravda.* "The independent activity of club members comes to naught, there are increasing numbers of street hooligans who are terrorizing . . . club members. Moreover, hooligan youth is corrupting club youth."[47] Fears of the spread of hooliganism from the "outside" to the "inside" lay behind much of the hysteria about the growth of hooliganism in this period. Hooliganism had always been present, but now it had moved from the streets to the workers' club. In other words, the hooligan was not entirely "other," but often, and most dangerously, a corrupted communist. He was likely to be a member of the Komsomol. A Komsomol secretary in the Sverdlovsk region was said to have organized a "cell of hooligans." Another "qualified worker, activist [and] secretary of a Komsomol circle" was censured for fighting while drunk.[48] Within the Komsomol, some of those most likely to be corrupted were the newest members of the youth league, who presumably had not been sufficiently inoculated against the disease of delinquency.[49] The corrupted Komsomol hooligan could be rehabilitated through better education and propaganda, but it was essential that the dangerous "outside" influences be kept away.

The language of disease used to describe hooliganism was part of what Naiman calls a "rhetoric of infection."[50] Local Komsomol surveys on problems of drunkenness, lack of discipline, sexual crimes, depression, and resignations from the youth league were often titled "On Illness in the Komsomol."[51] "It is obvious," Lunacharsky wrote, "that we are suffering from a sickness with the two symptoms of hooliganism and pessimism, both of which are devouring the very bones of our younger generation."[52] We have seen many other examples of this "rhetoric of infection," most especially in the discussion of the dangerous "contaminating" influences of urban street life and of the urban *besprizornye* on other, "healthy" youth. As Naiman notes, this discourse had implications far beyond youth, reflecting a broad-based preoccupation during NEP with purity, ideological control, and the danger of corruption and contagion. In this context, fears of hooliganism (or of syphilis, in Naiman's account) "represented other sorts of social infections which could lead to the stillbirth of the Revolution's most cherished hopes."[53]

AN "EPIDEMIC" OF SUICIDE

Hooliganism was a signifier of a variety of disagreeable and unacceptable attitudes and behaviors. Some so-called "hooliganism" was not the fighting and drinking described above, but growing apathy, withdrawal, and "disrespect." "This well-known drop in discipline," explained a local Komsomol committee in 1927, "has taken many forms . . . an irresponsible attitude toward basic Komsomol responsibilities, including not paying membership dues, not attending cell and other meetings, [and] not participating in demonstrations." "We have talked and talked" about these problems, and it is clear, concluded the committee, "that the authority of Komsomol rules has fallen."[54] Political authorities like Lunacharsky condemned the "complete abstinence" of increasing numbers of youth from the process of so-cialist state building.[55] Hesitation and doubt were deeply troublesome to revolutionary moralists who demanded full (and optimistic) commitment. The hooligan appeared disturbingly purposeless—even worse in this way than the criminal. "In contrast to criminal actions which always have a purpose, a logic and are usually done from necessity," explained Bulaiskii, "hooliganism is characterized by its lack of purpose, uselessness, and the fact that it does nothing but harm."[56] The danger specifically attributed to the uselessness of hooliganism is evident in the different meanings given to male and female delinquents. Women were considered much less likely to be involved in acts of hooliganism. Even when they were involved, their behavior was less threatening, because female hooligans were thought to be motivated by social or economic need.[57] The young male hooligan, on the other hand, was believed more dangerous because he behaved in an undisciplined fashion for inexplicable, perhaps even nonexistent, reasons.

Preoccupation with the pleasures of dance and dress was one form of withdrawal. Abandoning one's Komsomol responsibilities was more seri-ous. Most serious were depression and suicide. In 1926 and 1927, authori-ties were deeply concerned about what they called an "epidemic" of sui-cide.[58] Suicide was said to be so "wide-spread" in Leningrad that in 1926 a special committee of the Komsomol led an investigation into its causes. In early 1927, political and cultural authorities, including Lunacharsky, Karl Radek, and Vladimir Mayakovsky, organized a Moscow conference on "Depression among Youth."[59] Medical-forensic experts, moral statisticians, the Red Army's Political Administration, all were deeply involved in moni-toring and interpreting suicide.[60] Local Komsomol reports on hooliganism also often included a discussion of problems of depression and statistics on the number of suicides in their region. A Sverdlovsk bureau report was typical, describing an increase in suicides among youth in the Ural region from 26 in 1926 to 126 in 1928.[61]

Like hooliganism, suicide was seen as an illness threatening the health not just of the individual, but of society. The unhealthy individual lacked personal discipline and will power, was vulnerable therefore to despair and alienation, and could infect others with this illness. In a reassertion of the importance of the communal in Soviet discourse, suicides were said to be most likely among individuals lacking a strong connection to their com-munity. The very act of suicide demonstrated their isolation from Soviet society. Bourgeois students were said to be more likely than proletarian students to succumb to depression and suicide because they lacked the clear sense of revolutionary community and purpose available to work-ing-class youth.[62]

Bourgeois students were also said to be more likely to commit suicide because of their "social environment." Criminologists and social moralists argued that suicide would not exist once the Soviet Union was fully social-ist; it existed in the 1920s only because this was a society in transition. In his article "Are we threatened by an epidemic of suicides?" Semashko defended the revolutionary and collectivist ideals of the new Soviet order and insisted that suicide persisted only because it "fed" on leftovers from the "old capitalist system."[63] In a Komsomol account of what caused hooliganism and suicide in schools, the most important element was said to be the excessive influence of "bourgeois elements."[64] Like hooliganism, suicide came from the outside. The main sources of infection, according to V. M. Gur-Gurevich in his comparative account of suicide before and after the revolution, were schools where there was "not a strong Komsomol cell, a Pioneer detachment . . . The children of workers . . . are the least susceptible to suicide."[65] All of this was a change from 1921–1922, when suicides were often attributed to youthful despair among communist youth about the course of NEP. In late NEP (by which time many Komsomol members were no longer veterans of the Civil War) political authorities were more likely to blame the persistence of unhealthy bourgeois elements in NEP society.[66] Hooliganism and suicide were convenient targets for a state increasingly worried about its vulnerability to attack from either Western culture or Western armies. "Hooliganism is a declaration of war," wrote Professor L. G. Orshanskii. "It is a new, although of course short-lived, front."[67]

It is difficult to say with any certainty if there was a genuine increase in suicide in late NEP. In his work on suicide in Soviet Russia, Kenneth M. Pinnow rightly says very little about the social reality of suicide as reflected in numbers, and focuses instead on statistics as a form of politics with both discursive and disciplinary functions.[68] As important as this is, I believe we can say with some reliability that the proportion of young people committing suicide in Soviet Russia was higher than in some other societies. The suicide rate as a whole appears comparable to numbers in New York and Paris, but in the Soviet Union the largest number of suicides appear to have been young people; in other countries older people were more likely to commit suicide. Those between 20 and 24 years of age were most likely to kill themselves, followed by those 16 to 19 and then those 25 to 29.[69]

While supposed "hooligans" did not leave records describing their own activities, suicidal youth sometimes did. Young communists mailed letters or suicide notes to the Komsomol Central Committee, and local organizations sometimes forwarded copies of suicide notes. Although these notes are themselves a reflection of Soviet discourse (even as they sometimes repudiate Soviet power), they suggest a more complex picture than that painted by Bolshevik moralists. For one, it was often Komsomol youth who committed suicide, and they often expressed severe disappointment with the youth league. In his suicide note Grigorii Abramovich contrasted his early revolutionary experiences with the "self-serving" behavior of Komsomol'tsy after the revolution. He described his early eager participation in a "little group" who "every minute ran the risk of being killed" by anti-revolutionary forces. He remembered the intense comradeship of this group, whose members felt like they were part of a "single family." The individuals in the group were self-sacrificing and rose from their hospital beds to return to the revolutionary struggle. "It is still this way in the party," Abramovich writes, but in the Komsomol (which he joined after the Civil War) there are only "thousands of self-seeking people trying to worm their way into the party." The Komsomol is full of "unenlightened careerists and bureaucrats." He concluded that he had no strength left for his life or his work.[70] Abramovich's anger was clearly political, even if his behavior was self-destructive rather than outwardly rebellious.

Bolshevik experts were right that individual cases of suicide were indicative of a larger phenomenon: there were probably many more youth who felt despair but did not take their own lives. But the reasons were different from those given by Bolshevik social scientists. Indeed, for some young people it was the party campaigns against the United Opposition, and the tightening of party and Komsomol control that accompanied these campaigns, that signaled the end of a kind of revolutionary innocence. One Komsomol member remembered how arrests and official accusations of "counter-revolutionary" behavior forced him and his friends to give up their previously free and heated discussions of political subjects and the party leadership. None of them understood the meaning of "this word Trotskyism," he explained, but they knew enough to stop talking. "Not a trace remained of our former comradely sincerity and our youthful spontaneity."[71] Young people who committed suicide were sometimes believers, and as they considered suicide they still mourned their own failings and the ways in which they had failed to live up to the Komsomol ideals. A young woman who wrote despairingly in her notebook, "I am convinced that I am superfluous . . . that my life is without value," also noted that as a member of the Komsomol she knew that "it was necessary to fight against depression or she would not be fulfilling Lenin's behest."[72] Kolia Kiselev, who also felt "without value and superfluous," signed his suicide note "with Komsomol greetings."[73]

Some depressed and uncertain youth turned to the poetry of Sergei Esenin for comfort. As we saw earlier, Esenin was revered among some youth for his bohemian attributes, but he ricocheted between these bohemian excesses and a more somber effort to find meaning and purpose in a post-revolutionary world. Although he was just twenty-two in 1917, Esenin described himself as stuck between two generations:

> I am not a new man!
> Why should I hide it?
> I've remained with one leg in the past.
> And trying to overtake the steel army,
> I slip and fall with the other.[74]

A young Russian named Mikhail Koriakov wrote poignantly about his attraction to the ambivalence Esenin embodied: "Sergei Esenin was not just a poet, a literary figure . . . no, he was a part of our lives . . . like no other poet in the history of Russian literature."[75] For Koriakov, Esenin represented the concerns and fears of all those youth who did not feel a part of the new Soviet society, all those who did not understand the path of the revolution, but instead felt lost and anxious in the face of such monumental changes. Koriakov described his generation as disoriented, overwhelmed, and directionless in the "age of anxiety" [vek toski] following World War I. His anxiety reminds us what an impact war, and not just revolution, had on the children of this era. Koriakov's first memory was of women singing a song about soldiers, and the first word he remembered studying was "mobilization." His story resembles that of the so-called "lost generation," a term that was first applied to the American expatriate community in Paris after the war but later came to represent an entire generation of serious but pleasure-seeking young people who felt confused and disillusioned following the anti-climactic restoration of a staid post-war civilization.[76] According to Koriakov, however, there were those in Soviet Russia who felt this anxiety even more at the end of the 1920s. They sensed that they were approaching a "turning point" and were on the edge of a storm that would be even greater than that of 1917: "There was something in the air that lay heavy on the soul, that foretold a coming storm—a new revolution . . . " "We soviet youth of the 1920s needed these poems because as youth who were always sensitive and responsive—we were frightened at the approach of this turning point."[77]

Koriakov joined a group of young admirers of Esenin—one of many such circles where young men and women drank, danced, and read poems by the poet. These fan clubs sprang up in 1927 and 1928 among students and some working-class youth despite the fact that being branded as an Esenin supporter [Eseninshchinist] made it more difficult to get a job or enter a university. Koriakov himself was expelled from school three times for his "eseninist qualities." A warning on his school record describing him as "ideologically lacking self-control" made it impossible for him to enter university after leaving school, and he was told instead that he needed to work in a factory for three or four years to demonstrate his reliability.[78] Admiring secondary school students sometimes wrote their own poems about Esenin, which they transcribed into their school yearbooks. One student wrote of a life "without purpose": "Daydreams, one after the other / Fill the mind like a frightening swarm / Tell me why do we live, die / Who needs it." A tenth-grade student wrote about his "friendship with the bottle" and his depression: "a horrible cold penetrates my heart / I don't need this life / And it doesn't need me."[79] Young people gathered to memorialize Esenin in "suicide leagues," in which they contemplated suicide and sometimes committed it.[80]

Koriakov described the experiences of those young people who embraced Esenin because they felt in him the same hesitant ambivalence they had toward the upheavals of the revolutionary period. Enthusiasm for

Esenin was not limited to those who questioned the Soviet project. Some Komsomol members also loved and admired him. As one Komsomol student explained: "The poetry of a brilliant poet has a lot to give young people. In periods of internal confusion, when I don't have enough strength or words to express my feelings without changing or corrupting them, I turn to Esenin."[81] Although the Komsomol newspaper *Molodaia gvardiia* [Young Guard] would later express great reservations about the "Esenin cult," in January 1926 it published a tribute to the poet: "In your beloved new Soviet Russia your tender and clear-voiced poems will never be silenced."[82]

For concerned and committed communists, eseninism [*eseninshchina*] and hooliganism were a symbol of all that was wrong with youth in late NEP: apathy, individualism, a lack of commitment to the larger cause of Soviet socialism, doubt, degeneration. The eseninist was the opposite of the regulated, rational, and disciplined young communist so desired by Bolshevik moralists. Anxiety about youth's lack of discipline was, of course, not new to the late 1920s. We have seen how the Bolsheviks tried to discipline the ideological excesses of militant youth, the bodies of the flapper and the foxtrotter, and the public spaces of the urban street. But in late NEP an undisciplined personal life was increasingly described as a threat to politics, to modernization, to industrialization. A December 1925 party resolution on the Komsomol declared that the "old attitude" of ignoring the lack of discipline and anarchism in daily life categorically conflicted with the task of building a new economy.[83]

For some, the campaign against delinquency was at heart a campaign against the *causes* of depression and hooliganism, namely NEP. The campaigns against hooliganism and suicide must be understood, in other words, in terms of their symbolic discourses about NEP and anxieties about impropriety, impurity, and instability. There were those like Lunacharsky who continued to insist that NEP was still necessary, even while they admitted that the proliferation of bourgeois temptations and of NEPmen, and the ongoing economic difficulties, contributed to problems of depression and hooliganism.[84] But there were many others who took a more hostile approach to NEP. In 1926, V. Ermilov wrote, "We are in *a genuine war* against the hostile ideology of the kulak and the nepman . . . We must steadfastly replenish and enrich our arsenal of weapons in the fight against kulak-Nep ideology, against petit-bourgeois behavior [*meshchanstvo*], against depression."[85] For many committed communists, apolitical and apathetic youth symbolized increasing concerns about the possible defamation and destruction of the revolutionary agenda.

EPILOGUE

The variety of youthful responses to Bolshevik ideology and transformative efforts demonstrates both the "power and the fragility" of the Bolsheviks' attempted domination.[1] Some young enthusiasts were deeply committed to the Soviet project, but by the late 1920s it was evident that the massive cultural transformation the Bolsheviks had hoped for had yet to take place. A multiplicity of behaviors and beliefs persisted among youth, some that supported official ideals and many that did not. Some alternative cultural practices became forms of resisting the state. Other youth were more indifferent, but no less disturbing to the regime. Even those youth who supported communism could not always be relied on to obey party dictates. By late NEP, many young people no longer felt optimistic about the revolutionary endeavor, but were increasingly frustrated and depressed. Their NEP was not (or at least was no longer) the hopeful "revolutionary dream" of Stites's portrayal.[2]

The great distance between state and society suggested by the persistence of multiple resistant and disinterested youth cultures made it more difficult for political authorities to rapidly effect the kinds of transformative social and cultural programs they envisioned and to embark on necessary programs of industrialization and modernization. "Large-scale" expectations and ambitions were thwarted by the small-scale economic realities and social forces Roger Pethybridge describes in his *The Social Prelude to Stalinism,* but also by the "small-scale" cultural realities I have described here.[3] Despite the Bolsheviks' many educational efforts—propaganda, film, literature, revolutionary rituals—too many young people remained uncommitted. To be certain, youth posed a special challenge in this regard. By its nature age is not a very stable category, but a socially dynamic one. The generation the Bolsheviks addressed in 1917 had grown up by the tenth anniversary of the revolution; new generations had to be continually converted. Additionally, young people are often not very interested in stability. As we have seen, this made some youth a particular challenge for those committed to the gradualist goals of NEP.

Young people used languages of dress, of the body, and of everyday behavior to challenge the Bolshevik agenda, but more often their behavior was perceived as a challenge even when it was not meant to be. We have seen that the Bolsheviks often described youth in imaginary terms, either idealizing them or criminalizing them. Both positive imaginings of youth and negative anxieties about youth inhibited the active participation of young people in the Soviet project. The kind of activities planned for an imagined rational, non-pleasure-seeking, and disciplined Komsomol youth meant that few young people who did not fit this image would join. Anxieties about youth were similarly stunting, sometimes creating problems where there had been none, and generating a mood of intolerance and discipline which made it hard for real youth to get their needs and questions effectively addressed. In other words, both expectations of youth and anxieties about youth were out of synch with the realities, which in turn made it all the more difficult to transform these realities.

While there were hopeful, enthusiastic, utopian aspects to the period of the New Economic Policy, it was also a time of great anxiety. As Eric Naiman has so persuasively argued, much of this anxiety was directed against the pluralism and tolerance many were unhappily forced to accept in transitional NEP.[4] Although there were those who championed the diversity and openness of NEP, others were disgusted and disappointed by it. My work has explored the disciplinary aspects of this anxiety. Idealizing youth as "new men" was one aspect of this disciplinary effort; so was defining youth as hooligans. Primarily through discourse and propaganda, but also through coercion, party authorities and Bolshevik moralists tried to both prescribe what the Soviet state should look like and enforce this prescription. We should remember, however, that this imagining was multiple and the disciplining was not unidirectional. Discourses of youth reveal some fundamental consistencies in ideals about the Soviet project, but also some important disagreements about how best to achieve these ideals. This was a state in the process of becoming, and those who wanted to join in the Soviet project (youth included) were involved in a process of self-disciplining and definition as well.

Discipline was sometimes expressed as a kind of social puritanism. The revolution may have been liberating, but after the revolution, authorities wanted to reaffirm boundaries of acceptable behavior and belief. The relative openness of NEP to the popular cultures of the West only deepened Bolshevik preoccupation with ideological and cultural purity. Although many Bolsheviks embraced the modern and the progressive (equal rights for women, abortion, advances in science and technology), in other ways they were deeply conservative, particularly in their preoccupation with being "civilized" and in their distaste for the "popular." In part this reflected the power of entrenched cultural forms to resist change. It was as difficult for political authorities to change the values and habits of daily life as it was for youth, and many party leaders and educators had been shaped by the more traditional social expectations of the pre-revolutionary period. This meant that even in areas where the Bolsheviks did initiate revolutionary legislation—such as equality for women—inherited attitudes often inhibited any real transformation. And for political authorities concerned with conformity, youth culture was particularly troubling. Although it was youth who had to carry out the necessary revolutionary transformations, youth had an autonomy that could not be easily controlled.

The resistant behavior of youth (both real and imagined) had a special resonance for the Bolsheviks because of the intimate associations (again, both real and imagined) between the younger generation and the transition to a new socialist society. Soviet youth embodied all that was energetic and optimistic about the future. Soviet youth also represented all that could go wrong, be corrupted, and slide into "failure." Youth were a metaphor for social transformation, but they were also "an index for social anxiety."[5] If the younger generation was supposed to be the physical and spiritual representative of the socialist society, then the decadent and delinquent behavior of youth suggested the failure of this future.

It was the double-sided image of youth that made youth such an appropriate metaphor for this period of transition and transformation, especially for the double-edged dangers and opportunities of NEP. As described by Soviet developmental theorists the adolescent was an organism in transition, and as such was inherently vulnerable to internal disruptions as well as dangerous external influences. Youth could be good and contribute to the revolutionary struggle, or bad and succumb to delinquency and decadence. This discourse of adolescence was just the language applied to the uncertain imbalances of the New Economic Policy. It too was said to teeter between purity and impurity, revolutionary success and revolutionary failure. Although some young people complained that the moderate methods of NEP were too adult-like, in the larger framework of Soviet "development" NEP was itself an adolescent, immature and in transition, and therefore vulnerable like youth to dangerous influences, whether generated from within or "infecting" it from without.

The intimate relationship between youth and NEP has significance for our understanding of the reasons for NEP's demise and for the transition to rapid industrialization and collectivization. The ways in which the Bolsheviks responded to resistant and autonomous cultural and social forms had implications for the political process. NEP and the legalization of private business were introduced by the Bolsheviks to rescue a floundering Soviet economy, but by the end of the decade many were increasingly worried about the cultural implications of NEP for a younger generation constantly exposed to bourgeois attractions. It seemed increasingly likely that continued exposure to the gluttonous culture of NEP would inhibit the creation of a youth culture appropriate to the new socialist state. Some argued that the primary danger of NEP came from city streets that teemed with traders, beggars, wealthy NEPmen, and other manifestations of mixed economic policies. Others insisted that the rebellious and hedonistic behavior of young people could be attributed to the alienation of a younger generation inspired by the revolution and Civil War, and now confused by the complex transitional qualities of NEP. Either way it seemed that instead of moving closer together, state and society were moving further apart, and at an ever more rapid rate.

By the late 1920s, to those Bolsheviks worried about the rapid decline of the younger generation and implicitly, therefore, of the Soviet state, the moderate methods of NEP no longer seemed adequate. Youth's increasing problems were said to represent more general problems in Soviet society. Evgenii Preobrazhenskii, an opponent of NEP, described youth's depression and disillusionment as part of a general "crisis" in Soviet culture.[6] Between 1928 and 1932, the party increasingly responded to fears of decadence and antisocial behavior by limiting the cultural and recreational options open to young people. In 1928, "foreign and domestic pictures thought to glorify 'prostitution and debauchery'" were removed from film libraries. By 1932, there were no more foreign film imports into the Soviet Union, and American jazz bands no longer toured the country playing the latest dance tunes.[7] The frightening breakdown of cultural consensus suggested by the explosion of hooliganism and suicide, and general impatience with the apparent failure of NEP's gradualist approach to problems of cultural transformation, encouraged some people to support the authoritarian policies of Stalinism. Stalinism was in part a reassertion of parental authority over youth.

The young people described in this book provided the social and cultural foundation for the transformations of industrialization and collectivization in other ways as well. Sheila Fitzpatrick first gave the name "cultural revolution" to the militant, class-war politics of the period 1928 to 1931.[8] In her book *Cultural Revolution in Russia*, she describes this period as one of generational warfare, especially in the professions, and describes aggressive initiatives by youth "from below." There has been great controversy ever since about whether cultural revolution came "from above" or "from below." My book explores the relationship *between* above and below. I have shown how the actions and beliefs of young people helped shape official responses to them, and how in turn they responded to others' constructions of them. Young people were also themselves involved in the disciplining process; by telling others how to behave, they helped define themselves. So too certainly for the period of the First Five-Year Plan. As we have seen, militant youth were already agitating in the 1920s for some of the changes that were to follow in the period 1928 to 1931. The aggressive, iconoclastic cultural policies of the state were likely aimed in part at reengaging youth in support of party policy through explicit appeals to their militant and anti-bureaucratic inclinations. Youth brigades (often initiated by Komsomol'tsy) began to appear in isolated industries in 1926 and 1927. These efforts in socialist competition and shock work became part of a "sustained movement" in the fall of 1929.[9] The party mobilized young workers against bureaucrats in industry, in the arts, in universities. Communist youth were again referred to as the shock force of the party and as important anti-bureaucratic agents. Stalin, who had earlier brutally criticized Trotsky for calling youth the barometer of the party, in 1930 described Komsomol youth as "the nucleus of a new and numerous generation of Bolshevik destroyers of capitalism, of Bolshevik builders of socialism, of Bolshevik deliverers of all who are oppressed and enslaved." "Therein," he concluded, "lies our strength. And therein lies the pledge of our victory."[10]

Some also saw the industrialization campaigns as a way to reinvolve apathetic youth in the collective process of state building.[11] In 1927, there were approximately twenty-nine million youth between the ages of fourteen and twenty-three in the Soviet Union.[12] The party needed these youth to be actively involved if it was to have any hope of modernizing the country. In late NEP one frequently proposed solution to suicide among youth was to encourage social activism, to develop "a feeling of collectivism and interest in work, which would lead to an interest in life."[13] "Activism is a sign of health," asserted N. P. Brukhanskii. "Active participation in social construction is the best guarantee against suicide."[14] Party commentators on suicide were eager to fill any personal "emptiness" the potential suicide might feel with meaningful, collective activity.[15] These proposed solutions again point us in the direction of the First Five-Year Plan. The industrialization and collectivization campaigns were, after all, perfect examples of "meaningful and collective activity." In 1929, those younger than twenty-three formed 25 percent of the total number of workers; by 1933, they made up over 40 percent.[16]

It must be noted, however, that although appeals to youth during the period of the First Five-Year Plan resembled those of the Revolution and Civil War, Stalin was not as optimistic about the innate capacities of youth as these earlier adulators had been. Trotsky had suggested that youth had a great anti-bureaucratic role to play because of some quality inherent to youthfulness. Stalin praised the energy and initiative of youth in ways he had not done in 1924 and 1925, but he had little sense of them as having the capacity for, or right to, independent action outside the demands and discipline of the party. Thus, after listing the successes and achievements of the Komsomol in serving as successors to the Bolshevik Old Guard, Stalin reminded young communists that their achievements were fundamentally attributable to the party.[17] In an appeal to youth in late 1927, a party document listed the ways in which the Komsomol could help in the fight against bureaucratization, but specified that each committee of the Komsomol had to submit its anti-bureaucratic efforts to the local organ of the party.[18] In 1917, Soviet youth had been described as the new men (or women) of the future. A decade later it was clear that being the new men of the future meant that youth never became full participants in the present. Despite an early ideology of youth which promised a new social order with party and Komsomol together forming a vanguard, by the 1930s it was well established that the party had the need and the right to direct youth (even if youth still did not always do just as directed). The challenge of youth, that of constant questioning, renewal, even rebellion, was at best restrained, and at worst repressed.

It appears that, by adopting the Five-Year Plan and all of the cultural politics that went with it, the Bolsheviks hoped to move out of adolescence, as embodied by "transitional" NEP, and into adulthood. Stalin's declaration in 1936 that the USSR had reached socialism is the clearest example of this desire to finally "grow up." However, "adulthood" remained illusory, if by adulthood we mean the successful resolution of adolescent issues and the creation of a fully socialist society and culture. Rather than resolving the struggle over forms of daily life and problems of recreation and leisure, the politics of Stalinism largely ignored them. From 1928 to 1932, the transformative agenda of NEP was abandoned in favor of the bigger (and, I would argue, in some ways easier) tasks of economic and military construction. Emel'ian Iaroslavskii, who had been deeply interested in questions of personal behavior in the 1920s, condemned such a preoccupation in the early 1930s. When confronted with an account of one school that considered the moral behavior of students before giving them graduation certificates, Iaroslavskii responded, "Do our Party cells and CCC [Central Control Commission] exist for nothing better than to snoop around and find out how far men and women go in their private relationships? . . . Questions of private life should not be considered most important . . . We don't want always to be saying, 'What does so and so do badly?' We should ask, 'What does he do well?' It is the party member's work that counts."[19]

Scholars have commonly argued that the period that followed the First Five-Year Plan was even more of a "great retreat" from the struggle for personal transformation.[20] Some recent work challenges this thesis, describing instead a push to create a new "Stalinist" person.[21] More work will tell us just what this new Stalinist person was supposed to look like. Although the Stalinist period was one of pathological anxiety, the fears were different ones (as were the arenas of discipline and coercion). In the mid-1930s, for example, Western dances were again permitted, and were again very popular. A Komsomol report from 1936 describes popular dance parties, with as many as a thousand youth dancing the foxtrot and the tango. Although the report shows some mild anxiety that dance takes young people away from social work, the principal concern is that the "guy" who teaches dance "has no preparation and no training to teach West European dance." The author argues that some of the best Komsomol'tsy should be given a chance to teach dance too.[22]

I do not mean to suggest that the Bolsheviks' transformative agenda and gradualist approach during NEP completely failed to penetrate and transform youth culture. This is plainly not true; many young communists supported Bolshevik ideals of appropriate behavior and were as outraged as adults by the pleasure-seeking or bohemian behavior of their compatriots. Many clearly believed themselves to be good communists and felt entitled, therefore, to the supposed rewards of a socialist system: education, employment, social mobility, justice.[23] By March 1926, there were approximately 1,750,000 young people in the Komsomol; 62 percent of working-class youth in Leningrad were members, and 55 percent in Moscow.[24] The "private" sphere was penetrated in many other ways as well, and among many youth who would not call themselves communist. Interactions on the factory floor, in the family, and in the schoolyard were all influenced by Bolshevik categories and language. To give just one example, we know that school youth adopted the word "bourgeois" to denote habits such as wearing fine clothing, being polite, and using face powder. More suggestively, the word "bourgeois" was applied to "children who don't play the game, who aren't like the others. If a youngster doesn't like sport . . . he is 'bourjui'."[25]

Nonetheless, in the 1920s Komsomol youth remained a small percentage of the total number of eligible Komsomol-aged youth. Of the approximately twenty-nine million people between the ages of fourteen and twenty-two in the Soviet Union in 1926, only about 6 percent belonged to the Communist Youth League.[26] While the Bolsheviks clearly remained politically dominant, their inability to establish their cultural hegemony over the younger generation demonstrates the challenges of cultural transformation and the limits of the Bolsheviks' control over individual identity. The search for socialist transformation and communist hegemony would be long and difficult—not something that could be achieved in the single revolutionary moment of October 1917, or in the revolutionary decade following it.

INTRODUCTION

1. Ilia Erenburg, *Memoirs: 1921–1941,* trans. Tatiana Shebunina (New York: Grosset and Dunlap, 1966), p. 73.

2. Pierre Sorlin, *The Soviet People and Their Society: From 1917 to the Present* (New York: Frederick A. Praeger, 1968), pp. 5, 98.

3. V. Iakubson, "Khuliganstvo i sudebnaia repressiia protiv nego," in *Khuliganstvo i khuligany. Sbornik,* ed. V. N. Tolmacheva (Moscow: Izd. Narodnogo Komissariata Vnutrennikh Del RSFSR, 1929), pp. 86–87.

4. Frederick Thrasher's famous early survey of street gangs was published in 1927, for example. Frederick Milton Thrasher, *The Gang: A Study of 1,313 Gangs in Chicago* (Chicago: University of Chicago Press, [c. 1927]).

5. For an interesting discussion of statistics and the role of the scientific expert, see Kenneth M. Pinnow, "Making Suicide Soviet: Medicine, Moral Statistics, and the Politics of Social Science in Bolshevik Russia, 1920–1930" (Ph.D. diss., Columbia University, 1998).

6. Andrew Tolson, "Social Surveillance and Subjectification: The Emergence of 'Subculture' in the Work of Henry Mayhew," in *The Subcultures Reader,* ed. Ken Gelder and Sarah Thornton (London and New York: Routledge, 1997), p. 311. For another account of the process of subjectification by those researching youth, see Dick Hebdige, "POSING . . . THREATS, STRIKING . . . POSES: Youth, Surveillance, and Display," in the same collection. On the discursive creation of the other as subject, see also Michel Foucault, *Power/Knowledge: Selected Interviews and Other Writings 1972–1977,* ed. and trans. Colin Gordon (New York: Pantheon, 1980).

7. Susan Gross Solomon, "The Expert and the State in Russian Public Health: Continuities and Changes across the Revolutionary Divide," in *The History of Public Health and the Modern State,* ed. Dorothy Porter (Amsterdam: Editions Rodopi B. V., 1994); Francis L. Bernstein, "What Everyone Should Know about Sex: Gender, Sexual Enlightenment, and the Politics of Health in Revolutionary Russia, 1918–1931" (Ph.D. diss., Columbia University, 1998); Pinnow, "Making Suicide Soviet"; Peter Holquist, "Anti-Soviet *Svodki* from the Civil War: Surveillance as a Shared Feature of Russian Political Culture," *Russian Review* 56:3 (July 1997).

8. Derek Sayer, "Everyday Forms of State Formation: Some Dissident Remarks on 'Hegemony,'" in *Everyday Forms of State Formation: Revolution and the Negotiation of Rule in Modern Mexico,* ed. Gilbert M. Joseph and Daniel Nugent (Durham: Duke University Press, 1994), p. 371.

9. Ibid.

10. Iurii Lotman, "Conversations on Russian Culture: Russian Noble Traditions and Lifestyle in the Eighteenth and Early Twentieth Centuries," *Russian Studies in History* 35:4 (Spring 1997), pp. 7–15. Emphasis in the original.

11. See the discussion of subculture in Sarah Thornton, "General Introduction," in *The Subcultures Reader,* ed. Gelder and Thornton, pp. 1–5.

12. See, for example, Lawrence W. Levine, *Highbrow/Lowbrow: The Emergence of Cultural Hierarchy in America* (Cambridge, Mass.: Harvard University Press, 1988). For a discussion of some trends in cultural history, see Lawrence Grossberg, Cary Nelson, and Paula Treichler, eds., *Cultural Studies* (New York: Routledge, 1992); Lynn Hunt, ed., *The New Cultural History* (Berkeley: University of California Press,

1989); Chandra Mukerji and Michael Schudson, eds., *Rethinking Popular Culture: Contemporary Perspectives in Cultural Studies* (Berkeley: University of California Press, 1991); and Victoria Bonnell and Lynn Hunt, eds., *Beyond the Cultural Turn: New Directions in the Study of Society and Culture* (Berkeley: University of California Press, 1999).

13. Lawrence W. Levine, "William Shakespeare and the American People: A Study in Cultural Transformation," in *Rethinking Popular Culture: Contemporary Perspectives in Cultural Studies*, ed. Chandra Mukerji and Michael Schudson (Berkeley: University of California Press, 1991).

14. Mark D. Steinberg, "Worker-Authors and the Cult of the Person," in *Cultures in Flux: Lower-Class Values, Practices, and Resistance in Late Imperial Russia*, ed. Stephen P. Frank and Mark D. Steinberg (Princeton: Princeton University Press, 1994), p. 169.

15. Ibid., p. 174.

16. See James C. Scott, *Weapons of the Weak: Everyday Forms of Resistance* (New Haven: Yale University Press, 1985). For a discussion of the relationship between culture and power, see the introduction to *Culture/Power/History: A Reader in Contemporary Social Theory*, ed. Nicholas B. Dirks, Geoff Eley, and Sherry B. Ortner (Princeton: Princeton University Press, 1994).

17. On the British Cultural Studies tradition, see Stuart Hall, "Cultural Studies and the Centre: Some Problematics and Problems," in *Culture, Media, Language*, ed. Stuart Hall, Dorothy Hobson, Andrew Lowe, and Paul Willis (London: Hutchinson, 1980); Graeme Turner, *British Cultural Studies* (London: Unwin Hyman, 1990); and Ioan Davies, *Cultural Studies and Beyond: Fragments of Empire* (London and New York: Routledge, 1995).

18. Antonio Gramsci, *Selections from the Prison Notebooks of Antonio Gramsci*, ed. and trans. Quinton Hoare and Geoffrey Nowell Smith (New York: International Publishers, 1971).

19. Tony Bennett, "The Politics of 'The Popular' and Popular Culture," in *Popular Culture and Social Relations*, ed. Tony Bennett, Colin Mercer, and Janet Woollacott (Philadelphia: Open University Press, 1986), p. 19. See also Stuart Hall, "Notes on Deconstructing 'The Popular,'" in *People's History and Socialist Theory*, ed. Raphael Samuel (London: Routledge and Kegan Paul, 1981).

20. Researchers at the Centre for Contemporary Cultural Studies have made enormous contributions, but they have been extensively critiqued as well. Some of this material can be found, together with a helpful introduction to the work of the Centre and its critics, in Gelder and Thornton, *The Subcultures Reader*, parts 2 and 3.

21. See, for example, the articles on "Language and Meaning in Russian History" in *Russian Review* 55:3 (July 1996), and those on "Ideology, Resistance and Social Identity" in *Russian Review* 56:1 (January 1997). On pre-revolutionary Russia, see the bibliography in Frank and Steinberg, eds., *Cultures in Flux*.

22. Eric Naiman, *Sex in Public: The Incarnation of Early Soviet Ideology* (Princeton: Princeton University Press, 1997).

23. Sarah Davies, *Popular Opinion in Stalin's Russia: Terror, Propaganda, and Dissent, 1934–1941* (Cambridge: Cambridge University Press, 1997), p. 9.

24. Sheila Fitzpatrick, *Stalin's Peasants: Resistance and Survival in the Russian Village after Collectivisation* (Oxford: Oxford University Press, 1994), and Lynne Viola, *Peasant Rebels under Stalin: Collectivization and the Culture of Peasant Resistance* (New York: Oxford University Press, 1996). See also David L. Hoffmann, *Peasant Metropolis: Social Identities in Moscow, 1929–1941* (Ithaca: Cornell University Press, 1994); Stephen Kotkin, *Magnetic Mountain: Stalinism as a Civilization* (Berkeley: University of California Press, 1995); and Sheila Fitzpatrick, ed., *Stalinism: New Directions* (London: Routledge, 1999).

25. Welcome efforts to examine questions of culture and everyday life include Svetlana Boym, *Common Places: Mythologies of Everyday Life in Russia* (Cambridge, Mass.: Harvard University Press, 1994); Catriona Kelly and David Shepherd, eds., *Constructing Russian Culture in the Age of Revolution, 1881–1940* (Oxford: Oxford University Press, 1998); and Naiman, *Sex in Public.* Three important collections of articles on early Soviet culture are Sheila Fitzpatrick, Alexander Rabinowitch, and Richard Stites, eds., *Russia in the Era of NEP: Explorations in Soviet Society and Culture* (Bloomington: Indiana University Press, 1991); Abbott Gleason, Peter Kenez, and Richard Stites, eds., *Bolshevik Culture: Experiment and Order in the Russian Revolution* (Bloomington: Indiana University Press, 1985); and Sheila Fitzpatrick, *The Cultural Front: Power and Culture in Revolutionary Russia* (Ithaca: Cornell University Press, 1992). On the utopian aspects of Soviet culture, see Richard Stites, *Revolutionary Dreams: Utopian Vision and Experimental Life in the Russian Revolution* (New York: Oxford University Press, 1989); William G. Rosenberg, ed., *Bolshevik Visions: First Phase of the Cultural Revolution in Soviet Russia* (Ann Arbor: University of Michigan Press, 1990); and James von Geldern, *Bolshevik Festivals, 1917–1920* (Berkeley: University of California Press, 1993). On education and culture, see Sheila Fitzpatrick, *The Commissariat of the Enlightenment: Soviet Organization of Education and the Arts under Lunacharsky* (Cambridge: Cambridge University Press, 1970). On religion, see Daniel Peris, *Storming the Heavens: The Soviet League of the Militant Godless* (Ithaca: Cornell University Press, 1998), and Glennys Young, *Power and the Sacred in Revolutionary Russia: Religious Activists in the Village* (University Park: Pennsylvania State University Press, 1997). On the proletarian culture debate, see Lynn Mally, *Culture of the Future: The Proletkult Movement in Revolutionary Russia* (Berkeley: University of California Press, 1990). On propaganda, see Peter Kenez, *The Birth of the Propaganda State: Soviet Methods of Mass Mobilization, 1917–1929* (Cambridge: Cambridge University Press, 1985). Two books that focus explicitly on popular culture are Richard Stites, *Russian Popular Culture: Entertainment and Society since 1900* (Cambridge: Cambridge University Press, 1992), and Denise J. Youngblood, *Movies for the Masses: Popular Cinema and Soviet Society in the 1920s* (Cambridge: Cambridge University Press, 1992).

26. See, for example, Ralph Fisher, *Pattern for Soviet Youth: A Study of the Congresses of the Komsomol, 1918–1954* (New York: Columbia University Press, 1959); Allen Kassof, *The Soviet Youth Program: Regimentation and Rebellion* (Cambridge, Mass.: Harvard University Press, 1965); Isabel A. Tirado, *Young Guard! The Communist Youth League, Petrograd, 1917–1920* (New York: Greenwood Press, 1988); *Ocherki istorii Leningradskoi organizatsii VLKSM* (Leningrad: Lenizdat, 1969); *Slavnyi put Leninskogo komsomola*, vyp. 1 (Moscow: Molodaia gvardiia, 1974); Stanislav A. Pedan, *Partiia i Komsomol, 1918–1945* (Leningrad: Izd. Leningradskogo universiteta, 1979); and *50 let VLKSM, 1918–1968* (Moscow, 1969). An exception is an important work by N. B. Lebina, *Rabochaia molodezh' Leningrada. Trud i sotsial'nyi oblik, 1921–1925 gg.* (Leningrad: Izdatel'stvo Nauka, 1982), which portrays some of the complexities of youth culture and everyday life in the 1920s, but is focused on the working class and on the Komsomol. More recent work by Isabel Tirado (cited in the notes) is also in part about questions of culture. On contemporary youth culture, see especially Hilary Pilkington, *Russia's Youth and Its Culture: A Nation's Constructors and Constructed* (London and New York: Routledge, 1994).

27. Some interesting recent work by Russian historians does examine questions of daily life among youth, though largely still from an empirist perspective. See A. Iu. Rozhkov, "Molodoi chelovek i sovetskaia deistvitel'nost' 1920-kh godov. Formy povsednevnogo protesta," in *Sposoby adaptatsii naseleniia k novoi sotsial'no-ekonomicheskoi situatsii v Rossii*, ed. I. A. Butenko (Moscow: Moskovskii obshchestvennyi nauchnyi fond, 1999), and "Student kak zerkalo Oktiabr'skoi revoliutsii,"

Rodina 3 (March 1999); V. I. Isaev, *Kommuna ili kommunal'ka? Izmeneniia byta rabochikh sibiri v gody industrializatsii* (Novosibirsk: Nauka, 1996); and N. B. Lebina, "Molodezh' i NEP. Ot konflikta k edinstvu subkul'tur" (paper presented at a conference on "Youth in Soviet Russia, 1917–1941," Philipps-Universität, Marburg, Germany, May 1999).

28. On NEP more generally, see E. H. Carr, *The Bolshevik Revolution, 1917–1923,* vol. 2 (New York: Macmillan, 1952); Alan Ball, *Russia's Last Capitalists: The Nepmen, 1921–1929* (Berkeley: University of California Press, 1987); Stephen F. Cohen, *Bukharin and the Bolshevik Revolution: A Political Biography, 1888–1938* (New York: Alfred A. Knopf, 1973); Lewis Siegelbaum, *Soviet State and Society between Revolutions, 1918–1929* (Cambridge: Cambridge University Press, 1992).

29. Ball, *Russia's Last Capitalists,* chapter 2.

30. As cited in Ella Winter, *Red Virtue* (London: Victor Gollancz, 1933), p. 51. Richard Stites has the best descriptions of the "acrimonious arguments" over the utopian transformation of daily life. See his *Revolutionary Dreams,* p. 11.

31. Lebina, *Rabochaia molodezh',* p. 15. This is not to say that there were just 34 studies of everyday life, as these figures include only the 117 studies counted by Lebina. In the Stalinist period, the majority of works on youth were concerned with problems of work and with political and social activism. A valuable account of sociological studies of youth as primary sources can be found in E. A. Semenova, "Materialy sotsiologicheskikh obsledovanii detei i podrostkov kak istoricheskii istochnik po izucheniiu sovetskogo obraza zhizni (20-e gody)," *Istoriia SSSR* (September–October 1986), pp. 112–122. For a history of Soviet time budget studies, see Jiri Zuzanek, *Work and Leisure in the Soviet Union* (New York: Praeger, 1980).

32. Because of reduced funding during NEP, as well as shortages of paper and printing presses, most publishing organs were servicing only Moscow and Leningrad. See Katerina Clark, "The 'Quiet Revolution' in Soviet Intellectual Life," in *Russia in the Era of NEP,* ed. Fitzpatrick, Rabinowitch, and Stites, p. 218.

33. See the interesting work of Isabel Tirado on the Komsomol in the countryside for a discussion of some aspects of rural youth cultures. For example, Isabel A. Tirado, "The Komsomol and Young Peasants: The Dilemma of Rural Expansion, 1921–1925," *Slavic Review* 52:3 (Fall 1993), and "The Komsomol and the Kresti'anka: The Political Mobilization of Young Women in the Russian Village, 1921–1927," *Russian History/Histoire Russe* 23:1–4 (1996).

34. On students, see the work of Peter Konecny, including "Revolution and Rebellion: Students in Soviet Institutes of Higher Education, 1921–1928," *Canadian Journal of History* 27:3 (December 1992); "Chaos on Campus: The 1924 Student *Proverka* in Leningrad," *Europe-Asia Studies* 46:4 (1994); and "Library Hooligans and Others: Law, Order, and Student Culture in Leningrad, 1924–38," *Journal of Social History* 30:1 (Fall 1996). On youth in the workplace, see William J. Chase, *Workers, Society and the Soviet State: Labor and Life in Moscow, 1918–1929* (Urbana: University of Illinois Press, 1987); John Hatch, "The Politics of Mass Culture: Workers, Communists, and Proletkul't in the Development of Workers' Clubs, 1921–25," *Russian History/Histoire Russe* 13:2–3 (Summer–Fall 1986); Hiroaki Kuromiya, *Stalin's Industrial Revolution: Politics and Workers, 1928–1932* (Cambridge: Cambridge University Press, 1988); and the various important works of Diane Koenker cited throughout this study.

1. THE POLITICS OF GENERATION

1. Philip Abrams, "Rites de Passage: The Conflict of Generations in Industrial Society," *Journal of Contemporary History* 5:1 (1970), p. 178. See also Jürgen Reulecke, "Youth Protest: A Characteristic of the Twentieth Century," in *Jugendprotest und*

Generationenkonflikt in Europa im 20. Jahrhundert, ed. Dieter Dowe (Germany: Verlag Neue Gesellschaft, 1986), p. 356.

2. These figures are my own, based on a description of party resolutions found in Robert McNeal, *Guide to the Decisions of the Communist Party of the Soviet Union, 1917–1967* (Toronto: University of Toronto Press, 1972). Interestingly, in the "revolutionary" situation of contemporary Russia, youth are again being appealed to in much the same way. Igor Ilynsky, the rector of the Institute of Youth Studies in Moscow, wrote in 1995: "Not merely human beings but *young people as bearers of the future, the source of innovation and of change* should become the focus of contemporary politics." See Igor Ilynsky, "The Status and Development of Youth in Post-Soviet Society," in *Young People in Post-Communist Russia and Eastern Europe,* ed. James Riordan, Christopher Williams, and Igor Ilynsky (Brookfield, Vt.: Dartmouth Publishing Co., 1995), p. 26.

3. As cited in John Gillis, *Youth and History: Tradition and Change in European Age Relations* (New York: Academic Press, 1974), pp. 37–38.

4. David Raddock, *Political Behavior of Adolescents in China* (Tucson: University of Arizona Press, 1977), p. 42.

5. Robert Wohl, *The Generation of 1914* (Cambridge, Mass.: Harvard University Press, 1979), p. 180. The best discussion of youth under Italian fascism is Tracy Koon, *Believe, Obey, Fight: Political Socialization of Youth in Fascist Italy, 1922–1943* (Chapel Hill: University of North Carolina Press, 1985). On German youth politics, which have some similarities to those of Italy, see Walter Laqueur, *Young Germany: A History of the German Youth Movement* (London: Macdonald and James, 1962); and Peter D. Stachura, *The German Youth Movement, 1900–1945* (London: Macmillan, 1981). Although there are some similarities between communist and fascist youth, I do not want to conflate the two. As will become clear, I am also more interested in Bolshevik connections to other European and North American mentalities than to fascist ones.

6. As cited in Graham Murdock and Robin McCron, "Consciousness of Class and Consciousness of Generation," in *Resistance through Rituals: Youth Subcultures in Post-war Britain,* ed. Stuart Hall and Tony Jefferson (London: Hutchinson, 1976), p. 195.

7. Ibid.

8. Daniel J. Kevles, *In the Name of Eugenics: Genetics and the Uses of Human Heredity* (New York: Alfred A. Knopf, 1985); William H. Schneider, *Quality and Quantity: The Quest for Biological Regeneration in Twentieth Century France* (Cambridge: Cambridge University Press, 1990); Robert A. Nye, *Crime, Madness, and Politics in Modern France: The Medical Concept of National Decline* (Princeton: Princeton University Press, 1984).

9. Loren R. Graham, *Between Science and Values* (New York: Columbia University Press, 1981), pp. 231–245. See also Mark B. Adams, *The Wellborn Science: Eugenics in Germany, France, Brazil, and Russia* (New York: Oxford University Press, 1990), and "Eugenics as Social Medicine in Revolutionary Russia," in *Health and Society in Revolutionary Russia,* ed. Susan Gross Solomon and John F. Hutchinson (Bloomington: Indiana University Press, 1990).

10. See, for example, Vladimir Alekseevich Zaitsev, *Trud i byt rabochikh podrostkov* (Moscow: "Voprosy truda," 1926).

11. See the discussion of Gastev, below, as well as N. A. Semashko, *Novyi byt i polovoi vopros* (Moscow: Gos. izd., 1926), pp. 13–14, and M. Sobetskii, *Fizkul'tura v derevne* (Leningrad: Izd. Knizhnogosektora Gubono, 1925), p. 31.

12. Gillis argues that adolescence was "invented" in the nineteenth century. Others have since argued about the dating of the concept of adolescence, placing the arrival of "adolescence" in the sixteenth and seventeenth centuries. See Gillis,

Youth and History, p. 133. For a discussion of these debates, see John Springhall, *Coming of Age: Adolescence in Britain, 1860–1960* (Dublin: Gill and Macmillan, 1986).

13. Philip Cohen, "Historical Perspectives on the Youth Question Especially in Britain, " in *Jugendprotest und Generationenkonflikt in Europa*, ed. Dowe, p. 242. Hall makes this argument in his *Adolescence: Its Psychology and Its Relations to Physiology, Anthropology, Sociology, Sex, Crime, Religion and Education*, 2 vols. (New York, 1904).

14. V. E. Smirnov, *Rabochii podrostok* (Moscow-Leningrad: Molodaia gvardiia, 1924), p. 34.

15. Eric Naiman, *Sex in Public: The Incarnation of Early Soviet Ideology* (Princeton: Princeton University Press, 1997), p. 126, n. 9. See also David Joravsky, "Stalinist Mentality and Higher Learning," *Slavic Review* 42:4 (Winter 1983).

16. During NEP, some members of the Komsomol were older than twenty-three, especially those rural activists who were not accepted into the party. Isabel A. Tirado, *Young Guard! The Communist Youth League, Petrograd 1917–1920* (New York: Greenwood Press, 1988), pp. 4–5. The percentage of those older than twenty-three increased over the course of the 1920s; the increase concerned Komsomol leaders, who worried that too many of these were people who had been refused acceptance into the party. See B. A. Balashov and Nelepin, *VLKSM za 10 let v tsifrakh* (Moscow-Leningrad: Molodaia gvardiia, 1928), pp. 10–11. On definitions of child-hood and the Pioneers, see Margaret Kay Stolee, "A Generation Capable of Estab-lishing Communism: Revolutionary Child Rearing in the Soviet Union, 1917–1928" (Ph.D. diss., Duke University, 1982), pp. 7–8, and on Komsomol membership gen-erally see Ralph Fisher, *Pattern for Soviet Youth: A Study of the Congresses of the Kom-somol, 1918–1954* (New York: Columbia University Press, 1959).

17. A. Zalkind, "The Pioneer Youth Movement as a Form of Cultural Work among the Proletariat [1924]," in *Bolshevik Visions: First Phase of the Cultural Revolu-tion in Soviet Russia*, ed. William G. Rosenberg (Ann Arbor: University of Michigan Press, 1984), p. 351.

18. Yuri Olesha, *Envy*, in *The Portable Twentieth Century Reader*, ed. Clarence Brown (New York: Penguin Books, [1927] 1985), p. 248.

19. Nikolai Bukharin, *Kommunisticheskaia partiia Sovetskogo Soiuza, XIII s"ezd. Stenograficheskii otchet*, May 1924 (Moscow, 1963), p. 515.

20. Vladimir Lenin, "The Crisis of Menshevism," n.d., in *On Youth* (Moscow: Progress Publishers, 1970), p. 148. For a similar statement of the superiority of the younger generation over the old, see also Leon Trotsky, *Problems of Everyday Life and Other Writings on Culture and Science* (New York: Monad Press, 1973), p. 97.

21. Diane Koenker, "Urban Families, Working-Class Youth Groups and the 1917 Revolution in Moscow," in *The Family in Imperial Russia: New Lines of Historical Re-search*, ed. David L. Ransel (Urbana: University of Illinois Press, 1978), p. 281; Stephen A. Smith, *Red Petrograd: Revolution in the Factories, 1917–1918* (Cambridge: Cam-bridge University Press, 1983), p. 197; T. H. Rigby, *Communist Party Membership in the USSR, 1917–1967* (Princeton: Princeton University Press, 1968), p. 353.

22. Abrams, "Rites de Passage," p. 179.

23. Lenin, "The Working Class and Neo-Malthusianism," in *On Youth*, pp. 32–33. Emphasis in original.

24. Fisher, *Pattern for Soviet Youth*, pp. 41–42.

25. Isabel A. Tirado, "Nietzschean Motifs in the Komsomol's Vanguardism," in *Nietzsche and Soviet Culture: Ally and Adversary*, ed. Bernice Glatzer Rosenthal (Cambridge: Cambridge University Press, 1994), p. 240.

26. Leon Trotsky, "Youth Fills the Breach," March 5, 1920, in *Problems of Every-day Life*, p. 268. Leon Trotsky, *The First Five Years of the Communist International*, vol. 1 (New York: Monad Press, 1972), p. 311. Information on the military role of the Komsomol can be found in Fisher, *Pattern for Soviet Youth*, pp. 47–50.

27. Elizabeth A. Wood, *The Baba and the Comrade: Gender and Politics in Revolutionary Russia* (Bloomington: Indiana University Press, 1997), pp. 52–56.

28. See Reginald E. Zelnik, "On the Eve: Life Histories and Identities of Some Revolutionary Workers, 1870–1905," in *Making Workers Soviet: Power, Class and Identity*, ed. Lewis H. Siegelbaum and Ronald Grigor Suny (Ithaca: Cornell University Press, 1994).

29. As cited in Ava Baron, "On Looking at Men: Masculinity and the Making of a Gendered Working-Class History," in *Feminists Revision History*, ed. Ann-Louise Shapiro (New Brunswick, N.J.: Rutgers University Press, 1994), p. 154.

30. As cited in Naiman, *Sex in Public*, p. 70.

31. On Lenin's views after the revolution, see "The Crisis of Menshevism," in *On Youth*, p. 148. At the turn of the century, on the other hand, Bolshevik leaders had praised student activists; Lenin argued, for example, that students were the most responsive section of the intelligentsia. See Lenin, "The Tasks of Revolutionary Youth," September 1903, in *On Youth*, pp. 87–100.

32. From the first program of the Communist Youth League, as cited in Fisher, *Pattern for Soviet Youth*, p. 17.

33. Lenin, "The Tasks of the Youth Leagues," October 2, 1920, in *On Youth*, p. 250.

34. *Iunyi kommunist* 15–16 (September–October 1922), pp. 74–76.

35. Nikolai Bukharin, as cited in Fisher, *Pattern for Soviet Youth*, p. 42. Komsomol activists made similar kinds of statements. See N. Serebrennikov, "O komsomol'skom aktive," *Iunyi kommunist* 2 (November 1925), pp. 60–62.

36. *Iunyi kommunist* (September 1923), p. 38.

37. Vladimir Lenin, "On Cooperation," as cited in Trotsky, *Problems of Everyday Life*, p. 16.

38. Vladimir Lenin, "The Tasks of the Youth League," in *On Youth*, p. 242. See also "O rabote sredi molodezhi," May 1924, in *KPSS o Komsomole i molodezhi* (Moscow: Molodaia gvardiia, 1962), p. 47. See also Robert Tucker, "Lenin's Bolshevism as a Culture in the Making," in *Bolshevik Culture: Experiment and Order in the Russian Revolution*, ed. Abbott Gleason, Peter Kenez, and Richard Stites (Bloomington: Indiana University Press, 1985), p. 34.

39. Leon Trotsky, "The Position of the Republic and the Tasks of Young Workers," in *Report to the 5th All-Russian Congress of the Russian Communist League of Youth, 1922* (London: Young Socialists Publishers, 1972), p. 24. See also James McClelland, "Utopianism versus Revolutionary Heroism in Bolshevik Policy: The Proletarian Culture Debate," *Slavic Review* 39:3 (1980). A discussion of the conflicting views of the prioritization of culture over politics and economics can be found in Lynn Mally, *Culture of the Future: The Proletkult Movement in Revolutionary Russia* (Berkeley: University of California Press, 1990), and in Zenovia A. Sochor, "Was Bogdanov Russia's Answer to Gramsci?" *Studies in Soviet Thought* 22 (1981), pp. 59–81.

40. "On the Work of the Komsomol," April 25, 1923, as cited in Richard Gregor, ed., *Resolutions and Decisions of the Communist Party of the Soviet Union*, vol. 2 (Toronto: University of Toronto Press, 1974), p. 204.

41. Leon Trotsky, *Literature and Revolution* (Ann Arbor: University of Michigan Press, 1960), pp. 255–256.

42. A. Gastev, "Snariazhaites', molodye montery," *Iunyi kommunist* 1–2 (March 1923), p. 34–35. See also G. Lebgur, "NOT, Rabkrin i Komsomol," *Iunyi kommunist* 3 (June 1923), pp. 11–12. For more on Gastev, see Kendall E. Bailes, "Alexei Gastev and the Soviet Controversy over Taylorism, 1918–1924," *Soviet Studies* 19 (1977).

43. B. S. Sigal, *Trud i zdorov'e rabochei molodezhi* (Moscow-Leningrad: Molodaia gvardiia, 1925), pp. 3–5. See also P. I. Kurkin, *Moskovskaia rabochaia molodezh'*, vyp. 2 (Moscow: Izd. Moszdravotdela, 1925).

44. For examples of such artwork, see *Dorogi iunosti* (Moscow: "Sovetskii khudozhnik," 1988). Futurists such as Malevich also wanted to spread the idea of man as machine and wrote about the "industrial way of life" and the rationalization of art. See the discussion in V. I. Kas'ianenko, *Sovetskii obraz zhizni. Problemy issledovaniia* (Moscow: "Mysl'," 1982), p. 161.

45. As described by Klaus Mehnert, *Youth in Soviet Russia*, trans. Michael Davidson (Westport, Conn.: Hyperion Press, [1933] 1981), p. 88.

46. Yevgeny Zamyatin, *We*, trans. Mirra Ginsburg (New York: Avon Books, [1920–1921] 1972); Olesha, *Envy*. See also Vladimir Mayakovsky, *The Bedbug and Selected Poetry*, ed. Patricia Blake (New York: Meridian Books, 1960), and Mikhail Bulgakov, *Heart of a Dog*, trans. Mirra Ginsburg (New York: Grove Press, [1925] 1968). This new man of the 1920s was clearly different from the "new man" of the Russian fin-de-siècle. The Symbolists had, in contrast, seen the new man as the mystical poet, as an individual who through special powers could identify the heaven and earth of this existence and hope to somehow unite them.

47. As cited in Kas'ianenko, *Sovetskii obraz zhizni*, p. 163.

48. As cited in Lewis H. Siegelbaum, *Soviet State and Society between Revolutions, 1918–1929* (Cambridge: Cambridge University Press, 1992), p. 85.

49. On Stalin, see his "On the Contradictions in the Young Communist League," April 3, 1924, in *Collected Works*, vol. 6, pp. 67–68, and "Po organizatsionnomu voprosu," in *KPSS o Komsomole i molodezhi*, p. 28. For more on Trotsky and the debate about militant youth, see chapter 3.

50. *Pravda*, December 14, 1923, as cited in Sheila Fitzpatrick, *Education and Social Mobility in the Soviet Union, 1921–1934* (Cambridge: Cambridge University Press, 1979), p. 92.

51. Naiman, *Sex in Public*, p. 263.

52. Lunacharsky, as cited in Elizabeth Waters, "From the Old Family to the New: Work, Marriage, and Motherhood in Urban Soviet Russia, 1917–1931" (Ph.D. diss., University of Birmingham, 1985), p. 58, and Semashko, *Novyi byt i polovoi vopros*, p. 3. For an interesting discussion of the multiple meanings of *byt*, see Svetlana Boym, *Common Places: Mythologies of Everyday Life in Russia* (Cambridge, Mass.: Harvard University Press, 1994).

53. Trotsky, *Problems of Everyday Life*, p. 101.

54. V. Dmitriev and B. Galin, *Na putiakh k novomu bytu* (Moscow: "Novaia Moskva," 1927), p. 68.

55. G. Grigorov and S. Shkotov, *Staryi i novyi byt* (Moscow: Molodaia gvardiia, 1927), p. 89.

56. Of course, the "facilitation" of a working-class culture contained some contradictions of its own. If it was to be a working-class culture, why were intellectuals like Bogdanov needed to develop it? For more on this dilemma, see Sheila Fitzpatrick, "The Bolsheviks' Dilemma: Class, Culture, and Politics in the Early Soviet Years," *Slavic Review* 47:4 (Winter 1988), p. 602. On the Proletkult, see Mally, *Culture of the Future*. For more on the Bolsheviks' conflicted views of working-class culture, see Moshe Lewin, *The Making of the Soviet System: Essays in the Social History of Interwar Russia* (New York: Pantheon Books, 1985), pp. 193–194.

57. Leon Trotsky, "The Struggle for Cultured Speech," in *Problems of Everyday Life*; and Nikolai Semashko, "Kto vinovat—neriashlivost' ili bednost'?" as cited in Dmitriev and Galin, *Na putiakh*, pp. 55–57.

58. Mark D. Steinberg, *Moral Communities: The Culture of Class Relations in the Russian Printing Industry, 1867–1907* (Berkeley: University of California Press, 1992), p. 241. For more on pre-revolutionary anxiety about morality and culture, see Joan Neuberger, *Hooliganism: Crime, Culture, and Power in St. Petersburg, 1900–1914* (Berkeley: University of California Press, 1993); Charters Wynn, *Workers, Strikes, and*

Pogroms: The Donbass-Dnepr Bend in Late Imperial Russia, 1870–1905 (Princeton: Princeton University Press, 1992), chapter 3; Laura Engelstein, *The Keys to Happiness: Sex and the Search for Modernity in Fin-de-Siècle Russia* (Ithaca: Cornell University Press, 1992).

59. Helmut Gruber, *Red Vienna: Experiment in Working-Class Culture, 1919–1934* (New York and Oxford: Oxford University Press, 1991), p. 184.

60. Harry Hendrick, *Images of Youth: Age, Class, and the Male Youth Problem, 1880–1920* (Oxford: Clarendon Press, 1990), p. 175.

61. See, for example, Chris Waters, *British Socialists and the Politics of Popular Culture, 1884–1914* (Stanford: Stanford University Press, 1990).

62. On the mass culture debate, see, as a start, Raymond Williams, *Culture and Society* (Harmondsworth, England: Penguin, 1963); Patrick Brantlinger, *Bread and Circuses: Theories of Mass Culture as Social Decay* (Ithaca: Cornell University Press, 1983); Philip Slater, *The Origin and Significance of the Frankfurt School* (London: Routledge and Kegan Paul, 1977).

63. Mally describes Lenin's varying attitudes toward culture, by which he sometimes meant the "accumulated knowledge of educated elites" and other times "the civil accomplishments of modern industrial society, such as cleanliness and punctuality." Mally, *Culture of the Future*, p. xvi. See also David Joravsky, "Cultural Revolution and the Fortress Mentality," in *Bolshevik Culture*, ed. Gleason, Kenez, and Stites.

64. Stanley Cohen, *Folk Devils and Moral Panics: The Creation of the Mods and Rockers* (Oxford: Basil Blackwell, 1987).

65. Kathleen McDonnell, *Kid Culture: Children and Adults and Popular Culture* (Toronto: Second Story Press, 1994), pp. 111, 114.

66. Jeffrey Weeks, "AIDS and the Regulation of Sexuality," in *AIDS and Contemporary History*, ed. Virginia Berridge and Philip Strong (Cambridge: Cambridge University Press, 1993), p. 26.

67. Diane P. Koenker, "Class and Consciousness in a Socialist Society: Workers in the Printing Trades during NEP," in *Russia in the Era of NEP: Explorations in Soviet Society and Culture*, ed. Sheila Fitzpatrick, Alexander Rabinowitch, and Richard Stites (Bloomington: Indiana University Press, 1991), p. 45.

2. THE URBAN ENVIRONMENT

1. A. Kollontai, "The Family and the Communist State," in *Bolshevik Visions: First Phase of the Cultural Revolution in Soviet Russia*, ed. William G. Rosenberg (Ann Arbor: University of Michigan Press, 1990), p. 73. Kollontai headed the Women's Bureau (Zhenotdel) from 1920 to 1922.

2. Ibid., p. 76.

3. As late as 1926, there were only 88 males in Soviet Russia to every 100 females aged thirty or older. Wendy Z. Goldman, *Women, the State, and Revolution: Soviet Family Policy and Social Life, 1917–1936* (Cambridge: Cambridge University Press, 1993), p. 60; William G. Rosenberg, "NEP Russia as a 'Transitional' Society," in *Russia in the Era of NEP: Explorations in Soviet Society and Culture*, ed. Sheila Fitzpatrick, Alexander Rabinowitch, and Richard Stites (Bloomington: Indiana University Press, 1991), p. 5. On the social and demographic effects of the Civil War, see also Diane P. Koenker, William G. Rosenberg, and Ronald Grigor Suny, eds., *Party, State and Society in the Russian Civil War: Explorations in Social History* (Bloomington: Indiana University Press, 1989), especially the chapters by Koenker, Daniel R. Brower, and Barbara Evans Clements.

4. Lenin, "Introducing the New Economic Policy" (March 15, 1921), translated in Robert Tucker, ed., *The Lenin Anthology* (New York: W. W. Norton and Company, 1975), p. 508.

5. William J. Chase, *Workers, Society, and the Soviet State: Labor and Life in Moscow, 1918–1929* (Urbana: University of Illinois Press, 1987), p. 173.

6. Elizabeth A. Wood, *The Baba and the Comrade: Gender and Politics in Revolutionary Russia* (Bloomington: Indiana University Press, 1997), pp. 150–151.

7. Lewis H. Siegelbaum, *Soviet State and Society between Revolutions, 1918–1929* (Cambridge: Cambridge University Press, 1992), p. 93.

8. S. A. Zolotarev, *Chetyre smeny molodezhi, 1905–1925* (Leningrad: Izd. kooperativnoe, 1926), pp. 68–69, 72.

9. For more on the disease of Soviet nervousness, see Francis L. Bernstein, "What Everyone Should Know about Sex: Gender, Sexual Enlightenment, and the Politics of Health in Revolutionary Russia, 1918–1931" (Ph.D. diss., Columbia University, 1998), pp. 184–197.

10. Wendy Z. Goldman, "Working Class Women and the 'Withering Away' of the Family: Popular Responses to Family Policy," in *Russia in the Era of NEP,* ed. Fitzpatrick, Rabinowitch, and Stites, p. 126. On Soviet policy toward the family, see also David L. Ransel, ed., *The Family in Imperial Russia: New Lines of Historical Research* (Urbana: University of Illinois Press, 1978); Beatrice Farnsworth, "The Bolshevik Alternatives and Soviet Family Law: The 1926 Marriage Law Debate, " in *Women in Russia,* ed. Dorothy Atkinson, Alexander Dallin, and Gail Lapidus (Stanford: Stanford University Press, 1977); and Kent Geiger, *The Family in Soviet Russia* (Cambridge, Mass.: Harvard University Press, 1968).

11. Following further liberalization of divorce in 1927, three-quarters of all marriages in Moscow ended in divorce, and in Leningrad, two-thirds. Goldman, *Women, the State, and Revolution,* p. 297. For another interpretation of rising divorce rates and attitudes toward the family, see Barbara Evans Clements, "The Effects of the Civil War on Women and Family Relations," in *Party, State, and Society in the Russian Civil War,* ed. Koenker, Rosenberg, and Suny, p. 115.

12. Goldman, "Working Class Women," p. 130. Despite legal provisions for alimony, it proved very difficult to collect.

13. Goldman, *Women, the State, and Revolution,* pp. 127–128.

14. Speech by Comrade Beliaeva and Comrade Shtern in V. Dmitriev and B. Galin, *Na putiakh k novomu bytu* (Moscow: Izd. "Novaia Moskva," 1927), pp. 35, 40.

15. V. I. Kufaev, *Iunye pravonarushiteli,* 2nd ed. (Moscow, 1925), pp. 185, 188, as cited in Peter H. Juviler, "Contradictions of Revolution: Juvenile Crime and Rehabilitation," in *Bolshevik Culture: Experiment and Order in the Russian Revolution,* ed. Abbott Gleason, Peter Kenez, and Richard Stites (Bloomington: Indiana University Press, 1985), p. 264.

16. In 1924, Moscow working-class families had on average 1.3 working members. The average salary of the head of the household, 81.47 rubles, did not cover family expenses. E. O. Kabo, *Ocherki rabochego byta. Opyt monograficheskogo issledovaniia domashnego rabochego byta,* vyp. 1 (Moscow: VTsSPS, 1928), p. 24.

17. A. K. Pokrovskaia, "Domashniaia zhizn' moskovskikh detei," *Vestnik prosveshcheniia* 1 (1922), p. 13. Pokrovskaia studied the families with particular attention to the participation of adults in their children's education, hygiene, and everyday life.

18. Goldman, *Women, the State, and Revolution,* pp. 128–129.

19. Comrade Shtern in Dmitriev and Galin, *Na putiakh,* p. 39, and Comrade Petrova, ibid., pp. 29–30.

20. Jiri Zuzanek, *Work and Leisure in the Soviet Union* (New York: Praeger, 1980), pp. 177–180; Markoosha Fisher, *My Lives in Russia* (New York: Harper and Brothers, 1944), p. 71. Men spent less than two hours a day on household chores.

21. Susan M. Kingsbury and Mildred Fairchild, *Factory, Family, and Women in the Soviet Union* (New York: G. P. Putnam's Sons, 1935), p. 251. This is compared to

the two hours a day these women spent on cooking and two hours on travel and shopping. Although the survey is from 1931, proportions were little better during NEP.

22. Pokrovskaia, "Domashniaia zhizn'," p. 13.

23. As cited in M. Al'butskii, "Ideologiia sovetskogo shkol'nika," *Vestnik prosveshcheniia* 10 (1927), p. 51. From a survey of 900 school children, 92 percent of whom were working-class.

24. Sheila Fitzpatrick, *Education and Social Mobility in the Soviet Union, 1921–1934* (Cambridge: Cambridge University Press, 1979), p. 51. See also James McClelland, "Proletarianizing the Student Body: The Soviet Experience during the New Economic Policy," *Past and Present* 80 (August 1978).

25. M. M. Kucherenko, "Podgotovka kvalifitsirovannoi rabochei sily v SSSR (20-e–pervaia polovina 30-kh godov)," *Voprosy istorii* 10 (October 1985), p. 23.

26. I will return to the topic of juvenile delinquency in later chapters. For an example of the explicit association made between unemployment and delinquency, see, for example, the 15th Party Conference as discussed in L. S. Rogachevskaia, *Likvidatsiia bezrabotitsy v SSSR 1917–1930* (Moscow: Nauka, 1973), pp. 131–132.

27. Barskaia, Teleshevskaia, Truneva, Ianovich, and Iakunichkin, "Deiatel'nost' rebenka po obsluzhivaniiu sem'i," in *Trud i dosug rebenka*, ed. A. Gel'mont and A. Durikin (Moscow: "Novaia Moskva," 1927), pp. 26, 37.

28. Kabo, *Ocherki rabochego byta*, p. 50.

29. V. A. Zaitsev, *Trud i byt rabochikh podrostkov* (Moscow: "Voprosy truda," 1926), p. 258; P. I. Kurkin, *Moskovskaia rabochaia molodezh'* (Moscow: Moszdravotdela, 1925), pp. 20–21. Seventy-eight percent of working-class youth throughout urban Russia lived in apartments. In Leningrad the figure was slightly higher, 90 percent, and in Moscow lower, 70 percent. Twelve percent of working-class youth in Russia as a whole lived in communal living situations [*dom kommuny*], including 17 percent in Moscow and 4.4 percent in Leningrad. Zaitsev's 1923 survey was the first all-Russian medical inspection of adolescent workers. The majority of the 48,718 completed questionnaires were received from youth aged sixteen and seventeen. Kurkin's survey covered working-class boys and girls in Moscow and Moscow *guberniia*. The majority were between the ages of sixteen and eighteen.

30. Zaitsev, *Trud i byt*, p. 258. Approximately 10 percent of Russian working-class youth lived under these conditions. Zaitsev's and Kurkin's figures differ for Moscow. Kurkin argues that only 62 percent of Moscow youth lived in apartments, and 20.2 percent in barracks, while according to Zaitsev, 70 percent lived in apartments and only 13.5 percent in barracks. I have used Zaitsev's figures in order to have a consistent means of comparison among Moscow, Leningrad, and urban Russia as a whole.

31. I. S., "Gor'kii koren'," *Izvestiia*, March 8, 1928, p. 6.

32. *Trud, zdorov'e i byt Leningradskoi rabochei molodezhi* (Leningrad: Leningradskogo Gubzdravotdela, 1925), p. 15. In 1923, 59.3 percent of working-class youth in Leningrad and 52.5 percent in Moscow complained that their living conditions were unsatisfactory. This survey was carried out by a special youth department of the Leningrad Health Department [*Gubzdravotdela*]. In 1923, 6,184 adolescents between the ages of fourteen and nineteen were studied, and approximately 7,500 in 1924. See also Kurkin, *Moskovskaia rabochaia*, p. 20.

33. Kingsbury and Fairchild, *Factory, Family, and Women in the Soviet Union*, pp. 196–197; Walter Duranty, *I Write as I Please* (New York: Simon and Schuster, 1935), pp. 110–113.

34. Kurkin, *Moskovskaia rabochaia*, p. 20.

35. Kabo, *Ocherki rabochego byta*, p. 24; Zaitsev, *Trud i byt*, p. 32. Although I do not have any figures on the total number of urban youth throughout the Soviet

Union who lived with their families, in Leningrad the figure was 80 to 85 percent. Throughout Russia, 80 percent of all working-class youth ate with their families, suggesting that approximately this number also lived at home, except for students who lived and studied elsewhere but ate at home. See *Trud, zdorov'e i byt Leningradskoi rabochei molodezhi*, p. 12, and N. B. Lebina, *Rabochaia molodezh' Leningrada. Trud i sotsial'nyi oblik, 1921–1925 gg.* (Leningrad: Izdatel'stvo Nauka, 1982), p. 30.

36. Kabo, *Ocherki rabochego byta*, p. 173.

37. Students' abysmally poor conditions were the subject of numerous articles in the student and Komsomol press. The data cited here comes from *Krasnoe studenchestvo* 9 (May 1927), p. 49, and I. G. Vaisman, "Kul'tura i byt studenchestva," *Na fronte kommunisticheskogo prosveshcheniia* 12 (December 1932), p. 64.

38. Lebina, *Rabochaia molodezh'*, p. 153.

39. Clements, "The Effects of the Civil War on Women and Family Relations," p. 122, fn. 32; A. V. Kosareva and I. A. Kravalia, eds., *Molodezh' SSSR. Statisticheskii sbornik* (Moscow: TsUNKhU Gosplana SSSR i TsKVLKSM, 1936), pp. 320–321. Only 5 percent of young urban men got married before the age of twenty in 1926, and 24 percent of young women. In rural areas, 20 percent of men and 36 percent of women got married before the age of twenty. These figures are for 1926 in the European parts of the RSFSR, Ukraine, and Belorusiia.

40. On the influence of economic conditions, see S. Ia. Vol'fson, *Sotsiologiia braka i sem'i* (Minsk: Izd. Belorusskogo gosudarstvennogo universiteta, 1929), pp. 426–427.

41. *Trud, zdorov'e, i byt Leningradskoi rabochei molodezhi*, pp. 16–17.

42. Zaitsev, *Trud i byt*, p. 30.

43. *Krasnoe studenchestvo* 9 (May 1927), p. 48.

44. I. S., "Gor'kii koren'," *Izvestiia*, March 8, 1928, p. 6; *Krasnoe studenchestvo* 9 (November 1926), p. 32. See also D. I. Lass, "Byt Odesskogo studenchestva," *Nauchnyi rabotnik* 5–6 (May–June 1927), pp. 80–88.

45. N. Ognyov [Ognev], *Diary of a Communist Undergraduate*, trans. Alexander Werth (New York: Payson and Clarke, 1929), p. 132. The inhibiting impact of daily realities on revolutionary participation was informally confirmed in a series of interviews I conducted with senior citizens in a Soviet rest home. When I asked one women of eighty-one what her impressions had been of the revolution, she responded, "How could I even think about it? I thought only about how to survive, how to find milk for my aunt" (March 29, 1991).

46. Ivan T. Bobryshev, *Melkoburzhuaznye vliianiia sredi molodezhi* (Moscow-Leningrad: Molodaia gvardiia, 1928), p. 57.

47. W. I. Hryshko, "An Interloper in the Komsomol," in *Soviet Youth: Twelve Komsomol Histories*, ed. Nikolai K. Novak-Deker (Munich: Institute for the Study of the USSR, 1959), p. 91.

48. Kabo, *Ocherki rabochego byta*, p. 32.

49. M. Erogov, "Ekonomicheskoe i kul'turno-bytovoe polozhenie rabochei molodezhi," *Iunyi kommunist* 21 (November 1927), p. 53; Diane Koenker, "Urban Families, Working-Class Youth Groups and the 1917 Revolution in Moscow," in *The Family in Imperial Russia: New Lines of Historical Research*, ed. David L. Ransel (Urbana: University of Illinois Press, 1978), p. 292.

50. Chase, *Workers, Society and the Soviet State*, p. 141.

51. Figures vary on the precise number of unemployed juveniles. Unemployment data is based on those who registered at the Labor Exchanges; however, many adolescents did not register, and in some areas there was not even a Labor Exchange at which they could register. Information on the proportion of jobless who were juveniles can be found in Rogachevskaia, *Likvidatsiia*, p. 133, and Erogov, "Ekonomicheskoe," pp. 53, 57. According to Rogachevskaia, this figure varied from 16.9 percent in October 1924, to 13.2 percent in October 1925, to 17.6 percent in 1928.

52. Erogov, "Ekonomicheskoe," p. 53; Chase, *Workers, Society, and the Soviet State,* pp. 109, 150. On average, 55 percent of the unemployed adolescents were boys and 45 percent girls. In the Moscow industrial region that meant that girls and boys were unemployed at about the same rate. In 1923 in this region, girls between the ages of fifteen and twenty-four made up about 44 percent of the juvenile work force. See Rogachevskaia, *Likvidatsiia,* p. 134, and *Itogi vsesoiuznoi gorodskoi perepisi 1923 g.,* chast' 3, vyp. 1, *Naselenie gorodov soiuza S.S.R. po vozrastu, zaniatiiam i semeinomu sostoianiiu* (Moscow: Trudy tsentral'nogo statisticheskogo upravleniia, 1926), pp. 140–141.

53. Chase, *Workers, Society, and the Soviet State,* p. 151.

54. Nikolai Bokharin, *Kommunisticheskaia partiia Sovetskogo Soiuza. XIII s"ezd. Stenograficheskii otchet,* May 1924 (Moscow, 1963), p. 524.

55. Lebina, *Rabochaia molodezh',* p. 34.

56. Rogachevskaia, *Likvidatsiia,* pp. 133–134.

57. Lebina, *Rabochaia molodezh',* p. 34.

58. Vera Ketlinskaia, "Zdravstvui, molodost'!" *Novyi mir* 11 (November 1975), p. 56.

59. As cited in Lebina, *Rabochaia molodezh',* p. 35.

60. As cited in Bobryshev, *Melkoburzhuaznye vliianiia sredi molodezhi,* p. 102.

61. Tsentr Khraneniia Dokumentov Molodezhnykh Organizatsii (TsKhDMO), f. 1, op. 23, d. 506, l. 102.

62. TsKhDMO, f. 1, op. 23, d. 506, l. 36.

63. *Odinnadtsatyi s"ezd RKP(b). Stenograficheskii otchet* (Moscow, 1961), pp. 41–43.

64. Kucherenko, "Podgotovka kvalifitsirovannoi rabochei sily v SSSR," p. 23.

65. Ibid., p. 25.

66. See the discussion in Wood, *The Baba and the Comrade,* pp. 148–151.

67. Iu. Ia. Poborinskii, "Sviaz zhiznennykh uslovii s zabolevaemost'iu podrostkov," *Molodoi rabochii* 3 (September 1925), pp. 49–50.

68. *Trud, zdorov'e i byt Leningradskoi rabochei molodezhi,* p. 29. This information is from thirty-eight *guberniia* throughout the USSR in 1923. Although some youth still worked more than six hours, there had been a distinct improvement over pre-revolutionary conditions. In 1913, 69 percent of youth under the age of fifteen worked eight hours. Ninety-three percent of those between the ages of sixteen and nineteen worked nine hours or more.

69. *Iunyi kommunist* 6–7 (April 1922), p. 30. Reported by a Komsomol member in Smolensk.

70. V. Bylakh, "Voprosy truda molodezhi v svete kontrol'nykh tsifr gosplana," *Iunyi kommunist* 1 (October 1925), p. 19. In 1919, young workers were paid 98 percent of what adult workers were paid. In 1922, they were paid just 65 percent.

71. I. A. Ariamov, L. I. Odintsova, and E. I. Nechaeva, *Ditia rabochego* (Moscow: Novaia Moskva, 1926), p. 32.

72. L. I. Odintsova, "Idealy i interesy uchashchikhsia trudovykh shkol g. Moskvy," *Vestnik prosveshcheniia* 4 (1927), pp. 13–23. This was a survey of 1,054 young people, of whom 67 percent were working-class and 25 percent white-collar.

73. Odintsova, "Idealy i interesy," pp. 13–23. See also A. I. Kolodnaia, *Interesy rabochego podrostka* (Moscow-Leningrad: Molodaia gvardiia, 1929).

74. A. Lunacharsky, ed., *Upadochnoe nastroenie sredi molodezhi. Eseninshchina* (Moscow: Izd. kommunisticheskoi akademii, 1927), p. 74.

3. MAKING YOUTH COMMUNIST

1. Stephen Kotkin, *Magnetic Mountain: Stalinism as a Civilization* (Berkeley: University of California Press, 1995).

2. Ralph Fisher, *Pattern for Soviet Youth: A Study of the Congresses of the Komsomol, 1918–1954* (New York: Columbia University Press, 1959), and "The Soviet Model of the Ideal Youth," in *The Transformation of Russian Society,* ed. Cyril E. Black (Cambridge, Mass.: Harvard University Press, 1960). Isabel Tirado also describes the integration of an energetic and autonomous youth movement, largely dedicated to protecting youth's own interests, into an organization dominated by the party and by the party's military, propaganda, and education-related requirements. Isabel A. Tirado, *Young Guard! The Communist Youth League, Petrograd, 1917–1920* (New York: Greenwood Press, 1988). Tirado's later work on the Komsomol in the 1920s has more to say about the lived experiences of the Komsomol'tsy.

3. N. Lebina, *Rabochaia molodezh' Leningrada. Trud i sotsial'nyi oblik, 1921–1925 gg.* (Leningrad: Izdatel'stvo Nauka, 1982), p. 12. There were more than 320,000 youth of Komsomol age (between fourteen and twenty-three) and 32,000 working-class youth in Petrograd in 1918.

4. Fisher, *Pattern for Soviet Youth,* pp. 10, 26, 31; Lebina, *Rabochaia molodezh',* pp. 107–108.

5. In 1928, 8.7 percent of the delegates to the Eighth Komsomol Congress had joined the youth league in 1920 or earlier. Fisher, *Pattern for Soviet Youth,* p. 153. In 1930, the Komsomol had close to three million members and candidate members, and the party, just over a million and a half. Fisher, *Pattern for Soviet Youth,* p. 409, and T. H. Rigby, *Communist Party Membership in the USSR, 1917–1967* (Princeton: Princeton University Press, 1968), p. 52.

6. *Iunyi kommunist* 3–4 (February 1926), p. 51; *Biulleten' IV vsesoiuznoi konferentsii RLKSM,* N. 1–5 (Moscow: Molodaia gvardiia, n.d. [c. 1925]), p. 18.

7. Diane Koenker, "Urban Families, Working-class Youth Groups and the 1917 Revolution in Moscow," in *The Family in Imperial Russia,* ed. David L. Ransel (Urbana: University of Illinois Press, 1978), p. 286.

8. Interview with author, Moscow, May 1990.

9. Tsentr Khraneniia Dokumentov Molodezhnykh Organizatsii (TsKhDMO), f. 1, op. 23, d. 198, ll. 3–4 (on Zionist youth groups). Documents about non-communist youth groups and efforts to suppress them can be found in *Molodezhnoe dvizhenie v Rossii (1917–1928 gg.),* chast' 1, 2 (Moscow: Tsentr Khraneniia Dokumentov Molodeznykh Organizatsii, 1993). See also Margaret Kay Stolee, "A Generation Capable of Establishing Communism: Revolutionary Child Rearing in the Soviet Union, 1917–1928" (Ph.D. diss., Duke University, 1982), pp. 163–165; *Iunyi kommunist* 1–2 (March 1923), p. 54.

10. Vera Ketlinskaia, "Zdravstvui, molodost'!" *Novyi mir* 11 (November 1975), p. 56. This is an autobiographical memoir in the form of a novel.

11. Ibid., p. 58. See also S. A. Zolotarev, *Chetyre smeny molodezhi, 1905–1925* (Leningrad: Izd. kooperativnoe, 1926), p. 158.

12. Nicolai Lunev, "Blind Faith in a Bright Future," in *Soviet Youth: Twelve Komsomol Histories,* ed. Nikolai K. Novak-Deker (Munich: Institute for the Study of the USSR, 1959), p. 31.

13. Nikolai Bocharov, "Off the Beaten Track," in *Soviet Youth,* ed. Novak-Deker p. 43.

14. Ella Winter, *Red Virtue* (London: Victor Gallancz, 1933), p. 91.

15. Anastasyan Vairich, "Youth It Was That Led Us," in *Soviet Youth,* ed. Novak-Deker, p. 59.

16. Bocharov, "Off the Beaten Track," pp. 43–44.

17. For an interesting reading of student autobiographies, see Igal Halfin, "From Darkness to Light: Student Communist Autobiography during NEP," *Jahrbücher für Geschichte Osteuropas* 45, no. 2 (1997).

18. See, for example, TsKhDMO, f. 1, op. 23, d. 506, ll. 36, 102; Lebina, *Rabochaia molodezh',* p. 34.

19. As cited in Lebina, *Rabochaia molodezh'*, p. 108.

20. TsKhDMO, f. 1, op. 23, d. 3215, 1. 209.

21. Industrial workers made up 47.7 percent of the total membership, white-collar workers 33.4 percent, students 15 percent, and the unemployed 3.5 percent. In 1921, there were fewer Komsomol youth in the Petrograd metal factory than in the fifteenth city printing office, and in many city factories not more than 20 percent of the youth belonged to the Komsomol. Isabel Tirado, *Young Guard!*, p. 115, fn. 98. See also Lebina, *Rabochaia molodezh'*, pp. 78, 104. On changes to the working-class base of the party, see Sheila Fitzpatrick, "The Bolsheviks' Dilemma: Class, Culture, and Politics in the Early Soviet Years," *Slavic Review* 47 (Winter 1988), pp. 599–613.

22. Lebina, *Rabochaia molodezh'*, p. 101. Among those in leadership positions, the white-collar class was still more heavily represented. In 1925, 29 percent of provincial secretaries and 23 percent of regional secretaries were from this group, as compared to around 11 percent in the Komsomol as a whole. See *Biulleten' IV vsesoiuznoi*, p. 19.

23. N. B. Lebina, "Molodezh' i NEP. Ot konflikta k edinstvu subkul'tur" (paper presented at a conference on "Youth in Soviet Russia, 1917–1941," Marburg, Germany, May 1999), pp. 9–10.

24. Fisher, *Pattern for Soviet Youth*, p. 11.

25. Isabel A. Tirado, "The Komsomol and Young Peasants: The Dilemma of Rural Expansion, 1921–1925," *Slavic Review* 52:3 (Fall 1993), pp. 460, 465.

26. Joseph Stalin, "On the Contradictions in the Young Communist League," in *Collected Works*, vol. 6 (Moscow: Foreign Languages Publishing House, 1953), p. 70. See also "O rabote Komsomola v derevne" and "O rabote sredi molodezhi," in *KPSS o Komsomole i molodezhi* (Moscow: Molodaia gvardii, 1962), pp. 48–55, 61–64.

27. TsKhDMO, f. 1, op. 23, d. 315, ll. 119–120.

28. In 1918, at the first congress of the Komsomol, there were 2,000 rural members out of a total of 22,100. After the "turn to the village" in 1924, the number increased rapidly, doubling in the last six months of 1924 alone. B. A. Balashov and Nelepin, *VLKSM za 10 let v tsifrakh* (Moscow-Leningrad: Molodaia gvardiia, 1928), p. 8. Figures differ on the number of rural Komsomol members. Tirado writes that by 1926 "peasants accounted for 58.8 percent of the 1.8 million members." Tirado, "The Komsomol and Young Peasants," p. 474.

29. Tirado, "The Komsomol and Young Peasants," p. 474; Lebina, *Rabochaia molodezh'*, p. 109. Throughout the Soviet Union, the average was slightly lower. In a speech at the Fourth Komsomol Congress, the first secretary of the Komsomol, Chaplin, said that on average 50 percent of working-class youth had joined the Komsomol, and in Moscow, Leningrad, and Baku, 85 percent. See *Biulleten' IV vsesoiuznoi*, p. 14.

30. Friction between rural and urban Komsomol members is described in TsKhDMO, f. 1, op. 23, d. 313, ll. 106–107, and *Iunyi kommunist* 1 (January 1925): 12–13.

31. Hesitations about proletarian students derived in part from their support of Trotsky in the party debates of 1923–1924. See chapter 4.

32. *Krasnyi student* 1 (February 1923), p. 23.

33. Ibid., p. 21; Ketlinskaia, "Zdravstvui, molodost'!" p. 31. In 1923, of the approximately 40,000 higher education students in Moscow, a quarter were said to be communists, two-thirds of whom were of proletarian origin. See *Proletarskoe studenchestvo* 1 (April 1923), p. 110.

34. N. Vigilianskii, "O studencheskom byte," *Iunyi kommunist* 11–12 (June 1927), pp. 78–79.

35. L. Balabanov, "Zateriannaia tsennost'," in *Kakim dolzhen byt' kommunist*, ed. E. Iaroslavskii (Moscow-Leningrad: Molodaia gvardiia, 1925), p. 115.

36. A. Kollontai, "The Family and the Communist State," in *Bolshevik Visions*, ed. William G. Rosenberg (Ann Arbor: University of Michigan Press, 1990), pp. 75–76.

37. Lynn Mally, *Culture of the Future: The Proletkult Movement in Revolutionary Russia* (Berkeley: University of California Press, 1990), p. 180.

38. V. A. Murin, *Byt i nravy derevenskoi molodezhi* (Moscow: Izd. "Novaia Moskva," 1926), pp. 13–14; TsKhDMO, f. 1, op. 23, d. 315, l. 100. Parents sometimes mocked the Komsomol, laughing, for example, at the name of one of the Komsomol sports organizations, Spartak. "Spartak, Spartak!! It's a name for a dog. A human being won't come to such a name." Murin, *Byt i nravy*, p. 45.

39. Stephen A. Smith, *Red Petrograd: Revolution in the Factories, 1917–1918* (Cambridge: Cambridge University Press, 1983), p. 197. On young people in the revolution, see also Tsuyoshi Hasewaga, *The February Revolution: Petrograd, 1917* (Seattle: University of Washington Press, 1981). For an analysis of elements of youth culture during the war and revolution which contributed to the growing radicalization of youth in this period, see Koenker, "Urban Families," and Diane P. Koenker, "Urbanization and Deurbanization in the Russian Revolution and Civil War," in *Party, State, and Society in the Russian Civil War: Explorations in Social History*, ed. Diane P. Koenker, William G. Rosenberg, and Ronald Grigor Suny (Bloomington: Indiana University Press, 1989), pp. 88–89.

40. Koenker, "Urban Families," p. 300.

41. For a full discussion of this early history, see Tirado, *Young Guard!* pp. 18–24, and "The Socialist Youth Movement in Revolutionary Petrograd," *Russian Review* 46 (1987); Fisher, *Pattern for Soviet Youth*.

42. *KPSS o Komsomole i molodezhi*, pp. 7–9, 12, 15–16; *Biulleten' IV vsesoiuznoi*, pp. 14, 63. Of the 176 official delegates who attended the founding congress of the Komsomol in October 1918, 88 were members of the Bolshevik party, 38 were "Bolshevik sympathizers," and only 46 were without affiliation (Peter Kenez, *The Birth of the Propaganda State: Soviet Methods of Mass Mobilization, 1917–1929* [Cambridge: Cambridge University Press, 1985], p. 88). Young people were not as prominent in positions of party leadership. In city soviets throughout the Soviet Union, Komsomol members made up only 4.9 percent of those elected in 1926, and 6.3 percent in 1927. See Balashov and Nelepin, *VLKSM za 10 let v tsifrakh*, p. 24, and I. E. Liubimov, *Komsomol v sovetskom stroitel'stve, 1917–1927* (Moscow-Leningrad: Molodaia gvardiia, 1928).

43. The first quotation is from Aleksandra Kollontai and the second from Inessa Armand, both as cited in Elizabeth A. Wood, *The Baba and the Comrade: Gender and Politics in Revolutionary Russia* (Bloomington: Indiana University Press, 1997), pp. 76, 77.

44. Ibid., p. 208.

45. On these issues, see Diane P. Koenker, "Sons against Fathers on the Shop Floor in Early Soviet Russia: Generational Conflict in the Socialist Workplace" (paper presented at the annual meeting of the American Association for the Advancement of Slavic Studies, Seattle, November 1997), pp. 2–4.

46. V. Ermilov, "Komsomol'skaia pechat' i zaprosy molodezhi," *Molodaia gvardiia* 1 (1926), p. 235.

47. V. Dmitriev and B. Galin, *Na putiakh k novomu bytu* (Moscow: "Novaia Moskva," 1927), p. 68.

48. A. Stratonitskii, *Voprosy byta v komsomole* (Leningrad: "Priboi," 1926), p. 103.

49. TsKhDMO, f. 1, op. 5, d. 13, ll. 10, 11. It is unclear from archival sources whether such an organization was ever actually formed. Some argued that it was not necessary, given the number of other local groups dedicated to these issues.

50. Stratonitskii, *Voprosy byta v komsomole*, p. 95.

51. N. Krupskaia, "What a Communist Ought to Be Like," in *Bolshevik Visions*, p. 40, and N. Krupskaia, "O zadachakh khudozhestvennogo vospitaniia," Gosudarstvennyi Arkhiv Rossiiskoi Federatsii (GARF), f. 298, op. 1, g. 55, l. 331.

52. Lunev, "Blind Faith in a Bright Future," p. 31.

53. T. A. Retizova, *Kul'turno-prosvetitel'naia rabota v 1917–1925 gg.* (Moscow: Ministerstvo kul'tury RSFSR, 1968), pp. 37, 87; Lebina, *Rabochaia molodezh'*, p. 122; Stratonitskii, *Voprosy byta v komsomole*, p. 105.

54. *Pis'mo iz uteriannogo portfelia*, ed. L. Lebedev and L. Rubinshtein (Moscow: Molodaia gvardiia, 1928), p. 31.

55. Stratonitskii, *Voprosy byta v komsomole*, p. 108.

56. As cited in Fisher, *Pattern for Soviet Youth*, p. 41.

57. TsKhDMO, f. 1, op. 5, d. 13, ll. 2–4.

58. TsKhDMO, f. 1, op. 5, d. 13, l. 4. On Komsomol "police duties," see also Lev Kopelev's description in *The Education of a True Believer*, trans. Gary Kern (New York: Harper and Row, 1980), pp. 60–61.

59. Here I am manipulating Foucault's terms. See Michel Foucault, *Discipline and Punish: The Birth of the Prison*, trans. Alan Sheridan (New York: Vintage, 1979).

60. Vl. Dunaevskii, "Kommuny molodezhi," *Iunyi kommunist* 16 (November 1919), p. 6.

61. Richard Stites, *Revolutionary Dreams: Utopian Vision and Experimental Life in the Russian Revolution* (New York: Oxford University Press, 1989), pp. 207, 213, 216. On student communes during the 1860s, see Daniel R. Brower, *Training the Nihilists: Education and Radicalism in Tsarist Russia* (Ithaca: Cornell University Press, 1975), pp. 223–226.

62. M. Iankovskii, *Kommuna sta tridtsati trekh* (Leningrad: "Priboi," 1929), pp. 11, 33.

63. *Iunyi kommunist* 1 (January 1929), p. 45.

64. Ibid.

65. Stratonitskii, *Voprosy byta v komsomole*, p. 84.

66. Iankovskii, *Kommuna sta tridtsati trekh*, pp. 41–42.

67. Nikolai Kanin, *O druzhbe i tovarishchestve v komsomole* (Leningrad: "Krasnaia Gazeta," 1927), p. 4; Iankovskii, *Kommuny sta tridtsati trekh*, p. 50; Klaus Mehnert, *Youth in Soviet Russia*, trans. Michael Davidson (Westport, Conn.: Hyperion Press, [1933] 1981), p. 183. There are some interesting continuities in communal culture across national boundaries. Komsomol anxiety about relationships resembles that of the American community of Oneida, where children were taught "not to form exclusive friendships that left out other members of the peer group." Rosabeth Moss Kanter, *Commitment and Community: Communes and Utopias in Sociological Perspective* (Cambridge, Mass.: Harvard University Press, 1972), p. 89. See also the discussion of communes and their regulation of space and language in James C. Scott, *Domination and the Arts of Resistance: Hidden Transcripts* (New Haven: Yale University Press, 1990), pp. 127–128.

68. Mehnert, *Youth in Soviet Russia*, p. 174.

69. Stratonitskii, *Voprosy byta v komsomole*, pp. 82–84. See also P. G., "Kommuna 'Krasnyi kauchuk,'" *Smena* 4 (March 1924), p. 30.

70. Iankovskii, *Kommuna sta tridtsati trekh*, pp. 134–136.

71. Mehnert, *Youth in Soviet Russia*, p. 176; A. Naishtat, I. Rybkin, and I. Sosnovik, *Kommuny molodezhi* (Moscow: Molodaia gvardiia, 1931), pp. 59–60.

72. Mehnert, *Youth in Soviet Russia*, pp. 182–183.

73. Iankovskii, *Kommuna sta tridtsati trekh*, pp. 42–43, 60.

74. Mehnert, *Youth in Soviet Russia*, pp. 169–170.

75. *Iunyi kommunist* 9 (October 1923), p. 26; Mehnert, *Youth in Soviet Russia*, pp. 166; P. G., "Kommuna 'Krasnyi kauchuk,'" p. 30.

76. Iankovskii, *Kommuna sta tridtsati trekh*, p. 45.

206 Notes to pages 56–58

77. Dmitriev and Galin, *Na putiakh*, p. 17.

78. Iankovskii, *Kommuna sta tridtsati trekh*, pp. 55–56, 59.

79. Mehnert, *Youth in Soviet Russia*, pp. 164–165.

80. Like so many things, youth communes changed during the First Five-Year Plan. Fellow traveler Klaus Mehnert described returning to one student commune in 1933 that he had first visited in the 1920s. Whereas before men and women lived in single-sex rooms, now each couple had their own room. In part it may have been that the young people who had joined the commune as adolescents had now grown up and demanded allowances for their new, "personal" interests. Significantly, however, their personal interests now coincided with the new atmosphere of the 1930s, which emphasized industrialization and productivity rather than the egalitarianism of the communal movement. Mehnert's communards now criticized the communal vision of the 1920s as "petit-bourgeois, left-deviation, Trotskyist leveling mania." They defended their "right" to a three-room apartment as compensation for their contribution to the Five-Year Plan or their position as "First Engineer." On the other hand, not all efforts to organize communally ended with NEP. A book on youth communes published by the Komsomol press in 1931 still discussed the ways in which the communal movement could contribute to new ways of life, and some workers in the early years of industrialization organized themselves in production communes and collectives that shared wages equally among their members. However, these remaining efforts now ran against the Stalinist tide that explicitly emphasized differentials in wages and status as opposed to egalitarianism. Mehnert, *Youth in Soviet Russia*, p. 253. Naishtat, Rybkin, and Sosnovik, *Kommuny molodezhi;* Iu. Larin, *Stroitel'stvo sotsializma i kollektivizatsiia byta* (Leningrad: "Priboi," 1930); V. Kovanov, "Those Unforgettable Student Days," in *The Young in the Revolution*, ed. Vladimir Sevruk (Moscow: Progress Publishers, 1973), pp. 180–183; Lewis Siegelbaum, "Production Collectives and Communes and the 'Imperatives' of Soviet Industrialization, 1929–1931," *Slavic Review* 45:1 (Spring 1986).

81. Vl. Al'tman, "Pokolenie oktiabria v bor'be za novyi byt," in *Za novyi byt*, ed. M. S. Epshtein (Moscow: "Doloi negramotnost'," 1925), p. 293.

82. V. V. Mel'nikov, *Kul'turnaia revoliutsiia i Komsomol* (Rostov-on-Don: Izd. Rostovskogo universiteta, 1973), p. 49.

83. Factory clubs were attended by both Komsomol and non-Komsomol youth, while clubs in primary and secondary schools seem to have been attended almost exclusively by Komsomol youth. GARF, f. 5451, op. 7, d. 467, l. 87; Chepurnova and Nikitina, "Obshchestvennaia rabota shkol'nika," in *Trud i dosug rebenka*, ed. A. Gel'mont and A. Durikin (Moscow: "Novaia Moskva," 1927), p. 44.

84. Erogov, "Ekonomicheskoe i kul'turno-bytovoe polozhenie rabochei molodezhi," *Iunyi kommunist* 21 (November 1927), p. 60. See *Kluby Moskvy i gubernii* (Moscow: Izd. Moskovskii gubernskii sovet professional'nykh soiuzov "Trud i kniga," 1926), p. 10; GARF, f. 5451, op. 6, d. 460, ll. 1–2; John Hatch, "Workers' Clubs and the Search for a Socialist Working Class Culture" (unpublished paper, 1988), pp. 6, 7. See also *Iunyi kommunist* 3–4 (February 1926), p. 73; "Klubnaia rabota," TsKhDMO, f. 1, op. 23, d. 245, ll. 53–55; "Vsem proforganizatsiiam i organam RLKSM. O rabote iunosheskikh sektsii pri rabochikh klubakh," Komsomol Central Committee, September 25, 1925, TsKhDMO, f. 1, op. 23, d. 390, l. 29; Mel'nikov, *Kul'turnaia revoliutsiia*, p. 49.

85. "Ob organizatsii i rabote 'krasnykh ugolkov,'" GARF, f. 5451, op. 7, d. 467, ll. 113–115.

86. V. Leizerovich, ed., *Komsomol na kul'turnom fronte. Iz opyta Moskovskoi organizatsii komsomola* (Moscow: Molodaia gvardiia, 1928), pp. 25–26, 28.

87. V. Zamoskvoretskii, *Klub rabochei molodezhi* (Moscow: "Novaia Moskva," 1924), pp. 36–42; Leizerovich, *Komsomol na kul'turnom fronte*, pp. 62–63; Mehnert, *Youth in Soviet Russia*, p. 63; GARF, f. 5451, op. 6, d. 460, ll. 14–15.

88. V. I. Lenin, "The Tasks of the Youth League" (October 2, 1920), in *On Youth* (Moscow: Progress Publishers, 1970), pp. 250–251.

89. *KPSS o Komsomole i molodezhi,* pp. 53, 56; Peter Gooderham, "The Komsomol and Worker Youth: The Inculcation of 'Communist Values' in Leningrad during NEP," *Soviet Studies* 4 (October 1982), pp. 508, 510; GARF, f. 2316, op. 4, d. 169, l. 144; *IV s"ezd RKSM. Stenograficheskii otchet* (Moscow-Leningrad: Molodaia gvardiia, 1925), pp. 208–210.

90. Lebina, *Rabochaia molodezh',* pp. 120–121; GARF, f. 5451, op. 7, d. 467, l. 125.

91. *Krasnyi student* 2–3 (March–April 1923), pp. 22–23. The same young, politically active men were also the most likely to participate in other voluntary public demonstrations and mass holidays. Christel Lane, *The Rites of Rulers: Ritual in Industrial Society—The Soviet Case* (Cambridge: Cambridge University Press, 1981), p. 169.

92. GARF, f. 5451, op. 7, d. 467, ll. 60a–60b;TsKhDMO, f. 1, op. 23, d. 390, ll. 1–5.

93. Victoria Bonnell, *Roots of Rebellion: Workers' Politics and Organizations in St. Petersburg and Moscow, 1900–1914* (Berkeley: University of California Press, 1983), p. 331; Mark D. Steinberg, *Moral Communities: The Culture of Class Relations in the Russian Printing Industry, 1867–1907* (Berkeley: University of California Press, 1992), pp. 240, 243. For a discussion of the supposed acculturating function of "rational pastimes" in the countryside before the revolution, see Stephen P. Frank, "Confronting the Domestic Other: Rural Popular Culture and Its Enemies in Fin-de-Siècle Russia," in *Cultures in Flux: Lower-Class Values, Practices, and Resistance in Late Imperial Russia,* ed. Stephen P. Frank and Mark D. Steinberg (Princeton: Princeton University Press, 1994).

94. Gooderham, "The Komsomol and Worker Youth," p. 510. A good source for the broad outlines of the political education effort is Kenez, *The Birth of the Propaganda State.* Also see V. A. Zubkov, *Komsomol i kommunisticheskoe vospitanie molodezhi (1918–iiun' 1941 gg.)* (Leningrad: Izd. Leningradskovo universiteta, 1978).

95. Anne O'Hare McCormick, *The Hammer and the Scythe: Communist Russia Enters the Second Decade* (New York: Alfred A. Knopf, 1928), p. 179.

96. Richard Stites, "Bolshevik Ritual Building in the 1920s," in *Russia in the Era of NEP: Explorations in Soviet Society and Culture,* ed. Sheila Fitzpatrick, Alexander Rabinowitch, and Richard Stites (Bloomington: Indiana University Press, 1991), p. 287.

97. As cited in Kenez, *Birth of the Propaganda State,* pp. 91–92. See also Sidney Ploss, "From Youthful Zeal to Middle Age," *Problems of Communism* 7:5 (September–October 1958), pp. 11–12. For an interesting discussion of the relative roles of education and emotion in ritual in another revolutionary situation, see William H. Beezley, Cheryl English Martin, and William E. French, eds., *Rituals of Rule, Rituals of Resistance: Public Celebrations and Popular Culture in Mexico* (Wilmington, Del.: Scholarly Resources, 1994).

98. "The Young Guard" was written first as a poem by Aleksandr Bezymenskii in 1918 and soon after set to music. As cited in *Mass Culture in Soviet Russia,* ed. James von Geldern and Richard Stites (Bloomington: Indiana University Press, 1995), pp. 16–17.

99. Lane, *The Rites of Rulers,* p. 27.

100. Hatch, "Workers' Clubs and the Search for a Socialist Working Class Culture," p. 7; *Kluby Moskvy i guberniia,* pp. 20–34. Also popular were sports groups, radio clubs, and sewing. Political circles were reported to be of mixed interest. Generally less popular were the more instructional club activities, including those dedicated to health and social work. Surveys differed on the exact ranking of these activities, although the general trend remained constant until the end of NEP. A. G. Kagan, *Molodezh' posle gudka* (Moscow-Leningrad: Molodaia gvardiia, 1930), p. 152;

M. M. Rubinshtein, *Iunost'. Po dnevnikam i avtobiograficheskim zapisiam* (Moscow: Izd. vysshikh pedagogicheskikh kursov pri Moskovskom vysshem tekhnich. uchilishche, 1928), p. 119; GARF, f. 5451, op. 7, d. 467, l. 41.

101. Lynn Mally, "The Rise and Fall of the Soviet Youth Theater TRAM," *Slavic Review* 51:3 (Fall 1992), p. 416.

102. Ibid., p. 412. The first drama circle directly affiliated with a factory was established in Petrograd in 1922. By the end of the year there were 269 amateur art circles in city enterprises, and by late 1923 there were 500. Lebina, *Rabochaia molodezh'*, pp. 140–141.

103. L. A. Pinegina, *Sovetskii rabochii klass i khudozhestvennaia kul'tura 1917–1932* (Moscow: izd. Moscovskogo universiteta, 1984), p. 206.

104. Pinegina, *Sovetskii*, pp. 205. See also James von Geldern, "Nietzschean Leaders and Followers in Soviet Mass Theater, 1917–27," in *Nietzsche and Soviet Culture: Ally and Adversary*, ed. Bernice Glatzer Rosenthal (Cambridge: Cambridge University Press, 1994), p. 145.

105. Pinegina, *Sovetskii*, p. 207; Leizerovich, *Komsomol na kul'turnom fronte*, p. 94.

106. Lynn Mally, "Performing the New Woman: The Komsomolka as Actress and Image in Early Soviet Theater," *Journal of Social History* 30:1 (Fall 1996), p. 80; Pinegina, *Sovetskii*, pp. 204–207; Leizerovich, *Komsomol na kul'turnom fronte*, p. 95. See also V. Mironova, *TRAM. Agitatsionnyi molodezhnyi teatr 1920–1930-kh godov* (Leningrad: Iskusstvo, 1977).

107. Attendance at the lectures and discussions amounted to 850,000. GARF, f. 5451, op. 7, d. 467, ll. 73–74. On additional forms of Komsomol theater, especially the *Blue Blouses* [*Siniaia Bluza*], see Richard Stourac and Kathleen McCreery, *Theater as Weapon: Worker's Theater in the Soviet Union, Germany, and Britain, 1917–1934* (London: Routledge and Kegan Paul, 1986).

108. Anastasyan Vairich, "Youth It Was That Led Us," p. 59.

109. Komsomol clubs faced many challenges when they tried to make young people into new men and women. Some of these problems were practical in nature; in letters to the Komsomol Central Committee local club members frequently complained that they received little or no money and scant material assistance in the way of books or newspapers. They also lacked qualified teachers and trained club workers. These problems were particularly intense in the early years when both party and Komsomol were struggling to recover from the severe economic and social dislocations of war. See *Sputnik klubnogo rabotnika* (Moscow: Gos. izd., 1922); TsKhDMO, f. 1, op. 23, d. 390, l. 12; ibid., d. 247, l. 52; ibid., d. 247, ll. 52, 70; GARF, f. 5451, op. 7, d. 467, l. 63.

110. Kagan, *Molodezh' posle gudka*, pp. 26–28.

111. *Iunyi kommunist* 3–4 (February 1926), p. 71. The problem was particularly acute in rural areas. One report to the Komsomol Central Committee from a rural Komsomol group complained that of 175 members, only six or seven were active participants. TsKhDMO, f. 1, op. 23, d. 270, l. 5.

112. Derek Sayer, "Everyday Forms of State Formation: Some Dissident Remarks on Hegemony," in *Everyday Forms of State Formation: Revolution and the Negotiation of Rule in Modern Mexico*, ed. Gilbert M. Joseph and Daniel Nugent (Durham: Duke University Press, 1994), p. 370.

113. Enrollment went from 840,000 to 1,708,000. Fisher, *Pattern for Soviet Youth*, Appendix B, p. 409.

114. Vladimir Kuz'min, "O 'molodoi starosti,' asketizme i kazenshchine," in *Byt i molodezh'*, ed. A. Slepkov (Moscow: "Pravda" i "Bednota," 1926), p. 34. See also *Iunyi kommunist* 3–4 (February 1926), p. 70; GARF, f. 5451, op. 7, d. 467, l. 70; N. Ognyov [Ognev], *Diary of a Communist Schoolboy*, trans. Alexander Werth (New York: Payson and Clarke, 1928), pp. 24–25.

115. M. Danilevski, *Prazdniki obshchestvennogo byta* (Moscow-Leningrad: "Doloi negramotnost'," 1927), pp. 20–23. Stites has a thoughtful discussion of the challenges the Bolsheviks faced in making their rituals as meaningful as those they were meant to replace in "Bolshevik Ritual Building," pp. 306–307.

116. TsKhDMO, f. 1, op. 23, d. 506, ll. 163–164.

117. Kuz'min, "O 'molodoi starosti,' asketizme i kazenshchine," pp. 38–39.

118. Kagan, *Molodezh' posle gudka*, pp. 77–79.

119. Bocharov, "Off the Beaten Track," p. 52. See also Edel'shtein in *Khuliganstvo i ponozhovshchina*, ed. E. K. Krasnushkin, G. M. Segal, and Ts. M. Feinberg (Moscow: Izd. Moszdravotdela, 1927), p. 55.

120. TsKhDMO, f. 1, op. 23, d. 390, l. 6.

121. For a discussion of the debate over the role of entertainment versus education in workers' clubs, see John Hatch, "The Politics of Mass Culture: Workers, Communists, and Proletkult in the Development of Workers' Clubs, 1921–25," *Russian History/Histoire Russe* 13:2–3 (Summer–Fall 1986).

122. Mally, *Culture of the Future*, pp. 185, 189.

123. Lazar Shatskin at the Fourth Komsomol Congress, as quoted in Fisher, *Pattern for Soviet Youth*, p. 81.

124. N. Iu. Vostrikova, *Deiatel'nost' VLKSM po priobshcheniiu molodykh rabochikh k teatral'nomu iskusstvu v usloviiakh nachala sotsialisticheskoi industrializatsii (1926–1928)* (Saratov, 1986), pp. 7–8.

125. N. A. Semashko, *O svetlom i temnom v rabochem bytu* (Moscow: Gos. izd., 1928), p. 16. Like the Komsomol clubs, the pre-revolutionary People's Houses had the explicit purpose of "keeping working class youths from spending their free time in drinking, stealing and other debauches." Diane Koenker, *Moscow Workers and the 1917 Revolution* (Princeton: Princeton University Press, 1981), p. 83. On the social disciplining of pleasure, see John Fiske, *Understanding Popular Culture* (Boston: Unwin Hyman, 1989), p. 75. See also the discussions on pleasure in Hilary Pilkington, *Russia's Youth and Its Culture: A Nation's Constructors and Constructed* (London and New York: Routledge, 1994), pp. 42, 239.

126. Richard Taylor, "The Birth of the Soviet Cinema," in *Bolshevik Culture: Experiment and Order in the Russian Revolution*, ed. Abbott Gleason, Peter Kenez, and Richard Stites (Bloomington: Indiana University Press, 1985), p. 192.

127. A. E. Latsis and L. Keilina, *Deti i kino* (Moscow: Tea-kino-pechat', 1928), pp. 7–8; Leizerovich, *Komsomol na kul'turnom fronte*, p. 104. On the enormous popularity of the movies among adolescents, see also P. I. Liublinskii, *Kinematografiia i deti* (Moscow: "Pravo i zhizn'," 1925); Vladimir Vainshtok and Dm. Iakobson, *Kino i molodezh'* (Moscow-Leningrad: Gos. izd., 1926); and P. I. Liublinskii, *Bor'ba s prestupnost'iu v detskom i iunosheskom vozraste. Sotsial'no-pravovye ocherki* (Moscow: Narkomiust RSFSR, 1923), pp. 95–98. See the discussion of youth and film in Anne E. Gorsuch, "Soviet Youth and the Politics of Popular Culture," *Social History* 17:2 (May 1992), pp. 189–201.

128. Vostrikova, *Deiatel'nost' VLKSM*, pp. 17–18; Ketlinskaia, "Zdravstvui, molodost'!" p. 64.

129. Letter to "Brianskii Gyblit," marked "secret," GARF, f. 5451, op. 7, d. 467, l. 135.

130. GARF, f. 5451, op. 7, d. 467, ll. 66–67. See also N. Krupskaia, "O zadachakh khudozhestvennogo vospitaniia," GARF, f. 298, op. 1, d. 55, ll. 328–330.

131. "Byt, kak on est'," *Krasnoe studenchestvo* 6 (September 1926), p. 70.

132. G. Grigorov and S. Shkotov, *Staryi i novyi byt* (Moscow: Molodaia gvardiia, 1927), p. 103. "Kak vesti kruzhok (itogi odnogo opyta)," *Iunyi kommunist* 3 (June 1923), pp. 17–18. Pre-revolutionary workers were similarly anxious to maintain "order" and "discipline" in their union meetings. "[A] metalworker who attended

meetings of printers in Moscow in 1906–07 observed that they 'were pervaded with such seriousness and respectability . . . that it seemed as if you were attending some sort of *zemstvo* assembly and not a workers' meeting." See Steinberg, *Moral Communities*, p. 243.

133. This phrasing comes from the discussion of *byt* in Svetlana Boym, *Common Places: Mythologies of Everyday Life in Russia* (Cambridge, Mass.: Harvard University Press, 1994), p. 33.

134. M. S. Epshtein, ed., *Za novyi byt* (Moscow: Izd. "Doloi negramotnost'," 1925), p. 40; Stratonitskii, *Voprosy byta v komsomole*, p. 31.

135. Grigorov and Shkotov, *Staryi i novyi byt*, as cited in Stites, *Revolutionary Dreams*, p. 117.

136. Mel'nikov, *Kul'turnaia revoliutsiia*, p. 50. See also Gooderham, "The Komsomol and Worker Youth," p. 509.

137. *Krasnoe studenchestvo* 8 (November 1926), p. 24. For a similar complaint, see Vigilianskii, "O studencheskom byte," p. 76.

138. Stratonitskii, *Voprosy byta v komsomole*, p. 31.

139. Epshtein, ed. *Za novyi byt*, p. 97.

140. V. Kovanov, "Those Unforgettable Student Days," in *The Young in the Revolution*, ed. Vladimir Sevruk (Moscow: Progress Publishers, 1973), p. 178.

141. Lebina, *Rabochaia molodezh'*, pp. 145–146; Mel'nikov, *Kul'turnaia revoliutsiia*, pp. 50–51; Im. Iaroslavskii, "O bor'be s p'ianstvom," in *Byt i molodezh'* (Leningrad: Izd. Leningradskogo oblastnogo soveta profsoiuzov, 1928), p. 21.

142. Laura Lynne Phillips, "Everyday Life in Revolutionary Russia: Working-Class Drinking and Taverns in St. Petersburg, 1900–1929" (Ph.D. diss., University of Illinois, 1993), pp. 79–82. Despite anti-alcohol campaigns, alcohol abuse remained a tremendous problem among adult workers. Drunkenness was the primary cause of worker absenteeism. See William J. Chase, *Workers, Society, and the Soviet State: Labor and Life in Moscow, 1918–1929* (Urbana: University of Illinois Press, 1987), p. 221.

143. Young people were instructed, for example, to expose their parents if they drank. In mass anti-drinking demonstrations outside their parents' factories, Komsomol'tsy would surround the enterprise at closing time carrying placards and banners with anti-drinking slogans, and refuse to let their parents out until they had signed a pledge promising to stop drinking. Phillips, "Everyday Life in Revolutionary Russia," p. 170; William Henry Chamberlin, *Soviet Russia: A Living Record and a History* (Boston: Little, Brown and Co., 1935), p. 325.

144. Phillips, "Everyday Life in Revolutionary Russia," p. 173.

145. I. A. Ariamov, *Rabochii podrostok* (Moscow: Transpechat-NKPS, 1928), p. 26. Out of 238 working-class Komsomol youth surveyed in Moscow, 15 percent admitted that they still drank regularly. Thirty percent said that they drank on holidays and at parties.

146. TsKhDMO, f. 1, op. 23, d. 822, l. 87.

147. Phillips, "Everyday Life in Revolutionary Russia," p. 76, 82. On the manipulation of patriotic and revolutionary language to justify drinking, see Laura L. Phillips, "Message in a Bottle: Working-Class Culture and the Struggle for Revolutionary Legitimacy, 1900–1929," *Russian Review* 56:1 (January 1997), p. 37.

148. *Iunyi kommunist* 1–2 (March 1923), p. 80. Stites, *Revolutionary Dreams*, pp. 109–110.

149. TsKhDMO, f. 1, op. 23, d. 156, ll. 64, 65, 68.

150. This association between church and the tavern was made in the 1870s by Bakunin, but similar sentiments could be attributed to Lenin, who described religion as "stupefaction" and "stultification." See Stites, *Revolutionary Dreams*, pp. 101, 103.

151. Stites, *Revolutionary Dreams*, p. 109.

152. William Reswick, *I Dreamt Revolution* (Chicago: H. Regenery Co., 1952), p. 164. On rural resistance to anti-religious campaigns, see Glennys Young, *Power and the Sacred in Revolutionary Russia: Religious Activists in the Village* (University Park: Pennsylvania State University Press, 1997).

153. "How I Spent My Vacation," a school essay from Ugodskii Zavod. Nauchnyi Arkhiv Rossiiskoi Akademii Obrazovaniia (NA RAO), f. 1, op. 1, d. 243, l. 4.

154. Mikhail Bakhtin, *Rabelais and His World*, trans. Helene Iswolsky (Bloomington: Indiana University Press, 1984), p. 88.

155. Murin, *Byt i nravy*, pp. 37–38; *KPSS o Komsomole i molodezhi*, p. 80. As an example of "hooliganish" behavior, Murin described those youth who "gather in a crowd and head off to meet the church procession while playing the accordion and singing obscene songs."

156. Stites, *Revolutionary Dreams*, p. 110.

157. "O komsomol'skoi paskhe," February 26, 1923, TsKhDMO, f. 1, op. 23, d. 156, l. 56.

158. *Ocherki po istorii Sovetskoi shkoly i pedagogiki, 1921–1931* (Moscow: Izd. Ak. Ped. Nauk R.S.F.S.R., 1961), pp. 292–294.

159. Fisher, *Pattern for Soviet Youth*, pp. 130–131.

160. M. Neznamov, *Iunyi kommunist* 1–2 (January 15–February 1, 1922), p. 16. Emphasis in original. See also A. Mil'chakov, *Komsomol v bor'be za kul'turnyi byt* (Moscow-Leningrad: Molodaia gvardiia, 1927), pp. 30–31, and Il'ia Garkush, "O kul'trabote v soiuze i klube," *Iunyi kommunist* 3–4 (February 1926), p. 69.

161. TsKhDMO, f. 1, d. 2, op. 19, l. 106.

162. TsKhDMO, f. 1, d. 2, op. 19, l. 105.

163. TsKhDMO, f. 1, d. 2, op. 19, l. 106.

164. L. Stal'skii, "Upadochnye nastroenie sredi krest'ianskoi molodezhi," *Iunyi kommunist* 6 (March 1927), p. 54; *Iunyi kommunist* 6 (March 1927), p. 54; Kuz'min, "O molodoi starosti, asketizme i kazenshchine," p. 34.

165. Mil'chakov, *Komsomol v bor'be za kul'turnyi byt*, p. 30.

166. TsKhDMO, f. 1, op. 5, d. 9, l. 1.

167. Helmut Gruber, *Red Vienna: Experiment in Working-Class Culture, 1919–1934* (New York and Oxford: Oxford University Press, 1991), p. 127.

168. Latsis and Keilina, *Deti i kino*, pp. 26–41; Vainshtok and Iakobson, *Kino i molodezh'*, pp. 20, 44–50; TsKhDMO, f. 1, op. 23, d. 389, ll. 1, 5, 7, 36. For further descriptions of these movies, see Denise J. Youngblood, *Soviet Cinema in the Silent Era, 1918–1935* (Austin: University of Texas Press, 1991).

169. For a detailed discussion of these and other popular movies of the period, see Denise J. Youngblood, *Movies for the Masses: Popular Cinema and Soviet Society in the 1920s* (Cambridge: Cambridge University Press, 1992); Richard Taylor, "Soviet Cinema as Popular Culture; or, The Extraordinary Adventures of Mr. Nepman in the Land of the Silver Screen," *Revolutionary Russia* 1 (June 1988); Peter Kenez, *Cinema and Soviet Society, 1917–1953* (Cambridge: Cambridge University Press, 1992).

170. Richard Stites, *Russian Popular Culture: Entertainment and Society since 1900* (Cambridge: Cambridge University Press, 1992), p. 57.

171. Ven'iamin Iadin, "Posle Piati . . . ," *Iunyi Proletarii* 3 (February 1928), p. 14.

172. Letter to Komsomol Secretary Chaplin, November 3, 1925, TsKhDMO, f. 1, op. 23, d. 315, l. 194.

173. TsKhDMO, f. 1, op. 23, d. 680, l. 7.

174. Ognyov, *Diary of a Communist Schoolboy*, pp. 90–91.

175. Ketlinskaia, "Zdravstvui, molodost'! " p. 68.

176. Ibid., p. 33.

177. Ibid., p. 75.

178. Kagan, *Molodezh' posle gudka*, pp. 39, 44.

179. *Dovesti do kontsa bor'bu s nepmanskoi muzykoi* (Moscow-Leningrad: Gos. muzykal'noe izdatel'stvo, 1931), p. 82. For more complaints, see Vl. Kuz'min, "Pis'mo o novom byte," in *Komsomol'skii byt. Sbornik statei*, ed. I. Razin (Moscow-Leningrad: Molodaia gvardiia, 1927), p. 321.

180. O. Tarkhanov, "Ob ushcherbe," *Iunyi kommunist* 1–2 (1922), p. 13.

181. M. Tramp, "Pod fonarem 'El'dorado,'" in *Obyvatel'shchinu na pritsel! Sbornik statei i fel'etonov* (Leningrad: "Krasnaia gazeta," 1928), p. 31. See also *Iunyi kommunist* 3 (June 1923), p. 25.

182. N. Poznanskii, "Revoliutsiia i deti," *Vestnik prosveshcheniia* 1 (1923), pp. 116–125. The majority of students surveyed were in primary school. There was no breakdown by class. Unfortunately, Poznanskii does not tell us whom the rest of the youth admired, or what they wanted to be.

183. N. Rybnikov, "Ideologiia sovremennogo shkol'nika," *Pedologiia* 1 (1928), pp. 153–155. Most of the data included here was from a survey of 3,100 youth aged eight to eighteen from schools all over the Soviet Union, although the vast majority were in Russia.

184. N. Rybnikov, "Kak sovetskii shkol'nik otsenivaet sushchestvuiushchii poriadok," in *Deti i oktiabr'skaia revolutsiia*, ed. V. N. Shul'gina (Moscow: Rabotnik prosveshcheniia, 1928), pp. 139, 142–157. The data here is from a more detailed description of the same research described by Rybnikov above.

185. Iu. I. Kazhdanskaia, "Sotsial'no-politicheskie predstavleniia detei-shkol'nikov pervogo kontsentra trudovoi shkol gor. Odessy," *Pedologiia* 2 (1928). In 1924, the majority of youth surveyed were nine and ten years old; 68 percent of them were from working-class families.

186. Ibid., pp. 87–94.

187. TsKhDMO, f. 1, op. 5, d. 21, l. 13.

188. TsKhDMO, f. 1, op. 23, d. 247, l. 54.

189. Zolotarev, *Chetyre smeny molodezhi*, pp. 87–88.

190. See Sheila Fitzpatrick, *Education and Social Mobility in the Soviet Union, 1921–1934* (Cambridge: Cambridge University Press, 1979), pp. 36–37, for a discussion of relevant changes in educational policy. A sample of student responses to university entrance exams can be found in A. Lunacharsky, ed., *Upadochnoe nastroenie sredi molodezhi. Eseninshchina* (Moscow: Izd. Kommunisticheskoe akademii, 1927), pp. 106–107. For example: "Question: What do you know about the Octobrist Party? Answer: It was a party which existed at the time of the Great French Revolution. Question: Who were the Decembrists? Answer: They were a party which opposed freeing the peasants in 1861." This last answer is particularly illuminating, since the one-hundredth anniversary of the Decembrist uprising had been celebrated just a year earlier.

191. TsKhDMO, f. 1, op. 23, d. 247, l. 55.

192. See Michael David-Fox, "What Is Cultural Revolution?" *Russian Review* 58:2 (April 1999), p. 194.

193. Sayer, "Everyday Forms of State Formation," pp. 373–375.

194. Scott, as summarized by William Roseberry, "Hegemony and the Language of Contention," in *Everyday Forms of State Formation: Revolution and Negociation of Rule in Modern Mexico*, ed. Gilbert M. Joseph and Daniel Nugent (Durham and London: Duke University Press, 1994), p. 357.

4. EXCESSES OF ENTHUSIASM

1. Klaus Mehnert, *Youth in Soviet Russia*, trans. Michael Davidson (Westport, Conn.: Hyperion Press, [1933] 1981), p. 61.

2. For a discussion of the tension between didacticism and "transparency" and its application to culture in another revolutionary situation, see Lynn Hunt,

Politics, Culture, and Class in the French Revolution (Berkeley: University of California Press, 1984), pp. 74–76.

3. Vl. Slepkov, *Na bytovye temy* (Leningrad: "Krasnaia gazeta," 1927), pp. 8–11, 16. The enthusiasm of some youth for the Civil War was captured in a popular play by Kin, titled *Our Youth,* which describes two nineteen-year-old friends traveling to the "last front" against the Whites in 1922 (as cited in Mehnert, *Youth in Soviet Russia,* p. 120): "I know a lot who'd envy us. The war's finished west of the Urals, but here we are off again, back in 1919 . . . Our times—these are the most splendid and greatest of times . . . if I could choose when to live—now or in the Socialist epoch—I would choose the present without a second's consideration. Socialism will last a long time . . . but these years of fighting are already nearing their end. We are chasing them all across Siberia to get a last glimpse of them."

4. "Soiuz na mestakh" and O. Tarkhanov, "Na poroge novogo," both in *Iunyi kommunist* 6–7 (April 1922), pp. 30 and 4 respectively. Komsomol membership dropped dramatically in the post-war period. From the founding of the Komsomol in 1918 to the height of the Civil War in 1920, Komsomol membership had increased rapidly, from just 22,000 members to 400,000. Following the introduction of the New Economic Policy in March 1921, there was a sharp decline. By October 1922, the number of young people in the Komsomol had dropped by more than one-third to 260,000, which was about 1 percent of the eligible population between the ages of fourteen and twenty-three. See Peter Kenez, *The Birth of the Propaganda State: Soviet Methods of Mass Mobilization, 1917–1929* (Cambridge: Cambridge University Press, 1985), p. 168, and *Ocherki istorii Leningradskoi organizatsii VLKSM* (Leningrad: Lenizdat, 1969), p. 103.

5. Mark von Hagen, *Soldiers in the Proletarian Dictatorship: The Red Army and the Soviet Socialist State, 1917–1930* (Ithaca: Cornell University Press, 1990), pp. 191–195.

6. Markoosha Fisher, *My Lives in Russia* (New York: Harper and Brother, 1944), p. 11; Victor Serge, "Vignettes of NEP," in *Verdict of Three Decades,* ed. Julien Steinberg (New York: Duell, Sloan and Pearce, 1950), p. 138. See also O. Tarkhanov, "Ob ushcherbe," *Iunyi kommunist* 1–2 (1922), p. 14; S. A. Zolotarev, *Chetyre smeny molodezhi, 1905–1925* (Leningrad: Izd. kooperativnoe, 1926), pp. 105–108; and S. Shkotov, *Byt molodezhi* (Ivanovo-Voznesensk: "Osnova," 1925), p. 74.

7. See the discussion in Ivan T. Bobryshev, *Melkoburzhuaznye vliianiia sredi molodezhi* (Moscow-Leningrad: Molodaia gvardiia, 1928), p. 98.

8. N. Bukharin, as cited in Ralph Fisher, *Pattern for Soviet Youth: A Study of the Congresses of the Komsomol, 1918–1954* (New York: Columbia University Press), pp. 79–80. Similarly, see P. Shubin, "Molodezh' gorit," as cited in *Kakim dolzhen byt' kommunist,* ed. E. Iaroslavskii (Moscow-Leningrad: Molodaia gvardiia, 1925), pp. 79–80, and "O rabote RKSM" and "Pis'mo TsK RKP" from December 1920 in *KPSS o Komsomole i molodezhi* (Moscow: Molodaia gvardiia, 1962), pp. 14–16.

9. Vera Ketlinskaia, "Zdravstvui, molodost'!" *Novyi mir* 11 (November 1975), p. 46.

10. Letter to Lev Davidovich [Trotsky] from Dmitri Ignat'evich, October 15, 1925, Tsentr Khraneniia Dokumentov Molodezhnykh Organizatsii (TsKhDMO), f. 1, op. 23, d. 315, l. 192.

11. TsKhDMO, f. 1, op. 23, d. 315, l. 193. See also ibid., d. 679, l. 64.

12. Letter to Comrade Stalin from Nikolai Redoka, 1927, ibid., d. 679, l. 15.

13. As cited in Sheila Fitzpatrick, *Education and Social Mobility in the Soviet Union, 1921–1934* (Cambridge: Cambridge University Press, 1979), p. 94. See also a report by Komsomol Secretary Chaplin, June 1925, TsKhDMO, f. 37, op. 4, d. 6, l. 34. A similar sentiment could be found among some members of the Communist Youth International who saw themselves as having the role of "vanguard of the vanguard," dedicated to preventing the "ossification of the party." Richard Cornell, *Revolution-*

214 Notes to pages 82–85

ary Vanguard: The Early Years of the Communist Youth International, 1914–1924 (Toronto: University of Toronto Press, 1982), pp. 88–89.

14. Von Hagen, *Soldiers in the Proletarian Dictatorship*, p. 195.

15. As in a Komsomol poem from *Iunyi proletarii* (1917): "All that is old, powerless, and putrid, / Replacing the old with its own / Great beautiful, young creation." Cited in Isabel A. Tirado, "Nietzschean Motifs in the Komsomol's Vanguardism," in *Nietzsche and Soviet Culture: Ally and Adversary,* ed. Bernice Glatzer Rosenthal (Cambridge: Cambridge University Press, 1994), p. 243.

16. On the party, see T. H. Rigby, *Communist Party Membership in the USSR, 1917–1967* (Princeton: Princeton University Press, 1968), and Lewis H. Siegelbaum, *Soviet State and Society between Revolutions, 1918–1929* (Cambridge: Cambridge University Press, 1992), pp. 128–131.

17. *Trud, otdykh, son komsomol'tsa-aktivista. Po materialam vyborochnogo obsledovaniia biudzhetov vremeni aktivnykh rabotnikov RLKSM,* vyp. 6. (Moscow-Leningrad: Molodaia gvardiia, 1926), pp. 27, 28, 32, 36.

18. M. Teterin, "Protiv vseznaistva, uzkolobogo deiachestva i oblomovshchiny," *Iunyi kommunist* 2 (January 1927), p. 29.

19. Ibid., p. 26.

20. TsKhDMO, f. 1, op. 23, d. 680, l. 6.

21. O tekh, kto rukovodit," in *Komu doverit' rukovodstvo. Sbornik statei* (Moscow-Leningrad: Molodaia gvardiia, 1928), pp. 43–44.

22. *Iunyi kommunist* 7 (April 1927), pp. 61–62.

23. Nikonov, "Iz dnevnika aktivista," *Iunyi kommunist* 4 (July 1923), pp. 23–24.

24. TsKhDMO, f. 1, op. 23, d. 508, l. 51; N. Lebina, *Rabochaia molodezh' Leningrada. Trud i sotsial'nyi oblik, 1921–1925* (Leningrad: Izdatel'stvo Nauka, 1982), p. 109. For more on anarchism and syndicalism within the Komsomol, see TsKhDMO, *Molodezhnoe dvizhenie v Rossii (1917–1928 gg.),* chast' 1, 2 (Moscow, 1993).

25. Tarkhanov, "Na poroge novogo," p. 5; *Iunyi kommunist* 10–12 (July 1922), pp. 5f; TsKhDMO, f. 1, op. 23, d. 198, l. 2. These youth groups are reminiscent of the medieval buffoon societies described by Bakhtin, including one called "Carefree Lads." See Mikhail Bakhtin, *Rabelais and His World,* trans. Helene Iswolsky (Bloomington: Indiana University Press, 1984), p. 97.

26. Leon Trotsky, *The New Course* (Ann Arbor: University of Michigan Press, 1965), p. 24.

27. Ibid., p. 94. See also idem, "Youth and the Phase of Petty Jobs," in *Problems of Everyday Life and Other Writings on Culture and Science* (New York: Monad Press, 1973), and idem, "Vospitanie molodezhi i natsional'nyi vopros," in *Sochineniia* (Moscow-Leningrad: Gos. izd., 1925–27), vol. 21, p. 317.

28. A. I. Kriven'kii, *Komsomol v bor'be za edinstvo svoikh riadov (1921–1932 gg.)* (Moscow: Vysshaia komsomol'skaia shkola, 1980), p. 35. Kriven'kii does not explain how these 40 percent registered their support for Trotsky—whether by survey or vote. The degree of student support for Trotsky has been a matter of debate. On this question, see Peter Konecny, "Revolution and Rebellion: Students in Soviet Institutes of Higher Education, 1921–1928," *Canadian Journal of History* 27 (December 1992), pp. 469f.

29. Fitzpatrick, *Education and Social Mobility,* p. 96.

30. Most of the delegates at the Fourteenth Party Congress in late 1925 supported the moderate position of Stalin and Bukharin (in part because Stalin controlled the selection of delegates). Only 65 delegates voted for the more aggressive economic policies of Trotsky and the Left Opposition (versus 559 against). See Ronald Grigor Suny, *The Soviet Experiment: Russia, the USSR, and the Successor States* (New York: Oxford University Press, 1998), p. 155. On the conflicts in the party leadership in this period, see Isaac Deutscher, *Prophet Unarmed: Leon Trotsky, 1921–29* (New York: Random House, 1973); Stephen F. Cohen, *Bukharin and the Bolshevik Revolu-*

tion: A Political Biography, 1888–1938 (New York: Alfred A. Knopf, 1973); Alexander Erlich, *The Soviet Industrialization Debate, 1924–1928* (Cambridge, Mass.: Harvard University Press, 1960).

31. Joseph Stalin, May 1924, in *Collected Works*, vol. 6, pp. 234–238.

32. See Nikolai Bukharin in Trotsky, *The New Course*, p. 168. Bukharin's leadership in 1917 of the left communists, who were against the peace treaty with Germany and felt themselves to be more radical than Lenin, is described in Cohen, *Bukharin and the Bolshevik Revolution*, p. 64.

33. Fitzpatrick, *Education and Social Mobility*, p. 96, and generally Michael S. Fox, "Political Culture, Purges, and Proletarianization at the Institute of Red Professors, 1921–1929," *Russian Review* 52:1 (January 1993).

34. Fisher, *Pattern for Soviet Youth*, pp. 113–124; Kriven'kii, *Komsomol v bor'be*, pp. 38–46. At the Komsomol congresses in 1924 and 1926, 97 percent of the delegates were party members or candidate members. In addition, certain important members of the Komsomol Central Committee retained their posts for multiple terms.

35. Fitzpatrick, *Education and Social Mobility*, p. 96, and Konecny, "Revolution and Rebellion," pp. 470–472. For more on the purges see Fox, "Political Culture, Purges, and Proletarianization."

36. TsKhDMO, f. 1, op. 23, d. 506, ll. 37, 38, 80.

37. *Krasnoe studenchestvo* 8 (November 1926), p. 4.

38. TsKhDMO, f. 1, op. 23, d. 663, l. 89 (from October 5, 1927); ibid., d. 662, ll. 20, 21, 79 (December 19, 1927); ibid., d. 681, l. 49; ibid., d. 679, l. 17. One Komsomol member who had been expelled from the league in February 1927 returned to demand the release of "all Komsomol members, party and non-party workers who were arrested for being a part of the opposition." Ibid., d. 663, l. 90. See also Kriven'kii, *Komsomol v bor'be*, pp. 74, 78, 83.

39. Lev Kopelev, *Education of a True Believer*, trans. Gary Kern (New York: Harper and Row, 1980), p. 180.

40. Ibid., p. 179.

41. V. Kovanov in *The Young in the Revolution*, ed. Vladimir Sevruk (Moscow: Progress Publishers, 1973), p. 176.

42. TsKhDMO, f. 1, op. 23, d. 508, l. 14; Kriven'kii, *Komsomol v bor'be*, p. 74.

43. TsKhDMO. f. 1, op. 23, d. 820, ll. 41–42; *Slavnyi put' Leninskogo Komsomola*, vyp. 1 (Moscow: Molodia gvardiia, 1974), pp. 364–365.

44. I. Naimov, "Kuda idet Komsomol?" *Iunyi kommunist* 3 (February 1927), pp. 47–53.

45. Hunt, *Politics, Culture, and Class in the French Revolution*, pp. 53–54.

46. For a discussion of some of the multiple meanings of *meshchanstvo*, see Vera Dunham, *In Stalin's Time: Middleclass Values in Soviet Fiction* (Cambridge: Cambridge University Press, 1976), pp. 19–23.

47. L. Sosnovskii, "O kul'ture i meshchanstve," in *Byt' i molodezh*, ed. A. Slepkov (Moscow: "Pravda" i "Bednota," 1926), p. 13.

48. The term "idols of the establishment" comes from Richard Stites, *Revolutionary Dreams: Utopian Vision and Experimental Life in the Russian Revolution* (New York: Oxford University Press, 1989), chapter 3.

49. Vladimir Kuz'min, "O 'molodoi starosti,' asketizme i kazenshchine," in *Byt i molodezh'*, ed. A. Slepkov, p. 28; N. Ognyov [Ognev], *Diary of a Communist Undergraduate*, trans. Alexander Werth (New York: Payson and Clarke, 1929), p. 137; Panteleimon Romanov, *Without Cherry Blossoms*, trans. Leonide Zarine (London: Ernest Benn, 1930), p. 15.

50. A. Slepkov, as cited in S. I. Ploss, "From Youthful Zeal to Middle Age," *Problems of Communism* 7:5 (September–October 1958), p. 12.

51. Ekaterina Strogova, "Womenfolk: Factory Sketches," in *An Anthology of*

Russian Women's Writing, 1777–1992, ed. Catriona Kelly (Oxford: Oxford University Press, 1994), p. 282.

52. Speech from Comrade Shtern in V. Dmitriev and B. Galin, *Na putiakh k novomu bytu* (Moscow: "Novaia Moskva," 1927), p. 41.

53. Speech by Comrade Petrova in ibid., p. 29.

54. From a non-party delegate at a 1920 meeting of the Petrograd Soviet who said, "Comrades, under the bourgeoisie I wore a dirty blouse and the parasites who killed our working brothers and drank their blood wore ties and starched collars, and now our comrade members of the (union) organization have inherited those ties . . . and begun to look cleaner than the bourgeoisie . . . I propose that all leather jackets should be handed in and sent where they are needed." Quoted in Mary McAuley, "Bread without the Bourgeoisie," in *Party, State, and Society in the Russian Civil War: Explorations in Social History*, ed. Diane P. Koenker, William G. Rosenberg, and Ronald Grigor Suny (Bloomington: Indiana University Press, 1989), p. 175.

55. On revolutionary fashion, see John E. Bowlt, "Constructivism and Early Soviet Fashion Design," in *Bolshevik Culture: Experiment and Order in the Russian Revolution*, ed. Abbott Gleason, Peter Kenez, and Richard Stites (Bloomington: Indiana University Press, 1985).

56. T. Kostrov, "Kul'tura i meshchanstvo," *Revoliutsiia i kult'ura* 3–4 (1927), p. 22.

57. Kuz'min, "O 'molodoi starosti,' asketizme i kazenshchine," p. 28.

58. Fisher, *Pattern for Soviet Youth*, p. 83.

59. N. Ognyov [Ognev], *Diary of a Communist Schoolboy*, trans. Alexander Werth (New York: Payson and Clarke, 1929), pp. 19–27.

60. Sergei Nechaev as cited in Daniel R. Brower, *Training the Nihilists: Education and Radicalism in Tsarist Russia* (Ithaca: Cornell University Press, 1975), p. 15.

61. Brower, *Training the Nihilists*, p. 16.

62. On Russia, see Joan Neuberger, *Hooliganism: Crime, Culture, and Power in St. Petersburg, 1900–1914* (Berkeley: University of California Press, 1993); Stephen P. Frank and Mark D. Steinberg, eds., *Cultures in Flux: Lower-Class Values, Practices, and Resistance in Late Imperial Russia* (Princeton: Princeton University Press, 1994); and Laura Engelstein, *The Keys to Happiness: Sex and the Search for Modernity in Fin-de-Siècle Russia* (Ithaca: Cornell University Press, 1992). Of the large literature on this problem elsewhere, see, for example, the articles by Robert Bezucha and Michael Marrus in Jacques Beauroy, Marc Bertrand, and Edward T. Gargan, eds., *The Wolf and the Lamb: Popular Culture in France* (Saratoga, Calif.: Anma Libri and Co., 1976; Daniel Pick, *Faces of Degeneration: A European Disorder, 1848–1918* (Cambridge: Cambridge University Press, 1989); and Stephen Humphries, *Hooligans or Rebels? An Oral History of Working Class Childhood and Youth, 1889–1939* (Oxford: Basil Blackwell, 1981).

63. Shkotov, *Byt molodezhi*, p. 33.

64. Von Hagen, *Soldiers in the Proletarian Dictatorship*, p. 195.

65. Kostrov, "Kul'tura i meshchanstvo," pp. 24–25.

66. Dmitriev and Galin, *Na putiakh*, p. 65.

67. *Siniaia bluza* 34 (1926), p. 18.

68. A. Stratonitskii, *Voprosy byta v komsomole* (Leningrad: "Priboi," 1926), p. 19.

69. Stites, *Revolutionary Dreams*, p. 119.

70. Stratonitskii, *Voprosy byta v komsomole*, p. 104.

71. Fisher, *Pattern for Soviet Youth*, p. 82.

72. Geoff Eley, "Living the Future: The Left and Culture" (unpublished paper, 1991), p. 65. Anxiety about dirt and disease was not limited to European reformers. Mexican revolutionaries in the 1920s were similarly preoccupied with getting rid of "drink, blood sports, gambling, dirt, and disease" and improving the "physical and moral hygiene" of their population. See Alan Knight, "Revolutionary Project,

Recalcitrant People: Mexico, 1910–1940," in *The Revolutionary Process in Mexico*, ed. Jaime E. Rodriguez (Los Angeles: UCLA Latin American Center Publications, 1990), pp. 243–244.

73. Peter Stallybrass and Allon White, *The Politics and Poetics of Transgression* (Ithaca: Cornell University Press, 1986), pp. 126, 131. On the connections between cleanliness and "civilization," see also Frank Mort, *Dangerous Sexualities: Medico-Moral Politics in England since 1830* (London: Routledge and Kegan Paul, 1987).

74. Igal Halfin and Jochen Hellbeck, "Rethinking the Stalinist Subject: Stephen Kotkin's 'Magnetic Mountain' and the State of Soviet Historical Studies," *Jahrbücher für Geschichte Osteuropas* 44 (1996), p. 461.

75. Alan B. Spitzer, "The Historical Problem of Generations," *American Historical Review* 78:5 (December 1973), p. 1360. See also Philip Abrams, "Rites de Passage: The Conflict of Generations in Industrial Society," *Journal of Contemporary History* 5 (1970), and the essays in Dieter Dowe, *Jugendprotest und Generationenkonflikt in Europa im 20. Jahrhundert* (Germany: Verlag Neue Gesellschaft, 1986).

76. The term "the lost generation" has often been applied to the West European counterparts of these Russian youth, who like Russian men and women suffered and thrilled to their war experiences. In *The Generation of 1914*, Robert Wohl describes West European combatants' transition from the optimism of 1917–1920 to a severe disillusionment following the anticlimactic restoration of a staid postwar civilization. Despite this disappointment, for many young Europeans, as for many Soviet youth, the "dream of cultural and political renewal did not die," contributing to an inter-war passion for radicalism and the "creation of a new world and a new man." Despite the similarities, however, national discourses surrounding the experiences of war and revolution differed dramatically, and there are real dangers in overemphasizing the international aspects of a generational crisis. What the comparison does suggest, however, is the multiplicity of factors at work in this post-war period, some expressly related to Bolshevik policies and others reflecting complex calculations of age and generation. Robert Wohl, *The Generation of 1914* (Cambridge, Mass.: Harvard University Press, 1979), pp. 225, 231.

77. As cited in Eric Naiman, "Revolutionary Anorexia (NEP as Female Complaint)," *Soviet and East European Journal* 37:3 (1993), pp. 321f.

78. Walter Duranty, *Duranty Reports Russia* (New York: Viking Press, 1934), p. 93.

79. Sheila Fitzpatrick, "The Legacy of the Civil War," in *Party, State, and Society in the Russian Civil War: Explorations in Social History*, ed. Diane P. Koenker, William G. Rosenberg, and Ronald Grigor Suny (Bloomington: Indiana University Press, 1989), p. 393.

5. GENDER AND GENERATION

1. I. Iv., "Bez luny," *Izvestiia TsIK* 58 (March 8, 1928), p. 6.

2. S. Kirillov, "Devushka v komsomole," *Kommunistka* 9 (September 1928), p. 27.

3. See, for example, Wendy Z. Goldman, *Women, the State and Revolution: Soviet Family Policy and Social Life, 1917–1936* (Cambridge: Cambridge University Press, 1993), and Barbara Evans Clements, "The Effects of the Civil War on Women and Family Relations," in *Party, State, and Society in the Russian Civil War: Explorations in Social History*, ed. Diane P. Koenker, William G. Rosenberg, and Ronald Grigor Suny (Bloomington: Indiana University Press, 1989). A work that looks at discursive as well as political practices is Elizabeth A. Wood, *The Baba and the Comrade: Gender and Politics in Revolutionary Russia* (Bloomington: Indiana University Press, 1997).

4. B. A. Balashov and Nelepin, *VLKSM za 10 let v tsifrakh* (Moscow-Leningrad: Molodaia gvardiia, 1928), p. 10; Ralph Fisher, *Pattern for Soviet Youth: A Study of the Congresses of the Komsomol, 1918–1954* (New York: Columbia University Press, 1959),

p. 135; Tsentr Khraneniia Dokumentov Molodezhnykh Organizatsii (TsKhDMO), "O rabote sredi devushek," f. 1, op. 23. d. 864a, l. 2. The largest number of Komsomol women were found in the central industrial regions (22 percent in late 1925) and the smallest in the Muslim-dominated Central Asian republics (8.1 percent in 1925). TsKhDMO, "Report on the Condition of Women in the Komsomol," 1925, f. 1, op. 23., d. 391, l. 39.

5. Fisher, *Pattern for Soviet Youth*, p. 112. See also TsKhDMO, f. 1, op. 23, d. 391, l. 40, and T. H. Rigby, *Communist Party Membership in the USSR, 1917–1967* (Princeton: Princeton University Press, 1968), p. 361.

6. See Diane P. Koenker, "Men against Women on the Shop Floor in Early Soviet Russia: Gender and Class in the Socialist Workplace," *American Historical Review* 100:5 (December 1995).

7. The phrases "on the page" and "on the streets" come from Joan Neuberger in *Hooliganism: Crime, Culture, and Power in St. Petersburg, 1900–1914* (Berkeley: University of California Press, 1993), p. 5.

8. Histories of youth culture have typically had little to say about questions of gender, although the work of Angela McRobbie on British girl culture and that of Hilary Pilkington on contemporary Soviet girl cultures are notable exceptions. The imbalance was first pointed out in a chapter by Angela McRobbie and Jenny Garber titled "Young Women and Subcultures," in *Resistance through Rituals: Youth Subcultures in Post-war Britain*, ed. Stuart Hall and Tony Jefferson (London: Hutchinson, 1976). See also Hilary Pilkington, "Going Out in 'Style': Girls in Youth Cultural Activity," in *Perestroika and Soviet Women*, ed. Mary Buckley (Cambridge: Cambridge University Press, 1992), and Pilkington, *Russia's Youth and Its Culture: A Nation's Constructors and Constructed* (New York: Routledge, 1994).

9. Elizabeth Waters, "From the Old Family to the New: Work, Marriage, and Motherhood in Urban Soviet Russia, 1917–1931" (Ph.D. diss., University of Birmingham, 1985), pp. 59–60.

10. Speech by Comrade Petrova, "Iz stenogrammy soveshchaniia devushek-rabotnits moskovskikh fabrik," in V. Dmitriev and B. Galin, *Na putiakh k novomu bytu* (Moscow: Izd. "Novaia Moskva," 1927), p. 27.

11. Provincial activists spent an average of two hours and fifty-five minutes a day in meetings. *Trud, otdykh, son komsomol'tsa-aktivista. Po materialam vyborochnogo obsledovaniia biudzhetov vremeni aktivnykh rabotnikov RLKSM*, vyp. 6 (Moscow-Leningrad: Molodaia gvardiia, 1926), pp. 27–28, 32, 36.

12. See the speech by Comrade Beliaeva in Dmitriev and Galin, *Na putiakh*, p. 36.

13. Ibid., pp. 27–28.

14. Vera Ketlinskaia, *Devushka i komsomol* (Leningrad: "Priboi," 1927), p. 49.

15. G. Grigorov and S. Shkotov, *Staryi i novyi byt* (Moscow: Molodaia gvardiia, 1927), p. 99; Dmitriev and Galin, *Na putiakh*, pp. 27, 46; Petrova in Dmitriev and Galin, *Na putiakh*, p. 26. According to one author, the solution to such concerns was to show parents that the Komsomol was good for girls, that "we don't teach them just to sing the 'Internationale,' but also to sew, to knit, to cultivate two ears where before there was only one." V. A. Murin, *Byt i nravy derevenskoi molodezhi* (Moscow: Izd. "Novaia Moskva," 1926), p. 94. For more on rural parents and their opposition to their daughters' participation, see Isabel A. Tirado, "The Komsomol and the Krest'ianka: The Political Mobilization of Young Women in the Russian Village, 1921–1927," *Russian History/Histoire Russe* 23:1–4 (1996).

16. Murin, *Byt i nravy*, p. 35. Male rural youth were also more likely to travel to big cities like Moscow. The pedagogical archive has a series of letters describing young peasants' vacation trips to Moscow, the plays and movies they saw and the museums they visited. See Nauchnyi Arkhiv Rossiiskoi Akademii Obrazovaniia (NA RAO), f. 1, op. 1, d. 243, ll. 1–3.

17. Peasant girls were particularly underrepresented in the Komsomol. TsKhDMO, f. 1, op. 23, d. 391, l. 40. In 1925, peasants constituted 46.3 percent of the Komsomol but just 31.7 percent of its female membership.

18. Ketlinskaia, *Devushka i komsomol*, p. 48.

19. Murin, *Byt i nravy*, p. 94.

20. Ibid., p. 86.

21. Speech by Comrade Shtern in Dmitriev and Galin, *Na putiakh*, p. 40.

22. Carol Pateman, "The Fraternal Social Contract," as cited in Geoff Eley, "Nations, Publics, and Political Cultures: Placing Habermas in the Nineteenth Century," in *Culture/Power/History: A Reader in Contemporary Social Theory*, ed. Nicholas B. Dirks, Geoff Eley, and Sherry B. Ortner (Princeton: Princeton University Press, 1994), p. 313.

23. Mark D. Steinberg, *Moral Communities: The Culture of Class Relations in the Russian Printing Industry, 1867–1907* (Berkeley: University of California Press, 1992), pp. 78–79.

24. A. Stratonitskii, *Voprosy byta v komsomole* (Leningrad: "Priboi," 1926), p. 50, and TsKhDMO, f. 1, op. 23, d. 822, l. 83; I. Dubrovin, "Revoliutsionirovanie byta," *Iunyi kommunist* 8 (October 1923), pp. 20–21; Ivan T. Bobryshev, *Melkoburzhuaznye vliianiia sredi molodezhi* (Moscow-Leningrad: Molodaia gvardiia, 1928), p. 78.

25. Clements, "The Effects of the Civil War," pp. 105, 117.

26. Wood, *The Baba and the Comrade*, chapter 2.

27. Isabel A. Tirado, "Nietzschean Motifs in the Komsomol's Vanguardism," in *Nietzsche and Soviet Culture: Ally and Adversary*, ed. Bernice Glatzer Rosenthal (Cambridge: Cambridge University Press, 1994), p. 240. For more on visual images of male and female, see Victoria E. Bonnell, *Iconography of Power: Soviet Political Posters under Lenin and Stalin* (Berkeley: University of California Press, 1998), and Elizabeth Waters, "The Female Form in Soviet Political Iconography, 1917–1932," in *Russia's Women: Accommodation, Resistance, Transformation*, ed. Barbara Evans Clements, Barbara Alpern Engel, and Christine D. Worobec (Berkeley: University of California Press, 1991).

28. See Peter Konecny, "Creating the Responsible Husband: The Crisis of Masculinity among Soviet Students, 1924–36" (paper presented at the annual meeting of the American Association for the Advancement of Slavic Studies, Washington, D.C., October 1995).

29. TsKhDMO, f. 1, op. 5, d. 13, l. 13; Ketlinskaia, *Devushka i komsomol*, p. 21.

30. TsKhDMO, f. 1, op. 5, d. 13, l. 12.

31. TsKhDMO, f. 1, op. 23, d. 391, l. 59. Or, as another Komsomol Central Committee report concluded: "The influence of the old ways of life, of *meshchanstva*, is very strong among girls." Ibid., d. 864a, l. 14.

32. TsKhDMO, f. 1, op. 23, d. 391, ll. 41–42; ibid., d. 864a, ll. 6, 7. Similarly, young women heard the same tired presentations on "Girls and the Komsomol" so often that they complained they could not tell one meeting from the next.

33. TsKhDMO, f. 1, op. 23, d. 864a, ll. 26–27.

34. See, for example, Murin, *Byt i nravy*, p. 94. On men who did share household tasks with their wives, see Vera Ketlinskaia and Vladimir Slepkov, *Zhizn' bez kontrolia. Polovaia zhizn' i sem'ia rabochei molodezhi* (Moscow-Leningrad: Molodaia gvardiia, 1929), pp. 77–78, 80.

35. Ketlinskaia and Slepkov, *Zhizn' bez kontrolia*, p. 93. See also Kirillov, "Devushka v komsomole," pp. 29–30.

36. Ketlinskaia, *Devushka i komsomol*, p. 55.

37. TsKhDMO, f. 1, op. 23, d. 391, l. 61.

38. Ketlinskaia and Slepkov, *Zhizn' bez kontrolia*, p. 101. The survey was conducted among young women with children.

39. TsKhDMO, f. 1, op. 23, d. 864a, ll. 23–24; ibid., d. 822, l. 84; Kirillov, "Devushka

v komsomole," p. 29. It was also not uncommon for a young man whose advances were spurned to exact retribution by getting the young woman expelled from the Komsomol.

40. Richard Stites, *The Women's Liberation Movement in Russia: Feminism, Nihilism, and Bolshevism, 1860–1930* (Princeton: Princeton University Press, 1978), p. 360.

41. S. Smidovich, "Sem'ia i stroitel'stvo sotsializma," in *Byt i molodezhi*, ed. A. Slepkov (Moscow: "Pravda" i "Bednota," 1926), p. 55. Some blamed the transition from War Communism to NEP for the sexual excesses of youth, arguing that young people were demanding self-fulfillment after years of self-deprivation. S. Ia. Vol'fson, *Sotsiologiia braka i sem'i* (Minsk: Izd. Belorusskogo gosudarstvennogo universiteta, 1929), p. 418.

42. As cited in Richard Stourac and Kathleen McCreery, *Theater as Weapon: Workers' Theater in the Soviet Union, Germany, and Britain, 1917–1934* (London: Routledge and Kegan Paul, 1986), p. 32.

43. See A. Kollontai, "The Family and the Communist State," and Leon Trotsky, "From the Old Family to the New," in *Bolshevik Visions: First Phase of the Cultural Revolution in Soviet Russia*, ed. William G. Rosenberg (Ann Arbor: University of Michigan Press, 1990). For views of the family more generally, see Goldman, *Women, the State and Revolution*, and Waters, "From the Old Family to the New."

44. Ketlinskaia and Slepkov, *Zhizn' bez kontrolia*, p. 65.

45. TsKhDMO, f. 1, op. 23, d. 391, l. 64; *Iunyi kommunist* 2 (January 1927), p. 60. Observers like Ketlinskaia and Slepkov were most outraged by reports of secretaries of Komsomol collectives who made their wives leave the organization and stay home. *Zhizn' bez kontrolia*, pp. 64–68.

46. Ketlinskaia, *Devushka i komsomol*, p. 75.

47. TsKhDMO, f. 1, op. 23, d. 864a, l. 26.

48. See, for example, TsKhDMO, f. 1, op. 23, d. 864a, ll. 16, 23; ibid., d. 391, l. 50.

49. TsKhDMO, f. 1, op. 5, d. 13, l. 12. There are interesting correspondences between Komsomol views of young women as both "victim" and "villain" and Bolshevik views of prostitutes, especially in the late 1920s. See Elizabeth Waters, "Victim or Villain: Prostitution in Post-revolutionary Russia," in *Women and Society in Russia and the Soviet Union*, ed. Linda Edmondson (Cambridge: Cambridge University Press, 1992).

50. Lev Goomilevksy, *Dog Lane* (London, 1927), pp. 68, 102. In the pre-revolutionary period, radical worker Ivan Babushkin similarly "rejected two women's request to join his social democratic reading circle after asking himself, 'Would the presence of attractive members of the opposite sex not have a retarding effect on our studies?'" Charters Wynn, *Workers, Strikes, and Pogroms: The Donbass-Dnepr Bend in Late Imperial Russia, 1870–1905* (Princeton: Princeton University Press, 1992), p. 85.

51. The summary is from Klaus Mehnert, *Youth in Soviet Russia* (Westport, Conn.: Hyperion Press, [1933] 1981), pp. 86–87.

52. As cited in B. Galin, "Bytovye zametki," *Iunyi kommunist* 2 (January 1927), p. 63. See also TsKhDMO, f. 1, op. 23, d. 391, l. 50.

53. Petrova in Dmitriev and Galin, *Na putiakh*, pp. 31–32. In some cases, such as at the Moscow *Red October* candy factory, Komsomol men never went out with Komsomol women, but "always tried to chose good-looking non-party girls." For this reason some non-party women would not even join the youth league for fear that they would never get married. Beliaeva in Dmitriev and Galin, *Na putiakh*, p. 38.

54. Ketlinskaia and Slepkov, *Zhizn' bez kontrolia*, p. 96; TsKhDMO, f. 1, op. 23, d. 864a, l. 31.

55. Ketlinskaia, *Devushka i komsomol*, p. 77; N. Vigilianskii, "O studenche-

skom byte," *Iunyi kommunist* 11–12 (June 1927), p. 77; TsKhDMO, f. 1, op. 23, d. 391, l. 43.

56. TsKhDMO, f. 1, op. 23, d. 864a, ll. 17–19. See also Shtern in Dmitriev and Galin, *Na putiakh*, p. 40. On the percentage of young women holding qualified positions in the textile industry, see Kirillov, "Devushka v komsomole," p. 28.

57. Koenker, "Men against Women," p. 1463.

58. Petrova in Dmitriev and Galin, *Na putiakh*, p. 31. See also Ketlinskaia, *Devushka i komsomol*, p. 4. Places "reserved" for young women were called "mesta dlia iubok" ["places for skirts"].

59. As cited in Ella Winter, *Red Virtue* (London: Victor Gollancz, 1933), p. 99.

60. Beliaeva in Dmitriev and Galin, *Na putiakh*, p. 37. Other examples of women who succeeded in their leadership positions can be found in TsKhDMO, f. 1, op. 23, d. 864a, l. 22.

61. TsKhDMO, f. 1, op. 23, d. 864a, l. 21; Beliaeva in Dmitriev and Galin, *Na putiakh*, p. 37.

62. V. E. Maksimova, *IV s"ezd RKSM* (Moscow: Molodaia gvardiia, 1989), pp. 5, 9. Reports from the fifth congress in 1922 suggest it may have been even worse. *Iunyi kommunist* writes that there were only "a few girls" at that conference, and not a one at the following all-Russian congress. *Iunyi kommunist* 8 (October 1923), p. 22; TsKhDMO, "Devushka v aktive," January–October 1926, f. 1, op. 23, d. 580, l. 108; TsKhDMO, f. 1, op. 23, d. 864a, l. 21. For similar reports elsewhere, see TsKhDMO, f. 1, op. 23, d. 391, ll. 51–53, and TsKhDMO, f. 1, op. 23, d. 428, l. 94, as well as *Biulleten' IV vsesoiuznoi konferentsii RLKSM N. 1–5* (Moscow: Molodaia gvardiia, n.d. [c. 1925]), p. 19.

63. *Iunyi kommunist* 1 (January 1924), p. 27.

64. TsKhDMO, f. 1, op. 23, d. 864a, l. 20. For more on problems of promotion in rural areas, see Tirado, "The Komsomol and the Krest'ianka," pp. 16–19.

65. TsKhDMO, f. 1, op. 23, d. 864a, ll. 2, 5; ibid., d. 391, ll. 1, 8, 69. See also "O rabote komsomola sredi devushek" (March 17, 1927) and "O rabote sredi molodezhi" (May 1924), in *KPSS o Komsomole i molodezhi* (Moscow: Molodaia gvardiia, 1962), pp. 50, 117–120.

66. TsKhDMO, f. 1, op. 23, d. 864a, l. 6.

67. Ketlinskaia, *Devushka i komsomol*, p. 21. The party, too, argued that although the Komsomol was to make a special effort to bring young women into the league, there were to be no special women's sections. See Fisher, *Pattern for Soviet Youth*, p. 67.

68. TsKhDMO, f. 1, op. 23, d. 864a, l. 8.

69. As cited in Bobryshev, *Melkoburzhuaznye vliianiia sredi molodezhi*, pp. 80–81.

70. TsKhDMO, f. 1, op. 23, d. 833, l. 16. Original underlining deleted.

71. Goldman, *Women, the State, and Revolution*, pp. 242–245; Clements, "The Effects of the Civil War."

72. Petrova in Dmitriev and Galin, *Na putiakh*, p. 32.

73. Ketlinskaia and Slepkova, *Zhizn' bez kontrolia*, p. 89.

74. Stites, *The Women's Liberation Movement in Russia*, p. 322, fn. 11.

75. Petrova in Dmitriev and Galin, *Na putiakh*, p. 35.

76. Petrova and Shtern in Dmitriev and Galin, *Na putiakh*, pp. 34–35, 40.

77. Petrova in Dmitriev and Galin, *Na putiakh*, pp. 27–29. Despite her disapproval of young women who chose the "unrevolutionary" route, Petrova was not unsympathetic to the difficulties of their lives or their reasons for wanting to marry, admitting that economic conditions and parental pressures made it very difficult for a young woman to join the Komsomol. In this she differs from those Zhenotdel activists who rarely admitted that "very real problems were keeping most women occupied," insisting that "women's attitudes were the obstacle preventing them

from joining the revolution." See Barbara Evans Clements, "The Birth of the New Soviet Woman," in *Bolshevik Culture: Experiment and Order in the Russian Revolution*, ed. Abbott Gleason, Peter Kenez, and Richard Stites (Bloomington: Indiana University Press, 1985), p. 224.

78. Barbara Evans Clements, "The Utopianism of the Zhenotdel," *Slavic Review* 51:2 (Summer 1992), p. 487.

79. Ibid., p. 486.

80. N. Ognyov [Ognev],*The Diary of a Communist Undergraduate*, trans. Alexander Werth (New York: Payson and Clarke, 1929), p. 41. See also the description of the young daughter in A. Kollontai's *Love of Worker Bees*, trans. Cathy Porter (London: Virago, 1977).

81. As cited in M. M. Rubinshtein, *Iunost'. Po dnevnikam i avtobiograficheskim zapisiam* (Moscow: Izd. vysshikh pedagogicheskikh kursov pri Moskovskom vysshem tekhnich. uchilishche, 1928), p. 195.

82. As cited in Winter, *Red Virtue*, p. 128.

83. Ibid., p. 136.

84. Shtern in Dmitriev and Galin, *Na putiakh*, p. 42.

85. Kirillov, "Devushka v komsomole," p. 28.

86. N. Semashko, "Nuzhna li 'zhenstvennost'," *Molodaia gvardiia* 6 (1924), pp. 205–206.

87. As cited in Mehnert, *Youth in Soviet Russia*, p. 123. Anxiety about the "blurring of the sexes" was not particular to Soviet Russia. In France, according to Mary-Louise Roberts, "the blurring of a proper division between the sexes" was used "as a central metaphor for cultural crisis" and the "fragility of civilization" following World War I. Here it was the waistless, flat-chested dress of the flapper that most symbolized the masculinization of women. Mary-Louise Roberts, "'This Civilization No Longer Has Sexes': *La Garçonne* and Cultural Crisis in France after World War I," *Gender and History* 4:1 (Spring 1992), p. 52.

88. For more on the medical construction of sexual difference based on the sex glands, see especially Frances L. Bernstein, "What Everyone Should Know about Sex: Gender, Sexual Enlightenment, and the Politics of Health in Revolutionary Russia, 1918–1931" (Ph.D. diss., Columbia University, 1998), chapter 2. See also the discussion in Eric Naiman, *Sex in Public: The Incarnation of Early Soviet Ideology* (Princeton: Princeton University Press, 1997), pp. 143–147.

89. TsKhDMO, f. 1, op. 23, d. 391, l. 50.

90. Murin, *Byt i nravy*, p. 89

91. TsKhDMO, f. 1, op. 5, d. 13, l. 13.

92. TsKhDMO, f. 1, op. 5, d. 13, l. 20.

93. Ketlinskaia and Slepkov, *Zhizn' bez kontrolia*, p. 66.

6. FLAPPERS AND FOXTROTTERS

1. "Sotsial'noe polozhenie," *Bich* 5 (February 1928), p. 7.

2. William Reswick, *I Dreamt Revolution* (Chicago: H. Regnery, 1952), p. 52.

3. Walter Duranty, *Duranty Reports Russia* (New York: Viking Press, 1934), pp. 105–106.

4. Reswick, *I Dreamt Revolution*, p. 55. Although most of the descriptions of NEP life in this chapter refer to Moscow and Leningrad, other cities in the Soviet Union experienced some of the same changes. In his memoirs, a Komsomol activist sent to work in Rostov-on-Don remembered the busy restaurants with bright signs, the "dissolute variety shows," and the vulgar films of that city in the 1920s. See A. Mil'chakov, *Pervoe desiatiletie. Zapiski veterana komsomola* (Moscow: Molodaia gvardiia, 1965), pp. 73–74.

5. Alan M. Ball, *Russia's Last Capitalists: The Nepmen, 1921–1929* (Berkeley: University of California Press, 1987); Daniel R. Brower, "'The City in Danger': The Civil War and the Russian Urban Population," in *Party, State, and Society in the Russian Civil War,* ed. Diane P. Koenker, William G. Rosenberg, and Ronald Grigor Suny (Bloomington: Indiana University Press, 1989); *Izvestiia* 58–62 (March 1928); William J. Chase, *Workers, Society, and the Soviet State: Labor and Life in Moscow, 1918–1929* (Urbana: University of Illinois Press, 1987), pp. 124–125. In his memoirs, Ilia Erenburg described the mixed social background of some of these new entrepreneurs: "A former junior barrister, after working for two years in the Commissariat of Justice, suddenly started to trade in sleeping-car reservations. I knew a poet who in 1921 read semi-futurist verse at the Dominio. Now he was peddling French scent and cosmetics and Estonian brandy. A former worker at Goujon's factory, a veteran of the Civil War, was prosecuted . . . they found eight million rubles on him." Ilia Erenburg, *Memoirs: 1921–1941,* trans. Tatiana Shebunina (New York: Grosset and Dunlap, 1966), p. 68.

6. Victor Serge, "Vignettes of NEP," in *Verdict of Three Decades,* ed. Julien Steinberg (New York: Duell, Sloan and Pearce, 1950), p. 143.

7. On the growth of mass commercial culture in Europe and the United States, see, for example, Rosalind Williams, "The Dream World of Mass Consumption," in *Rethinking Popular Culture: Contemporary Perspectives in Cultural Studies,* ed. Chandra Mukerji and Michael Schudson (Berkeley and Los Angeles: University of California Press, 1991); Kathy Peiss, *Cheap Amusements: Working Women and Leisure in Turn-of-the-Century New York* (Philadelphia: Temple University Press, 1985); and Gareth Stedman-Jones, "Working-Class Culture and Working-Class Politics in London, 1870–1900: Notes on the Remaking of a Working Class," in *Languages of Class: Studies in English Working-Class History, 1832–1982,* ed. Gareth Stedman Jones (Cambridge: Cambridge University Press, 1983).

8. There is a growing literature on the body and its disciplining. Much of it stemmed originally from Foucault's work on the body as a place where social power is expressed and exerted: Michel Foucault, *The History of Sexuality, Volume 1,* trans. Robert Hurley (New York: Pantheon, 1978). My arguments about the disciplining of the pleasures of the body have also been informed by a chapter on "Offensive Bodies and Carnival Pleasures" in John Fiske, *Understanding Popular Culture* (Winchester: Unwin Hyman, 1989).

9. Vl. Slepkov, "Rytsari skorbi i pechali," in *Obyvatel'shchinu na pritsel! Sbornik statei i fel'etonov* (Leningrad: "Krasnaia gazeta," 1928), p. 84. Slepkov uses the term *bogema* in his description of NEP's aristocratic "golden youth." See Slepkov, "Rytsari skorbi i pechali," p. 86.

10. Ilia Erenburg, *First Years of Revolution, 1918–21,* trans. Anna Bostock (London: MacGibbon and Kee, 1962), pp. 62–63.

11. Walter Duranty, *I Write as I Please* (New York: Simon and Schuster, 1935), p. 241.

12. Gordon McKay, *Esenin: A Life* (Ann Arbor: Ardis, 1976), pp. 120–129.

13. As cited in Geoffrey Thurley, *Confessions of a Hooligan* (Cheshire, England: Carcanet Press, 1973), p. 53.

14. Dorothy Thompson, *The New Russia* (New York: Holt, 1928), pp. 55, 66.

15. Ibid., p. 66.

16. Erenburg, *First Years of Revolution,* pp. 66, 67, 159; Vladimir Lidin, *The Price of Life,* trans. Helen Chrouschoff Matheson (Westport, Conn: Hyperion Press, 1973), p. 55. See also S. Serov and L. Lebedev, *Molodezh' na sude* (Moscow-Leningrad: Molodaia gvardiia, 1927), pp. 52–54.

17. Dick Hebdige, *Subculture: The Meaning of Style* (London: Methuen, 1979), p. 122.

18. Edwin Ware Hullinger, *The Reforging of Russia* (New York: E. P. Dutton and Co., 1925), p. 319.

19. M. Tramp, "Pod fonarem 'El'dorado,'" in *Obyvatel'shchinu na pritsel! Sbornik statei i fel'etonov* (Leningrad: "Krasnaia gazeta," 1928), p. 31.

20. Vera Ketlinskaia, "Zdravstvui, molodost'!" *Novyi mir* 11 (November, 1975), p. 77.

21. V. A. Murin, *Byt i nravy derevenskoi molodezhi* (Moscow: Izd. "Novaia Moskva," 1926), p. 82.

22. Richard Stites, *Russian Popular Culture: Entertainment and Society since 1900* (Cambridge: Cambridge University Press, 1992), p. 15.

23. Hullinger, *The Reforging*, pp. 319–320.

24. S. Frederick Starr, *Red and Hot: The Fate of Jazz in the Soviet Union, 1917–1980* (New York: Oxford University Press, 1983), pp. 55–56.

25. "S nauchnoi tsel'iu," *Bich* 20 (May 1928), p. 9. Emphasis in original.

26. Starr, *Red and Hot*, p. 69.

27. Emma Goldman, *My Disillusionment in Russia* (New York: Thomas Y. Cromwell, 1970), vol. 2, p. 128.

28. Hullinger, *The Reforging*, p. 323.

29. Ibid., p. 65.

30. Tramp, "Pod fonarem 'El'dorado,'" pp. 28, 30.

31. Hullinger, *The Reforging*, pp. 326–327.

32. Ibid., pp. 323–324.

33. Lidin, *The Price of Life*, p. 122; N. Ognyov [Ognev], *The Diary of a Communist Undergraduate*, trans. Alexander Werth (New York: Payson and Clarke, 1929), pp. 118–124. A nonfictional account can be found in A. G. Kagan, *Molodezh' posle gudka* (Moscow-Leningrad: Molodaia gvardiia, 1930).

34. Ketlinskaia, "Zdravstvui, molodost'!" p. 77. See also E. D. Ivanova, ed., *Russkaia sovetskaia estrada, 1917–1929* (Moscow: Iskusstvo, 1976), p. 249, and Starr, *Red and Hot*, pp. 60–61.

35. Ketlinskaia, "Zdravstvui, molodost'!" p. 77. For a cultural history of the tango in Latin America and Western Europe, see Deborah L. Jakobs, "From Bawdyhouse to Cabaret: The Evolution of Tango as an Expression of Argentine Popular Culture," *Journal of Popular Culture* 18 (Summer 1984).

36. Robert A. Rothstein, "The Quiet Rehabilitation of the Brick Factory: Early Soviet Popular Music and Its Critics," *Slavic Review* 39:3 (September 1980), p. 376. See also Robert A. Rothstein, "Popular Song in the NEP Era," in *Russia in the Era of NEP: Explorations in Soviet Society and Culture*, ed. Sheila Fitzpatrick, Alexander Rabinowitch, and Richard Stites (Bloomington: Indiana University Press, 1991).

37. Stephanie Sandler, "Pleasure, Danger, and the Dance: Nineteenth-Century Russian Variations," in *Russia•Women•Culture*, ed. Helena Goscilo and Beth Holmgren (Bloomington: Indiana University Press, 1996), pp. 250–251.

38. Hullinger, *The Reforging*, p. 323.

39. Ognyov, *The Diary of a Communist Undergraduate*, pp. 122–123.

40. A. Stratonitskii, *Voprosy byta v komsomole* (Leningrad: "Priboi," 1926), p. 25.

41. *Dovesti do kontsa bor'bu s nepmanskoi muzykoi* (Moscow: Gos. muzykal'noe izdatel'stvo, 1931), pp. 51–52.

42. L. Kolesnikov, *Litso klassovogo vraga* (Moscow-Leningrad: Molodaia gvardiia, 1928), p. 84.

43. Eric Naiman, "Revolutionary Anorexia (NEP as Female Complaint)," *Slavic and East European Journal* 37:3 (1993).

44. My argument here has been influenced by Lewis A. Erenberg's thought-provoking description of the same dances in pre-war New York. See his *Steppin'*

Out: New York Nightlife and the Transformation of American Culture, 1890–1930 (Westport, Conn.: Greenwood Press, 1981), p. 81.

45. Lidin, *The Price of Life*, pp. 121–122.

46. Anna Zelenko, *Massovye narodnye tantsy* (Moscow: "Rabotnik prosveshcheniia," 1927), p. 3; *Iunyi proletarii* 1 (January 1924), p. 6; A. Lunacharsky, "Proletarskii muzykant," as cited in *Dovesti do kontsa*, p. 30.

47. Richard Maltby, ed., *Dreams for Sale: Popular Culture in the 20th Century* (London: Harrap, 1989) p. 72.

48. James Wickham, "Working-Class Movement and Working-Class Life: Frankfurt-am-Main during the Weimar Republic," *Social History* 8:3 (October 1983), p. 336.

49. As cited in Maltby, ed., *Dreams for Sale*, p. 72. An article in the American magazine *The New Republic* titled "Flapper Jane" might as well have had the title "Flapper Zhenia": "She is frankly, heavily made up, not to imitate nature, but for an altogether artificial effect—pallor mortis, poisonously scarlet lips, richly ringed eyes—the latter looking not so much debauched (which is the intention) as diabetic . . . " Elizabeth Stevenson, *Babbitts and Bohemians: The American 1920s* (New York: Macmillan, 1967), p. 141.

50. Stratonitskii, *Voprosy byta v komsomole*, p. 21.

51. N. Semashko, *Iskusstvo odevat'sia* (Moscow-Leningrad: Gos. izd., 1927), p. 3. For a discussion of the artistic and often utopian arena of Soviet fashion and textile design, see John E. Bowlt, "Constructivism and Early Soviet Fashion Design," in *Bolshevik Culture: Experiment and Order in the Russian Revolution*, ed. Abbott Gleason, Peter Kenez, and Richard Stites (Bloomington: Indiana University Press, 1985).

52. During the Civil War, most people wore whatever clothing they could find. According to Erenburg, those few with pretensions to high fashion wore dresses made of "wine colored curtains livened up with suprematist squares or triangles cut out of old loose-covers." Others wore "soldiers' faded greatcoats and green hats made of billiard table cloth." Erenburg, *First Years of Revolution*, p. 143.

53. Helena Goscilo, "Keeping A-Breast of the Waist-Land: Women's Fashion in Early Nineteenth-Century Russia," in *Russia•Women•Culture*, ed. Helena Goscilo and Beth Holmgren (Bloomington: Indiana University Press, 1996), p. 35; Christine Ruane, "Clothes Shopping in Imperial Russia: The Development of a Consumer Culture," *Journal of Social History* 28 (Summer 1995), pp. 765–82; *Zhenskoe delo* 1 (1910).

54. E. Stanichinskaia-Rozenberg, "Vliianie kino na shkol'nika," *Vestnik prosveshcheniia* 2 (1927); Tsentr Khraneniia Dokumentov Molodezhnykh Organizatsii (TsKhDMO), f. 1, op. 5, d. 9, ll. 34–35; Denise J. Youngblood, *Movies for the Masses: Popular Cinema and Soviet Society in the 1920s* (Cambridge: Cambridge University Press, 1992). Ironically, it was the party and the Soviet film studios who made Western films available to youth. The self-financing requirements of NEP forced the Soviet film studios to rely on the income generated by the more popular foreign imports to help support their own nascent efforts. Lenin himself called for all movie programs to include a "certain percentage" of films for profit and amusement (in order to attract an audience), as well as for education and propaganda. Of all the new films shown in 1926, 128 were foreign imports and 105 were Soviet productions. Peter Kenez, *Cinema and Soviet Society, 1917–1953* (Cambridge: Cambridge University Press, 1992), p. 39; Denise J. Youngblood, "The Fate of Soviet Popular Cinema during the Stalin Revolution," *Russian Review* 50:2 (April 1991), p. 153.

55. Paxton Hibben, "The Movies in Russia," *The Nation*, November 11, 1925, as cited in Jay Leyda, *Kino: A History of the Russian and Soviet Film*, 3rd ed. (Princeton: Princeton University Press, 1983), p. 185.

56. N. B. Lebina, *Rabochaia molodezh'. Trud i sotsial'nyi oblik, 1921–1925 gg.* (Leningrad: Izdatel'stvo Nauka, 1982), p. 135.

57. A. E. Latsis and L. Keilina, *Deti i kino* (Moscow: Tea-kino-pechat', 1928), pp. 12–13.

58. Ibid., p. 11.

59. *Pionerskaia pravda,* March 3, 1928, as cited in Latsis and Keilina, *Deti i kino,* p. 13.

60. Ivan T. Bobryshev, *Melkoburzhuaznye vliianiia sredi molodezhi* (Moscow-Leningrad: Molodaia gvardiia, 1928), p. 105.

61. T. Kostrov, "Kul'tura i meshchanstvo," *Revoliutsiia i kul'tura* 3–4 (1927), p. 28.

62. M. M. Rubinshtein, *Iunost'. Po dnevnikam i avtobiograficheskim zapisiam* (Moscow: Izd. vysshikh pedagogicheskikh kursov pri Moskovskom vysshem tekhnich. uchilishche, 1928), p. 222.

63. G. Grigorov and S. Shkotov, *Staryi i novyi byt* (Moscow: Molodaia gvardiia, 1927), p. 52, and N. B. Lebina, "Molodezh' i NEP. Ot konflikta k edinstvu subkul'tur" (paper presented at a conference on "Youth in Soviet Russia, 1917–1941," Marburg, Germany, May 1999), p. 12. See also T. Strizhenova, *Iz istorii sovetskogo kostiuma* (Moscow: "Sov. khudozhnik," 1972).

64. See advertisement on the back page of *Mody* 1 (1924).

65. See, for example, *Mody* 1 (1924), *Mody* 3 (1924), *Mody* 7 (1925).

66. *Mody sezona* 3–4 (1928), pp. 4, 22; *Mody sezona* 5–6 (1928). Russian fashion magazines were a few years behind their Western counterparts. In the United States and Western Europe, skirts were at their shortest from 1925 to 1927. See Maltby, ed., *Dreams for Sale,* p. 79.

67. Williams, "The Dream World of Mass Consumption," p. 203. For a description of the concept of "lifestyle advertising" and its development in the American context, see Martin Pumphrey, "The Flapper, the Housewife, and the Making of Modernity," *Cultural Studies* 1:2 (May 1987), p. 183.

68. Ekaterina Strogova, "Womenfolk: Factory Sketches," in *An Anthology of Russian Women's Writing, 1777–1992,* ed. Catriona Kelly (Oxford: Oxford University Press, 1994), p. 282. Getting "dressed up" for work was common in later periods as well, and was similarly condemned as unsuitable and immodest. See Ol'ga Vainstein, "Female Fashion, Soviet Style: Bodies of Ideology," in *Russia•Women• Culture,* ed. Goscilo and Holmgren, p. 69.

69. Advertisement from the back page of *Mody* 7 (1925). See Thompson, *The New Russia,* p. 46, and Alexander Wicksteed, *Life under the Soviets* (London: John Lane the Bodley Head, 1928), p. 12, for a description of young women making their clothing at home. One historian of modern fashion notes that the typical chemise dress of the flapper was easier to reproduce at home than earlier fashions had been because it used so little fabric and was so shapeless. See Elizabeth Ewing, *History of Twentieth Century Fashion* (London: B. T. Batsford, 1974), p. 96. For a similar effort by young working women in interwar Britain to make copies of fashionable clothing "with material a few pence a yard" see Sally Alexander, "Becoming a Woman in London in the 1920's and 1930's," in *Metropolis, London: Histories and Representations since 1800,* ed. David Feldman and Gareth Stedman Jones (London and New York: Routledge, 1989), pp. 263–264.

70. Thompson, *The New Russia,* p. 46.

71. Ibid., p. 30. In Europe and the United States, many women only began to wear cosmetics shortly before World War I. Excessive makeup was previously considered a sign of loose morals. By the end of the 1920s cosmetics "had become the norm rather than the exception, a sign of youth and up-to-dateness, a gauge of modern woman's independence." See Pumphrey, "The Flapper, the Housewife,"

p. 189. Although makeup's popularity also grew rapidly in the Soviet Union, Bolshevik moralists continued to oppose it, associating it with bourgeois behavior.

72. Ella Winter, *Red Virtue* (London: Victor Gollancz, 1933), p. 48.

73. Kolesnikov, *Litso klassovogo vraga*, p. 35.

74. Hullinger, *The Reforging*, p. 255.

75. Strogova, "Womenfolk," p. 282.

76. M. Rafail, *Za novogo cheloveka* (Leningrad: "Priboi," 1928), pp. 50, 51.

77. Ibid.; Bobryshev, *Melkoburzhuaznye vliianiia sredi molodezhi*, p. 68.

78. Grigorov and Shkotov, *Staryi i novyi byt*, pp. 107–108.

79. Bobryshev, *Melkoburzhuaznye vliianiia sredi molodezhi*, p. 68.

80. T. Kostrov, "Kul'tura i meshchanstvo," p. 27.

81. Bobryshev, *Melkoburzhuaznye vliianiia sredi molodezhi*, pp. 68–69.

82. Kostrov, "Kult'ura i meshchanstvo," p. 27. In his famous play *The Bedbug*, Vladimir Mayakovsky satirizes this drive to find a wealthy NEPman or -woman to marry. Mechanic: "I'm no deserter. You think I like wearing these lousy rags? Like hell I do! There are lots of us, you know, and there just aren't enough Nepmen's daughters to go around . . . We'll build houses for everybody! But we won't creep out of this foxhole with a white flag." Vladimir Mayakovsky, *The Bedbug and Selected Poetry*, ed. Patricia Blake (New York: Meridian Books, 1960), p. 256. Mark von Hagen similarly describes the widespread phenomenon of Red Army men marrying women from"non-toiling" backgrounds, and enthusiasts' condemnation of these "petit-bourgeois" marriages. Mark von Hagen, *Soldiers in the Proletarian Dictatorship: The Red Army and the Soviet Socialist State, 1917–1930* (Ithaca: Cornell University Press, 1990), pp. 192–193.

83. Stephen P. Frank, "Simple Folk, Savage Customs? Youth, Sociability, and the Dynamics of Culture in Rural Russia, 1856–1914," *Journal of Social History* 25:4 (1992), p. 718.

84. Iurii Sokolov, "Chto poet i rasskazyvaet derevnia," *Zhizn'. Zhurnal literatury, byta i obshchestvennoi zhizni* 1 (1924), p. 306. See also V. G. Tana-Bogoroza, ed., *Staryi i novyi byt. Sbornik* (Leningrad: Gos. izd., 1924).

85. Murin, *Byt i nravy*, pp. 82–83.

86. Peiss, *Cheap Amusements*, p. 65.

87. Diane P. Koenker, "Men against Women on the Shop Floor in Early Soviet Russia: Gender and Class in the Socialist Workplace," *American Historical Review* 100:5 (December 1995), p. 1463.

88. Ketlinskaia, "Zdravstvui, molodost'!," p. 31.

89. Kostrov, "Kul'tura i meshchantsvo," p. 27.

90. This is Stephen Frank's term for a similar phenomenon in the pre-revolutionary period among peasants. See Frank, "Simple Folk."

91. Bobryshev, *Melkoburzhuaznye vliianiia sredi molodezhi*, pp. 104–106.

92. Frank, "Simple Folk," p. 87.

93. Evgenii Iukon, "Devushka s belym sharfom," in *Obyvatel'shchinu na pritsel! Sbornik statei i fel'etonov* (Leningrad: "Krasnaia gazeta," 1928), pp. 89–90.

94. For a description of the NEPwomen in Kollontai's fiction, see Richard Stites, *The Women's Liberation Movement in Russia: Feminism, Nihilism, and Bolshevism, 1860–1930* (Princeton: Princeton University Press, 1978), pp. 356–357.

95. For a discussion of the meaning and "moral ambiguity" of cosmetics, see Elizabeth Wilson, *Adorned in Dreams: Fashion and Modernity* (Berkeley and Los Angeles: University of California Press, 1985), pp. 107–114.

96. Mary Louise Roberts, "Samson and Delilah Revisited: The Politics of Women's Fashion in 1920s France,"*American Historical Review* 98:3 (June 1993), p. 661.

97. Ibid., p. 683.

98. On Bukharin's policies toward the peasants, see Stephen F. Cohen, *Bukharin*

and the Bolshevik Revolution: A Political Biography, 1888–1938 (New York: Alfred A. Knopf, 1973).

7. LIFE AND LEISURE ON THE STREET

1. "When I Was Just a Small Lad," in *Yulya Sings Songs of Russian Street Urchins*, English lyrics by Thomas P. Whitney, Monitor Records, 1966 (MFS 759).

2. Joan Neuberger, *Hooliganism: Crime, Culture, and Power in St. Petersburg, 1900–1914* (Berkeley: University of California Press, 1993), pp. 178, 179. See also James von Geldern, "Life In-Between: Migration and Popular Culture in Late Imperial Russia," *Russian Review* 55:3 (July 1996).

3. The British Consultative Committee on Continuation Schools, as cited in Harry Hendrick, *Images of Youth: Age, Class, and the Male Youth Problem, 1880–1920* (Oxford: Clarendon Press, 1990), p. 124. Helmut Gruber explores the Austrian Socialist Party's preoccupation with "disorder, promiscuity, and decadence" in Gruber, *Red Vienna: Experiment in Working-Class Culture, 1919–1934* (New York and Oxford: Oxford University Press, 1991), p. 165. For a history of positive and negative views of the urban environment, see Andrew Lees, *Cities Perceived: Urban Society in European and American Thought* (New York: Columbia University Press, 1985).

4. James C. Scott, *Domination and the Arts of Resistance: Hidden Transcripts* (New Haven: Yale University Press, 1990), p. 121.

5. Ibid., p. xi.

6. Ibid. The relative freedom of subordinate groups such as youth in towns has a long history. See, for example, Paul Griffiths, *Youth and Authority: Formative Experiences in England, 1560–1640* (Oxford: Clarendon Press, 1996), pp. 362–363.

7. S. Shkotov, *Byt molodezhi* (Ivanovo-Voznesensk: "Osnova," 1925), pp. 46–47.

8. A. K. Pokrovskaia in a speech at a meeting of the Scientific-Pedagogical Institute of Aesthetic Education, April 4, 1922, Nauchnyi Arkhiv Rossiiskoi Akademii Obrazovaniia (NA RAO), f. 16, op. 1, d. 15, l. 11.

9. P. I. Liublinskii, *Bor'ba s prestupnost'iu v detskom i iunosheskom vozraste. Sotsial'no-pravovye ocherki* (Moscow: Narkomiust RSFSR, 1923), p. 93.

10. Liublinskii, *Bor'ba s prestupnost'iu*, pp. 93, 95. On anti-urbanism during the cultural revolution, see S. Frederick Starr, "Visionary Town Planning during the Cultural Revolution," in *Cultural Revolution in Russia, 1928–1931*, ed. Sheila Fitzpatrick (Bloomington: Indiana University Press, 1978). Worker-writers in the early revolutionary period were also ambivalent about urban industrial modernity. In their proletarian poems they admired the "vitality and promise" of the city, but feared its menacing and morally decadent aspects: "the 'bawling' of advertising and of the 'bazaar,' the depressing sight of prostitutes in the night gloom . . . and the sights and smells of the 'crowd, stinking and drunken.'" Mark D. Steinberg, "The Troubled Imagination of the Proletarian Poet" (paper presented at the annual meeting of the American Association for the Advancement of Slavic Studies, November 1997), p. 6.

11. L. M. Vasil'evskii, *Prostitutsiia i rabochaia molodezh'* (Moscow: "Novaia Moskva," 1924), p. 20.

12. Ibid.

13. As cited in Bertrand Mark Patenaude, "Bolshevism in Retreat: The Transition to the New Economic Policy, 1920–1922" (Ph.D. diss., Stanford University, 1987), pp. 341–342.

14. The estimation of the number of homeless youth is from A. Zalkind and M. Epshtein, "Besprizornost'," in *Bol'shaia Sovetskaia Entsiklopediia*, vol. 5 (Moscow: Aktsionernoe obshchestvo "Sovetskaia entsiklopediia," 1927), p. 786. It is difficult be certain how many *besprizornye* there were. See Alan Ball, *And Now My Soul Is*

Hardened: Abandoned Children in Soviet Russia, 1918–1930 (Berkeley: University of California Press, 1994), pp. 16–17.

15. Research on Arbat Lane, 20–21 June 1922, and Starokoniushennyi Lane, NA RAO, f. 16, op. 1, d. 15, l. 66. See also A. Gel'mont and A. Durikin, eds., *Trud i dosug rebenka* (Moscow: "Novaia Moskva," 1927), pp. 36–37.

16. "O literaturnom tvorchestve besprizornykh," E. G. Ershkovich, June 1927, NA RAO, f. 5, op. 1, d. 102.

17. B. S. Utevskii, *V bor'be s detskoi prestupnost'iu. Ocherk zhizhni i byta Moskovskogo trudovogo doma dlia nesovershennoletnikh pravonarushitelei* (Moscow: Izd. Narodnogo Komissariata Vnutrennikh Del RSFSR, 1927); M. N. Gernet, *Prestupnost' i samoubiistva vo vremia voiny i posle nee* (Moscow, 1927); V. I Kufaev, *Iunye pravonarushiteli* (Moscow: "Novaia Moskva," 1924). Some of the best material on daily life can be found in Mariia Isanovna Levitina, *Besprizornye. Sotsiologiia, byt, praktika raboty* (Moscow: "Novaia Moskva," 1925).

18. See, for example, M. N. Gernet, *Sotsial'nye faktori prestupnosti* (Moscow, 1905), and *Deti prestupniki. Sbornik statei* (Moscow, 1912).

19. On pre-revolutionary approaches to juvenile delinquency, see Dorena Caroli, "Les enfants abandonnés devant les tribunaux dans la russie pré-révolutionaire 1864–1917," *Cahiers du Monde Russe* 38:3 (July–September 1997), pp. 373–374. For an example of Soviet references to Western theorists, see, P. I. Liublinskii, "Khuliganstvo i ego sotsial'no-bytovye korni," in *Khuliganstvo i khuligany. Sbornik*, ed. V. N. Tolmacheva (Moscow: Izd. Narodnogo Komissariata Vnutrennikh Del RSFSR, 1929), p. 44. Professional connections were particularly strong with Germany. See Susan Gross Solomon, "The Soviet-German Syphilis Expedition to Buriat Mongolia, 1928: Scientific Research on National Minorities," *Slavic Review* 52:2 (Summer 1993).

20. Robert E. Park, as cited in *The Subcultures Reader*, ed. Ken Gelder and Sarah Thornton (London and New York: Routledge, 1997), p. 12.

21. The first study was of the Arbat in Moscow. It was supposed to be just a small part of a larger effort to study every aspect of children's everyday lives, including their ideals and dreams, religious attitudes, political beliefs, social life, and sexual relations. However, this first study is the only one the Commission's members appear to have completed. Eventually they hoped to compare the street life of Moscow to that of smaller provincial towns, but I can find no evidence that they did so. Information on the Institute's goals and projects can be found in NA RAO, f. 16, op. 1, d. 15. See also A. K. Pokrovskaia, "Domashniaia zhizn' moskovskikh detei," *Vestnik prosveshcheniia* 1 (1922).

22. Ball says that "roughly two-thirds to three-fourths of street children were boys." Ball, *And Now My Soul Is Hardened*, p. 60 and p. 227, fn. 83. A contemporary observer, Dorothy Thompson, concluded that although there were more boys than girls in the street "bands," "of the twenty thousand in Moscow institutions 40 percent are girls . . . On the whole girls are easier to keep than the boys." Dorothy Thompson, *The New Russia* (New York: Holt, 1928), pp. 251–252.

23. Kenneth M. Pinnow, "Making Suicide Soviet: Medicine, Moral Statistics, and the Politics of Social Science in Bolshevik Russia, 1920–1930" (Ph.D. diss., Columbia University, 1998), pp. 76.

24. Ibid., p. 114.

25. Vasil'evskii, *Prostitutsiia*, pp. 21–22.

26. NA RAO, f. 16, op. 1, d. 15, l. 66.

27. N. B. Lebina, *Rabochaia molodezh' Leningrada. Trud i sotsial'nyi oblik, 1921–1925 gg.* (Leningrad: Izdatel'stvo Nauka, 1982), pp. 146–147.

28. A. K. Pokrovskaia, "Ulitsa v zhizni detei," *Vestnik prosveshcheniia* 7 (1922), pp. 22–25.

29. Lebina, *Rabochaia molodezh'*, p. 148.

30. Ibid., p. 135.

31. Pokrovskaia, "Ulitsa v zhizni detei," p. 19.

32. A. G. Kagan, *Molodezh' posle gudka* (Moscow-Leningrad: Molodaia gvardiia, 1930), pp. 25–28.

33. E. Deichman, "Alkogolizm sredi shkol'nikov," *Vestnik prosveshcheniia* 2 (1927), pp. 87–88.

34. *Trud, zdorov'e, i byt Leningradskoi rabochei molodezhi* (Leningrad: Leningradskogo gubzdravotdela, 1925), p. 19. See also B. S. Segal, *Alkogolizm i molodezh'* (Moscow-Leningrad: Molodaia gvardiia, 1925).

35. Peter Gooderham, "The Komsomol and Worker Youth: The Inculcation of 'Communist Values' in Leningrad during NEP," *Soviet Studies* 4 (October 1982), p. 516. See also Kagan, *Molodezh' posle gudka*, p. 47.

36. Michael R. Marrus, as cited in Roy Rosenzweig, "The Rise of the Saloon," in *Rethinking Popular Culture: Contemporary Perspectives in Cultural Studies*, ed. Chandra Mukerji and Michael Schudson (Berkeley: University of California Press, 1991), p. 132. See also Andrew Davis, "Leisure in the 'Classic Slum,' 1900–1934," in *Workers' Worlds: Cultures and Communities in Manchester and Salford, 1880–1934*, ed. Andrew Davis and Steven Fielding (Manchester: Manchester University Press, 1992), pp. 108–109.

37. Laura Lynne Phillips, "Everyday Life in Revolutionary Russia: Working-Class Drinking and Taverns in St. Petersburg, 1900–1929" (Ph.D. diss., University of Illinois, 1993), pp. 76, 78; Mark D. Steinberg, *Moral Communities: The Culture of Class Relations in the Russian Printing Industry, 1867–1907* (Berkeley: University of California Press, 1992), pp. 73–74; Charters Wynn, *Workers, Strikes, and Pogroms: The Donbass-Dnepr Bend in Late Imperial Russia, 1870–1905* (Princeton: Princeton University Press, 1992), p. 81.

38. In 1865 in St. Petersburg, there was one drinking establishment for every 293 people. In 1923, in comparison, there were just seventy-six taverns in all (though the numbers did rise slightly after that). Reginald E. Zelnick, *Labor and Society in Tsarist Russia: The Factory Workers of St. Petersburg, 1855–1870* (Stanford: Stanford University Press, 1971), p. 247; Phillips, "Everyday Life in Revolutionary Russia," p. 154.

39. Kagan, *Molodezh' posle gudka*, pp. 61, 69.

40. Ibid., p. 52.

41. Ibid., p. 54.

42. *Komsomol'skaia pravda*, December 26, 1929, as cited in ibid., p. 50.

43. Ven'iamin Iadin, "Posle piati . . . ," *Iunyi proletarii* 3 (February 1928) p. 12.

44. See Wynn, *Workers, Strikes, and Pogroms*, pp. 88–89; Neuberger, *Hooliganism*, p. 64; Steinberg, *Moral Communities*, p. 73. On violence more generally, see Daniel R. Brower, "Labor Violence in Russia in the Late Nineteenth Century," *Slavic Review* 41:3 (Fall 1982), pp. 417–431.

45. Lebina, *Rabochaia molodezh'*, p. 146.

46. G. Grigorov and S. Shkotov, *Staryi i novyi byt* (Moscow: Molodaia gvardiia, 1927), p. 145. They describe a fight between two Komsomol boys, one of whom died with a knife through the heart.

47. L. B. Chernikova, "Deti gazetchiki i ikh sreda," *Pedologiia* 1–2 (1929), p. 172.

48. Lebina, *Rabochaia molodezh'*, p. 31.

49. See, for example, Detlev Peukert, "The Lost Generation: Youth Unemployment at the End of the Weimar Republic," in *The German Unemployed*, ed. Richard J. Evans and Dick Geary (London: Croom Helm, 1987), pp. 187–188, and Stephen Humphries, *Hooligans or Rebels? An Oral History of Working Class Childhood and Youth, 1889–1939* (Oxford: Basil Blackwell, 1981), p. 179.

50. *Moskovskii pechatnik* 24 (June 1924), p. 12, as cited in John Hatch, "Workers' Clubs and the Search for a Socialist Working Class Culture" (unpublished paper,

1988), p. 15; A. O. Edel'shtein, "Opyt izucheniia sovremennogo khuliganstva," in *Khuliganstvo i ponozhovshchina*, ed. E. K. Krasnushkin, G. M. Segal, and Ts. M. Feinberg (Moscow: Izd. Moszdravotdela, 1927), pp. 48, 67.

51. Lebina, *Rabochaia molodezh'*, p. 57. See also the discussion in L. S. Rogachevskaia, *Likvidatsiia bezrabotitsy v SSSR 1917–1930* (Moscow: Nauka, 1973), pp. 131–132.

52. N. Iu. Vostrikova, *Deiatel'nost' VLKSM po priobshcheniiu molodykh rabochikh k teatral'nomu iskusstvu v usloviiakh nachala sotsialisticheskoi industrializatsii (1926–1928)* (Saratov, 1986), pp. 7–8.

53. Chernikova, "Deti gazetchiki i ikh sreda," p. 176.

54. NA RAO, f. 5, op. 1, d. 102, l. 18. For additional *besprizornye* autobiographies, see O. Kaidanova, *Besprizornye deti. Praktika raboty opytnoi stantsii* (Moscow-Leningrad: Gos. izd., 1926), pp. 50–73.

55. In 1922, out of 2,592 homeless boys surveyed in Moscow, about half had been born in Moscow and half in other *gubernii*. Levitina, *Besprizornye*, p. 108. On the broader patterns of migration during the Civil War, see Daniel R. Brower, "'The City in Danger': The Civil War and the Russian Urban Population," and Diane P. Koenker, "Urbanization and Deurbanization in the Russian Revolution and Civil War," both in *Party, State, and Society in the Russian Civil War: Explorations in Social History*, ed. Diane P. Koenker, William G. Rosenberg, and Ronald Grigor Suny (Bloomington and Indianapolis: Indiana University Press, 1989). By the middle of the decade, only 10–20 percent of Moscow's *besprizornye* were native to the city. Ball, *And Now My Soul Is Hardened*, p. 23.

56. Zalkind and Epshtein, "Besprizornost'," pp. 786–787; Jennie Stevens, "Children of the Revolution: Soviet Russia's Homeless Children (Besprizorniki) in the 1920s," *Russian History* 9:2–3 (1982) p. 144; Gosudarstvennyi Arkhiv Rossiiskoi Federatsii (GARF), f. 5451, op. 6, d. 464, l. 1. On the causes of homelessness, see also Peter Juviler, "Contradictions of Revolution: Juvenile Crime and Rehabilitation," in *Bolshevik Culture: Experiment and Order in the Russian Revolution*, ed. Abbott Gleason, Peter Kenez, and Richard Stites (Bloomington: Indiana University Press, 1985); Ball, *And Now My Soul Is Hardened*; and Wendy Z. Goldman, *Women, the State, and Revolution: Soviet Family Policy and Social Life, 1917–1936* (Cambridge: Cambridge University Press, 1993), pp. 59–76.

57. Victor Serge, *Russia: Twenty Years After* (Westport, Conn.: Hyperion Press, 1973), p. 28.

58. See the discussion in the introduction to Stuart Hall and Tony Jefferson, eds., *Resistance through Rituals: Youth Subcultures in Post-war Britain* (London: Hutchinson, 1976), p. 15.

59. Sarah Thornton, "General Introduction," in *The Subcultures Reader*, pp. 4, 5.

60. Dick Hebdige, "POSING . . . THREATS, STRIKING . . . POSES: Youth, Surveillance and Display," in Gelder and Thornton, *The Subcultures Reader*, p. 404.

61. Sarah Thornton, "General Introduction," in *The Subcultures Reader*, p. 5.

62. As cited in Ball, *And Now My Soul Is Hardened*, pp. 82–83.

63. *Slovar' zhargona prestupnikov. Blatnaia muzyka* (Moscow: Narodnyi Komissariat Vnutrennikh Del, 1927); Levitina, *Besprizornye*, pp. 161, 170–172; NA RAO, f. 5, op. 1, d. 102, l. 25.

64. NA RAO, f. 5, op. 1, d. 102, l. 24; Utevskii, *Bor'ba s detskoi*, p. 76. Other common names for Komsomol youth included Komsomol'tsy, May, Danton, Spartak (the Komsomol sports organization), and Novobytnik ("One who has adopted a new way of life"). See *Iunyi kommunist* 3 (April 28, 1924), p. 44. Perhaps the most unusual name I found was "Anti-Christ," given to a new baby in a rural hospital. William Henry Chamberlin, *Soviet Russia: A Living Record and a History* (Boston: Little, Brown and Co., 1935), p. 331.

65. V. S. Krasuskii and A. M. Khaletskii, "Sreda besprizornika. Ee traditsii i

navyki," in *Nishchenstvo i besprizornost'*, ed. E. K. Krasnushkin, G. M. Segal, and Ts. M. Feinberg (Moscow: Izd. Moszdravotdela, 1929), pp. 230–231.

66. Utevskii, *V bor'be s detskoi*, pp. 80–82; Vyacheslav Shishkov, *Children of the Street*, trans. Thomas P. Whitney (Royal Oak, Mich.: Strathcona Publishing, 1979), p. 42.

67. Levitina, *Besprizornye*, p. 103. See also Vladimir Zenzinov, *Deserted: The Story of the Children Abandoned in Soviet Russia*, trans. Agnes Platt (Westport, Conn.: Hyperion Press, 1931), p. 127; Shishkov, *Children of the Street*, pp. 30, 35.

68. Utevskii, *V bor'be s detskoi*, p. 78.

69. Krasuskii and Khaletskii, "Sreda besprizornika," p. 236.

70. "Poseshchenie nochlezhki," January 10, 1924, NA RAO, f. 16, op. 1, d. 15, l. 244; K. Arkina, "Kokainizm, kak faktor prestupnosti," *Vestnik prosveshcheniia* 2 (1923), p. 70.

71. R. M. Ziman, "O kokainizme u detei," in *Voprosy narkologii*, ed. A. S. Sholomovich (Moscow: Izd. Moszdravotdela, 1926), p. 28. See also NA RAO, f. 5, op. 1, d. 195, l. 14.

72. On such places in pre-revolutionary Moscow, see Robert W. Thurston, *Liberal City, Conservative State: Moscow and Russia's Urban Crisis, 1906–1914* (New York: Oxford University Press, 1987); James H. Bater, *St. Petersburg: Industrialization and Change* (London: E. Arnold, 1976); and Joseph Bradley, "The Moscow Workhouse and Urban Welfare Reform in Russia," *Russian Review* 41:3 (October 1982).

73. Steinberg, *Moral Communities*, p. 72. See also Neuberger, *Hooliganism*, pp. 174–176.

74. Scott, *Domination and the Arts of Resistance*, pp. 129–131.

75. Krasuskii and Khaletskii, "Sreda besprizornika," pp. 228–229, 235; Utevskii, *V bor'be s detskoi*, pp. 76–77.

76. "Murka," *Yulya Sings Songs of Russian Street Urchins*.

77. Neuberger, *Hooliganism*, pp. 62–63.

78. Ilia Erenburg, *Memoirs: 1921–1941*, trans. Tatiana Shebunina (New York: Grosset and Dunlap, 1966), p. 104.

79. Walter Duranty, *Duranty Reports Russia* (New York: Viking Press, 1934), p. 54; Walter Duranty, *I Write as I Please* (New York: Simon and Schuster, 1935), p. 148.

80. Ball, *And Now My Soul Is Hardened*, pp. 141–142. For more on the theme of penetration in Soviet discourse, see Eric Naiman, *Sex in Public: The Incarnation of Early Soviet Ideology* (Princeton: Princeton University Press, 1997), chapter 2.

81. N. I. Ozeretskii, "Nishchenstvo i besprizornost' nesovershennoletnikh," in *Nishchenstvo i besprizornost'*, ed. Krasnushkin, Segal, and Feinberg, p. 163.

82. Shishkov, *Children of the Street*, p. 26.

83. Thompson, *The New Russia*, pp. 245–246.

84. Ball, *And Now My Soul Is Hardened*, p. 63.

85. Goldman, *Women, the State, and Revolution*, p. 81. Theft was the most common reason for adolescents to appear before the Juvenile Affairs Commission. Of a total of 25,425 youth appearing before the Commission in 1924, 16,218 (64 percent) were arrested for stealing. These figures are for the RSFSR, not including Moscow. Gernet, *Prestupnost'*, p. 35. See also L. Vasil'evskii, "Golod i detskaia prestupnost'," *Iunyi kommunist* 10–12 (June–July 1922), p. 17.

86. Gernet, *Prestupnost'*, p. 35. Of 1,794 crimes against people in 1924, 812 were for beatings and 217 for murder. According to one analyst, juveniles were most likely to commit murder for "vengeance" or to "conceal a criminal act." Kufaev, who was a perpetual optimist, argued that most killings resulted from "carelessness" during games, and the rest from fights, family quarrels, etc. V. D. Men'shagin, "Ubiistva," in *Ubiistva i ubiitsy*, ed. E. K. Krasnushkin, G. M. Segal, and Ts. M. Feinberg (Moscow: Izd. Moszdravotdela, 1928), p. 46; Kufaev, as cited in Gernet, *Prestupnost'*, p. 112.

87. Thompson, *The New Russia*, p. 250.

88. NA RAO, f. 5, op. 1, d. 102, l. 17.

89. Ozeretskii, "Nishchenstvo," pp. 157–190.

90. Levitina, *Besprizornye*, pp. 163, 168–170; Utevskii, *V bor'be s detskoi*, p. 78. For more on the various "professions" of the *besprizornye*, see Aleksandr Rozhkov, "Besprizorniki," *Rodina* 9 (Fall 1997), pp. 71–72.

91. Pokrovskaia, "Ulitsa v zhizni detei," pp. 20–21.

92. Alan Ball, "Private Trade and Traders during NEP," in *Russia in the Era of NEP: Explorations in Soviet Society and Culture*, ed. Sheila Fitzpatrick, Alexander Rabinowitch, and Richard Stites (Bloomington: Indiana University Press, 1991), p. 89. See also Chernikova, "Deti gazetchiki i ikh sreda," and Pokrovskaia, "Domashniaia zhizn'," p. 14.

93. Anne O'Hare McCormick, *The Hammer and the Scythe: Communist Russia Enters the Second Decade* (New York: Alfred A. Knopf, 1928), pp. 24–25.

94. NA RAO, f. 16, op. 1, d. 15, l. 252.

95. There were child prostitutes before the onslaught of homelessness. See Laurie Bernstein, *Sonia's Daughters: Prostitutes and Their Regulation in Imperial Russia* (Berkeley: University of California Press, 1995), pp. 42–46.

96. I. Zudin, K. Mal'kovskii, and P. Shalashov, *Melochi zhizni* (Leningrad, 1929), as cited in N. B. Lebina and M. V. Shkarovskii, *Prostitutsiia v Peterburge* (Moscow: Progress-Akademiia, 1994), p. 82.

97. This information is based in part on statistical data on where people contracted sexually transmitted diseases. After the revolution, people were eight times as likely to have caught a venereal disease "under the open skies" than they had been in the pre-revolutionary period. M. N. Gernet, "K statistike prostitutsii," *Statisticheskoe obozrenie* 7 (Moscow: Izd. TsSU Soiuz SSR, 1927), p. 87.

98. Duranty, *I Write as I Please*, pp. 147–148; Gernet, "K statistike," p. 89; N. B. Lebina, "Malen'kaia Vera obraztsa 20-kh godov," *Leningradskaia panorama* 9 (September 1989), p. 18. Many of these streets were also infamous sites of crime and hooliganism in the pre-revolutionary period.

99. Lebina, "Malen'kaia Vera," p. 18.

100. Lebina and Shkarovskii, *Prostitutsiia*, p. 66.

101. Ibid., p. 18. On female criminality (mostly adult) other than prostitution, see Louise Shelly, "Female Criminality in the 1920s: A Consequence of Inadvertent and Deliberate Change," *Russian History/Histoire Russe* 9:2–3 (1982), pp. 265–284.

102. Levitina, *Besprizornye*, pp. 118, 156.

103. Ibid., p. 120.

104. Lebina and Shkarovskii, *Prostitutsiia*, p. 67.

105. Gernet, "K statistike prostitutsii," p. 88; Levitina, *Besprizornye*, pp. 155, 170, 311–312; Vasil'evskii, *Prostitutsiia*, p. 23; Lebina and Shkarovskii, *Prostitutsiia*, pp. 67, 69.

106. S. Koporskii, "Vorovskoi zhargon v srede shkol'nikov," *Vestnik prosveshcheniia* 1 (1927), pp. 7–12.

107. A. Zalkind, "Psikhopaty li besprizornye?" *Vestnik prosveshcheniia* 9 (1924), p. 135. On fears of contamination, see also G. Shakhun'iants and F. Krotkov, "K trudovoi kommune," *Vestnik prosveshcheniia* 9 (1925), p. 89.

108. See the discussions in Walter D. Connor, *Deviance in Soviet Society: Crime, Delinquency, and Alcoholism* (New York: Columbia University Press, 1972), and Raymond A. Bauer, *The New Man in Soviet Psychology* (Cambridge, Mass.: Harvard University Press, 1952).

109. T. Simson, "Prichiny detskoi prestupnosti," *Vestnik prosveshcheniia* 2 (February 1923), pp. 64–66. See also Ozeretskii, "Nishchenstvo," pp. 182–183.

110. S. V. Poznyshev, *Kriminal'naia psikhologiia. Prestupnye tipy* (Leningrad: Gos. izd., 1926).

111. Neuberger, *Hooliganism*, p. 159.
112. V. E. Smirnov, *Rabochii podrostok* (Moscow-Leningrad: Molodaia gvardiia, 1924), p. 37.
113. Ibid. pp. 31, 32.
114. Bauer, *The New Man in Soviet Psychology*, pp. 80–83.
115. See Caroli, "Les enfants abandonnés," pp. 376–377, and "Les mineurs devant le tribunal tsariste," in *Reformen im Rußland des 19. und 20. Jahrhunderts*, ed. Dietrich Beyrau, Igor Čičurov and Michael Stolleis (Frankfurt am Main: Vittorio Klostermann, 1996).
116. Zalkind and Epshtein, "Besprizornost'," p. 783.
117. Levitina, *Besprizornye*, p. 130. See also O. L. Bem, "Detskaia besprizornost'," *Na putiakh k novoi shkole* 4–5 (April–May 1924).
118. Dorena Caroli, "Enfreindre la loi au temps du bolchevisme (1918–1924): le cas d'un enfant abandonné," *Rechtshistorisches Journal* 14 (1995), pp. 448f.
119. Zalkind and Epshtein, "Besprizornost'," p. 785.
120. Levitina, *Besprizornye*, p. 328.
121. Some German communists similarly idealized German youth gangs—which were also violent, aggressively masculine, and territorial—as "models of Bolshevik discipline and democratic centralism." Eve Rosenhaft, "Organizing the 'Lumpenproletariat': Cliques and Communists in Berlin during the Weimar Republic," in *The German Working Class, 1888–1933: The Politics of Everyday Life*, ed. Richard J. Evans (London: Croom Helm, 1982), p. 202.
122. Shishkov, *Children of the Street*, p. 113; Utevskii, *V bor'be s detskoi prestupnost'iu*, p. 77; Krasuskii and Khaletskii, "Sreda besprizornika," p. 232; Levitina, *Besprizornye*, pp. 163–164.
123. Zalkind, "Psikhopaty li besprizornye?" p. 136; Levitina, *Besprizornye*, p. 243; Zalkind and Epshtein, "Besprizornost'," p. 784. Emphasis in original.
124. "Proekt polozheniia o detskom dome, GUS" (1925), GARF, f. 298, op. 2, d. 58, ll. 10–11. For details on the workings of the *detdom* and other rehabilitation measures, see Ball, *And Now My Soul Is Hardened*, chapters 4–7.
125. N. Krupskaia, "K voprosu o detdomakh," *Na putiakh k novoi shkole* 7–8 (1924), p. 7.
126. Zorin, "Detdoma i detskoe kommunisticheskoe dvizhenie," in *Detskaia besprizornost' i detskii dom. Sbornik statei i materialov II vserossiiskogo s"ezda SPON po voprosam detskoi besprizornosti, detskogo doma i pravovoi okhrany detei i podrostkov*, ed. S. S. Tizanov, V. L. Shveitser, and V. M. Vasil'eva (Moscow: Otdel sotsial'no-pravovoi okhrany nesovershennoletnykh, 1926), p. 51; NA RAO, f. 5, op. 1, d. 102, ll. 25–26.
127. NA RAO, f. 5, op. 1, d. 102, ll. 25–27.
128. Ball, *And Now My Soul Is Hardened*, p. 95.
129. Most young people who appeared before the courts were supposed to be sent to labor homes like the Moscow Labor Home (Mostrudom), but by 1926, there were still only ten such facilities in Russia. This meant that the "overwhelming majority" of adolescents sentenced by the courts "had to go to regular adult places of confinement—prisons and labor camps," rather than special children's institutions. Even those educators who advocated a more disciplined approach to the "re-education" of criminal youth were anxious about the large number who went to adult prisons. Instead of transforming youth into better communist citizens, criminologists worried that exposure to adult criminals only further "corrupted" youth. Gernet, *Prestupnost'*, pp. 116–117; Utevskii, *V bor'be s detskoi*, pp. 7, 30–36; GARF, f. 298, op. 2, d. 58, ll. 1–2; Levitina, *Besprizornye*, pp. 180–183.
130. Anton Makarenko, *The Road to Life* (Moscow: Foreign Languages Publishing House, 1955), p. 40.
131. From a report by Mme. Kalinin to Dzerzhinskii in late 1920, as cited in

Zenzinov, *Deserted,* pp. 23–24; GARF, f. 2306, op. 13, d. 64, l. 31; G. A. Solonovich, "Ocherki sanitarnogo sostoianiia detskikh domov Khamovich raiona v sviazi s rezul'tatami obsledovaniia zdorov'ia detei," *Vestnik prosveshcheniia* 5–6 (1923), pp. 243–254.

132. G. Khranov-Shmarov, "Iz opyta raboty detskikh domov g. Tiumeni," *Na putiakh k novoi shkole* 7–8 (July–August 1924), p. 121. Some children were evidently able to joke about conditions in the *detdoma,* as can be seen by this "List of Members in Our Family" published in a *detdom* wall newspaper. NA RAO, f. 5, op. 1, d. 102, ll. 26–27.

Children	32
Leaders and other people	6
Dogs	6
And their relatives (cats)	5
Pigeons	2
Hedgehogs	1
A lot of bugs	15,798,974
Lice	All on vacation
Cockroaches	17
Flies	3 and one sickly one
Mice	one sickly one
Total	15,799,048

133. GARF, f. 2306, op. 13, d. 64, ll. 34, 39, 42; ibid., f. 1575, op. 6, d. 180, l. 5. See generally Ball, *And Now My Soul Is Hardened,* chapter 7, and Goldman, *Women, the State, and Revolution,* chapter 2. These conditions did not improve in the 1930s, when there were still serious problems of overcrowding, hunger, illness, and abuse. See Gábor T. Rittersporn, "Between Revolution and Daily Routine: Youth and Violence in the Prewar Soviet Union" (paper presented at the conference "Youth in Soviet Russia, 1917–1941," Philipps-Universität, Marburg, Germany, May 1999), pp. 5–6.

134. NA RAO, f. 16, op. 1, d. 15, l. 244. See also, P. Shimbirev, "Pravonarushiteli," *Vestnik prosveshcheniia* 2 (February 1923), p. 80.

135. Levitina, *Besprizornye,* p. 167. On the Komsomol raids of *besprizornye* hideouts, see *Pravda* (March 25, 1926), as cited in Zenzinov, *Deserted,* p. 172.

136. NA RAO, f. 16, op. 1, d. 15, l. 244.

137. Zenzinov, *Deserted,* p. 119; Ozeretskii, "Nishchenstvo," pp. 178–179; Chamberlin, *Soviet Russia,* p. 157.

138. NA RAO, f. 16, op. 1, d. 15, l. 246.

139. Makarenko, *The Road to Life,* p. 121.

140. NA RAO, f. 16, op. 1, d. 15, l. 238.

141. Thompson, *The New Russia,* p. 249.

142. Levitina, *Besprizornye,* p. 263.

143. Shimbirev, "Pravonarushiteli," pp. 81, 83.

144. Shishkov, *Children of the Street,* p. 114.

145. Utevskii, *V bor'be s detskoi,* p. 79.

146. Report from Cheliabinsk *guberniia* (November 16, 1920), GARF, f. 2306, op. 13, d. 64, l. 33; Makarenko, *The Road to Life,* pp. 95, 118; report on *detdoma* in Tambov and Kozlov (July–August 1921), GARF, f. 1575, op. 6, d. 89, l. 42.

147. Makarenko, *The Road to Life,* p. 20.

148. Utevskii, *Bor'ba s detskoi,* p. 17; Makarenko, *The Road to Life,* p. 94.

149. As cited in Levitina, *Besprizornye,* p. 260.

150. Goldman, *Women, the State, and Revolution,* pp. 304–310.

151. Paul Willis first made this point with respect to British youth cultures. Paul

Willis with Simon Jones, Joyce Canaan, and Geoff Hudd, *Common Culture: Symbolic Work at Play in the Everyday Cultures of the Young* (Buckingham, England: Open University Press, 1990), p. 103.

152. Iagoda's order was not enforced. David R. Shearer, "Crime and Social Order in Stalin's Russia: A Reassessment of the Great Retreat and the Origins of Mass Repression" (unpublished paper, August 1997), p. 23.

153. Rittersporn, "Between Revolution and Daily Routine," p. 4.

8. DISCOURSES OF DELINQUENCY

1. The word "hooligan" came from Ireland and entered common English usage in 1898. It may have first entered Russian via the London correspondent of a Moscow newspaper. See Ia. Bulaiskii, *Khuliganstvo kak sotsial'no-patologicheskoe iavlenie* (Moscow-Leningrad: Molodaia gvardiia, 1927), pp. 9f. See also Geoffrey Pearson, *Hooligan: A History of Respectable Fears* (London: Macmillan, 1983), pp. 74–75.

2. Gertsenzon reported that even as the absolute number of all crimes fell, hooliganism rose as a percentage of these crimes, from 2 percent in early 1925 to 6.5 percent in 1926. A. A. Gertsenzon, "Rost khuliganstva i ego prichiny," in *Khuliganstvo i ponozhovshchina*, ed. E. K. Krasnushkin, G. M. Segal, and Ts. M. Feinberg (Moscow: Izd. Moszdravotdela, 1927), pp. 12–13. Gertsenzon does not define what he means by the term "hooliganism," suggesting that he assumed the term to be so widely understood as to not need definition. Gertsenzon's criminal statistics need to be treated carefully, of course. Even Soviet criminologist A. O. Edel'shtein wondered whether the supposed increase in hooliganism in this period was real, or related to increasing rates of arrest and prosecution. See A. O. Edel'shtein, "Opyt izucheniia sovremennogo khuliganstva," in *Khuliganstvo i ponozhovshchina*, ed. Krasnushkin, Segal, and Feinberg, p. 47.

3. I could not find an order from the Central Committee asking for this information. I do have local reports, all from 1926 and 1927, which are similar enough in language and style to suggest that they may have resulted from a central inquiry about local conditions. I also found a brief covering note from the local organization in Tula which implies that it is sending its report in response to such an inquiry. See Tsentr Khraneniia Dokumentov Molodezhnykh Organizatsii (TsKhDMO), f. 1, op. 23, d. 664, l. 154.

4. References to many of these works can be found in the footnotes. For a summary of others, see Bulaiskii, *Khuliganstvo*, especially pp. 19–35.

5. G. M. Segal in *Khuliganstvo i ponozhovshchina*, ed. Krasnushkin, Segal, and Feinberg, p. 8.

6. V. Iakubson, "Khuliganstvo i sudebnaia repressiia protiv nego," in *Khuliganstvo i khuligany. Sbornik*, ed. V. N. Tolmacheva (Moscow: Izd. Narodnogo Komissariata Vnutrennikh Del RSFSR, 1929), p. 88.

7. TsKhDMO, f. 1, op. 23, d. 663, l. 89 (from October 5, 1927); ibid., d. 662, ll. 20, 21, 79 (December 19, 1927); ibid., d. 681, l. 49; ibid., d. 679, l. 17; ibid., d. 663, l. 90; A. Iu. Rozhkov, "Molodoi chelovek i sovetskaia deistvitel'nost' 1920-kh godov. Formy povsednevnogo protesta," in *Sposoby adaptatsii naseleniia k novoi sotsial'no-ekonomicheskoi situatsii v Rossii*, ed. I. A. Butenko (Moscow: Moskovskii obshchestvennyi nauchnyi fond, 1999), p. 134; A. I. Kriven'kii, *Komsomol v bor'be za edinstvo svoikh riadov (1921–1932 gg.)* (Moscow: Vysshaia komsomol'skaia shkola, 1980), pp. 74, 78, 83.

8. See the discussion in Eric Naiman, *Sex in Public: The Incarnation of Early Soviet Ideology* (Princeton: Princeton University Press, 1997), pp. 263–270.

9. TsKhDMO, f. 1, op. 23, d. 622, l. 86 and ibid., d. 663, ll. 17, 19, 90. *Slavnyi put' Leninskogo komsomola* (Moscow: Molodaia gvardiia, 1974), p. 368.

10. Andrew Pospielovsky, "Strikes during the NEP," *Revolutionary Russia* 10:1 (June 1997), p. 22. The Komsomol archive also contains reports of anti-communist, pro-fascist youth groups in the late 1920s. From the material I have seen, however, it is difficult to get a sense of the size or significance of these groups. TsKhDMO, f. 1, op. 23, d. 820, ll. 8, 44, 80, 100.

11. Rozhkov, "Molodoi chelovek," pp. 134, 137, 140.

12. Some Soviet observers were disturbed by these "excesses." E. Shirvindt complained that reports on hooliganism were "creating an excessively panicked and scarcely objective or well-grounded mood and inducing [journalists] to find hooliganism in every criminal." E. Shirvindt, "Nekotorye itogi bor′by s khuliganstvom," in *Khuliganstvo i khuligany*, ed. V. N. Tolamacheva, p. 169.

13. For multiple descriptions of all of these kinds of behaviors, see the articles and books already cited here, as well as TsKhDMO, f. 1, op. 23, d. 664, ll. 112–120, 130–131, 140–142, 154–163; ibid., d. 822, ll. 41–44, 76–77, 115; ibid., d. 833, l. 17. On the harassment of women, see also Ella Winter, *Red Virtue* (London: Victor Gollancz, 1933), p. 35.

14. Eric Naiman has explored the meaning of rape, especially collective rape, in this period in "The Case of Chubarov Alley: Collective Rape, Utopian Desire and the Mentality of NEP," *Russian History/Histoire Russe* 17:1 (Spring 1990). See also Bulaiskii, *Khuliganstvo*, pp. 68–69.

15. A. Zalkind, "O tak nazyvaemom 'khuliganstve' v shkole," *Vestnik prosveshcheniia* 1 (1927), p. 3. See also Edel'shtein, "Opyt izucheniia sovremennogo khuliganstva," p. 66, and L. G. Orshanskii, "Khuligan (psikhologicheskii ocherk)," in *Khuliganstvo i prestuplenie. Sbornik statei* (Moscow-Leningrad: Izd. Rabochii sud, 1927), pp. 73–74.

16. As cited in Peter Konecny, "Revolution and Rebellion: Students in Soviet Institutes of Higher Education, 1921–1928," *Canadian Journal of History* 27:3 (December 1992), p. 469.

17. As cited in M. Isaev, "Khuliganstvo (Iuridicheskii ocherk)," in *Khuliganstvo i khuligany*, ed. Tolmacheva, p. 11, emphasis in original. See also A. A. Zhizhilenko, "O khuligantsve (Iuridicheskii ocherk)," in *Khuliganstvo i prestuplenie*, pp. 83–90.

18. Isaev, "Khuliganstvo," p. 11.

19. N. V. Krulenko, "Chto takoe khuliganstvo," in *Khuliganstvo i prestuplenie*, p. 13.

20. Bulaiskii, *Khuliganstvo*, p. 7.

21. Shirvindt, "Nekotorye itogi bor′by s khuliganstvom," p. 170.

22. Stephen Humphries, *Hooligans or Rebels? An Oral History of Working Class Childhood and Youth, 1889–1939* (Oxford: Basil Blackwell, 1981), pp. 174–175.

23. Joan Neuberger, *Hooliganism: Crime, Culture, and Power in St. Petersburg, 1900–1914* (Berkeley: University of California Press, 1993), p. 276.

24. E. K. Krasnushkin, "K psikhologii khuliganstva," in *Khuliganstvo i ponozhovshchina*, ed. Krasnushkin, Segal, and Feinberg, pp. 154–156.

25. A. Lunacharsky, ed., *Upadochnoe nastroenie sredi molodezhi. Eseninshchina* (Moscow: Izd. kommunisticheskoi akademii, 1927), p. 14.

26. Yuri Slezkine, "The USSR as a Communal Apartment, or How a Socialist State Promoted Ethnic Particularism," *Slavic Review* 53:2 (Summer 1994), p. 424.

27. See Ronald D. LeBlanc, "A Russian Tarzan, or 'Aping' Jocko?" *Slavic Review* 46:1 (Spring 1987).

28. On Western views of the primitive, see Marianna Torgovnik, *Gone Primitive: Savage Intellects, Modern Lives* (Chicago: University of Chicago Press, 1990).

29. P. I. Liublinskii, "Khuliganstvo i ego sotsial'no-bytovye korni," in *Khuliganstvo i khuligany*, ed. Tolmacheva, p. 38. On racist language, see Pearson, *Hooligan*, p. 75.

30. Reports varied greatly as to the number of adolescent youth committing

acts of hooliganism, as compared to older youth. On the ages of hooligans, see Bulaiskii, *Khuliganstvo*, p. 28. See also Edel'shtein, "Opyt izucheniia sovremennogo khuliganstva," p. 48–50. He concluded that young people aged nineteen to thirty were 70 percent of the total number of hooligans, although they were just 30 percent of the general criminal population. Youth were overrepresented among the ranks of hooligans when compared to the Moscow population at large as well. 59.5 percent of the population were under thirty, while 74 percent of hooligans were thirty or younger. See also Gertsenzon, "Rost khuliganstva i ego prichiny," p. 17.

31. Bulaiskii, *Khuliganstvo*, pp. 28, 52.

32. Liublinskii, "Khuliganstvo," p. 45. Freud as cited in Torgovnick, *Gone Primitive*, p. 8. Hall's argument as summarized by Graham Murdock and Robin McCron, "Consciousness of Class and Consciousness of Generation," in *Resistance through Rituals: Youth Subcultures in Post-war Britain*, ed. Stuart Hall and Tony Jefferson (London: Hutchinson, 1976), p. 194.

33. Bulaiskii, *Khuliganstvo*, p. 60.

34. N. Semashko, *Iskusstvo odevat'sia* (Moscow-Leningrad: Gos. izd., 1927), p. 16.

35. Andrei Sobol', as cited in LeBlanc, "A Russian Tarzan," p. 70.

36. A. Stratonitskii, *Voprosy byta v komsomole* (Leningrad: "Priboi," 1926), p. 21.

37. Joan Neuberger, "Stories of the Street: Hooliganism in the St. Petersburg Popular Press," *Slavic Review* 48:2 (Summer 1989), p. 193.

38. Ibid., p. 194.

39. Joan Neuberger, "Crime and Culture: Hooliganism in St. Petersburg, 1900–1914" (Ph.D. diss., Stanford University, 1985), p. 289.

40. Krasnushkin, "K psikhologii khuliganstva," pp. 154–155. On rural hooligans, see also A. Mil'chakov, *Komsomol v bor'be za kul'turnyi byt* (Moscow-Leningrad: Molodaia gvardiia, 1927), pp. 41–43; Bulaiskii, *Khuliganstvo*, pp. 21–22; B. S. Man'kovskii, "Derevenskaia ponozhovshchina," in *Khuliganstvo i ponozhovshchina*, ed. Krasnushkin, Segal, and Feinberg; and the *chastushki* [topical songs in rhyme] on rural hooliganism cited by Iurii Sokolov, "Chto poet i rasskazyvaet derevnia," *Zhizn'. Zhurnal literatury, byta i obshchestvennoi zhizni* 1 (1924), p. 309.

41. See Naiman, "The Case of Chubarov Alley," pp. 10–11.

42. Michel Foucault, *Discipline and Punish: The Birth of the Prison*, trans. Alan Sheridan (New York: Vintage, 1977). See also, for example, Pearson, *Hooligan*; Humphries, *Hooligans or Rebels?*; and Jeffrey Weeks, *Coming Out: Homosexual Politics in Britain from the Nineteenth Century to the Present* (London: Quartet, 1977).

43. It went from 31 percent to 41 percent, TsKhDMO, f. 1, op. 23, d. 661, l. 39.

44. On opposition to this change in policy, see Shirvindt, "Nekotorye itogi bor'by s khuliganstvom," p. 170; Peter H. Juviler, *Revolutionary Law and Order: Politics and Social Change in the USSR* (New York: Free Press, 1976), p. 33; and "Khuliganstvo dolzhno byt' unichtozhno," *Pravda* (September 23, 1926). On the criminalization of hooliganism, see also T. Segalov, "Prestupnoe khuliganstvo i khuliganskie prestupleniia," in *Khuliganstvo i khuligany*, ed. Tolmacheva, p. 63.

45. Iakubson, "Khuliganstvo i sudebnaia repressiia protiv nego," pp. 86–87. Additional information on measures taken against hooligans in Moscow and Moscow province before and after June 1926 can be found in Gertsenzon, "Rost khuliganstva i ego prichiny," p. 24. See also John Hatch, "Workers' Clubs and the Search for a Socialist Working Class Culture" (unpublished paper, 1988), p. 14. *Pravda* (September 23, 1926) reported the arrest of 22,739 drunks and hooligans in Moscow over six months. The majority were between the ages of eighteen and twenty-five.

46. There were shifts in other policies as well in this period. Although private trade would not become illegal until 1930, increasing taxes and regulation in 1926–1927 were the first steps in what became, in Alan Ball's words, a "full-scale assault"

on the private sector by the end of the decade. Kulaks were also the victims of increased hostility in this period. Alec Nove, *An Economic History of the U.S.S.R.*, rev. ed. (Great Britain: Penguin Books, [1969]1982), pp. 137–138 and generally chapters 5 and 6; Alan M. Ball, *Russia's Last Capitalists: The Nepmen, 1921–1929* (Berkeley: University of California Press, 1987), chapter 3.

47. *Pravda* (January 7, 1926), as cited in Hatch, "Workers' Clubs and the Search for a Socialist Working Class Culture," p. 17.

48. Bulaiskii, *Khuliganstvo*, pp. 7, 24, 54.

49. TsKhDMO, f. 1, op. 23, d. 664, l. 133.

50. This phrase is from Naiman, "The Case of Chubarov Alley."

51. See the materials in TsKhDMO, f. 1, op. 23, d. 664, and the discussion below.

52. Lunacharsky, ed., *Upadochnoe nastroenie*, p. 13.

53. Naiman, "The Case of Chubarov Alley, " p. 17.

54. TsKhDMO, f. 1, op. 23, d. 664, l. 94.

55. A. Lunacharsky, *O komsomole i molodezhi* (Moscow: Molodaia gvardiia, n.d.), p. 326.

56. Bulaiskii, *Khuliganstvo*, p. 56.

57. According to one expert, women constituted just 8 percent of the hooligan population in cities and just 1.2 percent in the countryside. Gertsenzon, "Rost khuligantsva i ego prichiny," p. 17. See also S. Ukshe, "Zhenshchiny, osuzhdennye za khuliganstvo," in *Khuligantsvo i khuligany*, ed. Tolmacheva, p. 148.

58. For a few examples, see V. M. Gur-Gurevich, "Samoubiistva sredi detskogo i iunosheskogo vozrasta do i posle revoliutsiia," *Pedologiia* 1 (1930), p. 102; N. Semashko, "Ugrozhaet li nam epidemiia samoubiistva?" *Izvestiia*, (January 22, 1926), p. 5; Krasnushkin, "K psikhologii khuliganstva," p. 156. Semashko uses the term only to argue against it as an inaccurate description.

59. N. B. Lebina, "Malen'kaia Vera obraztsa 20-kh godov," *Leningradskaia panorama* 9 (September 1989), p. 19; Gur-Gurevich, "Samoubiistva"; V. Ermilov, *Protiv meshchantsva i upadochnichestva* (Moscow-Leningrad: Gos. izd., 1927), p. 7; M. N. Gernet, *Prestupnost' i samoubiistva vo vremia voiny i posle nee* (Moscow, 1927), p. 224. See also Leonard Shapiro, *The Communist Party of the Soviet Union*, 2nd ed. (New York: Vintage Books, 1971), pp. 313–314; Mark von Hagen, *Soldiers in the Proletarian Dictatorship: The Red Army and the Soviet Socialist State, 1917–1930* (Ithaca: Cornell University Press, 1990), pp. 305–308; Peter Konecny, "Library Hooligans and Others: Law, Order, and Student Culture in Leningrad, 1924–38," *Journal of Social History* 30:1 (Fall 1996), p. 115.

60. See Kenneth M. Pinnow, "Making Suicide Soviet: Medicine, Moral Statistics, and the Politics of Social Science in Bolshevik Russia, 1920–1930" (Ph.D. diss., Columbia University, 1998).

61. TsKhDMO, f. 1, op. 23, d. 822, ll. 123–124. For additional reports, see ibid., d. 822, l. 110; Lunacharsky, ed., *Upadochnoe nastroenie*, pp. 20–24, 30.

62. See speech by Komsomol Secretary Chaplin, March 25, 1927, in TsKhDMO, f. 37, d. 5, op. 6, l. 10; Ivan T. Bobryshev, *Melkoburzhuaznye vliianiia sredi molodezhi* (Moscow-Leningrad: Molodaia gvardiia, 1928), p. 98; L. Leonov in Lunacharsky, ed., *Upadochnoe nastroenie*, pp. 103–106.

63. Semashko, "Ugrozhaet li nam epidemiia samoubiistva?" p. 5.

64. TsKhDMO, f. 1, op. 23, d. 822, l. 48.

65. Gur-Gurevich, "Samoubiistva," pp. 104, 106.

66. On the need to find "new" ways to explain depression and suicide, see TsKhDMO, f. 1, op. 23, d. 822, l. 123.

67. Orshanskii, "Khuligan (Psikhologicheskii ocherk)," p. 56.

68. Pinnow, "Making Suicide Soviet," chapter 3. Russian experts also discussed

the challenges of relying on figures. As criminologist Gur-Gurevich noted, for example, it was difficult to compare the pre- and post-revolutionary periods, because the vast majority of statistics on suicide by young people before the revolution were collected by the Ministry of Education and principally concerned students, while post-revolutionary statistics focused on working-class youth. Gur-Gurevich, "Samoubiistva," p. 98. For published lists of numbers of suicides, see *Samoubiistva v SSSR, 1922–1925 gg.* (Moscow, 1927) and *Samoubiistva v SSSR v 1925 i 1926 gg.* (Moscow: Tsentral'noe statisticheskoe upravlenie SSSR, 1929).

69. G. T. Rittersporn, "Le message des données introuvables. L'État et les statistiques du suicide en Russia et en URSS," *Cahiers du Monde Russe* 38:4 (1997), pp. 517–518. On a comparison with other countries, see also N. P. Brukhanskii, *Samoubiitsy* (Leningrad: "Priboi," 1927), pp. 13, 17, f. 35.

70. Ibid., l. 171.

71. Anastasyan Vairich, "Youth It Was That Led Us," in *Soviet Youth: Twelve Komsomol Histories,* ed. Nikolai K. Novak-Deker (Munich: Institute for the Study of the USSR, 1959), p. 61. Although I have focused here on urban youth, rural youth also suffered from depression. For examples, see L. Stal'skii, "Upadochnoye nastroenie sredi krest'ianskoi molodezhi," *Iunyi kommunist* 6 (March 1927), pp. 48–55, and a letter found in the Komsomol archive from a rural activist, "Zdravstvuite, dorogie rebiata (samoubiistvo)," TsKhDMO, f. 1, op. 23, d. 315, l. 159.

72. TsKhDMO, f. 1, op. 23, d. 822, ll. 39–40.

73. TsKhDMO, f. 1, op. 23, d. 822, l. 163.

74. Sergei Esenin, "Departing Russia," as translated in Frances De Graaff, *Sergej Esenin: A Biographical Sketch* (The Hague: Mouton and Co., 1966), pp. 126–127. On Esenin, his poetry, and post-revolutionary angst, see also Bulaiskii, *Khuliganstvo,* pp. 72–73.

75. Mikhail Koriakov, "'Eseninshchina' i sovetskaia molodezh'," *Vozrozhdenie* 15 (Paris, 1951), pp. 96, 98. Koriakov later emigrated from the USSR.

76. See Reginald Pound, *The Lost Generation* (London: Constable, 1964), and Robert Wohl, *The Generation of 1914* (Cambridge, Mass.: Harvard University Press, 1979), pp. 225, 231.

77. Koriakov, "Eseninshchina," pp. 97, 105.

78. Ibid., pp. 97, 101.

79. TsKhDMO, f. 1, op. 23, d. 822, ll. 38–39. Emphasis in original.

80. TsKhDMO, f. 1, op. 23, d. 822, l. 123. On suicide groups, see also G. Bergman, "Esenin—znamia upadochnykh nastroenii," in *Protiv upadochnichestva. Protiv "Eseninshchiny"* (Moscow, 1926), pp. 6–7. See also Rozhkov, "Molodoi chelovek," p. 141.

81. Lunacharsky, ed., *Upadochnoe nastroenie,* p. 93. While most of these expressions of admiration were quietly personal, some youth were apparently influenced by the more aggressively rebellious qualities of Esenin's life and work. One group of young factory communists and Esenin-enthusiasts set up their own office, which they provocatively called a *buzbiuro,* next to the official bureau of the Komsomol. A fabricated word, *buzbiuro* literally means a "rowdy office," or a "place to kick up a row." Their inspiration apparently came from their readings of Esenin, about whom they said, "We are for Esenin. We think of him as our teacher." Ibid. p, 73.

82. V. Kirshon, "Sergei Esenin," *Molodaia gvardiia* (January 1926), p. 231.

83. "O rabote Komsomola," in *KPSS o komsomole i molodezhi* (Moscow: Molodaia gvardiia, 1962), p. 100. See also A. Mil'chakov, *Komsomol v bor'be za kul'turnyi byt,* p. 3.

84. Lunacharsky, ed., *Upadochnoe nastroenie,* pp. 20–24, 30, 39. According to Lunacharsky, the solution was to develop better cultural and political propaganda so as to make sure that youth understood the "path of the revolution" and the need for NEP.

85. Emphasis in original. Ermilov, *Protiv meshchanstva,* p. 9.

EPILOGUE

1. This phrase is from William Roseberry, "Hegemony and the Language of Contention," in *Everyday Forms of State Formation: Revolution and the Negotiation of Rule in Modern Mexico,* ed. Gilbert M. Joseph and Daniel Nugent (Durham: Duke University Press, 1994), p. 363.

2. Richard Stites, *Revolutionary Dreams: Utopian Vision and Experimental Life in the Russian Revolution* (New York: Oxford University Press, 1989).

3. Roger William Pethybridge, *The Social Prelude to Stalinism* (London: Macmillan, 1974).

4. Eric Naiman, *Sex in Public: The Incarnation of Early Soviet Ideology* (Princeton: Princeton University Press, 1997), especially the introduction.

5. This phrase comes from a discussion of moral panic about British youth culture in the 1970s. It seems as appropriate for Russia in the 1920s. See Stuart Hall, Charles Critcher, Tony Jefferson, and B. Roberts, *Policing the Crisis: Mugging, the State and Law and Order* (London: Macmillan, 1978), p. 235.

6. A. Lunacharsky, ed., *Upadochnoe nastroenie sredi molodezhi. Eseninshchina* (Moscow: Izd. kommunisticheskoi akademii, 1927), p. 47.

7. See Denise J. Youngblood, "The Fate of Soviet Popular Cinema during the Stalin Revolution," *Russian Review* 50:2 (April 1991), p. 157, and S. Frederick Starr, *Red and Hot: The Fate of Jazz in the Soviet Union, 1917–1980* (New York: Oxford University Press, 1983), chapter 5.

8. Sheila Fitzpatrick, "Editor's Introduction" and "Cultural Revolution as Class War," in *Cultural Revolution in Russia, 1929–1931* (Bloomington: Indiana University Press, 1978), pp. 1–40. For an intelligent, and provocative, reappraisal of the cultural revolution thesis, see Michael David-Fox, "What Is Cultural Revolution?" *Russian Review* 58:2 (April 1999), and the response by Fitzpatrick following.

9. Lewis H. Siegelbaum, *Soviet State and Society between Revolutions, 1918–1929* (Cambridge: Cambridge University Press, 1992), p. 209.

10. Joseph Stalin, "Letter to A. M. Gorky," January 17, 1930, in *Collected Works,* vol. 12 (Moscow: Foreign Languages Publishing House, 1953), p. 181.

11. Lunacharsky, ed., *Upadochnoe nastroenie,* pp. 38–40, 101.

12. Peter Kenez, *The Birth of the Propaganda State: Soviet Methods of Mass Mobilization, 1917–1929* (Cambridge: Cambridge University Press, 1985), p. 169.

13. N. Semashko, "Ugrozhaet li nam epidemiia samoubiistva?" *Izvestiia* (January 22, 1926), p. 5.

14. N. P. Brukhanskii, *Samoubiitsy* (Leningrad: "Priboi," 1927), p. 2.

15. On the fear of emptiness signified by suicides, see Anne Nesbet, "Suicide as Literary Fact in the 1920s," *Slavic Review* 50:4 (Winter 1991), pp. 830–831.

16. *Leninskii komsomol. Ocherki po istorii VLKSM* (Moscow: Molodaia gvardiia, 1963), p. 328; *Slavnyi put Leninskogo komsomola,* vyp. 1 (Moscow: Molodaia gvardiia, 1974), p. 441.

17. Stalin, "To the Leninist Young Communist League," October 28, 1928, in *Collected Works,* vol. 11, p. 252.

18. *KPSS o komsomole i molodezhi* (Moscow: Molodaia gvardiia, 1962), October 1927, pp. 128–129.

19. As cited in Ella Winter, *Red Virtue* (London: Victor Gollancz, 1933), pp. 31–32.

20. See especially Vera S. Dunham, *In Stalin's Time: Middleclass Values in Soviet Fiction* (Cambridge: Cambridge University Press, 1976).

21. See the discussion in David-Fox, "What Is Cultural Revolution?" p. 185, and the references therein, most importantly to Jochen Helbeck. See also Stephen Kotkin, *Magnetic Mountain: Stalinism as a Civilization* (Berkeley: University of California Press, 1995), and Vadim Volkov, "The Concept of *Kul'turnost':* Notes on the

Stalinist Civilizing Process," in *Stalinism: New Directions*, ed. Sheila Fitzpatrick (London: Routledge, 1999).

22. Tsentr Khraneniia Dokumentov Molodezhnykh Organizatsii (TsKhDMO), f. 1, op. 23, d. 1180, ll. 96–101. My thanks to Karen Petrone for showing this reference to me.

23. Rural Komsomol members believed similarly, though their precise expectations differed. See Isabel Tirado, "Letters from the Village: The Komsomol and the Bright Socialist Future" (paper presented at a conference on "Youth in Soviet Russia, 1917–1941," Philipps-Universität, Marburg, Germany, May 1999).

24. Ralph Fisher, *Pattern for Soviet Youth: A Study of the Congresses of the Komsomol, 1918–1954* (New York: Columbia University Press, 1959), p. 112; N. B. Lebina, *Rabochaia molodezh' Leningrada. Trud i sotsial'nyi oblik, 1921–1925 gg.* (Leningrad: Izdatel'stvo Nauka, 1982), p. 109.

25. Dorothy Thompson, *The New Russia* (New York: Holt, 1928), p. 221.

26. *Vozrast i gramotnost' naseleniia SSSR. Vsesoiuznaia perepis' naseleniia 17 dekabria 1926 g. Kratkie svodki* (Moscow: Izd. TsSU soiuza SSR, 1928), vyp. 7, p. 8. As I have described in chapter 2, one of the most obvious reasons for this was the overwhelmingly rural character of the Soviet Union.

BIBLIOGRAPHY

ARCHIVAL SOURCES

GARF: Gosudarstvennyi Arkhiv Rossiiskoi Federatsii
(formerly TsGAOR and TsA RSFSR)

Fond 298. Gosudarstvennyi uchenyi sovet Narkomprosa (GUS).
Fond 1575. Glavnoe upravlenie sotsial'nogo vospitaniia i politel'nicheskogo obrazovaniia detei (Glavsotsvas).
Fond 2306. Narodnyi komissariat po prosveshcheniiu RSFSR (Narkompros).
Fond 2313. Glavnyi politiko-prosvetitel'nyi komitet respubliki Narkomprosa (Glavpolitprosvet).
Fond 5451. Vsesoiuznyi tsentral'nyi sovet professional'nykh soiuzov.

NA RAO: Nauchnyi Arkhiv Rossiiskoi Akademii Obrazovaniia
(formerly NAAPNS)

Fond 1. Opytnaia stantsiia po narodnomu obrazovaniiu.
Fond 5. Nauchno-pedagogicheskii institut metodov vneshkol'noi raboty.
Fond 16. Nauchno-issledovatel'nyi institut detskogo chteniia.

TsKhDMO: Tsentr Khraneniia Dokumentov Molodezhnykh Organizatsii
(formerly TsVLKSM)

Fond 1. Tsentral'nyi komitet VLKSM.
Fond 5. Vsesoiuznye s"ezdy VLKSM.
Fond 6. Vsesoiuznye s"ezdy VLKSM.
Fond 37. Vsesoiuznye konferentsii VLKSM.

PERIODICALS AND JOURNALS

Bich
Buzoter
Iunyi kommunist
Izvestiia
Komsomol'skaia pravda
Krasnoe studenchestvo
Krasnyi student
Mody
Mody sezona
Molodaia gvardiia
Na putiakh k novoi shkole
Pedologiia
Pravda
Proletarskoe studenchestvo
Siniaia bluza
Smena
Sovetskoe studenchestvo
Vestnik prosveshcheniia
Zhenskoe delo

PRIMARY SOURCES

50 let VLKSM 1918–1968. Moscow, 1969.

Al'butskii, M. "Ideologiia sovetskogo shkol'nika." *Vestnik prosveshcheniia* 10 (1927).

Alpers, B. "Molodezh' i teatr." *Iunyi kommunist* 23–24 (December 1927).

Al'tman, Vl. "Pokolenie oktiabria v bor'be za novyi byt." In *Za novyi byt,* edited by M. S. Epshtein. Moscow: "Doloi negramotnost'," 1925.

Ariamov, I. A. "Osobennosti povedeniia sovremennogo podrostka." *Pedologiia* 1 (1928).

———. *Rabochii podrostok.* Moscow: Transpechat-NKPS, 1928.

Ariamov, I. A., L. I. Odintsova, and E. I. Nechaeva. *Ditia rabochego.* Moscow: "Novaia Moskva," 1926.

Arkina, K. "Kokainizm, kak faktor prestupnosti." *Vestnik prosveshcheniia* 2 (February 1923).

Balabanov, L. [L. Tol'm]. "Zateriannaia tsennost'." In *Kakim dolzhen byt' kommunist,* edited by E. Iaroslavskii. Moscow-Leningrad: Molodaia gvardiia, 1925.

Balashov, B. A., and W. Lutskii. "Komsomol." In *Great Soviet Encyclopedia.* New York: Macmillan, 1971.

Balashov, B. A, and Nelepin. *VLKSM za 10 let v tsifrakh.* Moscow-Leningrad: Molodaia gvardiia, 1928.

Barskaia, Teleshevskaia, Truneva, Ianovich, and Iakunichkin. "Deiatel'nost' rebenka po obsluzhivaniiu sem'i." In *Trud i dosug rebenka,* edited by A. Gel'mont and A. Durikin. Moscow: "Novaia Moskva," 1927.

Batkis, G. A. "Opyt podkhoda k izucheniiu problemy pola." *Sotsial'naia gigiena* 6 (1925).

Bem, O. L. "Detskaia besprizornost'." *Na putiakh k novoi shkole* 4–5 (April–May 1924).

———. "Ekonomicheskoe polozhenie gosudarstva i perspektivy bor'by s detskoi bezrabotsei i besprizornost'iu." In *Detskaia besprizornost' i detskii dom,* edited by S. S. Tizanov, V. L. Shveitser, and V. M. Vasil'eva. Moscow: Otdel sotsial'no-pravovoi okhrany nesovershennoletnykh, 1926.

Bergman, G. "Esenin—znamia upadochnykh nastroenii." In *Protiv upadochnichestva. Protiv "Eseninshchiny."* Moscow, 1926.

Bernshtein, M. S., and N. A. Rybnikov, eds. *Biudzhet vremeni nashego molodniaka.* Moscow-Leningrad: Gos. izd., 1927.

———. *Biudzhet vremeni shkol'nika. Sbornik statei.* Moscow-Leningrad: Gos. izd., 1927.

Bezrabotnye g. Moskvy. Vyp. 2. Moscow: Izd. TsSU soiuza SSR, 1927.

Biulleten' IV vsesoiuznoi konferentsii RLKSM N. 1–5. Moscow: Molodaia gvardiia, n.d. (c. 1925).

Bobryshev, Ivan T. *Melkoburzhuaznye vliianiia sredi molodezhi.* Moscow-Leningrad: Molodaia gvardiia, 1928.

Boguslavskii, M. S. *Deti ulitsy.* Moscow-Leningrad: Gos. izd. 1927.

Brukhanskii, N. P. *Samoubiitsy.* Leningrad: "Priboi," 1927.

Bukharin, Nikolai. "Bringing Up the Young Generation." In *Bolshevik Visions: First Phase of the Cultural Revolution in Soviet Russia,* edited by William G. Rosenberg. Ann Arbor: University of Michigan Press, 1989.

———. Report on Youth, 13th Party Congress, May 1924. *Kommunisticheskaia partiia Sovetskogo Soiuza. XIII s"ezd. Stenograficheskii otchet.* Moscow, 1963.

Bulaiskii, Ia. *Khuliganstvo kak sotsial'no-patologicheskoe iavlenie.* Moscow-Leningrad: Molodaia gvardiia, 1927.

Bulgakov, Mikhail. *Heart of a Dog.* Translated by Mirra Ginsburg. New York: Grove Press, [1925] 1968.

Bylakh, V. "Voprosy truda molodezhi v svete kontrol'nykh tsifr gosplana." *Iunyi kommunist* 1 (October 1925).

Byt i molodezh'. Leningrad: Izd. Leningradskogo oblastnogo soveta profsoiuzov, 1928.

Chamberlin, William Henry. *Soviet Russia: A Living Record and a History*. Boston: Little, Brown and Co., 1935.

Chepurnova and Nikitina. "Obshchestvennaia rabota shkol'nika." In *Trud i dosug rebenka*, edited by A. Gel'mont and A. Durikin. Moscow: "Novaia Moskva," 1927.

Chernikhova, L. B. "Deti gazetchiki i ikh sreda." *Pedologiia* 1–2 (1929).

Danilevskii, M. *Prazdniki obshchestvennogo byta*. Moscow-Leningrad: "Doloi negramotnost'," 1927.

Deichman, E. "Alkogolizm sredi shkol'nikov." *Vestnik prosveshcheniia* 2 (1927).

Dmitriev, V., and B. Galin. *Na putiakh k novomu bytu*. Moscow: "Novaia Moskva," 1927.

Dovesti do kontsa bor'bu s nepmanskoi muzykoi. Moscow-Leningrad: Gos. muzykal'noe izdatel'stvo, 1931.

Dreiser, Theodore. *Dreiser Looks at Russia*. New York: Horace Liveright, 1928.

Dubrovin, I. "Revoliutsionirovanie byta." *Iunyi kommunist* 8 (October 1923).

Dunaevskii, Vl. "Kommuny molodezhi." *Iunyi kommunist* 16 (November 1919).

Duranty, Walter. *Duranty Reports Russia*. New York: Viking Press, 1934.

———. *I Write as I Please*. New York: Simon and Schuster, 1935.

Edel'shtein, A. O. "Opyt izucheniia sovremennogo khuliganstva." In *Khuliganstvo i ponozhovshchina*, edited by E. K. Krasnushkin, G. M. Segal, and Ts. M. Feinberg. Moscow: Izd. Moszdravotdela, 1927.

Erogov, M. "Ekonomicheskoe i kul'turno-bytovoe polozhenie rabochei molodezhi." *Iunyi kommunist* 21 (November 1927).

Epshtein, M. S., ed. *Za novyi byt*. Moscow: Izd. "Doloi negramotnost'," 1925.

Erenburg, Ilia. *First Years of Revolution, 1918–21*. Translated by Anna Bostock. London: MacGibbon and Kee, 1962.

———. *Memoirs: 1921–1941*. Translated by Tatiana Shebunina. New York: Grosset and Dunlap, 1966.

Ermilov, V. "Komsomol'skaia pechat' i zaprosy molodezhi." *Molodaia gvardiia* 1 (1926).

———. *Protiv meshchantsva i upadochnichestva*. Moscow-Leningrad: Gos. izd., 1927.

Esenin, Sergei. *Confessions of a Hooligan*. Translated by Geoffrey Thurley. Cheshire, England: Carcanet Press, 1973.

Evdokimov, A. *V bor'be za molodezh'. Klassovaia bor'ba v derevne*. Leningrad: "Priboi," 1929.

Fisher, Markoosha. *My Lives in Russia*. New York: Harper and Brothers, 1944.

G., P. "Kommuna 'Krasnyi kauchuk.'" *Smena* 4 (March 1924).

Galin, B. "Bytovye zametki." *Iunyi kommunist* 2 (January 1927).

———. *Organizuem svoi dosug*. Moscow-Leningrad: Moskovskii rabochii, 1927.

Garkush, Il'ia. "O kul'trabote v soiuze i klube." *Iunyi kommunist* 3–4 (February 1926).

Gastev, A. "Snariazhaites', molodye montery." *Iunyi kommunist* 1–2 (March 1923).

Gel'man, I. *Polovaia zhizn' sovremennoi molodezhi*. Moscow-Petrograd: Gos. izd., 1923.

Gel'mont, A., and A. Durikin, eds. *Trud i dosug rebenka*. Moscow: "Novaia Moskva," 1927.

Gernet, M. N. "K statistike prostitutsii." *Statisticheskoe obozrenie* 7. Moscow: Izd. TsSU Soiuz SSR, 1927.

———. *Prestupnost' i samoubiistva vo vremia voiny i posle nee*. Moscow, 1927.

Gertsenzon, A. A. *Bor'ba s prestupnost'iu v RSFSR*. Moscow: Iuridicheskoe izd., 1928.

———. "Rost khuliganstva i ego prichiny." In *Khuliganstvo i ponozhovshchina*, edited by E. K. Krasnushkin, G. M. Segal, and Ts. M. Feinberg. Moscow: Moszdravotdela, 1927.

Goldman, Emma. *My Disillusionment in Russia*. New York: Thomas Y. Cromwell, 1970.

Goomilevsky, Lev. *Dog Lane.* London, 1927.
Gordon, G. "K voprosu o material'nom polozhenii nashego studenchestva." *Vestnik vospitaniia* 7 (October 1914).
Gor'kii, Maksim. *O molodezhi.* Moscow: Molodaia gvardiia, 1974.
Gregor, Richard, ed. *Resolutions and Decisions of the Communist Party of the Soviet Union.* Vol. 2. Toronto: University of Toronto Press, 1974.
Grigorov, G., and S. Shkotov. *Staryi i novyi byt.* Moscow: Molodaia gvardiia, 1927.
Gukhman, Boris Adol'fovich. *Chislennost' i zarabotnaia plata proletariata SSSR.* Moscow-Leningrad: Izd. voprosy truda, 1925.
Gur-Gurevich, V. M. "Samoubiistva sredi detskogo i iunosheskogo vozrasta do i posle revoliutsii." *Pedologiia* 1 (1930).
Gusev, S. I., ed. *Kakova zhe nasha molodezh'?* Moscow-Leningrad: Gos. izd., 1927.
Hullinger, Edwin Ware. *The Reforging of Russia.* New York: E. P. Dutton and Co., 1925.
Iadin, Ven'iamin. "Posle Piati . . . " *Iunyi Proletarii* 3 (February 1928).
Iakubson, V. "Khuliganstvo i sudebnaia repressiia protiv nego." In *Khuliganstvo i khuligany. Sbornik,* edited by V. N. Tolmacheva. Moscow: Izd. Narodnogo Komissariata Vnutrennikh Del RSFSR, 1929.
Iankovskii, M. *Kommuna sta tridtsati trekh.* Leningrad: "Priboi," 1929.
Iaroslavskii, E., ed. *Kakim dolzhen byt' kommunist.* Moscow-Leningrad: Molodaia gvardiia, 1925.
Ignatev, B. V., V. N. Shul'gin, and M. S. Epshtein, eds. *Letniaia shkola.* Gos. izd., 1927.
Isaev, M. "Khuliganstvo (Iuridicheskii ocherk)." In *Khuliganstvo i khuligany. Sbornik,* edited by V. N. Tolmacheva. Moscow: Izd. Narodnogo Komissariata Vnutrennikh Del RSFSR, 1929.
Itogi vsesoiuznoi gorodskoi perepisi 1923 g. Chast' 3, vyp. 1. *Naselenie gorodov soiuza S.S.R. po vozrastu, zaniatiiam i semeinomu sostoianiiu.* Moscow: Trudy tsentral'nogo statisticheskogo upravleniia, 1926.
Ittin, A. G. *Fizkul'tura i komsomol.* Moscow-Leningrad: Molodaia gvardiia, 1925.
Iukon, Evgenii. "Devushka s belym sharfom." In *Obyvatel'shchinu na pritsel! Sbornik statei i fel'etonov.* Leningrad: "Krasnaia gazeta," 1928.
IV s"ezd RKSM. Stenograficheskii otchet (September 21–28, 1921). Moscow-Leningrad: Molodaia gvardiia, 1925.
Kabo, E. O. *Ocherki rabochego byta. Opyt monograficheskogo issledovaniia domashnego rabochego byta.* Moscow: VTsSPS, 1928.
Kagan, A. G. *Molodezh' posle gudka.* Moscow-Leningrad: Molodaia gvardiia, 1930.
Kaidanova, O. *Besprizornye.* Moscow-Leningrad: Izdatel'stvo "Doloi negramotnost'," 1926.
——. *Besprizornye deti. Praktika raboty opytnoi stantsii.* Moscow-Leningrad: Gos. izd., 1926.
Kalinin, M. I. *On Communist Education.* Moscow: Foreign Languages Publishing House, 1950.
Kalmanson, S. M., ed. *Polovoi vopros.* Moscow-Leningrad: Molodaia gvardiia, 1924.
Kanin, Nikolai. *O druzhbe i tovarishchestve v komsomole.* Leningrad: "Krasnaia gazeta," 1927.
Kas'ianenko, V. I. *Sovetskii obraz zhizni. Problemy issledovaniia.* Moscow: "Mysl'," 1982.
Kataev, Valentine, *The Embezzlers.* Translated by Leonide Zarine. New York: Dial Press, 1929.
Kazhdanskaia, Iu. I. "Sotsial'no-politicheskie predstavleniia detei-shkol'nikov pervogo kontsentra trudovoi shkol gor. Odessy." *Pedologiia* 2 (1928).
Ketlinskaia, Vera. *Devushka i komsomol.* Leningrad: "Priboi," 1927.
——. "Zdravstvui, molodost'!" *Novyi mir* 11 (November 1975).

Ketlinskaia, Vera, and Vladimir Slepkov. *Zhizn' bez kontrolia. Polovaia zhizn' i sem'ia rabochei molodezhi.* Moscow-Leningrad: Molodaia gvardiia, 1929.
Khranov-Shmarov, G. "Iz opyta raboty detskikh domov g. Tiumeni." *Na putiakh k novoi shkole* 7–8 (July–August 1924).
Khuliganstvo i prestuplenie. Sbornik statei. Moscow-Leningrad: Izd. rabochii sud, 1927.
Kirillov, S. "Devushka v komsomole." *Kommunistka* 9 (September 1928).
Kirov, S. M. *O molodezhi.* Moscow: n.p., 1969.
Kirshon, V. "Sergei Esenin." *Molodaia gvardiia* (January 1926).
Kluby Moskvy i gubernii. Moscow: Izd. Moskovskii gubernskii sovet profession-al'nykh soiuzov "Trud i kniga," 1926.
Kogan, B. B., and M. S. Lebedinskii. *Byt rabochei molodezhi.* Moscow: Izd. Moszdra-votdela, 1929.
Kolesnikov, L. *Litso klassovogo vraga.* Moscow-Leningrad: Molodaia gvardiia, 1928.
Kollontai, A. "The Family and the Communist State." In *Bolshevik Visions: First Phase of the Cultural Revolution in Soviet Russia,* edited by William G. Rosenberg. Ann Arbor: University of Michigan Press, 1990.
———. *Love of Worker Bees.* Translated by Cathy Porter. London: Virago, 1977.
———. "Pis'ma k trudiasheisia molodezhi. Kakim dolzhen byt' kommunist?" *Molodaia gvardiia* 1–2 (April–May 1922).
Kolodnaia, A. I. *Interesy rabochego podrostka.* Moscow-Leningrad: Molodaia gvardiia, 1929.
Komsomol v derevne. Sbornik. Moscow: "Novaia Moskva," 1924.
Komu doverit' rukovodstvo. Sbornik statei. Moscow-Leningrad: Molodaia gvardiia, 1928.
Kopelev, Lev. *The Education of a True Believer.* Translated by Gary Kern. New York: Harper and Row, 1980.
Koporskii, S. "Vorovskoi zhargon v srede shkol'nikov." *Vestnik prosveshcheniia* 1 (1927).
Koriakov, Mikhail. "Eseninshchina i sovetskaia molodezh'." *Vozrozhdenie* 15 (Paris, 1951).
Kosareva, A. V. and I. A. Kravalia, eds. *Molodezh' SSSR. Statisticheskii sbornik.* Mos-cow: TsUNKhU Gosplana SSSR i TsKVLKSM, 1936.
Kostrov, T. "Kul'tura i meshchanstvo." *Revoliutsiia i kul'tura* 3–4 (1927).
KPSS o Komsomole i molodezhi. Moscow: Molodaia gvardiia, 1962.
Krasnushkin, E. K. "K psikhologii khuliganstva." In *Khuliganstvo i ponozhovshchina,* edited by E. K. Krasnushkin, G. M. Segal, and Ts. M. Feinberg. Moscow: Izd. Moszdravotdela, 1927.
Krasnushkin, E. K., G. M. Segal, and Ts. M. Feinberg, eds. *Khuliganstvo i pono-zhovshchina.* Moscow: Izd. Moszdravotdela, 1927.
———. *Nishchenstvo i besprizornost'.* Moscow: Izd. Moszdravotdela, 1929.
———. *Ubiistva i ubiitsy.* Moscow: Izd. Moszdravotdela, 1928.
Krasuskii, V. S., and A. M. Khaletskii. "Sreda besprizornika. Ee traditsii i navyki." In *Nishchenstvo i besprizornost',* edited by E. K. Krasnushkin, G. M. Segal, and Ts. M. Feinberg. Moscow: Izd. Moszdravotdela, 1929.
Krulenko, N. V. "Chto takoe khuliganstvo." In *Khuliganstvo i prestuplenie. Sbornik statei.* Moscow-Leningrad: Izd. rabochii sud, 1927.
Krupskaia, N. "K voprosu o detdomakh." *Na putiakh k novoi shkole* 7–8 (1924).
———. "What a Communist Ought to Be Like." In *Bolshevik Visions: First Phase of the Cultural Revolution in Soviet Russia,* edited by William G. Rosenberg. Ann Arbor: University of Michigan Press, 1984, 1990.
Kufaev, V. I. *Iunye pravonarushiteli.* Moscow: "Novaia Moskva," 1924.
———. "Prichiny detskoi besprizornosti." *Vestnik prosveshcheniia* 9 (1924).
Kurilovich, Sobolev, Sokolova, and Chepurnova. "Detskii dosug." In *Trud i dosug*

rebenka, edited by A. Gel'mont and A. Durikin. Moscow: "Novaia Moskva," 1927.

Kurkin, P. I. *Moskovskaia rabochaia molodezh'.* Vyp. 2. Moscow: Izd. Moszdravotdela, 1925.

Kuz'min, Vladimir. "O 'molodoi starosti,' asketizme i kazenshchine." In *Byt i molodezh',* edited by A. Slepkov. Moscow: "Pravda" i "Bednota," 1926.

———. "Pis'mo o novom byte." In *Komsomol'skii byt. Sbornik statei,* edited by I. Razin. Moscow-Leningrad: Molodaia gvardiia, 1927.

Larin, Iu. *Stroitel'stvo sotsializma i kollektivizatsiia byta.* Leningrad: "Priboi," 1930.

Lass, D. I. "Byt Odesskogo studenchestva." *Nauchnyi rabotnik* 5–6 (May–June 1927).

———. *Sovremennoe studenchestvo.* Moscow-Leningrad: Molodaia gvardiia, 1928.

Latsis, A. E., and L. Keilina. *Deti i kino.* Moscow: Tea-kino-pechat', 1928.

Lavrikov, K. *Komsomol v kul'turnoi estafete.* Moscow-Leningrad, 1931.

Lebedev, L., and L. Rubinshtein. *Pis'mo iz uteriannogo portfelia.* Moscow: Molodaia gvardiia, 1928.

Lebedev, L., and S. Serov. *Molodezh' na sude. Sudebno-bytovye ocherki.* Moscow-Leningrad: Molodaia gvardiia, 1927.

Lebgur, G. "NOT, Rabkrin i Komsomol." *Iunyi kommunist* 3 (June 1923).

Leizerovich, V., ed. *Komsomol na kul'turnom fronte. Iz opyta Moskovskoi organizatsii komsomola.* Moscow: Molodaia gvardiia, 1928.

Lenin, V. I. *The Emancipation of Women.* New York: International Publishers, 1934.

———. "Introducing the New Economic Policy" (March 15, 1921). Translated in *The Lenin Anthology,* edited by Robert Tucker. New York: W. W. Norton and Company, 1975.

———. *On Youth.* Moscow: Progress Publishers, 1970.

Leninskii Komsomol. Ocherki po istorii VLKSM. Moscow, 1969.

Lepeshinskii, P. "Chto takoe nravstvennost'." In *Voprosi zhizni i bor'by,* edited by E. Iaroslavskii. Moscow-Leningrad: Molodaia gvardiia, 1924.

Levitina, Mariia Isanovna. *Besprizornye. Sotsiologiia, byt, praktika raboty.* Moscow: "Novaia Moskva," 1925.

Lidin, Vladimir. *The Price of Life.* Translated by Helen Chrouschoff Matheson. Westport, Conn.: Hyperion Press, 1973.

Liubimov, I. E. *Komsomol v sovetskom stroitel'stve, 1917–1927.* Moscow-Leningrad: Molodaia gvardiia, 1928.

Liublinskii P. I. *Bor'ba s prestupnost'iu v detskom i iunosheskom vozraste. Sotsial'no-pravovye ocherki.* Moscow: Narkomiust RSFSR, 1923.

———. "Khuliganstvo i ego sotsial'no-bytovye korni." In *Khuliganstvo i khuligany. Sbornik,* edited by V. N. Tolmacheva. Moscow: Izd. Narodnogo Komissariata Vnutrennikh Del RSFSR, 1929.

———. *Kinematografiia i deti.* Moscow: "Pravo i zhizn'," 1925.

Lunacharsky, A. *O byte.* Moscow-Leningrad: Gos. izd., 1927.

———. *O komsomole i molodezhi.* Moscow: Molodaia gvardiia, n.d.

———, ed. *Upadochnoe nastroenie sredi molodezhi. Eseninshchina.* Moscow: Izd. kommunisticheskoi akademii, 1927.

Makarenko, Anton. *The Road to Life.* Moscow: Foreign Languages Publishing House, 1955.

Malashkin, Sergei. "Luna s pravoi storony ili neobyknovennaia liubov'." *Molodaia gvardiia* 9 (September 1926).

Mayakovsky, Vladimir. *The Bedbug and Selected Poetry.* Edited by Patricia Blake. New York: Meridian Books, 1960.

McCormick, Anne O'Hare. *The Hammer and the Scythe: Communist Russia Enters the Second Decade.* New York: Alfred A. Knopf, 1928.

Mehnert, Klaus. *Youth in Soviet Russia.* Translated by Michael Davidson. Westport, Conn.: Hyperion Press, [1933] 1981.

Men'shagin, V. D. "Ubiistva." In *Ubiistva i ubiitsy*, edited by E. K. Krasnushkin, G. M. Segal, and Ts. M. Feinberg. Moscow: Izd. Moszdravotdela, 1928.

Mil'chakov, A. *Komsomol v bor'be za kul'turnyi byt*. Moscow-Leningrad: Molodaia gvardiia, 1927.

———. *Pervoe desiatiletie. Zapiski veterana komsomola*. Moscow: Molodaia gvardiia, 1965.

Murin, V. A. *Byt i nravy derevenskoi molodezhi*. Moscow: Izd. "Novaia Moskva," 1926.

Naimov, I. "Kuda idet Komsomol?" *Iunyi kommunist* 3 (February 1927).

Naishtat, A., I. Rybkin, and I. Sosnovik. *Kommuny molodezhi*. Moscow: Molodaia gvardiia, 1931.

Narodnoe obrazovanie v RSFSR. Po dannym godovoi statisticheskoi otchetnosti mestnykh organov narodnogo komissariata po prosveshcheniiu na I/VI 1924 g. Moscow: Izd. "Doloi negramatnost'," 1925.

Naumov, I. "Kuda idet komsomol?" *Iunyi kommunist* (February 1927).

Neznamov, M. *Iunyi kommunist* 1–2 (January 15–February 1, 1922).

Nikonov. "Iz dnevnika aktivista." *Iunyi kommunist* 4 (July 1923).

Obyvatel'shchinu na pritsel! Sbornik statei i fel'etonov. Leningrad: "Krasnaia gazeta," 1928.

Odinnadtsatyi s"ezd RKP(b). Stenograficheskii otchet. Moscow, 1961.

Odintsova, L. I. "Idealy i interesy uchashchikhsia trudovykh shkol g. Moskvy." *Vestnik prosveshcheniia* 4 (1927).

Ognyov, N. [Ognev] (Mikhail Grigorevich Rozanov). *Diary of a Communist Schoolboy*. Translated by Alexander Werth. New York: Payson and Clarke, 1928.

———. *Diary of a Communist Undergraduate*. Translated by Alexander Werth. New York: Payson and Clarke. 1929.

Olesha, Yuri. *Envy*. In *The Portable Twentieth Century Reader*, edited by Clarence Brown. New York: Penguin Books, 1985.

Orshanskii, L. G. "Khuligan (psikhologicheskii ocherk)." In *Khuliganstvo i prestuplenie. Sbornik statei*. Moscow-Leningrad: Izd. rabochii sud, 1927.

Ozeretskii, N. I. "Nishchenstvo i besprizornost' nesovershennoletnikh." In *Nishchenstvo i besprizornost'*, edited by E. K. Krasnushkin, G. M. Segal, and Ts. M. Feinberg. Moscow: Izd. Moszdravotdela, 1929.

Petrov, V. V. *Byt derevni v sochineniiakh shkol'nikov*. Moscow: "Posrednik," 1927.

Poborinskii, Iu. Ia. "Sviaz zhiznennykh uslovii s zabolevaemost'iu podrostkov." *Molodoi rabochii* 3 (September 1925).

Pokrovskaia, A. K. "Domashniaia zhizn' moskovskikh detei." *Vestnik prosveshcheniia* 1 (1922).

———. "Ulitsa v zhizni detei." *Vestnik prosveshcheniia* 7 (1922).

Postanovichev, K. *Massovoe penie*. Moscow: Vserossiiskii proletkul't, 1925.

Poznanskii, N. "Revoliutsiia i deti." *Vestnik prosveshcheniia* 1 (1923).

Poznyshev, S. V. *Kriminal'naia psikhologiia*. Leningrad: Gos. izd., 1926.

Rafail, M. *Za novogo cheloveka*. Leningrad: "Priboi," 1928.

Razin, Izrail Mikhailovich. *Bibliografiia pionerskoi i detskoi knigi*. Moscow: Molodaia gvardiia, 1926.

———. *Partiia, Komsomol i detskoe dvizhenie*. Moscow: Molodaia gvardiia, 1928.

———, ed. *Komsomol'skii byt. Sbornik statei*. Moscow-Leningrad: Molodaia gvardiia, 1927.

Reswick, William. *I Dreamt Revolution*. Chicago: H. Regenery Co., 1952.

Rives, S. M. *Religioznost' i antireligioznost' v detskoi srede*. Moscow: Rabotnik prosveshcheniia, 1930.

Rodin, A. F., and V. G. Marts. *Kluby dlia detei i podrostkov*. Moscow: "Narodnyi uchitel'," 1919.

Romanov, Panteleimon. *Three Pairs of Silk Stockings*. Translated by Leonide Zarine. New York: Charles Scribner's Sons, 1931.

———. *Without Cherry Blossoms*. Translated by Leonide Zarine. London: Ernest Benn, 1930.

Rubinshtein, M. M. *Iunost'. Po dnevnikam i avtobiograficheskim zapisiam*. Moscow: Izd. vysshikh pedagogicheskikh kursov pri Moskovskom vysshem tekhnich. uchilishche, 1928.

Rybnikov, N. "Ideologiia sovremennogo shkol'nika." *Pedologiia* 1 (1928).

———. "Kak sovetskii shkol'nik otsenivaet sushchestvuiushchii poriadok." In *Deti i oktiabr'skaia revoliutsiia*, edited by V. N. Shul'gina. Moscow: "Rabotnik prosveshcheniia," 1928.

S., I. "Gor'kii koren'." *Izvestiia*, March 8, 1928.

Sakharov, A. "O vliianii teatra na sovremennogo shkol'nika." *Vestnik prosveshcheniia* 2–3 (1925).

Samoubiistva v SSSR 1922–1925. Moscow: Statistika SSSR, tom 35, vyp. 1, 1927.

Samoubiistva v SSSR v 1925 i 1926 gg. Moscow: Tsentral'noe statisticheskoe upravlenie SSSR, 1929.

Segal, B. S. *Alkogolizm i molodezh'*. Moscow-Leningrad: Molodaia gvardiia, 1925.

Segalov, T. "Prestupnoe khuliganstvo i khuliganskie prestupleniia." In *Khuliganstvo i khuligany. Sbornik*, edited by V. N. Tolmacheva. Moscow: Izd. Narodnogo Komissariata Vnutrennikh Del RSFSR, 1929.

Semashko, Nikolai A. "Alkogolizm i khuliganstvo." In *Khuliganstvo i khuligany. Sbornik*, edited by V. N. Tolmacheva. Moscow: Izd. Narodnogo Komissariata Vnutrennikh Del RSFSR, 1929.

———. *Iskusstvo odevat'sia*. Moscow-Leningrad: Gos. izd., 1927.

———. *Novyi byt i polovoi vopros*. Moscow: Gos. izd., 1926.

———. "Nuzhna li 'zhenstvennost'.'" *Molodaia gvardiia* 6 (1924).

———. *O svetlom i temnom v rabochem bytu*. Moscow: Gos. izd., 1928.

———. "Ugrozhaet li nam epidemiia samoubiistva?" *Izvestiia* (January 22, 1926).

Serge, Victor. *Russia: Twenty Years After*. Westport, Conn.: Hyperion Press, 1973.

———. "Vignettes of NEP." In *Verdict of Three Decades*, edited by Julien Steinberg. New York: Duell, Sloan and Pearce, 1950.

Serov, S., and L. Lebedev. *Molodezh' na sude*. Moscow-Leningrad: Molodaia gvardiia, 1927.

Shakhun'iants, G., and F. Krotkov. "K trudovoi kommune." *Vestnik prosveshcheniia* 9 (1925).

Shimbirev, P. "Pravonarushiteli." *Vestnik prosveshcheniia* 2 (February 1923).

Shirvindt, E. "Nekotorye itogi bor'by s khuliganstvom." In *Khuliganstvo i khuligany. Sbornik*, edited by V. N. Tolmacheva. Moscow: Izd. Narodnogo Komissariata Vnutrennikh Del RSFSR, 1929.

Shishkov, Vyacheslav. *Children of the Street*. Translated by Thomas P. Whitney. Royal Oak, Mich.: Strathcona Publishing, 1979.

Shkotov, S. *Byt molodezhi*. Ivanovo-Voznesensk: "Osnova," 1925.

Shokhin, A. *Komsomol'skaia derevnia*. Moscow: Molodaia gvardiia, 1923.

———. *Kratkii ocherk istorii Komsomola*. Moscow: Molodaia gvardiia, 1926.

Sholomovich, A. S., ed. *Voprosy narkologii*. Moscow: Izd. Moszdravotdela, 1926.

Shubin, P. "Molodezh' gorit." In *Kakim dolzhen byt' kommunist*, edited by E. Iaroslavskii. Moscow-Leningrad: Molodaia gvardiia, 1925.

Shul'gin, V. H., ed. *Deti i oktiabr'skaia revoliutsiia. Ideologiia sovetskogo shkol'nika*. Moscow: "Rabotnik prosveshcheniia," 1928.

Shvarts, Gr., and Vl. Zautsev. *Polozhenie truda rabochei molodezhi v SSSR v 1923–1925 gg*. Moscow-Leningrad: Molodaia gvardiia, 1926.

Shveitser, V. L., and A. M. Shabalova, eds. *Besprizornye v trudovykh kommunakh. Sbornik statei i materialov*. Moscow: Izd. Glavsotsvosa NKP, 1926.

Sigal, B. S. *Polovaia zhizn' rabochei molodezhi*. Moscow-Leningrad: Molodaia gvardiia, 1926.

———. *Trud i zdorov'e rabochei molodezhi.* Moscow-Leningrad: Molodaia gvardiia, 1925.
Simson, T. "Prichiny detskoi prestupnosti." *Vestnik prosveshcheniia* 2 (February 1923).
Slepkov, A., ed. *Byt i molodezh'.* Moscow: "Pravda" i "Bednota," 1926.
Slepkov, Vl. *Na bytovye temy.* Leningrad: "Krasnoi gazeta," 1927.
———. "Rytsari skorbi i pechali." In *Obyvatel'shchinu na pritsel! Sbornik statei i fel'etonov.* Leningrad: "Krasnaia gazeta," 1928.
Slovar' zhargona prestupnikov. Blatnaia muzyka. Moscow: Narodnyi Komissariat Vnutrennikh Del, 1927.
Smidovich, S. "Sem'ia i stroitel'stvo sotsializma." In *Byt i molodezhi,* edited by A. Slepkov. Moscow: "Pravda" i "Bednota," 1926.
Smirnov, V. E. *Rabochii podrostok.* Moscow-Leningrad: Molodaia gvardiia, 1924.
Sobetskii, M. *Fizkul'tura v derevne.* Leningrad: Izd. Knizhnogosektora Gubono, 1925.
"Soiuz na mestakh." *Iunyi kommunist* 6–7 (April 1922).
Sokolov, Iurii. "Chto poet i rasskazyvaet derevnia." *Zhizn'. Zhurnal literatury, byta i obshchestvennoi zhizni* 1 (1924).
Solonovich, G. A. "Ocherki sanitarnogo sostoianiia detskikh domov Khamovich raiona v sviazi s rezul'tatami obsledovaniia zdorov'ia detei." *Vestnik prosveshcheniia* 5–6 (1923).
Sol'ts, A. A. "Kommunisticheskaia etika." In *Kakim dolzhen byt' kommunist,* edited by E. Iaroslavskii. Moscow-Leningrad: Molodaia gvardiia, 1925.
Sosnovskii, L. "O kul'ture i meshchanstve." In *Byt i molodezh',* edited by A. Slepkov. Moscow: "Pravda" i "Bednota," 1926.
Sotsial'no-politicheskaia rabota v shkola-klubakh dlia podrostkov. 2nd ed. Moscow: Giz, 1920.
Sputnik klubnogo rabotnika. Moscow: Gos. izd., 1922.
Stalin, Joseph. *Collected Works.* Moscow: Foreign Languages Publishing House, 1952–55.
———. *O komsomole.* Moscow, 1935.
Stal'skii, L. "Upadochnoe nastroenie sredi krest'ianskoi molodezhi." *Iunyi kommunist* 6 (March 1927).
Stanichinskaia-Rozenberg, E. "Vliianie kino na shkol'nika." *Vestnik prosveshcheniia* 2 (1927).
Statisticheskii ezhegodnik. God vtoroi. Sostoianie narodnogo obrazovaniia v RSFSR za uch. 1924/25 god. Moscow: Izd. adm. org. upr. narkomprosa RSFSR, 1926.
Stel'makh, P. "Pod zashchitnym tsvetom." In *Obyvatel'shchinu na pritsel! Sbornik statei i fel'etonov.* Leningrad: "Krasnaia gazeta," 1928.
Stratonitskii, A. *Voprosy byta v komsomole.* Leningrad: "Priboi," 1926.
Strogova, Ekaterina. "Womenfolk: Factory Sketches." In *An Anthology of Russian Women's Writing, 1777–1992,* edited by Catriona Kelly. Oxford: Oxford University Press, 1994.
Tana-Bogoraza, V. G., ed. *Komsomol v derevne. Sbornik.* Moscow-Leningrad, 1926.
———. *Staryi i novyi byt. Sbornik.* Leningrad: Gos. izd., 1924.
Tarkhanov, O. "Na poroge novogo." *Iunyi kommunist* 6–7 (April 1922).
———. "Ob ushcherbe." *Iunyi kommunist* 1–2 (1922).
Teterin, M. "Protiv vseznaistva, uzkolobogo deiachestva i oblomovshchiny." *Iunyi kommunist* 2 (January 1927).
Thompson, Dorothy. *The New Russia.* New York: Holt, 1928.
Tizanov, S. S., and M. S. Epshtein, eds. *Gosudarstvo i obshchestvennost' v bor'be s detskoi besprizornost'iu.* Moscow: Gos. izd, 1927.
Tizanov, S. S., V. L. Shveitser, and V. M. Vasil'eva, eds. *Detskaia besprizornost' i detskii dom. Sbornik statei i materialov II vserossiiskogo s"ezda SPON po voprosam detskoi besprizornosti, detskogo doma i pravovoi okhrany detei i podrostkov.* Moscow: Otdel sotsial'no-pravovoi okhrany nesovershennoletnykh, 1926.

Tolmacheva, V. N., ed. *Khuliganstvo i khuligany. Sbornik.* Moscow: Izd. Narodnogo Komissariata Vnutrennikh Del RSFSR, 1929.

Tramp, M. "Pod fonarem 'El'dorado.'" In *Obyvatel'shchinu na pritsel! Sbornik statei i fel'etonov.* Leningrad: "Krasnaia gazeta," 1928.

Trotsky, Leon. *The First Five Years of the Communist International.* Vol. 1. New York: Monad Press, 1972.

———. "From the Old Family to the New." In *Bolshevik Visions: First Phase of the Cultural Revolution in Soviet Russia,* edited by William G. Rosenberg. Ann Arbor: University of Michigan Press, 1990.

———. *Literature and Revolution.* Ann Arbor: University of Michigan Press, 1960.

———. *The New Course.* Ann Arbor: University of Michigan Press, 1965.

———. "The Position of the Republic and the Tasks of Young Workers." *Report to the 5th All-Russian Congress of the Russian Communist League of Youth, 1922.* London: Young Socialists Publishers, 1972.

———. *Problems of Everyday Life and Other Writings on Culture and Science.* New York: Monad Press, 1973.

———. *Sochineniia.* Vol. 21. Moscow-Leningrad: Goz. izd., 1925–1927.

Trud, otdykh, son komsomol'tsa-aktivista. Po materialam vyborochnogo obsledovaniia biudzhetov vremeni aktivnykh rabotnikov RLKSM. Vyp. 6. Moscow-Leningrad: Molodaia gvardiia, 1926.

Trud, zdorov'e i byt Leningradskoi rabochei molodezhi. Leningrad: Leningradskogo gubzdravotdela, 1925.

Ukshe, S. "Zhenshchiny, osuzhdennye za khuliganstvo." In *Khuliganstvo i khuligany. Sbornik,* edited by V. N. Tolmacheva. Moscow: Izd. Narodnogo Komissariata Vnutrennikh Del RSFSR, 1929.

Utevskii, B. S. *V bor'be s detskoi prestupnost'iu. Ocherk zhizni i byta Moskovskogo trudovogo doma dlia nesovershennoletnikh pravonarushitelei.* Moscow: Izd. Narodnogo Komissariata Vnutrennikh Del RSFSR, 1927.

Vainshtok, Vladimir, and Dm. Iakobson. *Kino i molodezh'.* Moscow-Leningrad: Gos. izd., 1926.

Vasil'evskii, L. M. *Detskaia "prestupnost'" i detskii sud.* Tver: "Oktiabr'," 1923.

———. "Golod i detskaia prestupnost'." *Iunyi kommunist* 10–12 (June–July 1922).

———. *Prostitutsiia i rabochaia molodezh'.* Moscow: "Novaia Moskva," 1924.

Vigilianskii, N. "O studencheskom byte." *Iunyi kommunist* 11–12 (June 1927).

Vol'fson, S. Ia. *Sotsiologiia braka i sem'i.* Minsk: Izd. Belorusskogo gosudarstvennogo universiteta, 1929.

Vozrast i gramotnost' naseleniia SSSR. Vsesoiuznaia perepis' naseleniia 17 dekabria 1926 g. Kratkie svodki. Vyp. 7. Moscow: Izd. TsSU soiuza SSR, 1928.

Wicksteed, Alexander. *Life under the Soviets.* London: John Lane the Bodley Head, 1928.

Winter, Ella. *Red Virtue.* London: Victor Gollancz, 1933.

Yulya Sings Songs of Russian Street Urchins. English lyrics by Thomas P. Whitney. Monitor Records, 1966 (MFS 759).

Zaitsev, V. A. *Trud i byt rabochikh podrostkov.* Moscow: "Voprosy truda," 1926.

Zak, A. I. "Tipy detskoi besprizornosti, prestupnosti i prostitutsii." Vyp. 1, 2. *Vestnik vospitaniia* 7–8 (October–November 1914).

Zalkind, A. "O tak nazyvaemom 'khuliganstve' v shkole." *Vestnik prosveshcheniia* 1 (1927).

———. "The Pioneer Youth Movement as a Form of Cultural Work among the Proletariat [1924]." In *Bolshevik Visions: First Phase of the Cultural Revolution in Soviet Russia,* edited by William G. Rosenberg. Ann Arbor: University of Michigan Press, 1984.

———. "Psikhopaty li besprizornye?" *Vestnik prosveshcheniia* 9 (1924).

————. *Revoliutsiia i molodezh'*. Moscow: Izd. Kommunistich. un-ta. im. Sverdlova, 1925.

Zalkind, A., and M. Epshtein. "Besprizornost'." *Bol'shaia Sovetskaia Entsiklopediia*, vol. 5. Moscow: Aktsionernoe obshchestvo "Sovetskaia entsiklopediia," 1927.

Zamoskvoretskii, V. *Klub rabochei molodezhi*. Moscow: "Novaia Moskva," 1924.

Zamyatin, Yevgeny. *We*. Translated by Mirra Ginsburg. New York: Avon Books, [1920–1921] 1972.

Zelenko, Anna. *Massovye narodnye tantsy*. Moscow: Izd. "Rabotnik prosveshcheniia," 1927.

Zenzinov, Vladimir. *Deserted: The Story of the Children Abandoned in Soviet Russia*. Translated by Agnes Platt. Westport, Conn.: Hyperion Press, 1931.

Zhizhilenko, A. A. "O khuligantsve (Iuridicheskii ocherk)." In *Khuliganstvo i prestuplenie. Sbornik statei*. Moscow-Leningrad: Izd. rabochii sud, 1927.

Ziman, R. M. "O kakainizme u detei." In *Voprosy narkologii*, edited by A. S. Sholomovich. Moscow: Izd. Moszdravotdela, 1926.

Zinov'iev, Grigorii. *Studenchestvo i proletarskaia revoliutsiia*. Petrograd, n.p., 1921.

Zolotarev, S. A. *Chetyre smeny molodezhi, 1905–1925*. Leningrad: Izd. kooperativnoe, 1926.

Zorin. "Detdoma i detskoe kommunisticheskoe dvizhenie." In *Detskaia besprizornost' i detskii dom. Sbornik statei i materialov II vserossiiskogo s"ezda SPON po voprosam detskoi besprizornosti, detskogo doma i pravovoi okhrany detei i podrostkov*, edited by S. S. Tizanov, V. L. Shveitser, and V. M. Vasil'eva. Moscow: Otdel sotsial'nopravovoi okhrany nesovershennoletnykh, 1926.

SECONDARY SOURCES

Abrams, Philip. "Rites de Passage: The Conflict of Generations in Industrial Society." *Journal of Contemporary History* 5:1 (1970).

Adams, Mark B. "Eugenics as Social Medicine in Revolutionary Russia." In *Health and Society in Revolutionary Russia*, edited by Susan Gross Solomon and John F. Hutchinson. Bloomington: Indiana University Press, 1990.

————. *The Wellborn Science: Eugenics in Germany, France, Brazil, and Russia*. New York: Oxford University Press, 1990.

Alexander, Sally. "Becoming a Woman in London in the 1920s and 1930s." In *Metropolis, London: Histories and Representations since 1800*, edited by David Feldman and Gareth Stedman Jones. London and New York: Routledge, 1989.

Andrea, Philippe. "Lenin et la jeunesse." *Quatrième Internationale* 11 (1983).

Atkinson, Dorothy, Alexander Dallin, and Gail Lapidus. *Women in Russia*. Stanford: Stanford University Press, 1977.

Atsarkin, A. N. *Komsomol v bor'be s trotskizom, 1923–1927*. Moscow, 1985.

————. *Pod Bol'shevistskoe znamia. Soiuzy rabochei molodezhi v Petrograde v. 1917g.* Leningrad: Molodaia gvardiia, 1958.

Bailey, Victor. *Delinquency and Citizenship: Reclaiming the Young Offender, 1914–1948*. Oxford: Clarendon Press, 1987.

Bakhtin, Mikhail. *Rabelais and His World*. Translated by Helene Iswolsky. Bloomington: Indiana University Press, 1984.

Ball, Alan M. *And Now My Soul Is Hardened: Abandoned Children in Soviet Russia, 1918–1930*. Berkeley: University of California Press, 1994.

————. "Private Trade and Traders during NEP." In *Russia in the Era of NEP: Explorations in Soviet Society and Culture*, edited by Sheila Fitzpatrick, Alexander Rabinowitch, and Richard Stites. Bloomington: Indiana University Press, 1991.

————. *Russia's Last Capitalists: The Nepmen, 1921–1929*. Berkeley: University of California Press, 1987.

Baron, Ava. "On Looking at Men: Masculinity and the Making of a Gendered Work-ing-Class History." In *Feminists Revision History,* edited by Ann-Louise Shapiro. New Brunswick, N.J.: Rutgers University Press, 1994.

Bater, James A. *St. Petersburg: Industrialization and Change.* London: E. Arnold, 1976.

Bauer, Raymond A. *The New Man in Soviet Psychology.* Cambridge, Mass.: Harvard University Press, 1952.

Beezley, William H., Cheryl English Martin, and William E. French, eds. *Rituals of Rule, Rituals of Resistance: Public Celebrations and Popular Culture in Mexico.* Wilmington, Del.: Scholarly Resources, 1994.

Bennett, Tony. "The Politics of 'The Popular' and Popular Culture." In *Popular Culture and Social Relations,* edited by Tony Bennett, Colin Mercer, and Janet Wollacott. Philadelphia: Open University Press, 1986.

Bernstein, Francis L. "What Everyone Should Know about Sex: Gender, Sexual Enlightenment, and the Politics of Health in Revolutionary Russia, 1918–1931." Ph.D. dissertation, Columbia University, 1998.

Bernstein, Laurie. *Sonia's Daughters: Prostitutes and Their Regulation in Imperial Russia.* Berkeley: University of California Press, 1995.

Bocharov, Nikolai. "Off the Beaten Track." In *Soviet Youth: Twelve Komsomol Histories,* edited by Nikolai K. Novak-Deker. Munich: Institute for the Study of the USSR, 1959.

Bodek, Richard. "The Not-So-Golden Twenties: Everyday Life and Communist Agitprop in Weimar-Era Berlin." *Journal of Social History* 30 (Fall 1996).

Bonnell, Victoria. "The Representation of Women in Early Soviet Political Art." *Russian Review* 50:3 (1991).

———. *Roots of Rebellion: Workers' Politics and Organizations in St. Petersburg and Moscow, 1900–1914.* Berkeley: University of California Press, 1983.

Bordiugov, G. A. "Nekotorye problemy kul'turnogo byta v kontse 20-x–30-e gody." In *Dukhovnyi potentsial SSSR nakanune velikoi otechestvennoi voiny. Iz istorii sovetskoi kul'tury 1917–1941.* Moscow: Institut istorii SSSR AN SSSR, 1985.

Bowen, James. *Soviet Education: Anton Makarenko and the Years of Experiment.* Madison: University of Wisconsin Press, 1965.

Bowlt, John E. "Constructivism and Early Soviet Fashion Design." In *Bolshevik Culture: Experiment and Order in the Russian Revolution,* edited by Abbott Gleason, Peter Kenez, and Richard Stites. Bloomington: Indiana University Press, 1985.

Boym, Svetlana. *Common Places: Mythologies of Everyday Life in Russia.* Cambridge, Mass.: Harvard University Press, 1994.

Bradley, Joseph. "The Moscow Workhouse and Urban Welfare Reform in Russia." *Russian Review* 41:3 (October 1982).

Brake, Michael. *Comparative Youth Cultures: The Sociology of Youth Cultures and Youth Subcultures in America, Britain, and Canada.* Boston: Routledge and Kegan Paul, 1985.

Broer, Lawrence R., and John D. Walther. *Dancing Fools and Weary Blues: The Great Escape of the Twenties.* Bowling Green, Ohio: Bowling Green State University Popular Press, 1990.

Brooks, Jeffrey. "The Breakdown in Production and Distribution of Printed Materials." In *Bolshevik Culture: Experiment and Order in the Russian Revolution,* edited by Abbott Gleason, Peter Kenez, and Richard Stites. Bloomington: Indiana University Press, 1985.

———. "Studies of the Reader in the 1920s." *Russian History/Histoire Russe* 9 (1982).

Brower, Daniel R. "Labor Violence in Russia in the Late Nineteenth Century." *Slavic Review* 41:3 (Fall 1982).

———. *Training the Nihilists: Education and Radicalism in Tsarist Russia.* Ithaca: Cornell University Press, 1975.

Brown, Edward. *The Proletarian Episode in Russian Literature, 1928–1932.* New York: Columbia University Press, 1953.

Caroli, Dorena. "Les enfants abandonnés devant les tribunaux dans la russie pré-révolutionaire 1864–1917." *Cahiers du Monde Russe* 38:3 (July–September 1997).

———. "Enfreindre la loi au temps du bolchevisme (1918–1924): le cas d'un enfant abandonné." *Rechtshistorisches Journal* 14 (1995).

———. "Les mineurs devant le tribunal tsariste." In *Reformen im Rußland des 19. und 20. Jahrhunderts,* edited by Dietrich Beyrau, Igor Čičurov and Michael Stolleis. Frankfurt am Main: Vittorio Klostermann, 1996.

Carr, E. H. *The Bolshevik Revolution, 1917–1923.* Vol. 2. New York: Macmillan, 1952.

———. *Socialism in One Country, 1924–1926.* 3 vols. New York and London: Macmillan, 1958–1964.

Chase, William J. *Workers, Society, and the Soviet State: Labor and Life in Moscow, 1918–1929.* Urbana: University of Illinois Press, 1987.

Clements, Barbara Evans. "The Birth of the New Soviet Woman." In *Bolshevik Culture: Experiment and Order in the Russian Revolution,* edited by Abbott Gleason, Peter Kenez, and Richard Stites. Bloomington: Indiana University Press, 1985.

———. "The Effects of the Civil War on Women and Family Relations." In *Party, State, and Society in the Russian Civil War: Explorations in Social History,* edited by Diane P. Koenker, William G. Rosenberg, and Ronald Grigor Suny. Bloomington: Indiana University Press, 1989.

———. "The Utopianism of the Zhenotdel." *Slavic Review* 51:2 (Summer 1992).

Cohen, Philip. "Historical Perspectives on the Youth Question Especially in Britain." In *Jugendprotest und Generationenkonflikt in Europa im 20. Jahrhundert,* edited by Dieter Dowe. Germany: Verlag Neue Gesellschaft, 1986.

Cohen, Stanley. *Folk Devils and Moral Panics: The Creation of the Mods and Rockers.* Oxford: Basil Blackwell, 1987.

———. *Images of Deviance.* Harmondsworth, England: Penguin, 1970.

Cohen, Stephen F. *Bukharin and the Bolshevik Revolution: A Political Biography, 1888–1938.* New York: Alfred A. Knopf, 1973.

Conner, Walter D. *Deviance in Soviet Society: Crime, Delinquency, and Alcoholism.* New York: Columbia University Press, 1972.

Cornell, Richard. *Revolutionary Vanguard: The Early Years of the Communist Youth International, 1914–1924.* Toronto: University of Toronto Press, 1982.

David-Fox, Michael. "What Is Cultural Revolution?" *Russian Review* 58:2 (April 1999).

Davies, Ioan. *Cultural Studies and Beyond: Fragments of Empire.* London and New York: Routledge, 1995.

Davies, Sarah. *Popular Opinion in Stalin's Russia: Terror, Propaganda, and Dissent, 1934–1941.* Cambridge: Cambridge University Press, 1997.

Davis, Andrew. "Leisure in the 'Classic Slum,' 1900–1934." In *Workers' Worlds: Cultures and Communities in Manchester and Salford, 1880–1934,* edited by Andrew Davis and Steven Fielding. Manchester: Manchester University Press, 1992.

Deak, Frantisek. "Blue Blouse." *The Drama Review* 17 (March 1973).

Dowe, Dieter. *Jugendprotest und Generationenkonflikt in Europa im 20. Jahrhundert.* Germany: Verlag Neue Gesellschaft, 1986.

Dunham, Vera S. *In Stalin's Time: Middleclass Values in Soviet Fiction.* Cambridge: Cambridge University Press, 1976.

Eley, Geoff. "Living the Future: The Left and Culture." Unpublished paper, 1991.

———. "Nations, Publics, and Political Cultures: Placing Habermas in the Nineteenth Century." In *Culture/Power/History: A Reader in Contemporary Social Theory,* edited by Nicholas B. Dirks, Geoff Eley, and Sherry B. Ortner. Princeton: Princeton University Press, 1994.

Emerson, Caryl. "New Words, New Epochs, Old Thoughts." *Russian Review* 55:3 (July 1996).

Erenberg, Lewis A. *Steppin' Out: New York Nightlife and the Transformation of American Culture, 1890–1930.* Westport, Conn.: Greenwood Press, 1981.

Esler, Anthony. *Bombs, Beards, and Barricades: 150 Years of Youth in Revolt.* New York: Stein and Day, 1971.

Evans, Richard J., and Dick Geary, eds. *The German Unemployed.* London: Croom Helm, 1987.

Ewing, Elizabeth. *History of Twentieth Century Fashion.* London: B. T. Batsford, 1974.

Fisher, Ralph. *Pattern for Soviet Youth: A Study of the Congresses of the Komsomol, 1918–1954.* New York: Columbia University Press, 1959.

———. "The Soviet Model of the Ideal Youth." In *The Transformation of Russian Society,* edited by Cyril E. Black. Cambridge, Mass.: Harvard University Press, 1960.

Fitzpatrick, Sheila. "The Bolsheviks' Dilemma: Class, Culture, and Politics in the Early Soviet Years." *Slavic Review* 47:4 (Winter 1988).

———. *The Commissariat of the Enlightenment: Soviet Organization of Education and the Arts under Lunacharsky.* Cambridge: Cambridge University Press, 1970.

———. *The Cultural Front: Power and Culture in Revolutionary Russia.* Ithaca: Cornell University Press, 1992.

———. *Education and Social Mobility in the Soviet Union, 1921–1934.* Cambridge: Cambridge University Press, 1979.

———. "The Legacy of Civil War." In *Party, State, and Society in the Russian Civil War: Explorations in Social History,* edited by Diane P. Koenker, William G. Rosenberg, and Ronald G. Suny. Bloomington: Indiana University Press, 1989.

———. "Sex and Revolution: An Examination of Literary and Statistical Data on the Mores of Soviet Students in the 1920s." *Journal of Modern History* 50 (June 1978).

———, ed. *Cultural Revolution in Russia, 1928–1931.* Bloomington: Indiana University Press, 1978.

Fitzpatrick, Sheila, Alexander Rabinowitch, and Richard Stites, eds. *Russia in the Era of NEP: Explorations in Soviet Society and Culture.* Bloomington: Indiana University Press, 1991.

Foucault, Michel. *Discipline and Punish: The Birth of the Prison.* Translated by Alan Sheridan. New York: Vintage, 1979.

———. *The History of Sexuality, Volume 1.* Translated by Robert Hurley. New York: Pantheon, 1978.

Fox, Michael S. [David-Fox]. "Political Culture, Purges, and Proletarianization at the Institute of Red Professors, 1921–1929." *Russian Review* 52:1 (January 1993).

Frank, Stephen P. "Simple Folk, Savage Customs? Youth, Sociability, and the Dynamics of Culture in Rural Russia, 1856–1914." *Journal of Social History* 25:4 (1992).

Frank, Stephen P., and Mark D. Steinberg, eds. *Cultures in Flux: Lower-Class Values, Practices, and Resistance in Late Imperial Russia.* Princeton: Princeton University Press, 1994.

Gelder, Ken, and Sarah Thornton, eds. *The Subcultures Reader.* London and New York: Routledge, 1997.

Gillis, John. *Youth and History. Tradition and Change in European Age Relations.* New York: Academic Press, 1974.

Gleason, Abbott, Peter Kenez, and Richard Stites, eds. *Bolshevik Culture: Experiment and Order in the Russian Revolution.* Bloomington: Indiana University Press, 1985.

Goldman, Wendy Z. *Women, the State, and Revolution: Soviet Family Policy and Social Life, 1917–1936.* Cambridge: Cambridge University Press, 1993.

————. "Working Class Women and the 'Withering Away' of the Family: Popular Responses to Family Policy." In *Russia in the Era of NEP: Explorations in Soviet Society and Culture,* edited by Sheila Fitzpatrick, Alexander Rabinowitch, and Richard Stites. Bloomington: Indiana University Press, 1991.

Gooderham, Peter. "The Komsomol and Worker Youth: The Inculcation of 'Communist Values' in Leningrad during NEP." *Soviet Studies* 4 (October 1982).

Gorsuch, Anne E. "Soviet Youth and the Politics of Popular Culture." *Social History* 17:2 (May 1992).

Goscilo, Helena. "Keeping A-Breast of the Waist-Land: Women's Fashion in Early Nineteenth-Century Russia." In *Russia•Women•Culture,* edited by Helena Goscilo and Beth Holmgren. Bloomington: Indiana University Press, 1996.

Goscilo, Helena, and Beth Holmgren, eds. *Russia•Women•Culture.* Bloomington: Indiana University Press, 1996.

de Graff, Frances. *Sergei Esenin: A Biographical Sketch.* The Hague: Mouton and Co., 1966.

Graham, Loren R. *Between Science and Values.* New York: Columbia University Press, 1981.

Gramsci, Antonio. *Selections from the Prison Notebooks of Antonio Gramsci.* Edited and translated by Quintin Hoare and Geoffrey Nowell Smith. New York: International Publishers, 1971.

Griffiths, Paul. *Youth and Authority: Formative Experiences in England 1560–1640.* Oxford: Clarendon Press, 1996.

Grossberg, Lawrence, Cary Nelson, and Paula Treichler, eds. *Cultural Studies.* New York: Routledge, 1992.

Gruber, Helmut. *Red Vienna: Experiment in Working-Class Culture, 1919–1934.* New York and Oxford: Oxford University Press, 1991.

Halfin, Igal. "From Darkness to Light: Student Communist Autobiography during NEP." *Jahrbücher für Geschichte Osteuropas* 45:2 (1997).

Halfin, Igal, and Jochen Hellbeck. "Rethinking the Stalinist Subject: Stephen Kotkin's 'Magnetic Mountain' and the State of Soviet Historical Studies." *Jahrbücher für Geschichte Osteuropas* 44 (1996).

Hall, Stuart. "Cultural Studies and the Centre: Some Problematics and Problems." In *Culture, Media, Language,* edited by Stuart Hall, Dorothy Hobson, Andrew Lowe, and Paul Willis. London: Hutchinson, 1980.

————. "Notes on Deconstructing 'The Popular.'" In *People's History and Socialist Theory,* edited by Raphael Samuel. London: Routledge and Kegan Paul, 1981.

Hall, Stuart, Charles Critcher, Tony Jefferson, and B. Roberts. *Policing the Crisis: Mugging, the State and Law and Order.* London: Macmillan, 1978.

Hall, Stuart, and Tony Jefferson, eds. *Resistance through Rituals: Youth Subcultures in Post-war Britain.* London: Hutchinson, 1976.

Halttunen, Karen. *Confidence Men and Painted Women: A Story of Middle-Class Culture in America, 1830–1870.* New Haven: Yale University Press, 1982.

Harvey, Elizabeth. *Youth and the Welfare State in Weimar Germany.* Oxford: Clarendon Press, 1993.

Hatch, John. "The Politics of Mass Culture: Workers, Communists, and Proletkul't in the Development of Workers' Clubs, 1921–25." *Russian History/Histoire Russe* 13:2–3 (Summer–Fall 1986).

————. "Worker's Clubs and the Search for a Socialist Working Class Culture." Unpublished paper, 1988.

Hebdige, Dick. "POSING . . . THREATS, STRIKING . . . POSES: Youth, Surveillance, and Display." In *The Subcultures Reader*, edited by Ken Gelder and Sarah Thornton. London and New York: Routledge, 1997.

———. *Subculture: The Meaning of Style*. London: Methuen, 1979.

Hendrick, Harry. *Images of Youth: Age, Class, and the Male Youth Problem, 1880–1920*. Oxford: Clarendon Press, 1990.

Holquist, Peter. "Anti-Soviet *Svodki* from the Civil War: Surveillance as a Shared Feature of Russian Political Culture." *Russian Review* 56:3 (July 1997).

Hryshko, W. I. "An Interloper in the Komsomol." In *Soviet Youth: Twelve Komsomol Histories*, edited by Nikolai K. Novak-Deker. Munich: Institute for the Study of the USSR, 1959.

Humphries, Stephen. *Hooligans or Rebels? An Oral History of Working Class Childhood and Youth, 1889–1939*. Oxford: Basil Blackwell, 1981.

Hunt, Lynn, ed. *The New Cultural History*. Berkeley: University of California Press, 1989.

———. *Politics, Culture, and Class in the French Revolution*. Berkeley: University of California Press, 1984.

Ilynsky, Igor. "The Status and Development of Youth in Post-Soviet Society." In *Young People in Post-Communist Russia and Eastern Europe*, edited by James Riordan, Christopher Williams, and Igor Ilynsky. Brookfield, Vt.: Dartmouth Publishing Co., 1995.

Institute for the Study of the USSR (Institut zur Erforschung der UdSSR). *Komsomol. Sbornik statei*. Munich, 1960.

Isaev, V. I. *Kommuna ili kommunal'ka? Izmeneniia byta rabochikh sibiri v gody industrializatsii*. Novosibirsk: Nauka, 1996.

Ivanova, E. D., ed. *Russkaia sovetskaia estrada 1917–1929*. Moscow: Iskusstvo, 1976.

Jakobs, Deborah L. "From Bawdyhouse to Cabaret: The Evolution of the Tango as an Expression of Argentine Popular Culture." *Journal of Popular Culture* 18 (Summer 1984).

Joravsky, David. "Stalinist Mentality and Higher Learning." *Slavic Review* 42:4 (Winter 1983).

Joseph, Gilbert M., and Daniel Nugent, eds. *Everyday Forms of State Formation: Revolution and the Negotiation of Rule in Modern Mexico*. Durham: Duke University Press, 1994.

Juviler, Peter. "Contradictions of Revolution: Juvenile Crime and Rehabilitation." In *Bolshevik Culture: Experiment and Order in the Russian Revolution*, edited by Abbott Gleason, Peter Kenez, and Richard Stites. Bloomington: Indiana University Press, 1985.

———. *Revolutionary Law and Order: Politics and Social Change in the USSR*. New York: Free Press, 1976.

Kanter, Rosabeth Moss. *Commitment and Community: Communes and Utopias in Sociological Perspective*. Cambridge, Mass.: Harvard University Press, 1972.

Kasatov, Aleksandr Anatol'evich. "Deiatel'nost' VLKSM po osushchestvlenliiu politiki kommunisticheskoi partii v oblasti fizicheskoi kul'tury osnov sotsializma v SSSR (1921–1932 gg)." Avtoreferat. Moscow: Vysshaia komsomol'skaia shkola, 1985.

Kas'ianenko, V. I. *Sovetskii obraz zhizni. Problemy issledovaniia*. Moscow: "Mysl'," 1982.

Kassof, Allen. *Revolutionary Law and Order: Politics and Social Change in the USSR*. New York: Free Press, 1976.

———. *The Soviet Youth Program: Regimentation and Rebellion*. Cambridge, Mass.: Harvard University Press, 1965.

Kelly, Catriona, and David Shepherd, eds. *Constructing Russian Culture in the Age of Revolution, 1881–1940.* Oxford: Oxford University Press, 1998.

Kenez, Peter. *The Birth of the Propaganda State: Soviet Methods of Mass Mobilization, 1917–1929.* Cambridge: Cambridge University Press, 1985.

———. *Cinema and Soviet Society, 1917–1953.* Cambridge: Cambridge University Press, 1992.

Kevles, Daniel J. *In the Name of Eugenics: Genetics and the Uses of Human Heredity.* New York: Alfred A. Knopf, 1985.

Kingsbury, Susan M., and Mildred Fairchild. *Factory, Family, and Women in the Soviet Union.* New York: G. P. Putnam's Sons, 1935.

Knight, Alan. "Revolutionary Project, Recalcitrant People: Mexico, 1910–1940." In *The Revolutionary Process in Mexico,* edited by Jaime E. Rodriguez. Los Angeles: UCLA Latin American Center Publications, 1990.

Koenker, Diane P. "Class and Consciousness in a Socialist Society: Workers in the Printing Trades during NEP." In *Russia in the Era of NEP: Explorations in Soviet Society and Culture,* edited by Sheila Fitzpatrick, Alexander Rabinowitch, and Richard Stites. Bloomington: Indiana University Press, 1991.

———. "Men against Women on the Shop Floor in Early Soviet Russia: Gender and Class in the Socialist Workplace." *American Historical Review* 100:5 (December 1995).

———. *Moscow Workers and the 1917 Revolution.* Princeton: Princeton University Press, 1981.

———. "Sons against Fathers on the Shop Floor in Early Soviet Russia: Generational Conflict in the Socialist Workplace." Paper presented at the annual meeting of the American Association for the Advancement of Slavic Studies, Seattle, November 1997.

———. "Urban Families, Working-Class Youth Groups and the 1917 Revolution in Moscow." In *The Family in Imperial Russia: New Lines of Historical Research,* edited by David L. Ransel. Urbana: University of Illinois Press, 1978.

Koenker, Diane P., William G. Rosenberg, and Ronald Grigor Suny, eds. *Party, State, and Society in the Russian Civil War: Explorations in Social History.* Bloomington: Indiana University Press, 1989.

Komsomol i molodezhnaia pechat'. Moscow: Molodaia gvardiia, 1973.

Konecny, Peter. "Chaos on Campus: The 1924 Student *Proverka* in Leningrad." *Europe-Asia Studies* 46:4 (1994).

———. "Library Hooligans and Others: Law, Order, and Student Culture in Leningrad, 1924–38." *Journal of Social History* 30:1 (Fall 1996).

———. "Revolution and Rebellion: Students in Soviet Institutes of Higher Education, 1921–1928." *Canadian Journal of History* 27:3 (December 1992).

Koon, Tracy. *Believe, Obey, Fight: Political Socialization of Youth in Fascist Italy, 1922–1943.* Chapel Hill: University of North Carolina Press, 1985.

Kotkin, Stephen. *Magnetic Mountain: Stalinism as a Civilization.* Berkeley: University of California Press, 1995.

Kovanov, V. "Those Unforgettable Student Days." In *The Young in the Revolution,* edited by Vladimir Sevruk. Moscow: Progress Publishers, 1973.

Kriven'kii, A. I. *Komsomol v bor'be za edinstvo svoikh riadov (1921–1932 gg).* Moscow: Vysshaia komsomol'skaia shkola, 1980.

Krivoruchenko, V. K. "Istoriografiia i istochnikovedenie. Nekotorye voprosy nauchnoi razrabotki istorii Leninskogo komsomola." *Voprosi istorii KPSS* 11 (1974).

Kucherenko, M. M. "Podgotovka kvalifitsirovannoi rabochei sily v SSSR (20-e–pervaia polovina 30-kh godov)." *Voprosi istorii* 10 (October 1985).

Kulagin, A. S. "Komsomol i molodaia nauchno-tekhnicheskaia intelligentsiia (opyt konkretnogo sotsiologicheskogo issledovaniia)." *Istoriia SSSR* 5 (September–October 1968).

Kuromiya, Hiroaki. *Stalin's Industrial Revolution: Politics and Workers, 1928–1932.* Cambridge: Cambridge University Press, 1988.

Lane, Christel. *The Rites of Rulers: Ritual in Industrial Society—The Soviet Case.* Cambridge: Cambridge University Press, 1981.

Lapidus, Gail Warshofsky. "Educational Strategies and Cultural Revolution: The Politics of Soviet Development." In *Cultural Revolution in Russia, 1928–1931,* edited by Sheila Fitzpatrick. Bloomington: Indiana University Press, 1978.

———. *Women in Soviet Society: Equality, Development, and Social Change.* Berkeley: University of California Press, 1978.

Laqueur, Walter. *Young Germany: A History of the German Youth Movement.* London: Macdonald and James, 1962.

Lebina, N. B. "Malen'kaia Vera obraztsa 20-kh godov." *Leningradskaia panorama* 9 (September 1989).

———. "Molodezh' i NEP. Ot konflikta k edinstvu subkul'tur." Paper presented at the conference "Youth in Soviet Russia, 1917–1941," Marburg, Germany, May 1999.

———. *Rabochaia molodezh' Leningrada. Trud i sotsial'nyi oblik, 1921–1925 gg.* Leningrad: Izdatel'stvo Nauka, 1982.

Lebina, N. B., and M. B. Shkarovskii. *Prostitutsiia v Peterburge.* Moscow: Progress-Akademiia, 1994.

LeBlanc, Ronald. "A Russian Tarzan, or 'Aping' Jocko?" *Slavic Review* 46:1 (Spring 1987).

Leninskii komsomol. Ocherki po istorii VLKSM. Moscow: Molodaia gvardiia, 1963.

Lewin, Moshe. *The Making of the Soviet System: Essays in the Social History of Interwar Russia.* New York: Pantheon Books, 1985.

Leyda, Jay. *Kino: A History of Russian and Soviet Film.* 3rd ed. Princeton: Princeton University Press, 1983.

Lotman, Iurii. "Conversations on Russian Culture: Russian Noble Traditions and Lifestyle in the Eighteenth and Early Twentieth Centuries." *Russian Studies in History* 35:4 (Spring 1997).

Lunev, Nicolai. "Blind Faith in a Bright Future." In *Soviet Youth: Twelve Komsomol Histories,* edited by Nikolai K. Novak-Deker. Munich: Institute for the Study of the USSR, 1959.

Maksimova, V. E. *IV s"ezd RKSM.* Moscow: Molodaia gvardiia, 1984.

Mally, Lynn. *Culture of the Future: The Proletkult Movement in Revolutionary Russia.* Berkeley: University of California Press, 1990.

———. "Performing the New Woman: The Komsomolka as Actress and Image in Early Soviet Theater." *Journal of Social History* 30:1 (Fall 1996).

———. "The Rise and Fall of the Soviet Youth Theatre TRAM." *Slavic Review* 51:3 (Fall 1992).

Maltby, Richard, ed. *Dreams for Sale: Popular Culture in the 20th Century.* London: Harrap, 1989.

Maquire, Robert. *Red Virgin Soil: Soviet Literature in the 1920s.* Princeton: Princeton University Press, 1968.

Marinichik, P. F. *Rozhdenie komsomol'skogo teatra.* Moscow: Molodaia gvardiia, 1969.

McAuley, Mary. "Bread without the Bourgeoisie." In *Party, State, and Society in the Russian Civil War: Explorations in Social History,* edited by Diane P. Koenker, William G. Rosenberg, and Ronald Grigor Suny. Bloomington: Indiana University Press, 1989.

McClelland, James. "Bolshevik Approaches to Higher Education, 1917–1921." *Slavic Review* 30:4 (December 1971).

———. "Proletarianizing the Student Body: The Soviet Experience during the New Economic Policy." *Past and Present* 80 (August 1978).

———. "Utopianism versus Revolutionary Heroism in Bolshevik Policy: The Proletarian Culture Debate." *Slavic Review* 39:3 (1980).

McDonnell, Kathleen. *Kid Culture: Children and Adults and Popular Culture.* Toronto: Second Story Press, 1994.

McKay, Gordon. *Esenin: A Life.* Ann Arbor: Ardis, 1976.

McNeal, Robert. *Guide to the Decisions of the Communist Party of the Soviet Union, 1917–1967.* Toronto: University of Toronto Press, 1972.

McRobbie, Angela. "Girls and Subcultures." In *Resistance through Rituals: Youth Subcultures in Post-war Britain,* edited by Stuart Hall and Tony Jefferson. London: Hutchinson and Co., 1976.

McRobbie, Angela, and Mica Nava. *Gender and Generation.* New York: Macmillan, 1984.

Mehnert, Klaus. "Changing Attitudes of Russian Youth." In *The Transformation of Russian Society,* edited by Cyril E. Black. Cambridge, Mass.: Harvard University Press, 1960.

Mel'nikov, V. V. *Kul'turnaia revoliutsiia i komsomol.* Rostov-on-Don: Izd. Rostovskogo universiteta, 1973.

Mironova, V. *TRAM. Agitatsionnyi molodezhnyi teatr 1920–1930-kh godov.* Leningrad: Iskusstvo, 1977.

Molodezhnoe dvizhenie v Rossii (1917–1928 gg). Chast' 1, 2. Moscow: Tsentr Khraneniia Dokumentov Molodezhnykh Organizatsii, 1993.

Mort, Frank. *Dangerous Sexualities: Medico-Moral Politics in England since 1830.* London: Routledge and Kegan Paul, 1987.

Mukerji, Chandra, and Michael Schudson, eds. *Rethinking Popular Culture: Contemporary Perspectives in Cultural Studies.* Berkeley: University of California Press, 1991.

Mungham, G., and G. Pearson, eds. *Working Class Youth Cultures.* London: Routledge and Kegan Paul, 1976.

Murdock, Graham, and Robin McCron. "Consciousness of Class and Consciousness of Generation." In *Resistance through Rituals: Youth Subcultures in Post-war Britain,* edited by Stuart Hall and Tony Jefferson. London: Hutchinson, 1976.

Naiman, Eric. "The Case of Chubarov Alley: Collective Rape, Utopian Desire and the Mentality of NEP." *Russian History/Histoire Russe* 17:1 (Spring 1990).

———. "Revolutionary Anorexia (NEP as Female Complaint)." *Soviet and East European Journal* 37:3 (1993).

———. *Sex in Public: The Incarnation of Early Soviet Ideology.* Princeton: Princeton University Press, 1997.

Nesbet, Anne. "Suicide as Literary Fact in the 1920s." *Slavic Review* 50:4 (Winter 1991).

Neuberger, Joan. "Crime and Culture: Hooliganism in St. Petersburg, 1900–1914." Ph.D. dissertation, Stanford University, 1985.

———. *Hooliganism: Crime, Culture, and Power in St. Petersburg, 1900–1914.* Berkeley: University of California Press, 1993.

———. "Stories of the Street: Hooliganism in the St. Petersburg Popular Press." *Slavic Review* 48:2 (Summer 1989).

Novak-Deker, Nikolai K., ed. *Soviet Youth: Twelve Komsomol Histories.* Munich: Institute for the Study of the USSR, 1959.

Nove, Alec. *An Economic History of the U.S.S.R.* Rev. ed. Great Britain: Penguin Books, [1969] 1982.

Nye, Robert A. *Crime, Madness, and Politics in Modern France: The Medical Concept of National Decline.* Princeton: Princeton University Press, 1984.

Ocherki istorii leningradskoi organizatsii VLKSM. Leningrad: Lenizdat, 1969.

Ocherki po istorii sovetskoi shkoly i pedagogiki, 1921–1931. Moscow: Izd. Ak. Ped. Nauk R.S.F.S.R., 1961.

Patenaude, Bertrand Mark. "Bolshevism in Retreat: The Transition to the New Economic Policy, 1920–1922." Ph.D. dissertation, Stanford University, 1987.

Pearson, Geoffrey. *Hooligan: A History of Respectable Fears.* London: Macmillan, 1983.

Pedan, Stanislav A. *Partiia i Komsomol, 1918–1945.* Leningrad: Izd. Leningradskogo universiteta, 1979.

Peiss, Kathy. *Cheap Amusements: Working Women and Leisure in Turn-of-the-Century New York.* Philadelphia: Temple University Press, 1986.

Peris, Daniel. *Storming the Heavens: The Soviet League of the Militant Godless.* Ithaca: Cornell University Press, 1998.

Pethybridge, Roger. *The Social Prelude to Stalinism.* London: Macmillan, 1974.

Peukert, Detlev. "The Lost Generation: Youth Unemployment at the End of the Weimar Republic." In *The German Unemployed,* edited by Richard J. Evans and Dick Geary. London: Croom Helm, 1987.

Phillips, Laura Lynne. "Everyday Life in Revolutionary Russia: Working-Class Drinking and Taverns in St. Petersburg, 1900–1929." Ph.D. dissertation, University of Illinois, 1993.

————. "Message in a Bottle: Working-Class Culture and the Struggle for Revolutionary Legitimacy, 1900–1929." *Russian Review* 56:1 (January 1997).

Pick, Daniel. *Faces of Degeneration: A European Disorder, 1848–1918.* Cambridge: Cambridge University Press, 1989.

Pilkington, Hilary. "Going Out in 'Style': Girls in Youth Cultural Activity." In *Perestroika and Soviet Women,* edited by Mary Buckley. Cambridge: Cambridge University Press, 1992.

————. *Russia's Youth and Its Culture: A Nation's Constructors and Constructed.* New York: Routledge, 1994.

Pinegina, L. A. *Sovetskii rabochii klass i khudozhestvennaia kul'tura 1917–1932.* Moscow: izd. Moscovskogo universiteta, 1984.

Pinnow, Kenneth M. "Making Suicide Soviet: Medicine, Moral Statistics, and the Politics of Social Science in Bolshevik Russia, 1920–1930." Ph.D. dissertation, Columbia University, 1998.

Platt, Anthony. *The Child Savers: The Invention of Delinquency.* Chicago: University of Chicago Press, 1969.

Ploss, Sidney. "From Youthful Zeal to Middle Age." *Problems of Communism* 7:5 (September–October 1958).

Pospielovsky, Andrew. "Strikes during the NEP." *Revolutionary Russia* 10:1 (June 1997).

Pumphrey, Martin. "The Flapper, the Housewife, and the Making of Modernity." *Cultural Studies* 1:2 (May 1987).

Rabiniants, N. *Teatr iunosti. Ocherk istorii Leningradskogo gosudarstvennogo teatr imeni Leninskogo komsomola.* Leningrad, 1959.

Raddock, David. *Political Behavior of Adolescents in China.* Tucson: University of Arizona Press, 1977.

Ransel, David L., ed. *The Family in Imperial Russia: New Lines of Historical Research.* Urbana: University of Illinois Press, 1978.

Retisova, T. A. *Kul'turno-prosvetitel'naia rabota v 1917–1925 gg.* Moscow: Ministerstvo kul'tury RSFSR, 1968.

Reulecke, Jürgen. "Youth Protest: A Characteristic of the Twentieth Century." In *Jugendprotest und Generationenkonflikt in Europa im 20. Jahrhundert,* edited by Dieter Dowe. Germany: Verlag Neue Gesellschaft, 1986.

Rigby, T. H. *Communist Party Membership in the USSR, 1917–1967.* Princeton: Princeton University Press, 1968.

Riordan, James. *Sport in Soviet Society: Development of Sport and Physical Education in Russia and the USSR.* Cambridge: Cambridge University Press, 1977.

Riordan, James, Christopher Williams, and Igor Ilynsky, eds. *Young People in Post-Communist Russia and Eastern Europe.* Brookfield, Vt.: Dartmouth Publishing Co., 1995.

Rittersporn, Gábor T. "Between Revolution and Daily Routine: Youth and Violence in the Prewar Soviet Union." Paper presented at the conference "Youth in Soviet Russia, 1917–1941," Philipps-Universität, Marburg, Germany, May 1999.

———. "Le message des données introuvables. L'État et les statistiques du suicide en Russia et en URSS." *Cahiers du Monde Russe* 38:4 (1997).

Roberts, Mary-Louise. "Samson and Delilah Revisited: The Politics of Women's Fashion in 1920s France." *American Historical Review* 98:3 (June 1993).

———. "'This Civilization No Longer Has Sexes': *La Garçonne* and Cultural Crisis in France after World War I." *Gender and History* 4:1 (Spring 1992).

Rogachevskaia, L. S. *Likvidatsiia bezrabotitsy v SSSR 1917–1930.* Moscow: Nauka, 1973.

Roseberry, William. "Hegemony and the Language of Contention." In *Everyday Forms of State Formation: Revolution and Negotiation of Rule in Modern Mexico,* edited by Gilbert M. Joseph and Daniel Nugent. Durham: Duke University Press, 1994.

Rosenberg, William G. "NEP Russia as a 'Transitional' Society." In *Russia in the Era of NEP: Explorations in Soviet Society and Culture,* edited by Sheila Fitzpatrick, Alexander Rabinowitch, and Richard Stites. Bloomington: Indiana University Press, 1991.

———, ed. *Bolshevik Visions: First Phase of the Cultural Revolution in Soviet Russia.* 2nd ed. Ann Arbor: University of Michigan Press, 1990.

Rosenhaft, Eve. "Organizing the 'Lumpenproletariat': Cliques and Communists in Berlin during the Weimar Republic." In *The German Working Class, 1888–1933: The Politics of Everyday Life,* edited by Richard J. Evans. London: Croon Helm, 1982.

Rosenthal, Bernice Glatzer, ed. *Nietzsche and Soviet Culture: Ally and Adversary.* Cambridge: Cambridge University Press, 1994.

Rosenzweig, Roy. "The Rise of the Saloon." In *Rethinking Popular Culture: Contemporary Perspectives in Cultural Studies,* edited by Chandra Mukerji and Michael Schudson. Berkeley: University of California Press, 1991.

Rothstein, Robert. "The Quiet Rehabilitation of the Brick Factory: Early Soviet Popular Music and Its Critics." *Slavic Review* 39:3 (September 1980).

Rozhkov, A. Iu. "Besprizorniki." *Rodina* 9 (Fall 1997).

———."Molodoi chelovek i sovetskaia deistvitel'nost' 1920-kh godov. Formy povsednevnogo protesta." In *Sposoby adaptatsii naseleniia k novoi sotsial'no-ekonomicheskoi situatsii v Rossii,* edited by I. A. Butenko. Moscow: Moskovskii obshchestvennyi nauchnyi fond, 1999.

———. "Student kak zerkalo Oktiabr'skoi revoliutsii." *Rodina* 3 (March 1999).

Ruane, Christine, "Clothes Shopping in Imperial Russia: The Development of a Consumer Culture." *Journal of Social History* 28 (Summer 1995).

Russell, Robert. "Red Pinkertonism: An Aspect of Soviet Literature in the 1920's." *Soviet and East European Review* 60 (July 1982).

Sandler, Stephanie. "Pleasure, Danger, and the Dance: Nineteenth-Century Russian Variations." In *Russia•Women•Culture,* edited by Helena Goscilo and Beth Holmgren. Bloomington: Indiana University Press, 1996.

Sartori, Rosalind. "Stalinism and Carnival: Organization and Aesthetics of Political Holidays." In *The Culture of the Stalin Period,* edited by Hans Gunther. London: Macmillan Press, 1990.

Sayer, Derek. "Everyday Forms of State Formation: Some Dissident Remarks on 'Hegemony.'" In *Everyday Forms of State Formation: Revolution and the Negotiation of Rule in Modern Mexico,* edited by Gilbert M. Joseph and Daniel Nugent. Durham: Duke University Press, 1994.

Schneider, William H. *Quality and Quantity: The Quest for Biological Regeneration in Twentieth Century France.* Cambridge: Cambridge University Press, 1990.

Scott, James C. *Domination and the Arts of Resistance: Hidden Transcripts.* New Haven: Yale University Press, 1990.

———. *Weapons of the Weak: Everyday Forms of Resistance.* New Haven: Yale University Press, 1985.

Selivanov, A. M. *Sotsial'no-politicheskoe razvitie sovetskoi derevni posle perekhoda v NEPU. Derevenskii komsomol v 1921–1925 gg.* Iaroslavl': Iaroslavskii gosudarstvennyi universitet, 1983.

Semenova, E. A. "Materialy sotsiologicheskikh obsledovanii detei i podrostkov kak istoricheskii istochnik po izucheniiu sovetskogo obraza zhizni (20-e gody)." *Istoriia SSSR* (September–October 1986).

Sevruk, Vladimir, ed. *The Young in the Revolution.* Moscow: Progress Publishers, 1973.

Shapiro, Leonard. *The Communist Party of the Soviet Union.* 2nd ed. New York: Vintage Books, 1971.

Shelley, Louise. "Female Criminality in the 1920s: A Consequence of Inadvertent and Deliberate Change." *Russian History/Histoire Russe* 9:2–3 (1982).

Siegelbaum, Lewis. "Production Collectives and Communes and the 'Imperatives' of Soviet Industrialization, 1929–1931." *Slavic Review* 45:1 (Spring 1986).

———. *Soviet State and Society between Revolutions, 1918–1929.* Cambridge: Cambridge University Press, 1992.

Slavnyi put Leninskogo komsomola. Vyp. 1. Moscow: Molodaia gvardiia, 1974.

Slezkine, Yuri. "The USSR as a Communal Apartment, or How a Socialist State Promoted Ethnic Particularism." *Slavic Review* 53:2 (Summer 1994).

Smith, Stephen A. *Red Petrograd: Revolution in the Factories, 1917–1918.* Cambridge: Cambridge University Press, 1983.

Sochor, Zenovia A. "Was Bogdanov Russia's Answer to Gramsci?" *Studies in Soviet Thought* 22 (1981).

Solomon, Peter H. "Criminalization and Decriminalization in Soviet Criminal Policy, 1917–1941." *Law and Society Review* 16 (1981–1982).

Solomon, Susan Gross. "The Expert and the State in Russian Public Health: Continuities and Changes across the Revolutionary Divide." In *The History of Public Health and the Modern State,* edited by Dorothy Porter. Amsterdam: Editions Rodopi B.V., 1994.

———. "The Soviet-German Syphilis Expedition to Buriat Mongolia, 1928: Scientific Research on National Minorities." *Slavic Review* 52:2 (Summer 1993).

Solomon, Susan Gross, and John F. Hutchinson, eds. *Health and Society in Revolutionary Russia.* Bloomington: Indiana University Press, 1990.

Sorlin, Pierre. *The Soviet People and Their Society: From 1917 to the Present.* New York: Frederick A. Praeger, 1968.

Spitzer, Alan. B. "The Historical Problem of Generations." *American Historical Review* 78:5 (December 1973).

Springhall, John. *Coming of Age: Adolescence in Britain, 1860–1960.* Dublin: Gill and Macmillan, 1986.

————. *Youth, Empire and Society: British Youth Movements, 1883–1940*. London: Croom Helm, 1977.

Stachura, Peter D. *The German Youth Movement, 1900–1945*. London: Macmillan, 1981.

Stallybrass, Peter, and Allon White. *The Politics and Poetics of Transgression*. Ithaca: Cornell University Press, 1986.

Stargardt, Nicholas. "Male Bonding and the Class Struggle in Imperial Germany." *The Historical Journal* 38 (1995).

Starr, S. Frederick. *Red and Hot: The Fate of Jazz in the Soviet Union, 1917–1980*. New York: Oxford University Press, 1983.

Steele, Valerie. *Fashion and Eroticism: Ideals of Feminine Beauty from the Victorian Era to the Jazz Age*. New York: Oxford University Press, 1985.

Steinberg, Mark D. *Moral Communities: The Culture of Class Relations in the Russian Printing Industry, 1867–1907*. Berkeley: University of California Press, 1992.

————. "The Troubled Imagination of the Proletarian Poet." Paper presented at the annual meeting of the American Association for the Advancement of Slavic Studies, November 1997.

————. "Worker-Authors and the Cult of the Person." In *Cultures in Flux: Lower-Class Values, Practices, and Resistance in Late Imperial Russia*, edited by Stephen P. Frank and Mark D. Steinberg. Princeton: Princeton University Press, 1994.

Stepanov, Z. V. *Kul'turnaia zhizn' Leningrada 20-k–nachala 30-kh godov*. Leningrad, 1976.

Stevens, Jennie. "Children of the Revolution: Soviet Russia's Homeless Children (Besprizorniki) in the 1920s." *Russian History/Histoire Russe* 9:2–3 (1982).

Stevenson, Elizabeth. *Babbitts and Bohemians: The American 1920s*. New York: Macmillan, 1967.

Stites, Richard. "Bolshevik Ritual Building in the 1920s." In *Russia in the Era of NEP: Explorations in Soviet Society and Culture*, edited by Sheila Fitzpatrick, Alexander Rabinowitch, and Richard Stites. Bloomington: Indiana University Press, 1991.

————. *Revolutionary Dreams: Utopian Vision and Experimental Life in the Russian Revolution*. New York: Oxford University Press, 1989.

————. *Russian Popular Culture: Entertainment and Society since 1900*. Cambridge: Cambridge University Press, 1992.

————. *The Women's Liberation Movement in Russia: Feminism, Nihilism, and Bolshevism, 1860–1930*. Princeton: Princeton University Press, 1978.

Stolee, Margaret Kay. "A Generation Capable of Establishing Communism: Revolutionary Child Rearing in the Soviet Union, 1917–1928." Ph.D. dissertation, Duke University, 1982.

Stourac, Richard, and Kathleen McCreery. *Theatre as Weapon: Workers' Theatre in the Soviet Union, Germany, and Britain, 1917–1934*. London: Routledge and Kegan Paul, 1986.

Strizhenova, T. *Iz istorii sovetskogo kostiuma*. Moscow: "Sov. khudozhnik," 1972.

Suny, Ronald Grigor. *The Soviet Experiment: Russia, the USSR, and the Successor States*. New York: Oxford University Press, 1998.

Taylor, Richard. "The Birth of the Soviet Cinema." In *Bolshevik Culture: Experiment and Order in the Russian Revolution*, edited by Abbott Gleason, Peter Kenez, and Richard Stites. Bloomington: Indiana University Press, 1985.

————. *The Politics of Soviet Cinema, 1917–1929*. Cambridge: Cambridge University Press, 1979.

————. "Soviet Cinema as Popular Culture; or, The Extraordinary Adventures of Mr. Nepman in the Land of the Silver Screen." *Revolutionary Russia* 1 (June 1988).

Thurley, Geoffrey. *Confessions of a Hooligan.* Cheshire, England: Carcanet Press, 1973.

Thurston, Robert W. *Liberal City, Conservative State: Moscow and Russia's Urban Crisis, 1906–1914.* New York: Oxford University Press, 1987.

Tirado, Isabel. "The Komsomol and the Krest'ianka: The Political Mobilization of Young Women in the Russian Village, 1921–1927." *Russian History/Histoire Russe* 23:1–4 (1996).

———. "The Komsomol and Young Peasants: The Dilemma of Rural Expansion, 1921–1925." *Slavic Review* 52:3 (Fall 1993).

———. "Letters from the Village: The Komsomol and the Bright Socialist Future." Paper presented at the conference "Youth in Soviet Russia, 1917–1941," Philipps-Universität, Marburg, Germany, May 1999.

———. "Nietzschean Motifs in the Komsomol's Vanguardism." In *Nietzsche and Soviet Culture: Ally and Adversary*, edited by Bernice Glatzer Rosenthal. Cambridge: Cambridge University Press, 1994.

———. "The Socialist Youth Movement in Revolutionary Petrograd." *Russian Review* 46 (1987).

———. *Young Guard! The Communist Youth League, Petrograd, 1917–1920.* New York: Greenwood Press, 1988.

Tolson, Andrew. "Social Surveillance and Subjectification: The Emergence of 'Subculture' in the Work of Henry Mayhew." In *The Subcultures Reader*, edited by Ken Gelder and Sarah Thornton. London and New York: Routledge, 1997.

Torgovnik, Marianna. *Gone Primitive: Savage Intellects, Modern Lives.* Chicago: University of Chicago Press, 1990.

Trushenko, N. V. "'V. I. Lenin o komsomole i molodezhi v sovetskoi istoriograficheskoi literature." *Pozyvnye istorii* (1969).

Tucker, Robert. "Lenin's Bolshevism as a Culture in the Making." In *Bolshevik Culture: Experiment and Order in the Russian Revolution*, edited by Abbott Gleason, Peter Kenez, and Richard Stites. Bloomington: Indiana University Press, 1985.

Vainstein, Ol'ga. "Female Fashion, Soviet Style: Bodies of Ideology." In *Russia• Women•Culture*, edited by Helena Goscilo and Beth Holmgren. Bloomington: Indiana University Press, 1996.

Vairich, Anastasyan. "Youth It Was That Led Us." In *Soviet Youth: Twelve Komsomol Histories*, edited by Nikolai K. Novak-Deker. Munich: Institute for the Study of the USSR, 1959.

Viola, Lynne. *The Best Sons of the Fatherland: Workers in the Vanguard of Soviet Collectivization.* New York: Oxford University Press, 1986.

von Geldern, James. *Bolshevik Festivals, 1917–1920.* Berkeley: University of California Press, 1993.

———. "Life In-Between: Migration and Popular Culture in Late Imperial Russia." *Russian Review* 55:3 (July 1996).

———. "Nietzschean Leaders and Followers in Soviet Mass Theater, 1917–27." In *Nietzsche and Soviet Culture: Ally and Adversary*, edited by Bernice Glatzer Rosenthal. Cambridge: Cambridge University Press, 1994.

von Geldern, James, and Richard Stites, eds. *Mass Culture in Soviet Russia.* Bloomington: Indiana University Press, 1995.

von Hagen, Mark. *Soldiers in the Proletarian Dictatorship: The Red Army and the Soviet Socialist State, 1917–1930.* Ithaca: Cornell University Press, 1990.

Vostrikova, N. Iu. *Deiatel'nost' VLKSM po priobshcheniiu molodykh rabochikh k teatral'nomu iskusstvu v usloviiakh nachala sotsialisticheskoi industrializatsii (1926–1928).* Saratov, 1986.

Waters, Chris. *British Socialists and the Politics of Popular Culture, 1884–1914.* Stanford: Stanford University Press, 1990.

Waters, Elizabeth. "From the Old Family to the New: Work, Marriage, and Mother-
hood in Urban Soviet Russia, 1917–1931." Ph.D. dissertation, University of Birmingham, 1985.
———. "Victim or Villain: Prostitution in Post-revolutionary Russia." In *Women
and Society in Russia and the Soviet Union*, edited by Linda Edmondson. Cam-
bridge: Cambridge University Press, 1992.
Weeks, Jeffrey. "AIDS and the Regulation of Sexuality." In *AIDS and Contemporary
History*, edited by Virginia Berridge and Philip Strong. Cambridge: Cambridge
University Press, 1993.
Wickham, James. "Working-Class Movement and Working-Class Life: Frankfurt-
am-Main during the Weimar Republic." *Social History* 8:3 (October 1983).
Williams, Raymond. *Culture and Society*. Harmondsworth, England: Penguin, 1963.
Williams, Rosalind. "The Dream World of Mass Consumption." In *Rethinking Popular
Culture: Contemporary Perspectives in Cultural Studies*, edited by Chandra Mukerji
and Michael Schudson. Berkeley and Los Angeles: University of California
Press, 1991.
Willis, Paul, with Simon Jones, Joyce Canaan, and Geoff Hudd. *Common Culture:
Symbolic Work at Play in the Everyday Cultures of the Young*. Buckingham, En-
gland: Open University Press, 1990.
Wilson, Elizabeth. *Adorned in Dreams: Fashion and Modernity*. Berkeley: University
of California Press, 1985.
Wohl, Robert. *The Generation of 1914*. Cambridge, Mass.: Harvard University Press,
1979.
Wood, Elizabeth A. *The Baba and the Comrade: Gender and Politics in Revolutionary
Russia*. Bloomington: Indiana University Press, 1997.
Wynn, Charters. *Workers, Strikes, and Pogroms: The Donbass-Dnepr Bend in Late Impe-
rial Russia, 1870–1905*. Princeton: Princeton University Press, 1992.
Young, Glennys. *Power and the Sacred in Revolutionary Russia: Religious Activists in
the Village*. University Park: Pennsylvania State University Press, 1997.
Youngblood, Denise J. "The Fate of Soviet Popular Cinema during the Stalin Revo-
lution." *Russian Review* 50:2 (April 1991).
———. *Movies for the Masses: Popular Cinema and Soviet Society in the 1920s*. Cam-
bridge: Cambridge University Press, 1992.
———. *Soviet Cinema in the Silent Era, 1918–1935*. Austin: University of Texas Press,
1991.
Zelnick, Reginald E. *Labor and Society in Tsarist Russia: The Factory Workers of St.
Petersburg, 1855–1870*. Stanford: Stanford University Press, 1971.
———. "On the Eve: Life Histories and Identities of Some Revolutionary Workers,
1870–1905." In *Making Workers Soviet: Power, Class and Identity*, edited by Lewis
H. Siegelbaum and Ronald Grigor Suny. Ithaca: Cornell University Press, 1994.
Zhukova, L. A. "Narkomzdrav RSFSR v bor'bu s detskoi besprizornost'iu (1917–
1935)." *Sovetskoe zdravookhranenie* 4 (1980).
Zubkov, V. A. *Komsomol i kommunisticheskoe vospitanie molodezhi (1918–iiun' 1941
gg)*. Leningrad: Izd. Leningradskovo universiteta, 1978.
Zubkov, V. A., and S. A. Pedan. *Leninskii komsomol v gody vostanovleniia narodnogo
khoziaistva (1921–1925)*. Leningrad, 1975.
Zuzanek, Jiri. *Work and Leisure in the Soviet Union*. New York: Praeger, 1980.

INDEX

Page numbers in italics indicate illustrations.

ANNE E. GORSUCH is Associate Professor in History
at the University of British Columbia.